Ecological Studies

D0203335

Analysis and Synthesis

Edited by

W. D. Billings, Durham (USA) F. Golley, Athens (USA)

O. L. Lange, Würzburg (FRG) J. S. Olson, Oak Ridge (USA)

H. Remmert, Marburg (FRG)

Volume 48

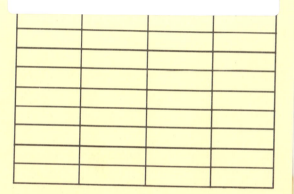

Ecological Effects of Fire in South African Ecosystems

Edited by
P. de V. Booysen and N. M. Tainton

With 54 Figures

Springer-Verlag
Berlin Heidelberg New York Tokyo 1984

PETER DE V. BOOYSEN
Professor Emeritus in Grassland Science
University of Natal, King George V Avenue
Durban 4001, South Africa

NEIL M. TAINTON
Professor and Head of Department of Grassland Science
University of Natal, P.O. Box 375
Pietermaritzburg 3200, South Africa

ISBN 3-540-13501-4 Springer-Verlag Berlin Heidelberg New York Tokyo
ISBN 0-387-13501-4 Springer-Verlag New York Heidelberg Berlin Tokyo

Library of Congress Cataloging in Publication Data. Main entry under title: Ecological effects of fire in South African ecosystems. (Ecological studies; v. 48) Includes bibliographical references and indexes. 1. Fire ecology – South Africa. 2. Wildfires – Environmental aspects – South Africa. 3. Prescribed burning – Environmental aspects – South Africa. I. Booysen, P. de V. II. Tainton, N.M. (Neil Melbourne), 1934–. III. Series: Ecological studies series; v. 48. QH195.S6E36 1984   574.5′264′0968   84-5575

Printing and binding: Brühlsche Universitätsdruckerei, Giessen
2131/3130-543210

Foreword

This is a stimulating tale of the interplay of observation, experimentation, working hypotheses, tentative conclusions, niggling and weightier doubts and great aspirations, on the part of some score of students, on varied ecological and other aspects of the regime and role of fire in relevant biomes and ecosystems – mainly in South Africa – and on other pertinent features of fire ecology.

The impressive contents is a tribute to conveners and authors alike. One can expect a profound range and depth of investigation and interpretation, a closeknit fabric of knowledge, delicately interwoven with wisdom, an exposition and quintessence of information.

Admirable is the collective vision responsible for selecting appropriate topics: the wide sweeps of the brush picturing the nature of the biomes; ably describing the fire regimes – whether in grassland, savanna, fynbos or forest; skillfully defining the effects of such regimes – according to ecosystem – upon aerial and edaphic factors of the habitat, upon constituent biota, individually, specifically and as a biotic community; elucidating the basic implications in the structure and dynamics of the plant aspect of that community ... and unravelling to some degree the tangled knot of the conservation and dissipation of moisture and nutrients. Moreover, gratitude is owed for efforts exerted to understand the interplay of fire and faunal behaviour and dynamics as well as composition, together with the principle of adaptive responses of organisms of diverse kinds.

Philosophically and pragmatically pleasing is the intermittent treatment of historical and sociological features of the responses of man down the millenia to that dangerous but glorious gift from Prometheus: fire!

All this is excellent, but would be all the finer were subsequent action intended to further refine and graft these branchlets of knowledge and to model into holistic vignettes what is already written.

With this higher level of scholarship in mind, it is all the more encouraging that future research priorities – themselves inevitably appreciably conjectural – are discussed by a notable investigator and academic administrator.

A "Straggler Musketeer of the 1930's" – the frontier times of the art, science and discipline of fire ecology – who is sincerely grateful for the honour paid him in this invitation to add a few thoughts to this book, ventures several comments, probably valedictory!

We knew very little about fire ecology in 1929 when I drafted, on a mountain massif at the edge of the Massai Steppe, Tanganyika, the paper later published in the South African Journal of Science, 1930, "Fire: its influence on biotic communities and physical factors in South and East Africa", but this volume blazons the fact that our knowledge is much greater today. May A.D. 2030 commemorate that those to follow will have not only added rich stores of Knowledge but also garnered priceless Wisdom.

As "A Straggler" it behoves me humbly and gratefully to record the debt owed – often unknowingly – to several giants of the past who furthered, through their very eminence, the cause of learning something about the history, role, regime, ecology of fire in South and East Africa: General J C Smuts and I B Pole-Evans in our country and the redoubtable naturalist and famous student of tsetsefly, C F M Swynnerton of Rhodesia, Mocambique and East Africa. My service with Swynnerton sharpened my wits for what awaited me in my own land ... but it did more, it led me to find Hamish Scott, himself now also a "Straggler Musketeer", who has wrought right well in fire ecology and related fields of learning.

We were a tiny band in 1931 ... and for long remained so. According to their respective spheres and responsibilities, the General and Pole-Evans were strict, firm but inspiring mentors. Those who may remember those days "full of old hat and gunpowder" will not bewail what we did not have but, rather, will remember with pride what was attempted and achieved. Bless those who have contributed toward this book ... also all those others – men and women alike – whose labours unobtrusively are intermeshed therein ... although exerted perhaps long, long ago. Finally, it is fitting that the name of Dr E V Komarek, Tall Timbers Fire Ecology Research Station, Florida, should be remembered: he has made it possible for so many to be stimulated in their studies of fire ecology in Africa south of the Sahara, and by no means least in southern Africa.

JOHN F. V. PHILLIPS

Preface

The Scientific Committee on Problems of the Environment (SCOPE) was established in 1969 by the International Council of Scientific Unions (ICSU) – an international, non-governmental scientific organization – as a consequence of a concern for the environment. SCOPE sets as its objectives (i) the advancement of knowledge of the influence of man on the environment and the effect of these environmental changes on people, and (ii) the provision of service and advice on environmental problems. In the pursuit of these objectives, particular attention is given to those influences and effects which are either global or shared by several nations, and which require an interdisciplinary approach.

Over the years, SCOPE has established a number of projects covering a wide range of environmental topics. One such project concerns fire in the ecosystem. At a SCOPE meeting in Washington in 1976 an international project to synthesize knowledge on the ecological effects of fire was initiated. Fifteen countries designated national correspondents and five initiated contributory projects. These contributions have taken various forms but all are short-term projects aimed at bringing together existing information in the field of fire ecology.

The SCOPE project has already produced three major review volumes – published as *Proceedings of the symposium on environmental consequences of fire and fuel management in Mediterranean ecosystems* (Mooney and Conrad 1977), *Fire in the Australian biota* (Gill et al. 1981) and *The role of fire in northern circumpolar ecosystems* (Wein and MacLean 1983). The present volume provides a further regional contribution to our knowledge, while a major global synthesis is currently in an advanced stage of preparation as the final product of the international cooperative effort.

Fire has long been recognized as a natural phenomenon in African ecosystems and as an essential tool in the management of these systems by man (Phillips 1930). It is therefore not surprising that the South African National Committee for Environmental Sciences, which is the adhering body for SCOPE in this country, became actively involved in the fire ecology project at an early stage. The South African project aimed at providing a mechanism for the review of research, and the synthesis of knowledge, on the ecological effects of fire in South African ecosystems, with particular emphasis on the ecological processes whereby fire influences, and is influenced by, ecosystem characteristics and by management strategies employed in fire-regulated ecosystems. This objective was in the end to be realized in the publication of a book on the *Ecological effects of fire in South African ecosystems*. Early in the review process it was realized that there were significant gaps in the spectrum of knowledge on fire ecology in southern Africa.

So, concurrent with the process of gathering and reviewing current knowledge was the complementary objective of identification of gaps in current fire ecological knowledge, and promoting and funding short-term research projects in an effort to fill in these gaps where possible. This process delayed the anticipated date of achieving the primary objective. However, the delay was considered to be worthwhile even though it was clear from the start that with the limitations on funds, time and manpower, many gaps could not be researched and few, if any, could be comprehensively filled.

When the initial period of research promotion had run its course, a symposium was held with invited papers covering, firstly, fire in each of the five major biomes of South Africa, and then a series of papers dealing with fire in relation to ecological processes and management strategies. These papers have provided the basis for the chapters which constitute this book.

In the end, in an attempt to produce a book which provides as comprehensive and cohesive a documentary on fire as possible, the chapters of the book have been structured on more than just the above two categories of papers. The first four chapters provide the platform from which fire in relation to biomes, ecological processes and management strategies can be seen in better perspective. The two major tiers of that platform are situational, describing the biomes that are being dealt with and the fire regime characteristic of each, and historical, outlining past events, practices and researches concerning fire in South Africa.

The second group of four chapters also constitutes a set, this time reviewing what is known about the fire factor in the ecology of each of four biomes – fynbos, grassland, savanna and forest. The karoo biome has been omitted. It was found that the only information available on fire in the karoo pertains to the essentially grassland margins of the biome and to the outliers of grassland which occur on the mountains which rise out of the karoo plains. The fuel load in the dwarf shrub vegetation of the karoo proper is so low that fires are an extremely rare occurrence, and the cover is so sparse that when fires do occur they are very localized. It is true, though, that when such fires do occur they have an extremely harmful effect on the susceptible shrub vegetation. Clearly then, fire is indeed a factor of some significance in the karoo biome, and it is a great pity that so little is known about its occurrence and effects that a chapter could not be included in this book. In a sense a similar situation pertains in the forest biome in that fires of significance to the forest are essentially fires of the grassland margins surrounding the forests. Here, too, fires in the forest itself are rare and tend to be localized, not because of low fuel loads and sparsity of cover, but rather because of high moisture content and low flammability of the evergreen trees. As in the karoo, when fires do occur, they have an extremely harmful effect on the vulnerable forest species. Also, as in the karoo, information on fire in forests is relatively scant, as little experimental data are available. However, the influence of fire on this dwindling resource has attracted sufficient attention and comment to warrant a chapter on this topic, albeit a chapter including much speculation.

The fynbos, grassland and savanna biomes are characterized by a highly inflammable ground layer and so the fire factor has been much more evident. Fire also has been used as a management tool on a large scale, particularly since settlement and particularly in the grassland and savanna areas. Thus the fire factor has invoked the interest not only of the ecologist but also of those concerned with management and production, that is, the agriculturalist and the forester. Considerably more information and data are available on fire in these biomes, although the gaps in our knowledge are still considerable.

Inserted between this group of chapters and the next is one looking at the nature of fire itself – its characteristics and behaviour. This is a subject which has not been well researched in South Africa and so here, too, there is a significant lack of critical data. But the chapter is an important one as it draws attention to the variability of fire and the considerable diversity of its effects consequent upon this range in its characteristics and behaviour. This discussion provides an appropriate introduction to the consideration of the effects of fire on specific ecological processes and management strategies.

Now ignoring biome boundaries, another series of four chapters attempts to bring together the information relating to the influences of fire on the structure and dynamics of the floral and faunal components of the ecosystem. The relationship between fire and the production of forage is singled out for particular treatment within the context of the fire/flora interaction because of the particular emphasis which has been given to fire as a tool in the management of the veld of South Africa. This tradition stems from the early post-settlement days, and has been maintained in sharp focus over the years, and essentially encompasses the role of fire in the maintenance of a particular condition of the vegetation and the effect of fire on the quantity and quality of forage for livestock. The discussion of the interrelationships and interactions between fire and the biota of the ecosystem is then concluded by an evaluation of the adaptive responses and survival mechanisms of plants and animals to the incidence of fire. While there is, of course, much information in the literature which provides a basis for such an evaluation, it is largely of a qualitative and speculative nature. Nevertheless, the application of deductive reasoning to the association between fire and traits of organisms is of considerable importance to a better understanding of the biotic influences of fire in the ecosystem.

The influences of fire within the ecosystem are more obviously seen in terms of the floral and faunal components of the system. In many instances of fire in the ecosystem these effects on plants and animals are not longlived, and even those that are more drastic are seldom irreversible. So in the biota being dealt with, resources show obvious responses to fire but nevertheless are renewable in response to even drastic perturbations. The soil is a different matter. The effects of fire are less obvious but can be far more serious, as the cumulative effects of fire can reduce cover and expose the soil to such an extent that soil loss occurs, and in the time scales of human endeavour this resource must be seen as non-renewable. Two chapters are devoted to the influences of fire upon the soil, the microclimate and the hydrological cycle – matters which are deserving of much greater attention than they have received in the past.

The use of fire as a management tool probably dates back to the time when man first learned to control fire – perhaps as long ago as 180,000 B.C. The use of fire by man in pre-settlement and early post-settlement times is dealt with in earlier chapters in the book. The penultimate chapter concerns current issues regarding the application of fire by man in the management of the natural resource ecosystems which he manipulates and manages. In these manipulations his objectives may be, inter alia, agricultural, afforestation, conservation or recreation. Whatever the interest and whatever the management philosophy, fire will need to be considered as one of the range of tools available to the manager. To use it properly with due regard to the stability and permanence of the system requires that it be understood. Hopefully this synthesis of available information on the ecology of fire will place in perspective the use of fire as a tool and will aid in the development of the best mechanisms for the application of the tool.

This book thus represents the culmination of an extended period of research, review and synthesis. That there is still much not known and much research to be done is clear. It is hoped that the ordering of existing knowledge in these chapters will stimulate interest and further research in this important area of ecological study, and will provide a sound basis for the development of further research programmes. The concluding remarks are an attempt to offer a few pointers in this direction.

P. DE V. BOOYSEN

Acknowledgements

We wish to acknowledge the help we have received from many colleagues who have assisted us in so many ways. First and foremost, our thanks to Mr P.J.K. Zacharias for the enormous amount of work which he has done in copy editing the contents of this volume. His many hours of meticulous work have contributed greatly to its final format.

Our thanks are also due to Margaret Orton, who has been responsible for the production of the camera-ready copy, and to Leslie le Roux for producing the graphs, diagrams and maps.

A number of colleagues were involved in reviewing individual chapters, and have contributed greatly to the content of many of the submissions. In this regard, we wish to thank R.C. Bigalke, T.E. Bosman, H.J. Deacon, R. Dillon, D. Edwards, the late P.J. Edwards, P.G.H. Frost, W.P.D. Gertenbach, J.E. Granger, F.J. Kruger, I.A.W. Macdonald, M.T. Mentis, P.W. Roux, R.E. Schulze, J.S.B. Scotcher, W.R. Siegfried and W.S.W. Trollope. A number of institutions and their staff have played a major role in encouraging and financing work on fire in South Africa. In particular, the Department of Agriculture, the CSIR, conservation bodies and in particular the National and Provincial Parks Boards, the Department of Cooperation and Development and a number of South African Universities. To these organizations we extend our grateful thanks.

Finally, the Cooperative Scientific Programmes Unit of the CSIR provided much of the stimulus and the finance leading to the publication of *The ecological effects of fire in South African ecosystems*. In particular, Mr Brian Huntley has personally done much to stimulate and coordinate its production. It was he who organized the Fire Ecology Research under the auspices of the Cooperative Scientific Programmes Section of the CSIR which encouraged work on fire ecology in southern Africa, and it fell to him to organize workshops and generally encourage authors to embark on a programme of reviewing work on fire ecology in South Africa.

Contents

Contributors

BIGALKE R.C. Department of Nature Conservation, Faculty of Forestry, University of Stellenbosch, Stellenbosch 7600, South Africa

BOOYSEN P. DE V. University of Natal, King George V Avenue, Durban 4001, South Africa

BOSCH J.M. Jonkershoek Forestry Research Station, Private Bag X5011, Stellenbosch 7600, South Africa

CASS A. Department of Soil Science and Agrometeorology, University of Natal, P.O. Box 375, Pietermaritzburg 3200, South Africa

EDWARDS D. Botanical Research Institute, Private Bag X101, Pretoria 0001, South Africa

EDWARDS P.J. Late of Cedara College of Agriculture. All correspondence to N. M. Tainton, South Africa

FROST P.G.H. c/o Savanna Ecosystem Project, P.O. Box 540, Naboomspruit 0560, South Africa

GRANGER J.E. Department of Botany, University of Transkei, Private Bag X5092, Umtata, Transkei

HALL M. Department of Archaeology, South African Museum, P.O. Box 61, Cape Town 8000, South Africa

HUNTLEY B.J. CSP, CSIR, P.O. Box 395, Pretoria 0001, South Africa

KRUGER F.J. South African Forestry Research Institute, P.O. Box 727, Pretoria 0001, South Africa

MENTIS M.T. Department of Grassland Science, University of Natal, P.O. Box 375, Pietermaritzburg 3200, South Africa

SAVAGE M.J. Department of Soil Science and Agrometeorology, University of Natal, P.O. Box 375, Pietermaritzburg 3200, South Africa

SCHULZE R.E. Department of Agricultural Engineering, University of Natal, P.O. Box 375, Pietermaritzburg 3200, South Africa

SCOTT J.D.
2 Bridmore, 57 Cordwalles Road, Pietermaritzburg 3200, South Africa

TROLLOPE W.S.W.
Department of Agronomy, Faculty of Agriculture, University of Fort Hare, Private Bag X1314, Alice 5700, Ciskei

WALLIS F.M.
Department of Microbiology and Plant Pathology, University of Natal, P.O. Box 375, Pietermaritzburg 3200, South Africa

WILLAN K.
Department of Zoology, University of Fort Hare, Private Bag X1314, Allice 5700, Ciskei

TAINTON N.M.
Department of Grassland Science, University of Natal, P.O. Box 375, Pietermaritzburg 3200, South Africa

Chapter 1 Characteristics of South African Biomes

B. J. HUNTLEY

INTRODUCTION

The development of integrated cooperative ecological research programmes on a national scale demands the use of major biotic divisions rather than political or administrative units as a basis to the organizational framework. Such a framework should bring together research on those ecosystems which share floristic, faunistic, climo-edaphic and dynamic characteristics and which are consequently subject to the same kinds of environmental problems. For this reason the National Programme for Environmental Sciences has followed the tradition initiated in the International Biological Programme in developing its activities within the major biomes of South Africa.

The term biome has been little used in South Africa, indeed, with the exception of an unpublished note on the topic by Edwards (1977a), no formal account of South African biomes exists in the literature. The term has been variously defined and interpreted - essentially it relates to "the largest land community convenient to recognize ... where the life form of the climatic climax vegetation is uniform ... and reflects the major features of climate and determines the structural nature of the habitat for animals ... the biome is a total community unit and not a unit of vegetation alone" (Odum 1971).

The value of using the traditional Clementsian concept of the "climatic climax" to identify "the largest land community" is questionable where fire subclimax communities are both dominant and ancient features of the landscape. Thus in this account the grassland biome includes the moist grasslands of the escarpment slopes of the eastern seaboard which, according to Acocks (1975) and others, are seral to Afromontane forest, while the moist savanna biome, in central and west Africa at least, develops to a Guineo-Congolian forest climax with the exclusion of fire. Yet these grasslands and savannas today cover more than 95% of the land area in which they occur, with the "climatic climax" forests remaining as relict patches. Furthermore, palaeoecological evidence suggests that the moist grasslands of Natal and the moist savannas of central Africa have been dominant features of the landscape for the Holocene at least. It is therefore evident that strict adherence to the climatic climax philosophy in characterizing biomes is no longer tenable if the concept is used to define "the largest land community convenient to recognize".

DISTRIBUTION OF SOUTH AFRICAN BIOMES

The first map of African biomes (Odum 1971), based on a sketch map of Moreau (1952), included four biomes for South Africa. The more recent map produced by Moreau (1966), based on the AETFAT map of the vegetation of Africa south of the tropic of Cancer (Keay 1959), is far more useful. Moreau reduced the 35 vegetation types of the AETFAT map to six viz : montane, lowland forest, moist woodlands and savannas, dry woodlands and steppe, desert and semidesert, and macchia. These divisions constitute the major plant formations of Africa (although omitting natural grasslands) and correspond very closely to the biomes defined in this account.

Based on Moreau's work, and on the extensive discussions in Werger (1978), the following classification of South African biomes is recommended.

1   Fynbos biome – the evergreen sclerophyllous heathlands and shrublands of the southwestern and southern Cape.

2   Karoo biome – the arid to desertic regions occupied by low shrubs, succulents and desert grasses.

3   Grassland biome – the natural grasslands of the South African highveld and the "false" grasslands of the higher rainfall areas.

4   Savanna biomes – (a) Arid savanna biome – the spinescent, usually fine-leaved wooded grasslands and thickets of base-rich substrates in hotter, drier regions, and (b) Moist savanna biome – the deciduous broadleaf savannas and woodlands of acid substrates and mesic to moist rainfall regimes.

5   Forest biomes – (a) Lowland forest biome – the forests of the Zululand coast with strong affinities to the Guineo-Congolian flora and fauna – in most cases the South African examples of this biome form transitional complexes with the forests of the next type; (b) Afromontane forest biome – the forests dominated by *Podocarpus* spp and usually at altitudes exceeding 1 500 m but occurring at much lower altitudes at the southern limit of their distribution.

The above definitions are of necessity simplistic and will be expanded in the biome descriptions which follow. The classification should, however, provide for the coordination of ecosystem research on an ecological rather than regional or thematic basis.

A map of South African biomes would be most useful, but its compilation is rendered extremely difficult by the wide differences between the Veld Type concept of Acocks (1975) and the biome concept adopted in this account. A first approximation based on the classification and definitions given here is presented in Figure 1. The allocation of Veld Types within the biomes recognized in this account is indicated in Table 1. From the listing it will be clear that much of South African vegetation forms a small-scale mosaic, most pronounced where geomorphic surfaces, soil types and climatic gradients are steep, such as in Natal, the eastern and southern Cape and the eastern Transvaal. The existence of this mosaic accounts for the generally confused interpretation of biotic relations existing in the South African literature, written almost entirely by authors who have not witnessed the broad patterns present in central and equatorial Africa.

Features of the main biomes are illustrated in Figures 3 to 8.

4

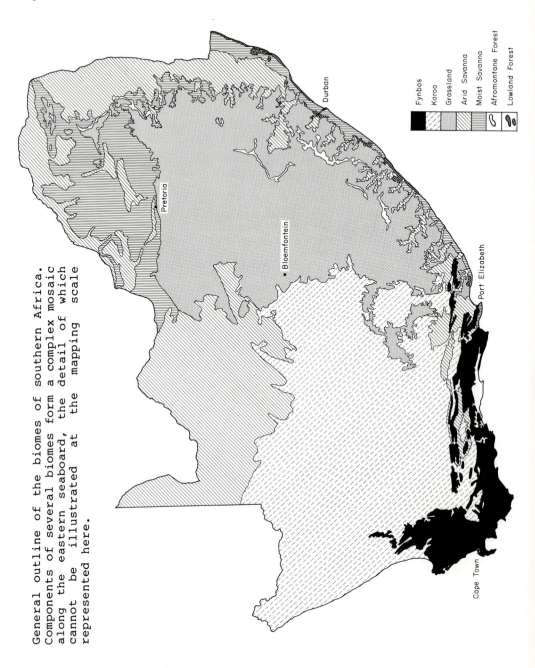

Figure 1 General outline of the biomes of southern Africa. Components of several biomes form a complex mosaic along the eastern seaboard, the detail of which cannot be illustrated at the mapping scale represented here.

Fynbos
Karoo
Grassland
Arid Savanna
Moist Savanna
Afromontane Forest
Lowland Forest

Pretoria
Bloemfontein
Durban
Port Elizabeth
Cape Town

Table 1   Allocation of Acocks's (1975) Veld Types within the
          biomes recognized in this account.

Veld Types

Fynbos biome	Fynbos proper	47, 69, 70
	Coastal renosterbosveld	46
	West coast strandveld	34 (south of St Helena Bay)
Karoo biome	Succulent karoo	31, 33, parts of 26, 28, 29, 32, 34
	Karoo proper	27, 28, 30, 32
	"False" karoo	35-43
Grassland biome	Grassland proper	48-59
	"False" grassland	60-68, patches of 1, 3, 5-8, 22, 45, 49
Savanna biomes	Arid savanna biome	11-16, 23, patches of 1, 10, 17, 21, 22, 24, 25
	Moist savanna biome	9, 18-20, patches of 1, 6, 7, 10, 21, 22
Forest biomes	Lowland forest biome	patches of 1, 3, 6, 7
	Afromontane forest biome	2, 4, patches of 3, 5, 7, 8, 44, 45

FYNBOS BIOME

This biome comprises evergreen sclerophyllous heathlands and shrublands in which fine-leaved low shrubs and leafless tufted grasslike plants are typical. Trees and evergreen succulent shrubs are rare, while grasses form an insignificant part of the biomass.

The biome occupies 59 282 km^2 or 5,3%[1] of South Africa, almost exclusively in the southwest and southern Cape. It includes (a) fynbos (Veld Types 47, 69 and 70), comprising coastal fynbos on recent coastal deposits, and mountain fynbos on quartzitic and leached granitic soils, (b) coastal renosterbosveld (Veld Type 46) on base-saturated soils of the lowlands, and (c) the west coast strandveld (Veld Type 34, south of St Helena Bay), on recent sands.

[1]The per cent values quoted in this chapter are based on the area of the Republic of South Africa, Transkei, Bophuthatswana and Venda.

6

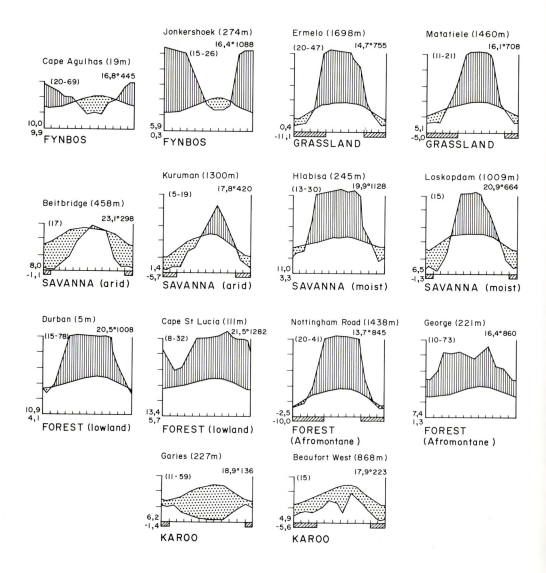

Figure 2　　Representative climate diagrams for stations in the various biomes of South Africa.

The climate of the fynbos biome is variable (Figure 2). Rainfall ranges from about 200 to over 3 000 mm yr^{-1}, with a typical winter regime in the west, but with spring and autumnal peaks in the east. Mean annual temperature ranges from less than 12°C to about 19°C. Frosts are rare except in intermontane valleys and on high plateaux. Snow falls frequently on the high mountains but does not persist.

The fynbos flora is dominated by the families Asteraceae, Ericaceae, Proteaceae, Leguminosae, Iridaceae, Cyperaceae, Restionaceae and a number of others. Predominant genera are *Erica*, *Restio*, *Ficinia*, *Senecio*, *Cliffortia*, *Aspalathus* and many more. These diverse genera are characterized by a high degree of endemism.

Plant communities are very rich in species. The restioid and the ericoid elements are invariably present while proteoid shrubs are common. Communities range from tall broad-sclerophyllous (proteoid) or sometimes narrow-sclerophyllous (ericoid) scrub through low ericoid heathland or open shrub communities, to restionaceous herbland. Coastal renosterbosveld and west coast strandveld differ somewhat from fynbos sensu strictu, especially in terms of the importance of the restioid growth form, the higher base-status of their soils and the lower frequency of fires (Kruger 1978).

Coastal Renosterbosveld shows affinities not only with the fynbos flora, but also with the savanna and karoo floras. Communities are dominated by the shrub *Elytropappus rhinocerotis* (renosterbos), 0,5 to 1,5 m high. Grasses often form a significant component and patches of tall scrub 3 to 4 m high are scattered through the landscape.

West coast strandveld comprises semisucculent and broad-sclerophyllous shrubs. Floristic affinities are found with fynbos, karoo and savanna floras.

The zoogeography of the fynbos biome is briefly reviewed by Jarvis (1979). Floristic diversity is not paralleled by an equally rich fauna; the fynbos biome nevertheless possesses a wide variety of endemic vertebrates which include 9 mammals, 6 birds, 19 freshwater fishes, 9 frogs and toads and approximately 20 reptiles. The invertebrate fauna has high levels of endemism in some orders, particularly within the Mollusca, Lepidoptera and Coleoptera, while primitive groups such as the Onychophora and Megaloptera are of particular zoogeographic interest. Thus, although the faunal identity of fynbos is not as clear as the floral, there is a growing body of evidence to support the concept of a distinctive "fynbos fauna".

Above-ground biomass and production data for fynbos communities are given by Kruger (1977a). Biomass values of between 2 000 to 26 000 kg ha^{-1} were reported for stands of from 2 to 17 yr of age, the mature communities usually ranging from 12 000 to 16 000 kg ha^{-1}. Estimates of annual above-ground production vary from 1 000 kg ha^{-1} to 4 000 kg ha^{-1} with average above-ground production of the order of 2 500 kg ha^{-1} (Kruger 1977a).

Fynbos communities generally require from 4 to 6 yr to accumulate sufficient fuel to burn and fires occur at random within 6 to 40 yr rotations (Kruger 1979a). Fires are most prevalent during the dry summer months (in the west) while late summer and autumn fires are frequent in the southern Cape.

Figure 3   Coastal fynbos on recent sands near Mamre, Cape. Rainfall occurs almost entirely in winter, totalling 570 mm per annum. This low heathland comprises a rich diversity of ericoid, restioid and proteoid species. Approximately five years post-fire.

Figure 4   False Upper Karoo (sensu Acocks 1975), Middelburg, Cape. The dwarf shrubland is dominated by *Pentzia*, *Pteronia* and *Eriocephalus* species. Low trees of *Acacia karroo* along seasonal watercourses. The fire scar on ·the mountain indicates the position of a burn following a series of summers with unusually high rainfall. Mean rainfall is 360 mm per annum. (Photo P W Roux).

KAROO BIOME

The karoo biome is characterized by dwarf and low open shrublands in which xerophytic, fine-leaved and succulent shrubs predominate. Depending on topography and substrate, varying densities of small trees are present, being most abundant in the rocky brokenveld (Veld Types 26 and 33) of the Great Karoo, Little Karoo and the Robertson Karoo.

The karoo biome occupies 369 946 km^2 or 31,9% of the Republic and includes Namaqualand, the Little Karoo, the Great Karoo, the central and upper Karoo, Bushmanland, the Cape Midlands, the eastern mixed Karoo and the southwestern Orange Free State.

The topography of the vast central plateau region is dominated by wide peneplains with scattered mesas, buttes and inselbergs. The greater area of the biome lies on sediments of the Karoo System, throughout which dolerite intrusions are common. The northern region is a featureless rolling plain covered by gravel, with sands of the Kalahari System in the far north, while a rugged mountain complex predominates on the eastern boundary. The southern and southwestern region of the biome interdigitates with the fold mountains of the Cape System.

The climate is characterized by extremes of most weather variables. Severe frost and snow on the higher mountains during winter contrast with high air and soil temperatures and high light intensities in summer. The average rainfall ranges from 50 mm in the west to 350 mm in the east. Winter rainfall from 50 to 200 mm predominates in the west.

The general monotony of the karoo landscape belies its floristic and ecological complexity. The flora is relatively rich, with the families Asteraceae, Mesembryanthemaceae, Scrophulariaceae and Gramineae best represented. The boundaries of the region grade into grassland, fynbos and arid savanna.

The biome has been variously subdivided according to climatic, edaphic, floristic and dynamic characteristics. In broad terms, three main divisions can be recognized:-

1   The western, arid succulent karoo - which falls mainly within the zone of winter rainfall.

2   The central and upper karoo - the karoo sensu strictu, which falls mainly within the summer rainfall zone, but extends into nonseasonal rainfall areas in the south and west.

3   The "false" karoo - vast areas of formerly different vegetation transformed during the last few centuries to a form in which karroid dwarf shrubs have become dominant due to their greater competitive ability under excessive grazing pressure.

Within these three main karoo types, the basic structural components of low, often succulent, fine-leaved shrubs, short grasses and low trees occur in varying densities.

The western karoo is very rich in succulent species, belonging mainly to the families Mesembryanthemaceae, Crassulaceae and Euphorbiaceae. Desert grasses, especially *Stipagrostis* spp predominate in the northwest.

The karoo proper has few succulents, with xeromorphic dwarf shrubs of the genera *Pentzia, Eriocephalus, Plinthus, Pteronia, Salsola* and many more. Grasses become taller and more common from west to east, with species of *Eragrostis, Aristida* and *Stipagrostis* being more prevalent. Scattered trees, which are most conspicuous on the numerous dolerite intrusions and other low hills, include the genera *Euclea, Olea, Rhus* and *Boscia*. *Acacia karroo* (sweet thorn), *Rhus lancea* (karee), *Salix mucronata* (Cape willow) etc, form short woodlands along the sandy riverbeds which drain the biome.

The "false" karoo includes nine Veld Types which, while retaining many of their original floristic characteristics, have been structurally transformed by the reduction in the grass and palatable shrub component and their replacement by unpalatable karroid dwarf shrubs. The transformation has been most extensive in the southern Orange Free State, where "False Upper Karoo" now occupies 65 777 km^2 of former grassland.

A distinctive contemporary karoo fauna has not been recognized by modern zoogeographers, although 19 bird species endemic to South Africa are largely confined to the biome as described in this account. Typical of these are Ludwig's bustard *(Neotis ludwigii)*, karoo korhaan *(Eupodotis vigorsii)*, black korhaan *(E. afra)*, karoo lark *(Mirafra albescens)*, karoo chat *(Cercomela schlegelii)* and karoo robin *(Erythropygia coryphaeus)*.

The indigenous large mammal fauna, comprising vast herds of migratory springbok *(Antidorcas marsupialis)*, black wildebeest *(Connochaetes gnou)*, quagga *(Equus quagga)* and blesbok *(Damaliscus dorcas phillipsi)* until the late 19th century, have been largely replaced by domestic stock, in particular by merino sheep.

Few reliable biomass data are available for the karoo biome (Rutherford 1978). Estimates of above-ground biomass range from 3 700 kg ha^{-1} to 7 500 kg ha^{-1} for the less arid parts of the karoo – figures for the extremely arid western karoo are not available but would be much lower.

Due to the low productivity of karoo vegetation, the accumulation of combustible fuel seldom reaches levels sufficient to support a fire. Following unusually high rainfall seasons, however, production might surpass utilization and fires might occur. During 1975 widespread fires were experienced in many "false karoo" areas where grass production in particular had been unusually high following a series of very good rain seasons. Such fires, despite their infrequency, probably exercise a far greater influence on the dynamics of karoo vegetation than their rarity would suggest.

GRASSLAND BIOME

Grasslands are defined as those areas where the vegetation is dominated by grasses and occasionally by other plants of grassy

appearance (eg Cyperaceae, Juncaceae) and in which woody plants
are absent or rare.

The grassland biome of South Africa, as recognized in this
account, occupies 280 047 km^2 or 24,1% of the country's area.
Two main types of grassland may be distinguished: (a) "True"
grasslands - grasslands occurring over extensive areas where the
climatic climax appears to be grassland. These areas can be
said to have a grassland climate inducing winter dormancy.
Succession does not normally proceed beyond the grassland
climax. (b) "False" grasslands - those grasslands occurring in
areas where there is evidence that the climate will permit
succession to proceed beyond the grassland stage into shrubland,
savanna, woodland or forest but which are maintained as grassland
by biotic factors such as grazing and fire or edaphic factors
such as seasonal waterlogging.

The grassland biome of South Africa occurs on flat to gently
rolling upland plateaux at 1 000 to 1 800 m above sea level to
the west of the escarpment, and on the steeply sloping escarpment
faces of the eastern seaboard usually at altitudes exceeding
500 m. Alpine grasslands, related to the Afro-alpine biome of
East Africa, occur in the Lesotho highlands and marginally within
Natal, eastern Cape and Orange Free State, but will not be
discussed here. For the greater part, grassland areas are
underlain by Karoo System rocks, consisting mostly of sedimentary
rocks with dolerite intrusions and extrusive basalt and
rhyolites, or of Precambrian sedimentary and intrusive rocks.

Most grasslands occur in the summer rainfall area. Winters
are relatively dry, frosty to very cold with snow at the higher
altitudes. Mean annual rainfall varies from less than 500 mm to
well over 1 000 mm, but the precipitation of most grasslands lies
within this range.

The "true" grasslands vary from short sour[1] grasslands,
usually at the higher altitudes, which are largely dominated by
the tribes Andropogoneae, Chlorideae, Eragrosteae, Arundinelleae
and Paniceae, and with a component of geophytes, to taller and
less sour grasslands with a preponderance of Andropogoneae at
lower altitudes. In those "false" grasslands which occur in
potential forest climax areas with leached soils the grassland is
sour. In areas of potential savanna, the grassland may be sour,
mixed or sweet following a trend from moist through mesic to arid
savannas. Grasslands adjacent to the karoo biome are generally
short and sweet. In many areas these grasslands are being
replaced by "false" karoo due to selective overgrazing of the
palatable grass species.

The original ungulate fauna of the highveld grasslands
included vast herds of blesbok, black wildebeest and springbok.

---

[1]In South African stock farming terminology "sour" implies a
significant decrease in acceptability and nutritive value in
winter; "sweet" implies that the acceptability and nutritive
value of constituent species remains relatively unchanged from
summer to winter.

These migratory herds have been reduced in numbers and distribution during the last century, but large numbers still occur in nature reserves throughout the biome. The wild migratory ungulate biomass has been replaced by an equal or larger biomass of sedentary domestic species such as cattle, sheep and goats.

The grassland biome possesses a surprisingly rich "endemic" avifauna. Twenty one species of birds are confined essentially to the biome, including threatened species such as bald ibis (*Geronticus calvus*), blue crane (*Anthropoides paradisea*), blue korhaan (*Eupodotis caerulescens*), ground woodpecker (*Geocolaptes olivaceus*), Botha's lark (*Spizocorys fringillaris*) and Rudd's lark (*Mirafra ruddi*).

Numerous production estimates are available for the grassland biome. Mean figures for 10 yr periods quoted by Rutherford (1978) range from 630 kg ha^{-1} yr^{-1} for grasslands around Bloemfontein receiving 500 mm mean annual rainfall, to 3 900 kg ha^{-1} yr^{-1} in the higher rainfall (721 mm yr^{-1}) grasslands near Pietermaritzburg. Considerable variation occurs from season to season in accordance with rainfall, while production also varies significantly according to soil type within the same rainfall regime.

SAVANNA BIOME

Savannas are here defined as wooded C4 grasslands of the tropics and subtropics in which the density, height and growth form characteristics of both woody and grass components vary markedly between the two principal types of savanna in southern Africa - ie arid eutrophic savannas and moist dystrophic savannas.

ARID SAVANNA BIOME

The arid savannas occupy 270 220 km^2 or 24,2% of South Africa, usually occurring on base-rich soils of hotter, drier, lowland valleys and rejuvenated upland situations. Calcretes are a common feature of arid savanna soils. Rainfall is usually restricted to 5 or 6 months of the year and ranges typically from 250 to 650 mm yr^{-1}. Elements of arid savanna extend into moist savanna on termitaria or other base-rich substrates.

Arid savannas are physiognomically diverse and include open sparse grassland with scattered shrubs and short trees to dense thorn thickets in which the herbaceous layer might be insignificant. The woody component is dominated by spinescent nano- and microphylls, in particular the genera *Acacia* and *Commiphora*. Xerophytic tussock grasses of the Eragrosteae and Paniceae predominate, with a large percentage of annuals in the driest areas.

The nutritive value of arid savanna is high and supports large concentrations of indigenous ungulates. Typical arid savanna species include kudu (*Tragelaphus strepsiceros*), impala (*Aepyceros melampus*) and black rhinoceros (*Diceros bicornis*). Birds typical of arid savannas include Cape penduline tit (*Anthoscopus minutus*), southern grey tit (*Parus afer*), Marico flycatcher (*Melaenornis mariquensis*) and whitebrowed sparrowweaver (*Plocepasser mahali*).

13

Figure 5   Highland Sourveld (sensu Acocks 1975) at Thabamhlope,
Natal.   These short grasslands are dominated by
Themeda triandra, *Tristachya hispida* and *Heteropogon
contortus*.   Rainfall averages 900 mm, altitude
1500 m.   (Photo M Mentis).

Figure 6   Arid eutrophic savanna on alluvial soil on the margins
of the Nyl river floodplain, northern Transvaal. Open
short tree savanna with *Acacia tortilis*, *A. nilotica*,
Euclea undulata and clumps of *Sansevieria cylindrica*
and *Carissa bispinosa*.   Dominant grasses include
Eragrostis lehmanniana and *Sporobolus iocladus*.

Production estimates for the herbaceous component of arid savanna indicate an average of between 500 to 1 000 kg ha^{-1} yr^{-1}. Woody component biomass values ca 20 000 kg ha^{-1}.

Fire is an infrequent but significant phenomenon. In some arid savannas such as those of the Kalahari sandveld of the northern Cape, fire was seldom recorded until extensive fires occurred in 1974 to 1977 following seasons of above average rainfall. Damage to many large *Acacia erioloba* (camel thorn) trees was severe, markedly influencing community structure (M G L Mills, personal communication, 1981). Succession advances towards an open woodland or shrub savanna climax but under disturbed conditions a dense thicket might develop.

MOIST SAVANNA BIOME

The moist or mesic savannas occupy 115 579 km^2 or 9,9% of South Africa and occur typically on plateaux at 500 to 1 000 m above sea level. The soils of these planation surfaces are nutrient poor, leached and occasionally waterlogged during the rainy season which ranges from 6 to 9 months with from 500 to 1 100 mm rainfall yr^{-1}. Elements of moist savanna extend into arid savanna on acidic sands. Laterites are a prominent feature of moist savanna soils.

The vegetation comprises a catena of tall closed nonspinescent mesophyllous to microphyllous deciduous woodland, and open drainage-line grasslands. Geoxylic suffrutices are a prominent feature in moist savanna and are absent from arid savannas. The tall perennial mesophytic grasses which dominate in moist savannas are mainly of the tribe Andropogoneae. Woody genera include *Burkea, Terminalia and Ochna*. The vegetation is of low nutritive value and low density indigenous ungulate species such as roan *(Hippotragus equinus)*, sable *(H. niger)*, common reedbuck *(Redunca arundinum)* and oribi *(Ourebia ourebi)* are typical. Birds include grey penduline tit *(Anthoscopus caroli)*, pallid (mousecoloured) flycatcher *(Melaenornis pallidus)* and southern black tit *(Parus niger)*.

Moist savannas have high levels of herbaceous productivity, with annual production values of up to 4 800 kg ha^{-1} for central African miombo being reported by Rutherford (1978). In South African moist savannas the herbaceous production is much less, probably closer to 2 200 kg ha^{-1} yr^{-1}. Estimates for the biomass of the woody component range from ca 20 000 kg ha^{-1} for *Burkea africana* (red syringa) savanna at Nylsvley to 40 000 kg ha^{-1} for *Brachystegia* woodland in Zambia.

Fire is a regular phenomenon in moist savannas, annual winter burns being the normal pattern in central Africa but in South Africa fire might be as infrequent as once in 5 yr in the Transvaal Waterberg which receives about 600 mm rainfall yr^{-1}.

FOREST BIOME

The forest biome includes the indigenous evergreen and semideciduous closed forests of the coastal lowlands and escarpment slopes which occupy less than 1% of the Republic's

Figure 7   Moist dystrophic savanna on shallow sands at Nylsvley,
            northern Transvaal. Rainfall averages 630 mm. Mosaic
            of dense woodland with grass understorey interspersed
            with open grass patches. *Burkea africana*, *Terminalia
            sericea* and *Ochna pulchra* dominate the woody
            component, *Eragrostis pallens* and *Panicum maximum*
            dominate the herb layer in the open and under trees
            respectively. (Photo P G H Frost).

Figure 8
Moist evergreen Afromontane
forest near George, southern
Cape. Rainfall approximates
1100 mm and is non-seasonal.
Dominant canopy trees of up
to 22 m include *Podocarpus
latifolius*, *P. falcatus*, *Olea
capensis* and *Ocotea bullata*.
(Photo C J Geldenhuys).

land area. Forests are here distinguished from closed canopy moist savannas on the basis of the absence of C4 grasses from the herb layer and the absence of fire within forests. Floristically forests comprise elements of the Guineo-Congolian or Afromontane Regions while savannas comprise components of the Sudano-Zambezian Region.

With a few exceptions, such as the forests of the southern Cape and the Zululand coast dune systems, forests occur in South Africa as small (usually less than 10 km^2) relict patches scattered throughout the higher rainfall areas. The total area of forest in South Africa is probably less than 2 000 km^2, although the extent of the Veld Types in which they occupy a significant area is 50 962 km^2 or 4,4% of the country.

The forests of South Africa are related to the lowland Guineo-Congolian and upland Afromontane forests of tropical Africa. Elements of both these types tend to intergrade over much of the forest biome in South Africa and a clear distinction of the two types can only be made when comparing examples such as the coast dune forests of Tongaland with the montane forests of the Drakensberg escarpment.

Biomass and production estimates are not available for indigenous forests in South Africa. Estimates of basal area summarized by Rutherford (1978) provide an idea of the relative densities of woody cover in savanna and forest. Basal area ranges from 5 m^2 ha^{-1} for open shrubby arid savanna, 5 to 10 m^2 ha^{-1} in moister savanna to between 10 and 16 m^2 ha^{-1} for central African miombo. Comparative figures for South African forests are 40 m^2 ha^{-1} for lowland forest in Zululand to between 40 to 50 m^2 ha^{-1} for Afromontane forest of the southern Cape.

Fire is an important determinant of the dynamics of forest margin communities, but seldom, if ever, penetrates extensive patches of mature forest. Presence of charcoal within the soil profiles of some southern Cape forests (F J Kruger, personal communication, 1980) might indicate that fires such as that of 1866 reported by Scott (this volume, chapter 4) might well sweep through forests at intervals of perhaps several hundreds of years.

LOWLAND FOREST BIOME

The lowland forests, such as those of the coast dunes and lowlands (Tongaland, Dukuduku, Ngoye) have tall (20 to 35 m) closed canopies with fairly dense understoreys of shrubs and lianes. Epiphytes are present but not abundant. Plants and animals of particular biogeographic interest, showing their Guineo-Congolian/Indian Ocean Coast Belt affinities, are *Blighia unijugata* (triangle tops), *Pseudobersama mossambicensis* (false white ash), *Alchornea hirtella* (Zulu bead-string), *Olyra latifolia* (wild olive), Delegorgue's (bronze-naped) pigeon (*Columba delegorguei*), Woodwards' (green) barbet (*Cryptolybia woodwardi*), red bush squirrel (*Paraxerus palliatus*) and *Bitis gabonica* (gaboon viper). Birds typical of these forests are sombre bulbul (*Andropadus importunus*), purplecrested lourie (*Tauraco porphyreolophus*), Natal robin (*Cossypha natalensis*), spotted thrush (*Turdus fischeri*), forest weaver (*Ploceus bicolor*).

AFROMONTANE FOREST BIOME

The Afromontane forests of South Africa occur along the Drakensberg escarpment, in the Natal and eastern Cape midlands and on the coast of the southern Cape. The canopies of these forests are generally lower (10 to 25 m) and less dense than those of the lowland forests, while the understorey is generally open. Epiphytes are often abundant while lianes are rare. These forests are usually found on steep, often south-facing slopes, and orographic fog and rainfall are important features of their climate.

Genera which are common to most of these forests are *Podocarpus*, *Olea*, *Ilex*, *Pittosporum*, *Rapanea*, *Xymalos*, etc. Although the Afromontane forests of tropical Africa have a very rich endemic avifauna, those of South Africa have none. The mammalian fauna of these forests is also without notable characteristic species, but birds typically restricted to these forests include bush blackcap *(Lioptilus nigricapillus)*, Knysna lourie *(Tauraco corythaix)*, chorister robin *(Cossypha dichroa)* and rameron pigeon *(Columba arquatrix)*.

The above description of South African biomes provides a first approximation to a more rigorous treatment of the subject. It might be argued that the Namib Desert biome and Afroalpine biome should be included in this account. Their very limited extent in the geographic area under consideration, and the absence or insignificance of fire in their functioning, accounts for their omission.

Chapter 2 Fire Regimes in the Biomes of South Africa

D. EDWARDS

INTRODUCTION

Evidence of ancient fires is available from the Palaeozoic, Mesozoic and Tertiary Periods in various parts of the world (West 1965; Komarek 1971a; Kozlowski and Ahlgren 1974). In South Africa modern evidence shows that most plant formations are subject to burning at one time or another but the frequency with which this may take place differs greatly. Biomes such as the grassland, savanna and fynbos are adapted to regular and frequent firing and have many plant species whose evolutionary development accords with community behavioural responses to fire (Bews 1925; Bayer 1955; Bean 1962; Levyns 1966a; Gordon-Gray and Wright 1969). Other biomes such as the evergreen forest and karoo, however, are rarely subject to fires.

In characterizing the main fire regimes into which the biomes may be grouped, emphasis has been placed on outlining their historical development from pre-colonial times through the post-colonial period. This comparative treatment involves broad consideration of available natural fuels, general climatically induced causes of fires, and the general history of fire in the post-colonial period dating from 1652. Man-induced fires are discussed in detail by Hall (this volume, chapter 3).

AVAILABLE NATURAL FUELS, CLIMATE AND WEATHER CONDITIONS

Primary production, a functional parameter of the ecosystem referring to the rate of production of biomass, and above-ground biomass, and a structural parameter of vegetation, determine the potential natural fuels of biomes and of the various communities within a biome. Thus, the quantity and quality of fuels available for fires vary widely in South Africa primarily in relation to climate and weather but also in relation to the degree of use by man and herbivores. Unfortunately, little work has been undertaken on the relationships of fire either to net primary production or the kind and amount of functional biomass and the amount of dead material. At present, therefore, available biomass and yield data serve to indicate the potential, type and quantities of fuel available under various climatic and weather conditions in the different biomes. Such biomass and production data given here are largely based on the recent review by Rutherford (1978) and on the references cited by Rutherford (see also subsequent chapters).

FYNBOS BIOME

Fuels in the fynbos biome consist mainly of those provided by evergreen, sclerophyllous, fine to broadleaved shrubs and small trees and by the sclerophyllous restioid growth form. Eastwards, grasses contribute progressively more to biomass and production. Plant mass is usually concentrated in the first 1,5 m above ground, with evergreen tall shrubs and small trees emergent up to 3 to 5 m. Compared with the grasslands and the grass layer of savanna, the bulk of the biomass in fynbos is distinctly coarser, more woody (twiggy), and with aromatic oils and thick cuticular waxes that may contribute combustible properties. Whereas grass and low shrub components of the grasslands, grassy savannas and karoo are grazed over most of their area, in the fynbos herbivore use is almost entirely restricted to certain parts of the lowland area, such as in the Bredasdorp region, where intensive agronomy is not practised. Most of the annual net primary production of fynbos that is not lost to other natural processes therefore becomes available as fuel for fires. Biomass is related to the age of the fynbos communities relative to the previous fire and in mature communities is amongst the highest recorded in South Africa.

In mountain fynbos where the mean annual rainfall commonly exceeds 1 000 mm and at some sites exceeds 3 000 mm, the biomass is between 11 000 and 26 000 kg ha^{-1} for 10 to 17 yr old mesophy-llous evergreen broad sclerophyll scrub, heath and restioid communities, but low values of around 5 000 kg ha^{-1} are also found in certain mature mountain fynbos communities. The lowest biomass is possibly found in the low rainfall areas (200 to 300 mm yr^{-1}) dominated by *Elytropappus rhinocerotis* (renosterbos), though in the extreme southwestern karoo biome in the Mountain Renosterbos veld type, Rutherford (1979) recorded a biomass of 11 000 kg ha^{-1}.

Rutherford (1978) cites Kruger as stating that the average production for the first two years of growth in fynbos is about 2 500 kg ha^{-1} yr^{-1}, ranging from 1 000 kg ha^{-1} yr^{-1} for a heath community to 4 000 kg ha^{-1} yr^{-1} for an *Elegia-Osmitopsis* swamp community. These values are higher than for much of the grass-land of South Africa but, with the exception of the swamp fynbos community, are about half as much as that attained by moist grasslands.

In addition to the unique fuel aspects of the fynbos, the climate of the fynbos biome is also unique in the co-incidence of the dry period with high summer[1] temperatures and a high incid-ence of southeasterly winds. Together with the periodic occurr-ence of hot, dry fohn-like Berg winds that occur mainly during spring over most of South Africa, southeasterly winds and dry summer and autumn periods, provide a highly favourable climate for fire.

KAROO BIOME

Compared to the fynbos and other biomes in South Africa, the potential fuel loads in the karoo biome are low and concentrated in usually widely dispersed dwarf shrubs with low aerial cover.

---

[1]Throughout this chapter the four seasons are those used by the Weather Bureau (1957), namely summer = December, January and February; autumn = March, April and May; winter = June, July and August; spring = September, October and November. Seasons are also used to describe the time when fires occur. The terms early, mid and late season refer to the first, second and third months, respectively, of any season. January (mid-summer) is usually the hottest month and July (mid-winter) is usually the coldest month.

In the western and southern karoo where the winter rainfall averages 50 to 300 mm yr^{-1}, non-flammable succulent dwarf shrubs are either dominant or make up a large part of the vegetation. Eastwards, with the shift towards a mean annual summer rainfall of 500 mm, grasses become increasingly more important, especially in the karoo mountain areas, and provide a continuity of fuel for potential fires.

Local stands of *Tetrachne dregei* grassland on moist sites near Middelburg, Cape, can accumulate 5 100 kg ha^{-1} over 3 yr and similar values probably occurred formerly in karoo mountain grass vegetation. However, grazing and the highly variable rainfall (the mean deviation from the annual mean ranges from 25% in the east to 80% in the northwest) are such that fuels seldom attain sufficient biomass and continuity to support more than a localized burn under present day conditions. The few data available indicate a biomass of 3 700 kg ha^{-1} for shrub vegetation under about 200 mm rainfall near Carnarvon, of 4 800 to 5 600 kg ha^{-1} for the higher, 300 to 400 mm rainfall area near Middelburg, Cape, and of 7 500 kg ha^{-1} for a non-flammable succulent karoo scrub near Robertson with a winter rainfall of ca 300 mm yr^{-1}. If the data of Walter (cited by Rutherford 1979, 1980) for South West Africa/Namibia may be extrapolated to similar dwarf shrub and desert grass of the adjoining northwest Cape region of 100 to 200 mm mean annual rainfall, low biomass values of 600 to 1 700 kg ha^{-1} may be expected in these regions.

GRASSLAND AND SAVANNA BIOMES

Fuels of the grasslands and the grass layer in savannas in the summer rainfall parts of the country contrast with those of the fynbos and karoo.

The intensity and duration of the dry winter season and the frost period determine the degree of inflammability during autumn, winter and spring. Based on Stevenson screen temperatures of less than 0°C, the average duration of the frost period is 60 to over 90 days for grasslands of the central plateau and the Drakensberg escarpment and its foothill regions, decreasing east, west and south to no frost along the coast (Schulze 1965).

Most of the grassland and savanna biomes do not normally receive measurable rainfall for 2 to 4 months during winter. However, due to the effect of the eastern escarpment in increasing the quota of winter rainfall (Schulze 1965), the grasslands associated with the montane forests from the southeastern Cape through Natal to the eastern Transvaal have mean monthly rainfalls even during the dry season of at least 10 mm. Also, no severe dry season is experienced along the narrow coastal strip from the southern and eastern Cape to Natal, in that no monthly means are less than 25 mm (Edwards 1967; Schulze and McGee 1978). This winter rain together with the absence of frost along the coastal regions results in these grasslands being less inflammable than those further inland and, especially, the intensely frosty highveld plateau grassland. Rainfall variability is less than 25% mean deviation from the annual mean for the grasslands and moist savanna (Weather Bureau 1957).

Most of the grasslands are short with foliage concentrated in the first 0,5 m above ground. In the warmer and moister areas, including the savannas, the grass layer is medium-high with the foliage concentration extending up to 1 m above ground over extensive areas. Tall grasslands up to 2 m high are localized but not uncommon in the moister regions. Virtually all the grasslands are of a bunch grass type with a closed or nearly closed canopy when mature and well managed by graziers, but with basal cover generally less than 20% so that if closely grazed the fuel mass is dispersed as well as reduced. Grazing is a major influence on the biomass and potential fuel mass. Under conditions of low rainfall and/or unleached fertile soils, the so-called "sweet-veld" grasslands and savannas are palatable to stock for most of the year, and fuel mass is commonly severely reduced by grazing. In the so-called "sourveld" grasslands of moist climates and leached and low nutrient soils, which are prevalent in the moist grassland and moist savanna regions, palatability is limited to about 4 months of the year so that plant material accumulates to provide greater fuel mass and inflammability during the dry season.

Mean annual rainfall ranges from less than 500 mm to over 1 000 mm in the grassland biome with annual production values from 560 to 5 560 kg ha^{-1} yr^{-1}. There is considerable variation of potential fuel mass according to soil type and annual rainfall. At Bloemfontein on the frosty central highveld plateau under a 500 to 600 mm rainfall, production on three different soils was 4 900, 3 300 and 3 100 kg ha^{-1} yr^{-1}, while at Pietermaritzburg in Natal under a rainfall of ca 800 mm the 15 yr average production was 3 900 kg ha^{-1} yr^{-1}, ranging from 2 880 to 5 560 kg ha^{-1} yr^{-1}.

Herbaceous layer production (chiefly grass) of the savanna biome is related to the density of the woody tree and shrub layers and to rainfall, which ranges from arid (250 to 500 mm) to moist (500 to 1 100 mm). Rainfall in the northern regions of South Africa is almost exclusively a summer phenomenon. Winter precipitation increases southwards. Northwards to beyond the Tropic the dry season is therefore extended to the high temperatures and atmospheric saturation deficits of late spring and early summer to provide a more consistently and more highly inflammable vegetation than southwards. The herbaceous layer is more inflammable than the deciduous woody layer and dense woody vegetation with a low herbaceous biomass is less prone to fire than a mixed grass-woody vegetation.

In the relatively dry moist savanna community of *Burkea africana* (red syringa) woodland at Nylsvley in the northern Transvaal, irregularly burnt about every 5 yr, the mean aboveground woody biomass of 18 132 kg ha^{-1} was found to be composed of 14 937 kg ha^{-1} wood, 236 kg ha^{-1} current season's twigs and 1 100 kg ha^{-1} leaves. Necromass comprised 1 859 kg ha^{-1} dead wood attached to trees and shrubs. Shrub sized individuals of less than 2,5 m height within reach of browsing animals constituted 11,5% of the total woody biomass and 29,7% of the leaf biomass (Rutherford 1979). In savanna types of average rainfall (ca 500 mm yr^{-1}) it appears that herbaceous layer growth is roughly 1 000 kg ha^{-1} yr^{-1} or more, and the woody species leaf and current twig production is about 1 500 kg ha^{-1} yr^{-1} (Rutherford 1978). In the arid northeast Cape savanna (400 to 500 mm rainfall yr^{-1}) potential fuel loads are lower. Herbaceous layer production ranges from 119 to 1 071 kg ha^{-1} yr^{-1} in inverse relation to the density of *Acacia mellifera* subsp. *detinens* (black thorn) trees and shrubs. Only 51 kg ha^{-1} yr^{-1} was recorded during a season of severe drought. In the eastern Cape Province, probably under a fairly similar mean annual rainfall, similar herbaceous layer production was found to range from 70 to 1 000 kg ha^{-1} under *Acacia karroo* (sweet thorn) densities of 1 000 individuals ha^{-1} over a number of seasons with widely differing rainfall.

Despite the high total biomass, fires in the South African savanna are mainly close to the ground, though crown fires do sometimes occur in woody vegetation above 3 to 4 m. This may be attributed to the open distribution and lower flammability of the often microphyllous woody plant material and to low herbaceous biomass and its discontinuous distribution. Red syringa woodland data at Nylsvley in the northern Transvaal illustrate the lateral discontinuity of herbaceous biomass of a savanna community: from 640 kg ha^{-1} under shrubs, to 970 kg ha^{-1} under trees, and 1 230 kg ha^{-1} between trees and shrubs.

FOREST BIOME

No biomass data appear to be available for the evergreen forest biomes. These forests are of limited area in South Africa and seldom burn, except under rare conditions of weather and drought stress and when so modified by human activity as to allow the entry of fire. They are fundamentally an ecosystem of species intolerant of fire. Thus, this biome will not be considered further here. However, it should not be thought that fire has had no influence on forest vegetation in South Africa. On the contrary, fire in the surrounding vegetation has had a marked effect on the forest margin and on the extent of the forest (Granger, this volume, chapter 8).

PHYSICALLY INDUCED NATURAL FIRES

The variety of physical causes of fire ignition in vegetation includes falling boulders, earthquake activity, spontaneous combustion and volcanic action. Volcanic activity is absent from South Africa and there is little evidence for significant spontaneous combustion taking place in vegetation.

Despite scepticism by some ecologists, there is good evidence for falling boulders and earthquake activity as ignition sources. Wicht (1945) cites direct evidence of a fire that on the 19th October 1937 was started by a falling rock accidentally dislodged by a labourer constructing a mountain path at Jonkershoek in the fynbos. The rock struck a spark on a boulder scree covered with highly inflammable dry grass and the resulting fire burnt a considerable area of veld. He notes that natural falls of rock, as well as those caused by baboons who have been observed to dislodge and roll rocks from precipices, might also cause fires. Falling rock from earth tremors can also cause fires and numerous fires were observed after the recent severe Ceres earth tremor (Forestry Department, 1969/70). Tremors have occurred in the southern Cape about 53 times over the past 50 yr (Theron 1974). Nanni (1956) also notes that fires started by rock falls are on record at the Cathedral Peak Forest Station in the Natal Drakensberg. Apart from Luckhoff (1971), who records that out of 80 accidental fires in the present century in the Cedarberg Mountains of the western Cape, 5% could be ascribed to rock falls, and Andrag (1977) who records 12 (23%) out of 53 fires as due to rolling rocks in the Cedarberg for the period 1958 to 1974, there is little evidence of the frequency with which boulders and earth tremors cause fires. It appears that though fires ignited by rock falls do occur, they are limited to mountainous areas where there is adequate inflammable plant material during dry weather conditions.

LIGHTNING INDUCED FIRES

Lightning is generally considered the most significant of the natural causes (excluding man) of veld fires in South Africa (Phillips 1930; West 1965, 1971; Scott 1970; Komarek 1971a). But although accepted as an ignition source, opinions differ as to the frequency and importance of lightning induced fires in natural ecosystems.

The incidence of thunderstorm activity over South Africa is shown in Figure 1 (Schulze 1965). The ground lightning flash densities recorded from over 300 lightning counters in South Africa by the CSIR National Lightning Recording Scheme during 1975 to 1978 are depicted in Figures 2 and 3 (Anderson 1965a; Anon 1977; Anderson et al 1978; Eriksson 1978; Kroninger 1978). Records of thunderstorm activity and ground lightning flash density show similar patterns of high and low incidence, being highest mainly at altitudes over 1 000 m in the predominantly grassland and Afro-alpine areas of Lesotho, Natal, the Transvaal and the Orange Free State and lowest in the southwestern and southern Afro-montane forest and fynbos. Ground lightning flash densities range from less than 1 km^{-2} yr^{-1} to over 10 km^{-2} yr^{-1}. Table 1 for State Forest land in South Africa, and Table 2 for Southern Cape State Forest lands, show the actual incidence of fires that have been ascribed to lightning as well as to other causes (Annual Reports of Department of Forestry 1959/60 to 1977/78; le Roux 1979). Annual reports for the Kruger National Park (18 800 km^2) also testify to the incidence of lightning fires where, for example, on the 2nd February 1968, 13 fires were recorded after a dry thunderstorm near Tshokwane, of which three that could not be reached in time caused considerable damage. It is reported that while 25 lightning fires caused considerable damage during the summer of 1967/68 in that area, the total number of lightning induced fires was considerably greater.

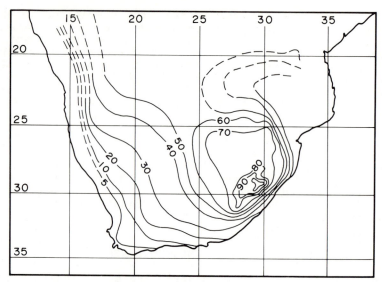

Figure 1   Average number of days yr^{-1} with thunder (generalized) (Schulze 1965).

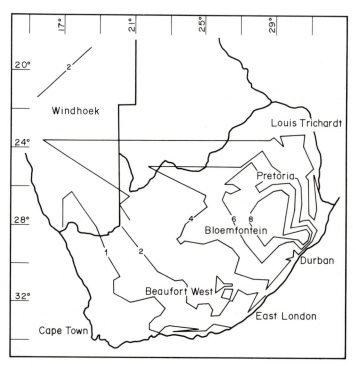

Figure 2   Lightning flash densities during 1975 to 1978 (No. of flashes to ground km^{-2} yr^{-1}) (after Kroninger 1978).

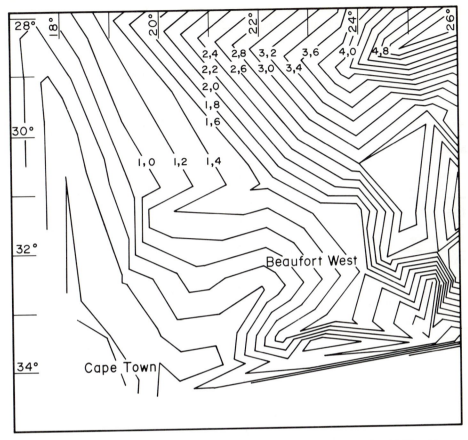

Figure 3   Lightning flash densities during 1975 to 1978 (No. of flashes to ground km^{-2} yr^{-1}) (after Kroninger 1978).

Compared with recorded lightning ground flash densities, the number of recorded lightning fires is low. Table 1 shows a mean of 0,002 lightning fires km^{-2} yr^{-1} for the State Forest areas of South Africa as a whole while there is a lower frequency of about 0,001 lightning fires km^{-2} yr^{-1} for the 2 372 km^2 of all-year rainfall fynbos catchments in the southern Cape according to the data of le Roux (1979). For a region with a mean flash density of 1 km^{-2} yr^{-1}, a frequency of lightning fires of 0,002 km^{-2} yr^{-1} is equivalent to one successful lightning induced veld fire out of 500 ground flashes km^{-2} yr^{-5}. However, such a fire could quite conceivably burn in excess of 100 km^2 of land. Although nearly half as much, and bearing in mind that nearly a quarter of fires are due to unknown causes (Table 1), the South African estimate of the incidence of lightning fires are not very

Table 1   Causes of fires in 16 317 km^2 of State Forest land in South Africa during 1959/60 to 1977/78 (compiled from Annual Reports of Department of Forestry).

	Lightning	Man-made	Unknown	Total
Total (19 yr)	555	3 020	1 093	4 668
Mean annual no. (mean total area = 16 317 km^2)	29,2(12%)	159(65%)	57(23%)	245,7
Mean annual no fires km^{-2}	0,002	0,01	0,004	0,015
1965/66: highest no. fires and man-made fires	38(8%)	360(74%)	89(18%)	487
1963/64: highest no. lightning fires	63(20%)	181(59%)	64(21%)	308
1971/72: lowest no. fires and man-made fires	11(16%)	42(61%)	16(23%)	69
1973/74: lowest no. lightning fires and highest % man-made fires	2(3%)	66(81%)	13(16%)	81

Table 2   Causes of fires in 2 372 km^2 of fynbos in southern Cape State Forest lands during 1966/67 to 1975/76 (le Roux 1979).

Cause	Number	%	Total area burnt (ha)	Av. area burnt per fire (ha)	% of total area burnt
Lightning	23	27,4	5 589	243	14,3
Trains	20	23,8	660	33	1,7
Unknown	13	15,5	22 555	1 735	57,6
Prescribed	10	11,9	6 450	645	16,5
Camp fires, squatters, etc.	9	10,7	2 385	265	6,1
Arson	6	7,1	1 278	213	3,3
Smokers	2	2,4	296	148	0,5
Honey hunters	1	1,2	2	2	0,0
TOTAL	84	100,0	39 215	410,5	100,0

dissimilar from those calculated from the data of Komarek (1967) for the incidence of lightning induced fires in National Forest areas in the United States. For the 22 yr period from 1945 to 1966, 932 485 km^2 of National Forests experienced an average of 4 871 lightning fires per year or 0,005 lightning fires km^{-2} yr^{-1}, while the California National Forests experienced 725 lightning fires per year, equivalent to a mean of 0,008 lightning fires km^{-2} yr^{-1}.

A considerable difference may be expected between ground lightning flash densities and veld ignition for a number of reasons. These include the difficulty of recording with certainty the occurrence of a lightning fire, as well as of the cause of any veld fire, as shown by the 23% annual mean for fires of unknown origin for State Forest lands in South Africa (Table 1). Further, the ignition of the veld by a ground lightning strike, and the subsequent sustained combustion, obviously depend on the availability of a suitable quality and quantity of fuel and on weather conditions. Also, for the lightning strike itself the most destructive cloud-positive form with high incendiary properties is known to occur as a not precisely established but relatively small proportion of the total number of ground flashes (Anon 1977; Anderson et al 1978).

While most lightning induced fires cover relatively small areas under present day conditions (2,43 km^2 per fire average for the southern Cape according to le Roux (1979) (Table 2)) there are a number of modern instances of fires having burnt large areas. Pienaar (1968, cited by Komarek 1971a) for example, reported a lightning fire in the Kruger National Park area of the savanna biome that burned nearly 780 km^2 (300 square miles). On present evidence, in pre-colonial times with low human population densities, lightning induced fires could have burned extensive tracts of country, especially when they occurred under conditions favourable for veld fires (see next section).

CURRENT FIRE REGIMES AND THEIR POST SETTLEMENT DEVELOPMENTS

The fire regimes of South Africa are determined primarily by climate, vegetation and fuel and three main fire regime categories can be recognized:-

1   The winter rainfall fynbos fire regime of regular fires occurring chiefly in the dry summer and autumn months in continuous, woody, sclerophyllous vegetation with high fuel masses. The fynbos and montane forests of the southern Cape year-round rainfall region are also included in this category. Data by le Roux (1979, Table 3) show that 58,2% of the fires occur in the summer-autumn period from December to May in this southern Cape region.

Table 3 Monthly occurrence of fires in 2 372 km^2 of fynbos in southern Cape State Forest lands during 1966/67 to 1975/76 (le Roux 1979).

Month	Total number	%	Total area burnt (ha)	Av. area burnt per fire (ha)	% of total area burnt area burnt
January	16	19,0	6 224	389	15,9
February	9	10,7	4 842	538	12,4
March	5	5,9	400	80	1,0
April	9	10,7	11 088	1 232	28,4
May	4	4,8	696	174	1,8
June	3	3,6	2 250	750	5,8
July	7	8,3	609	87	1,6
August	5	5,9	2 015	403	5,1
September	3	3,6	6 513	2 171	16,6
October	5	5,9	710	142	1,8
November	12	14,3	3 612	301	9,2
December	6	7,1	168	28	0,4
TOTAL	84	99,8	39 127	–	100,0
Ave/month	7		3 260		

2 The summer rainfall grassland-savanna fire regime of regular fires occurring chiefly during late autumn, winter and spring in a continuous herbaceous field layer composed mainly of grasses. In savanna the grass layer is complemented by a woody tree-shrub layer, these two layers varying in amount in inverse proportion to each other. This vegetation is characterized by moderate to high fuel masses.

3 The arid karoo fire regime of irregular fires after occasional periods of rainfall sufficient to provide adequate continuity and mass of fuel in this area of variable low rainfall and dispersed low fuel masses.

WINTER RAINFALL FYNBOS FIRE REGIME

Prior to 1652, during pre-colonial times, the winter rainfall fynbos fire regime may be considered to have been a natural one in which the chief causes of fire were lightning and falling rock in mountain areas, the latter being considerably the less significant. On the assumption that climates and available fuels from the best primary sites available today did not differ radically from those of fairly immediate pre-colonial times, it should be possible to arrive at some general estimates of fire frequency. Three factors are, however, important in the shrubby fynbos vegetation: (i) the longer return period of fire, of several years at least, than occurs in grassland; (ii) a relatively low level of herbivore utilization of the predominantly shrubby fynbos vegetation; and (iii) in pre- colonial times of low human population density, the absence of man as an agent controlling the spread of fires once started, either directly and deliberately, or indirectly as a consequence of his modification of the landscape by means such as roads, railways and cultivation. Based on southern Cape data (Table 2), which show a probability of 0,01 lightning fires $km^{-2} yr^{-1}$, for a region with a low ground flash density of 1 $km^{-2} yr^{-1}$ (Figure 3), one successful lightning induced fire may be expected, for example, every 100 km^2 once in 10 yr, or one lightning fire 50 km^{-2} once in 20 yr. Together with the fires set by the local inhabitants in pre-colonial times (Hall, this volume, chapter 3), an average fire frequency of 15 to 20 yr, or less, is not unlikely and possibly conservative for the winter rainfall fynbos fire regime since the dry season is more pronounced over the greater part of the biome area than for the all-year rainfall southern Cape area. It will also be apparent that as the vegetation ages under the low herbivore utilization prevalent in the fynbos vegetation, the likelihood of extensive unchecked fires occurring would become greater, especially where the vegetation has remained unburnt for at least 10 yr.

After settlement in 1652, the early Cape farmers learned the practice of veld burning from the local Khoikhoi (Hottentots). Thus, the advent of the European settlers and permanent farmers resulted in an overall marked increase in the frequency of burning (Tables 1 to 3). In 1658 burning was forbidden during the dry season. In 1687 a new law provided scourging as a penalty for a first offence and death by hanging for a second offence, nobody having the right to burn any grazing, wheatland or forest without permission (Agricola 1947). A notable feature of the early laws from 1658 onwards against unpermitted burning, however, was that their purpose was not veld conservation as such, but to protect the grain, houses and other possessions of the inhabitants against fire, and to prevent depletion of the wood supplies (Agricola 1948). Little attention was paid to these laws and to subsequent re-enactments during the seventeenth, eighteenth and nineteenth centuries under both the Dutch and British governments (Brown 1877; Botha 1924). Deliberate burning was common early in the dry season, but often indiscriminate with regard to season. Frequently the veld was burnt as often as possible with the objectives of providing fresh grazing for stock and as insurance against accidental fires. It is interesting to note that even before 1707, the Governor Willem Adriaan van der Stel recommended that if burning was needed it should be done in February as the best month to prevent damage to the grass roots (Agricola 1948). Injudicious cutting opened up the evergreen forests and enabled fire to enter and in 1854 the Colonial Botanist Pappe warned against destruction of the forests by fire.

By 1865, under the influence of the Colonial Botanist, Brown, burning was being restricted on the crown forest lands. The consequences of injudicious protection were not always realized, however, to the extent that a certain Captain Harrison (Brown 1875), after a destructive December fire in the Tsitzikamma that started in "dry bushy veld of seven years' growth", recorded: "On my first arrival...veld was regularly burnt in winter, without any damage to the forest, but ensuring their protection against accidental fires. Science then said I was wrong and burning was prohibited. The result is the late disastrous fire". At van Staadens River at the same time the massive smoke pall from another bush and forest fire was noted by the inhabitants of Bedford and Adelaide 150 km away.

In February 1869 there occurred the most extensive fires recorded in South Africa (Brown 1875, 1877). Good veld growth provided by a higher than normal rainy season in 1866 was followed by another wet season in 1868. This was in turn succeeded by a hot dry period of six weeks that reached its climax on the 9th February 1869 with a scorching hot dry northerly Berg wind and high temperatures that attained 33,9°C (93°F) at 08h00, 38,3°C (101°F) at 09h00 and 45°C (113°F) at 14h00 at Humansdorp. At about 15h00 the wind changed to a very strong southwesterly. Numerous fires that had broken out travelled rapidly and were carried large distances to start new fires. The fires swept through a tract of country some 640 km (400 miles) long and 24 to 240 km (15 to 150 miles) wide through the districts of Swellendam, Riversdale, Mossel Bay, George, Knysna, Oudtshoorn, Humansdorp and Uitenhage, causing loss of life and much damage to property and to the natural forests. In the Humansdorp and Tsitzikamma districts alone, 20 homesteads were burned to the ground and 20 persons died. When the wind veered to the south and then southeast, soaking rains that lasted till the next afternoon fell and extinguished the fires. The 1869 fire provides a graphic illustration of the extensive spread of veld fires under particular hot dry weather conditions following wet seasons of fuel accumulation, aided by the policy of injudiciously applied protection of vegetation against burning.

The controversy between the government and scientists on the one hand who viewed the burning of fynbos as highly detrimental, and the farmers and landowners on the other hand who considered fire as necessary for grazing and as unavoidable to avoid catastrophic accidental fire, raged until the 1940's. As a result of a memorandum to the Royal Society of South Africa by J S Henkel in 1943 recommending controlled burning, Wicht (1945), as head of a special committee, presented an extensive report which pointed out the natural occurrence of fire and of adaptations of the Cape flora to fire. Evidence was put forward favouring a system of controlled burning and research requirements were suggested. Catchment hydrological studies incorporating burns were undertaken and, resulting from observations of the effects of longterm protection from fire on the composition and structure of the fynbos, scheduled burning was accepted as part of catchment and conservation management for State Forests and farming areas. Uncertainty still exists as to the optimal frequency and timing of burning for different fynbos communities, but overall there has been a real decline in the frequency of burns during the twentieth century compared to the eighteenth and nineteenth centuries. As discussed in detail by Kruger and Bigalke (this volume, chapter 5), most fires occur during summer with a widely varying frequency ranging from less than 10 yr to about 40 yr, the longer periods of fire absence having resulted from management directed towards the exclusion of fires.

SUMMER RAINFALL GRASSLAND-SAVANNA FIRE REGIME

Apart from climatic and fuel differences, other primary factors differentiating the natural summer rainfall grassland-savanna fire regime from the winter rainfall fynbos fire regime are the short return period of fires (since the perennial grass component can rapidly re-establish a canopy cover) and the natural presence of large herds of antelope and other indigenous herbivores. As in the fynbos regime the natural causes of fires were chiefly lightning and man, and falling rock locally in mountain areas. In the absence of fire and grazing and other forms of defoliation, the inability of the grasses to shed their leaves tends to result in accumulation of self-smothering dead material. Accumulation is rapid in the productive moist and "sour" grasslands, but slow in the generally less productive dry and palatable "sweet" grasslands. Three years of protection from fire, grazing and other defoliation is usually sufficient in moist grasslands to cause a marked deterioration in structure and species composition. Because of these basic functional attributes of grassland ecosystems, grazing alone may suffice to maintain the sweetveld grasslands and the grass component of dry savannas, but under natural conditions fire is necessary to maintain the vitality of moist and sourveld grasslands.

Fires could burn large areas (as still occurs today when unchecked by man and man-made barriers (National Parks Board of Trustees 1967/68)) and such fires were reported by early travellers (Barker 1852 and Perestrello 1575, cited by Edwards 1967). The highest ground lightning flash densities in the country are centred over the area of grassland distribution (Figure 2), being over 4 km^{-2} yr^{-1} for the higher altitude grasslands of the Cape Province, Natal, Orange Free State and Transvaal, suggesting that the potential for lightning fires is more than four times that of the fynbos fire regime. Results from the National Lightning Recording Survey also indicate that the late spring and summer months, chiefly November and January, have the highest lightning occurrence in the summer rainfall parts of the country, but that for September and October, and March and April, there is also considerable ground lightning activity.

Evidence for the frequency and importance of lightning induced fires in the natural fire regime of the summer rainfall parts of the country is conflicting for different regions and according

to different workers. Killick (1963) considered lightning induced fires to have been a feature of early spring when the grass
sward is dry and inflammable in the Cathedral Peak area of the
Drakensberg, citing evidence from Forestry Department records.
Also, the behaviour of vernal aspect forbs in grassland suggests
that spring burning (presumably caused by lightning) was a natural factor of the climate (Bews 1925; Bayer 1955; Gordon-Gray and
Wright 1969). Similar evidence, including that of occasional
thunderstorms from April to August, was given by Edwards (1967)
for the Drakensberg foot-hill montane forest and grassland regions. West (1971) also had a similar view, recording that a
lightning induced fire during a particularly good rainy season
in grassland that had been protected for some years with much
old dry grass in the Inyanga montane forest area of Zimbabwe
burnt more than 20 ha before being put out. Van Wyk (cited by
Gertenbach and Potgieter 1979) considered that, dependent upon
rainfall, the resultant grass growth and grazing pressure, lightning fires were most likely more frequent than three yearly in
the Kruger National Park savanna biome. Gertenbach and Potgieter
(1979) concluded that, for the Kruger National Park, lightning
fires during a wet climatic cycle were more frequent for the
months from August to December, possibly biennial, than for the
months from January to April. During the dry climatic cycle
lightning fires were less frequent, three to five yearly, and
chiefly in early summer.

However, Scotcher et al (1980a) were able to establish, on
the basis of existing fire records for five Natal Drakensberg
nature reserves with a total area of 50 515 ha, only six lightning fires for periods ranging between 12 to 73 yr. Two occurred
each in January and September and one each in February and
July. Since these constituted less than 1% of the fires they
concluded (as did Mentis et al 1974) that lightning induced fires
were unimportant. Berry and Macdonald (1979) came to similar
conclusions for the 91 820 ha Hluhluwe-Umfolozi Game Reserve
complex of Zululand. Of 772 recorded fires only eight (1%) were
definitely caused by lightning over a 24 yr period. Six of the
fires occurred during the rainy period October to March and two
during the remaining dry period. They further concluded that the
natural climatic incidence of fire was insufficient to maintain
the fire induced communities of the area and that they had
evolved primarily from man initiated fires.

Apart from the physical and climatically induced fires of the
natural pre-colonial regime, man-induced fires are of considerable antiquity (Hall, this volume, chapter 3). There is general
agreement that primitive man was a potent fire agent. The early
San (Bushmen) used fire in hunting, and the Khoikhoi (Hottentot)
tribes and later Bantu-speaking peoples also used fire in hunting
as well as to provide grazing for their livestock. Shipwrecked
Portuguese, such as Perestrello who in 1575 trekked through the
length of Natal, described extensive areas of burning (Mackeurton
1930, cited by Edwards 1967). While he described the country as
'well-peopled', population densities were certainly not comparable with those found 300 yr later when they could be estimated
at 1,9 km^{-2} (5 $mile^{-2}$) and their potential for causing a higher
burning frequency was corespondingly greater (Edwards 1967).

Although conclusive evidence is lacking it may well be that man was the major factor causing fire from very early times.

Whereas in the winter rainfall fynbos fire regime the post-colonial period dates from 1652, that of the summer rainfall grassland and savanna regime started over 150 yr later with the arrival of the British settlers in 1820 in the eastern Cape and with the opening up of the Orange Free State and Transvaal by the Voortrekkers of the Great Trek in 1836. As in the southwestern Cape, the European settlers continued the old custom of veld burning practised by the Khoikhoi (Hottentot) and Bantu-speaking peoples to promote grazing for stock. Shortly after the Voor-trekkers established themselves in the Transvaal, an open meeting held at Derdepoort near Pretoria on 23 May 1849 requested, without success, that the magistrates notify the field cornets that no veld burning should take place without punishment. Twenty years later in a 'Proposal of a Law' it was suggested that to counter the careless and unnecessary burning of grass it should not be permissible to set the veld alight between the 20th of April and the 31st of August. Between the 1st of September and the 19th April 48 hours notification of intention to burn was to be given to neighbours and disobedience of the proposed legislation was to be subject to a heavy fine or a jail sentence and compensation for any damage caused was to be paid. The law was eventually passed in 1870 in a very much watered down form that essentially gave anyone the right to burn veld on his own farm provided that damage caused to others was compensated for (Agricola 1947).

From early historical writings and from a knowledge of the practices that have persisted even up to the present time it is clear that as in the winter rainfall fynbos fire regime, the post settlement period of the summer rain grassland and savanna regime was characterized by an increasingly fixed land settlement patt-ern in which veld burning during the dry season from mid autumn to early spring was common practice. Only with the advent of experimental work comparing the effects of different times and frequencies of burns that culminated in the work of Scott (1952a), was there a decline in the general incidence of burning as a whole and of burning in late summer, autumn and early winter to obtain out of season grazing for livestock.

The extent of veld burning in the grassland and savanna regions of South Africa is summarized in Figures 4 and 5 from available satellite imagery of Landsat 1 and 2 for the September to January period of 1972/73 and the June to January period of 1975/76 (Edwards 1977b). The occurrence of veld burns totalling approximately 500 ha or more in extent per 15 minute square of latitude and longitude (equivalent to roughly 67 500 ha) is shown. The Landsat 1 imagery also shows extensive veld burns in the southwestern Cape fynbos and in the southern Cape fynbos and montane forest regions (Figure 4). The absence of veld burns in the karoo biome in the southwestern section of the satellite image cover in Figure 5 is also clearly seen. In a more recent 1981 study of veld burning using satellite imagery covering 193 941 km^2 (16% of South Africa) of grassland and savanna in the eastern Cape Province, Natal, Orange Free State and central Transvaal, 1 096 burns covering an area of 4 128 km^2, or 2,1% of

the area covered by the image scenes, indicate an overall low
amount of burning (Edwards et al 1983).

THE ARID KAROO FIRE REGIME

Prior to the inland penetration of the European settlers from
the southwest Cape, the karoo had a far greater proportion of
grass and supported large herds of migrating antelope (Acocks
1975), but there is little evidence to suggest the regular
occurrence of extensive natural fires. Lightning ground flash
densities from 1 to 3 km^{-2} yr^{-1} are intermediate between those of
the winter rainfall fynbos and the summer rainfall grassland and
savanna fire regimes. The incidence of lightning fires is most
likely to have been highest in the grassy transitional mountain
karoo, where veld burning became an established practice in the
post-colonial period (Brown 1875, 1877). In the northwestern
Namaqualand area of the karoo, Brown (1877) cites an 1863 letter
by the missionary Tindall, a resident of 25 years in the area: "I
have seldom if ever known the Namaquas set any tract of country
on fire, and fires rarely occur by accident. The exception is
when they are in pursuit of young locusts, when the bushes in
which the insects rest at night in dense masses are fired, and in

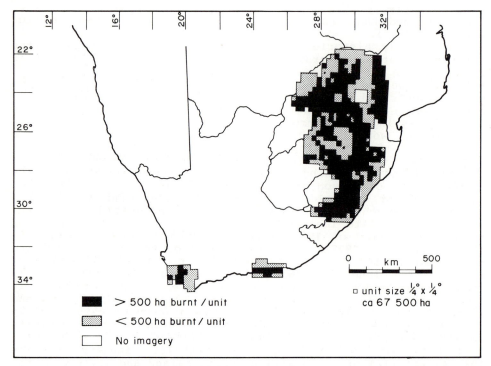

Figure 4   Distribution of veld burning: Landsat 1 imagery for
the period 8 September 1972 to 19 January 1973.

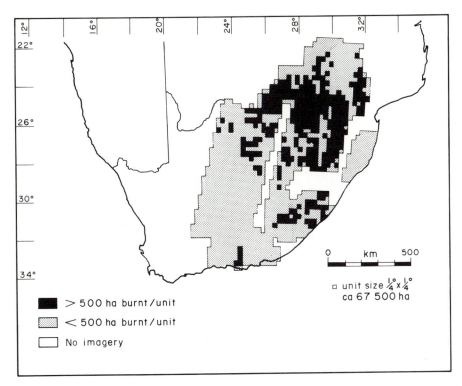

Figure 5   Distribution of veld burning: Landsat 2 imagery for
the period 25 June 1975 to 8, 11 and 29 January 1976.

this way millions are caught for food, but then the conflagration
is very partial...".   Eastwards it is probable that nomadic
Khoikhoi (Hottentot) pasturalists periodically burned the veld.
In the northern transition from the karoo to the arid savanna,
the missionary Moffat recorded that "the Natives have the yearly
custom of burning the grass..." (Brown 1877).

In the post-colonial period deliberate veld burning was
again standard practice, chiefly in the grassy eastern areas
and mountains of the karoo (Anon 1961).   In the southeastern
Jansenville karoo, the Civil Commissioner in 1874 recorded that
the spiny succulent *Euphorbia coerulescens* (noorsdoring) was
frequently burnt to provide food for goats and cattle during
times of drought when "... the long grass between readily burns
...", but at this time the introduction of sheep had already lead
to the widespread replacement of grassveld by karroid dwarf
shrubs (Brown 1877), so that fuel loads were limiting to firing.
Under present day conditions burning is virtually absent from the
karoo, except locally after exceptionally good years and on the
mountains where it may occur at three to fifteen year intervals.

Chapter 3 Man's Historical and Traditional Use of Fire in Southern Africa

M. HALL

"Fire is the image of youth and blood,
the symbolic colour in the ruby and
cinnabar, and in ochre and haematite with
which men painted themselves
ceremonially. When Prometheus in Greek
mythology brought fire to man, he gave
him life and made him into a demigod —
that is why the gods punished
Prometheus." (Bronowski 1973)

INTRODUCTION

Fire is of course far older than mankind and has been a major
agent in the environment since the earth's formative stages. It
must have been perceived as a major force by the earliest
hominids, as part of the consciousness of the australopithecines
and their progeny, modern man. But the point of the Promethean
myth is its emphasis on control, for the divine gift was the
ability to use fire as an artefact, thus transforming parts of
the environment at will. It is not surprising that Olympus
decreed a severe punishment, for the effects of anthropogenic
fire have been considerable: "The historic records from around
the world leave no room to doubt that primitive hunting and
gathering peoples, as well as ancient farmers and herders, for a
number of reasons, frequently and intentionally set fire to
almost all the vegetation around them which would burn." (Stewart
1963). The purpose of this chapter is to examine the role of
such fires in southern Africa in the broader context, beyond its
use in modern commercial farming systems and land management.

THE EARLIEST USE OF FIRE BY MAN

It is difficult to establish when man first began to control
fire systematically, for it is usually impossible from evidence
such as pollen spectra and soil profiles to distinguish between
anthropogenic fires and those initiated by climatic or physical
factors. The clearest indicator is the presence of hearths in
dwelling sites, for this shows that the prehistoric community was
either able to make fire or to transport it to a particular place
and subsequently control it for domestic purposes. Particularly
early sites are Choukoutien, near Peking, where hearths are
associated with bones of *Homo erectus*, Vertesszollos, in Hungary,
which was also occupied by *H. erectus*, and the hearths excavated
in the Escale cave in southern France. This evidence indicates
that man was able to control fire from the Middle Pleistocene
(Coles and Higgs 1969). Hearths as early as this, however, are
unknown in Africa and it may be that the ability to create
favourable microclimates in dwelling sites was an essential aid
in the expansion northwards into cold environments, but less
crucial in tropical and subtropical regions (Jelinek 1977).
The evidence from southern Africa is consistent with this
global pattern. For although it has been claimed, on the basis
of evidence from the Transvaal site of Makapansgat, that

australopithecines made controlled use of fire, the stratigraphy
and associations of material from this locality have been shown
to be equivocal (Sampson 1974).

Hearths are associated with Early Stone Age artefacts at
Kalambo Falls in Zambia (Clark 1969) and in the Cave of Hearths,
Transvaal (Mason 1969) but as Inskeep (1978) has noted, other
carefully investigated Early Stone Age sites in southern Africa
have failed to yield such evidence. Thus although fire was used
by communities of the Early Stone Age, it may be that it was not
widely employed until the succeeding Middle Stone Age. The
interface between these two technological traditions appears to
lie between about 150 000 and 180 000 BC (Maggs 1977).

THE SYMBOLISM OF FIRE

Two broad roles may be recognized for anthropogenic fire.
Fire is an agent which man has used and continues to use in
changing his environment, but it is also a source of symbolism.

This role, which could also be described as the social ecology of fire, clearly has its origin deep in the mythologies of
many societies. Thus in both the Old and New Testaments fire is
used in representations of relationships between man and God, for
example in the form of offerings, which took a new status when
burnt: "The offering was then no longer considered mutual food,
which man shared with God after having offered it to him, but was
mingled with the smoke and the incense as it rose up to Yahweh"
(Maertens 1964). Similarly, fire plays an important part in the
processes of eastern religions such as Hinduism (Hinnells and
Sharpe 1972).

The place of fire as a symbol in the indigenous social systems of southern Africa varies. Thus Bryant (1949) commented that
fire plays little part in the rituals of the Zulu, while for the
Pedi it is of considerable importance. In this tribal confed-
eracy of the central Transvaal, fire has a central role in the
ritual of marriage of a woman of the paramount house to a chief
of a subordinate group, and thus in the maintenance of political
control. Hearth fires were first extinguished and then rekindled
by order of rank with brands taken from the paramount's
homestead. In this way the royal brides "put out the powers of
one reign and brought in the flame of its successor" (Sansom
1974). The ceremonial fireplace was also the focus of day-to-day
administration: "The men's fire and the area surrounding it ...is
the site for the political jural activities of the men. Here
they meet and discuss the affairs of their group, and to arbitr-
ate in any differences between members of the group ... any new
unit seceding from the parent body has to take an ember of fire
from this fire place to light its own first fire" (Monnig 1967).
The domestic hearth also reflects kinship relations, as the term
for the agnatic kin group can be translated as "children of my
fire place" (Monnig 1967).

The symbolic importance of fire has been recorded in a number
of other southern African communities. Junod (1962) recorded
that the Thonga of southern Mozambique have taboos associated
with fire, including prohibition of the maintenance of the

hearthfire of a deceased tribesman after the mourning period and the belief that the lighting of fresh fires will cancel severe misfortunes. In Thonga myths of origin the name of one of the two original ancestors is *Likalahumba*, which means "the origins of fire" (Junod 1962). The Bemba of Zambia, when establishing a new village, first place and light a sacred hearth (Richards 1939). San (Bushmen) communities living in the Etosha area believe that all fire is property of the head of the group and that the first fire he kindles, which is not allowed to go out, is essential for the welfare of the community (Schapera 1930). A parallel belief held by the !Kung of Nyae Nyae in the Namib is recorded by Marshall (1976): "New fire is associated with fresh hope, fresh chance for good fortune. To build new fires on old sites might nullify the fresh chance and invite misfortune".

FIRE AND THE HUMAN ENVIRONMENT

In addition to any symbolic function that they might have, domestic fires are of course also important in food preparation. For although wild fruits, dried meat and similar food items collected and prepared by both hunter/gatherer and farming populations are of considerable economic significance, most plant and animal staples are cooked to increase their palatability. In some cases, cooking is also essential to render toxic foods edible (see Scudder 1971 for examples from the diet of farming communities in Zambia). Because of such domestic importance fireplaces are often focal points for routine activities in the settlement.

This consideration of domestic function leads to the second major human use of fire-transformation of man's environment. Fires so used are invariably adjuncts to food procuration, either to increase the productivity of important food supplies or to remove vegetation and allow the planting of fields with domestic crops. "Fire was the first forceful tool for energy input and ecosystem manipulation used deliberately by primitive man" (Naveh 1974a), and it has continued to be so used until the present day. For convenience, such fires may be divided into two categories. "Extensive regimes" are those where fire is used in grassland and heath in order to remove litter and encourage seasonal regeneration, while "intensive regimes" are followed in savanna and forest where field systems are to be sited. Such fire systems are not exclusive and may be used in conjunction with one another, nor are they restricted to fixed areas, as an intensive regime which results in the removal of closed vegetation may be replaced by an extensive regime in subsequent secondary grasslands or open woodlands. They are, however, associated with broad economic categories, for whereas farmers have used fires of both types, hunter/gatherer communities in southern Africa have been responsible only for fires on an extensive scale.

EXTENSIVE FIRE REGIMES

Of these two regimes, extensive burning is undoubtedly the older. Before the arrival of the first farming communities in the second century AD, most southern African economies were variants of the hunter/gatherer type. In such systems, and varying with availability and preference, a range of animal species was hunted and snared and plant foods, which often provided greater food intake, were collected. Inskeep (1978) has provided a general summary of such Stone Age economies while examples of specific and regional studies are; for the Cape, Deacon (1976), Klein (1979a) and Parkington (1972); for the Drakensberg, Carter (1978); and for the eastern and southeastern margins of the sub-continent, Beaumont (1978) and Plug (1978). Such hunter/gatherer communities were either absorbed into or obliterated by successive Iron Age and colonial farmers, although some populations have survived in extreme environments and have been the subject of recent anthropological study (Lee and DeVore 1968; Marshall 1976).

The details of Stone Age economic strategies are not of concern here, but a general observation requires emphasis. With some minor exceptions, hunter/gatherer communities exploited the surplus of plant and animal populations without significantly altering the web of interactions controlling the distribution and abundance of resource species. Within such economies, there is unlikely to have been concern to change the structure of the environment by the use of fire. Burning would have been employed where there was adequate natural accumulation of combustible fuels, such as in seasonally dry grasslands and savannas, but there would be little reason to introduce fire into closed woodlands or forest.

Archaeological evidence is generally too ephemeral to definitely indicate the way in which fire was used during the Stone Age, although Deacon (1976) has suggested that burning was a conscious management technique in the southern Cape during the earlier Holocene, favouring the regeneration of hemicryptophytes and geophytes. Ethnographic observations provide further information. In November 1811 Burchell, travelling in West Griqualand and on the margins of the highveld grasslands, noted that "In some parts of the plain the Bushmen had burnt away the old grass, for the purpose of attracting the game by the young herbage which subsequently springs up. At this time it had already begun to sprout, and had given to many extensive patches the beautiful verdure of a field of wheat. In places which had not been in this manner cleared by burning, the green blades were concealed by the old withered grass" (Burchell 1822). Marshall, working among the !Kung in more recent years, has made a parallel observation: "Veld fires are a common sight. Bushmen set the fires to attract game. After the fire has passed, the grasses put forth green shoots and the game come to graze. The fires run raging before the winds till the winds shift and blow them back on themselves. We have seen around us as many as eight fires at a time" (Marshall 1976).

At other times there is some suggestion that San (Bushmen) communities used fire with more purpose. Schapera (1930) noted that in the Okavango area, the veld was normally burnt at the end of the dry season: "This, it is said, is done primarily in order that the edible bulbs, roots, etc, should come up better during the approaching rain season. It is also used, however, as a means of hunting, for the men spread round the fire in a semi-circle and drive all the game rushing from it before them in a certain direction where some hunters are lying in wait; moreover, the new grass growing soon after the burning attracts the game, which returns to the area, and thus makes it good hunting ground".

A number of other writers have noted considerable conflagrations such as these which have been started by hunter/gatherers. There is, however, no evidence for the manipulation of fuels; burning of this kind rather substitutes for climatically and physically induced fires in situations where ignition has not taken place and quantities of dry litter have accumulated.

Although one of the characteristics of the hunter/gatherer life is pronounced mobility, with camps occupied for short periods and readily abandoned in accordance with the fluctuating availability of resources, recent research has shown that such movement was not random. There were in the past, and are today, regularities in the seasonal round, and these in turn imply regularities in the location, timing and frequency of anthropogenic fires, a suggestion also made for the southern Cape region by Deacon (1976).

Excavations at a number of rock shelters in the western Cape have shown that such sites were occupied on a seasonal basis throughout the Stone Age, with winter months spent on the coast and coastal plain and spring and summer spent in the mountainous inland regions (Parkington 1972). A similar model has been proposed for the southeast, with annual movement between the Drakensberg and lower regions (Carter 1970) and it is a reasonable suggestion that such strategies were adopted by Stone Age communities around much of the shieldlike escarpment which separates the coastal areas from the interior basin of southern Africa. As upland grasses tend to be palatable only early in their growing season, animal populations would have moved to these regions early in spring and the hunters would have followed them, moving back when fauna returned to winter grazing areas in the lowlands. Such a model implies that, in the summer rainfall region, anthropogenic fires would have been more frequently initiated in the lowland areas during autumn and winter, when grass productivity was low and fire could be used to encourage out of season new growth in order to attract game. Upland vegetation would, in contrast, have been burnt more frequently in early spring.

Frequency of burning would have depended on whether Stone Age communities visited the same areas every year, or ranged widely within each topographical region. This is difficult to establish firmly, but differences in the nature of dwelling sites suggest a pattern. Thus, in the sandstone horizons exposed in the Drakensberg escarpment, erosion has created rock shelters which have favourable microclimatic conditions and which were used repeatedly as living sites through the Stone Age. It can be argued that hunter/gatherer communities returned repeatedly to the same sites in the early summer months, and therefore that nearby vegetation was consistently burnt on an annual basis. In lower topographical regions, rock shelters also occur, but these are far less frequent, and numerous scatters of stone artefacts indicate that communities often camped in the open, presumably in temporary shelters. Although the same areas may have been visited each winter, there were clearly fewer constraints on the location of settlement, and it is possible that anthropogenic fires in the lowland areas were less regular in their occurrence.

Such a model is, however, clearly unsuitable for the whole of southern Africa, for although topographical and seasonal variation in resource abundance co-occur in many situations, other localities must have been subject to different constraints in the Stone Age. For instance, the southern Cape, with its winter rainfall regime, must have allowed different adaptations while in the arid semideserts of the west coast and the interior Kalahari basin, the need to obtain water would have been a primary factor affecting both man and the resources upon which he depended. Indeed, research with hunter/gatherer communities in such dry areas gives some indication of the probable patterns of anthropogenic fires. Parkington (1977) has studied the records of the travellers who, from the mid-17th century, travelled northwards from Table Bay to Namaqualand and made important comments concerning indigenous populations. Parkington has suggested that the Soaqua, a hunter/gatherer community occupying the middle reaches of the Olifants River, were concentrated around the main river and its water supply during the dry season, but when water was more widely available they spread into a wider area. In this situation, regular fires would have occurred in the immediate river valley, as indeed Parkington (1977) notes: "Taking advantage of the dry condition of the veld and anticipating the plant growth of the wet season, the Soaqua burned the grass along the banks of the river in the late summer of 1661 and presumably in other years too".

Lee's (1968) study of the !Kung of the semi-arid northwestern region of the Kalahari suggests a similar pattern. Thus although some patterns have undoubtedly recurred over many millenia, there must also have been considerable variation in the distribution and frequency of extensive man-made fires.

It was mentioned earlier that extensive burning of more open vegetation was not exclusive to hunter/gatherer communities but has also been practised for many centuries by farmers. In these economic systems the aim was still to encourage new grass growth, but to provide grazing for domestic livestock rather than to attract game for hunting. Again, there is no direct archaeological evidence to indicate those techniques which were employed, but it is reasonable to assume that fire has been used in association with animal husbandry ever since domestic animals were first part of southern African economic systems. Herding is now known to have been practised for almost 2 000 yr in the southern Cape (Maggs 1977) and although the presence of sheep further north has not yet been firmly identified at such an early period it is quite possible that research will demonstrate still earlier dates in these areas.

The first farmers, who moved into the eastern and southeastern parts of the subcontinent in the 2nd century AD, were firmly established in the valleys of the major rivers and along the southern coastal plain beyond the Transkei by the 8th century AD (Hall and Vogel 1980; Maggs 1980). Although it is possible that the earliest communities were agriculturalists without domestic livestock, there is evidence from sites that cattle and sheep were present throughout the area by the 6th century. After AD 1 000, farmers settled the higher regions of the subcontinent, including the lower slopes of the escarpment and high grasslands of the interior basin within the summer rainfall region (Maggs 1976, 1980; Hall and Vogel 1980). At important sites, such as the political centres of Great Zimbabwe and Mapungubwe, considerable herds were kept.

Again, some insight into burning practices is provided by the ethnographic literature. Marwick (1940) has described the extensive use of fire by the Swazi: "Grass is burnt in the autumn and is then called *mshakwindla* (burnt in the autumn), and is ready for the stock early in the spring. The grass which is not burnt in the autumn is called *sikotsa sokuhlala ubusika* (the grass to defeat the winter). The stock will graze this until the *mshakwindla* is ready. Grass which has been left over and not burnt is called *umlale* and burnt grass is called *liklunga*. The burning of grass takes place at the discretion of the chief on the advice of his followers". Similar veld management has been recorded in a number of other instances among stock keepers in southern Africa, and it is clear that planning, in order to allow best advantage to be taken of grassland resources, is careful.

If the settlement of the subcontinent by Iron Age farmers early in the first millenium is seen as the first major transition in the economic history of southern Africa, then the second was the colonization of the Cape by farmers from Europe in the mid-17th century, and their subsequent radiation during the following two centuries. But although these events eventually led to the development of a dual economy with subsistence agriculture paralleled by commercial farming, with the use of fire in a far more systematic and regulated manner, many of the early white farmers adopted local lore and followed practices established centuries before their arrival.

Botha (1924) noted that early colonial farmers in the Cape learned the art of veld burning from Khoisan communities and persisted with this method of seasonal veld improvement despite severe legislation by successive governments. Burchell (1822), travelling from Genadendal to Tulbagh in April 1811, noticed the practice and disapproved. Firewood was scarce "and, in all the grazing parts of the colony, it is rendered much more so by the wasteful and destructive practice of annually setting fire to the old withered grass, as the means of clearing the pastures". A few years later, Backhouse (1844) also noticed burning, this time in February: "On the more elevated land, the grass was long and sour. In some places the people were burning it off, in order to obtain a tender blade, and the atmosphere was laden with smoke".

Further north, in Natal, colonial practice in the 19th century was much the same. Brooks (1876), in a general description of the area, observed that "the old colonists secure a constant source of tender young grass by continually burning the grass in large patches as soon as it gets dry and unduly coarse.

This leads to the 'grass fires' which are regular and frequent accompaniments of the 'dry season' throughout the colony, and which occasionally, under bad management or accidentally adverse conditions, become dangerous and destructive conflagrations." Oates (1889), writing of the area near Pretoria in June 1873, noted that "this part of Africa is no timber country. On the high veldt (sic), there is nothing but parched grass, in many places burnt for a whole day's trek, as fires are of everyday occurrence".

Thus although much of the evidence is insubstantial and reconstruction of patterns speculative, it is reasonable to conclude that man has been introducing fire into the more open vegetation types of southern Africa for more than 150 000 yr and that such fires have often been extensive. Thus anthropogenic fires, first a factor in Late Pleistocene environments, have been part of southern African ecosystems throughout the Holocene and therefore throughout the period that the plant and animal species comprising these ecosystems have been adapting to contemporary climatic conditions. Perhaps, given this antiquity, it would be better to see anthropogenic fire as a central component in some heath and grassland communities, rather than as an extraneous factor.

INTENSIVE FIRE REGIMES

The intensive anthropogenic fire regime is, in contrast, of far more recent origin and has probably been less widespread. Nevertheless, any shortcomings in chronological and geographical scope have been adequately compensated by effect, for intensive fire has probably been the instrument which drastically transformed large areas of the southern African biota.

As defined earlier in this chapter, intensive fire regimes are those associated with the clearance of savanna and forest for fields by farming communities. In contrast to extensive burns in open vegetation, however, farmers using fire intensively have been manipulating their environments, changing the structure of the biota in order to allow the cultivation of crops and for livestock grazing. Archaeological research, which has already been reviewed, has shown that the first farming settlements were in the lower-lying southeastern parts of the subcontinent during the 3rd century AD and it may be deduced that these communities introduced the practice of swidden cultivation which, in the subsequent one and a half millenia, has had a pronounced effect on the southern African biota.

Evidence for the nature of Early Iron Age farming is still for the most part indirect, implied by the size of archaeological sites of this period, suggesting semipermanent villages, and the frequency with which grindstones and pits, which were probably used for crop storage, have been found. At a few sites, however, identifiable remains of crops have been recovered. At the Natal site of Shongweni, dated to the 1st millenium AD, there are preserved specimens of *Eleusine coracana* (finger millet), *Pennisetum americanum* (bullrush millet), *Lagenaria siceraria* (bottle gourd), *Sorghum* spp (sorghum) and *Citrullus lanatus*

(Tsamma melon) (Maggs 1980). Further north, seed impressions in pottery found at the early farming settlement of Silver Leaves have been identified as bullrush millet (Klapwijk 1974), while beyond the Limpopo direct evidence for the components of farming systems has been recovered from a number of excavated Early Iron Age settlements (Maggs 1980). Thus, although collected wild plant foods were clearly still of importance, these first farming communities were cutting fields for the propagation of domesticated staple crops.

A first problem in assessing the effect of such swidden cultivation is a lack of evidence for the nature of the southern African biota immediately before the Early Iron Age. There are no relevant palynological data for the southeastern coastal and riverine areas and it is thus impossible to identify specific plant communities of the 1st and 2nd centuries AD. It can be argued, however, that there would have been few factors to prevent the development of climatic climax vegetation for this part of the subcontinent. On the coastal plain and forelands of Mozambique, Zululand, Natal and the Transkei the subtropical and near subtropical climates, with high precipitation and lack of a severe dry season and high temperatures, would have encouraged the development of closed forest communities, similar to remnants still surviving in parts of Zululand today. Further inland, in the river valleys of the southeast and beneath the eastern escarpment, there is a pronounced arid season which could have inhibited tree growth in places, resulting in a mosaic of forest and more open savanna. It is nevertheless noticeable that closed woodlands do survive in parts of such interior lowland habitats, for example, the *Spirostachys africana* (tamboti) woodland and *Celtis africana* (white stinkwood)/ *Euclea schimperi* (bush guarri) forest of the Umfolozi and Hluhluwe Reserves in Zululand (Whateley and Porter 1979).

This evidence suggests that only intercession by limiting factors other than aridity and extreme temperature would prevent forest development in these low-lying areas. Such a factor could have been lightning-induced fire, but available evidence suggests that this was not the case. Berry and Macdonald (1979) in an extensive study of the history of fire in parts of the Umfolozi and Hluhluwe River valleys concluded that lightning fires were inadequate for the maintenance of subclimax plant communities. A similar conclusion on a more general level has been reached by Granger (this volume, chapter 8). Thus it is logical to deduce that forests and woodlands were widespread in these areas early in the 1st millenium.

If, then, Early Iron Age farmers were colonizing areas with relatively closed vegetation, fire must have been a vital tool in the necessary felling and clearing of plots for fields. Again, the archaeological record is deficient in direct evidence and it is ethnographic observation which suggests some of the methods that were employed. The best example for this purpose is provided by the *chitemene* system of cultivation of the Bemba of the northeastern Zambian plateau. These farmers chose as field locations areas that are more densely wooded, "arguing that soil which yields good trees will give good food" (Richards 1939). The timber itself is, however, also vital. Branches are cut from trees over a wide area, stacked on the plot and fired. "Burning disposes of the wood and brush, provides nutrients to be washed down into the soil with the rains... The relatively deep ash garden can then be used for more years than the shallower ash deposits of other systems" (Puzo 1978). The *chitemene* system uses between 0,6 and 1,2 ha per person per yr, necessitating a relatively low population density of about 5 km^{-2} (Puzo 1978). As such, large areas of woodland and forest are required if critical population densities are not to be reached.

Assuming a broadly similar system of swidden agriculture, an attempt has been made to model the effects of the intensive fire regime on the primeval vegetation of Zululand (Hall 1980). In this study, distinction was drawn between two basic Early Iron Age habitats – the coast and the river valley. Field studies in the St Lucia region showed that the earliest Iron Age villages were confined to the lower inland slopes of the coastal dune cordon and the slopes of relict dunes lying slightly inland. Neither the immediate coast nor the coastal plain seem to have been occupied during the 1st millenium. When the probable distribution of plant communities before the Iron Age is taken into account, it is clear that settlement was concentrated largely along the narrow ecotone between the Coastal Dune Forest covering the dune cordon, and the hygrophilous grasslands of the lagoon area, where the high water table prevents forest development. It has been suggested that the first farming communities built their villages on the edge of the forests and cut the fields in the dune cordon. These areas would have been particularly suited to swidden agriculture, as the high phytomass would confer high productivity when converted to usable nutrients by burning. The inherently low productivity of the coastal sandy soils and the rapid leaching resulting from high rainfall would, however, have rapidly destroyed the agricultural value of such fields, and new clearing would have been necessary after only a few seasons' cultivation. Such a system, it was suggested, would lead to rapid clearance of coastal vegetation, while the constant necessity for livestock grazing would have encouraged farmers to prevent secondary regeneration, again through the use of fire. Such a model would seem to provide a reasonable explanation for the extensive secondary grasslands found today in this part of Zululand.

The Zululand riverine environment is somewhat different from that of the coast, and it has been suggested that this was reflected in the ecology of Iron Age farming (Hall 1980). The immediate valleys of the major rivers, the preferred habitats of early farmers in Natal and Zululand (Maggs 1980), have deep, rich alluvial soils which would have supported crops far longer than the coastal sands. This durability is perhaps reflected in archaeological deposits, for riverine sites of this period tend to be significantly larger than their coastal counterparts. Nevertheless, clearance, probably by burning, would have been necessary before fields could be planted and there would have been the same interest in maintaining open grassland for livestock. Over the centuries, the natural expansion of the Iron Age population would have increased agricultural requirements and accelerated the clearance of forest. Thus although swiddens would probably have been longer-term in the valleys than on the coast, Iron Age activity has undoubtedly resulted in the replacement of substantial tracts of woodland with a floral mosaic of predominantly open structure.

Little archaeological research of this nature has been done in areas other than Zululand and so it is difficult to estimate the extent to which this model can be applied elsewhere, although patterns of settlement distribution do seem similar in Natal.

In the eastern parts of the subcontinent, on the coastal plain of Mozambique and beneath the escarpment in the Transvaal, there has been little research into the distribution of archaeological sites and the effect of Iron Age communities on the structure of the biota. However, because of the many similarities between the ecological characteristics of these areas and those of the Zululand coastal and riverine habitats, the use of fire by early agriculturalists may well have been much the same.

The implication of a model such as this is, of course, that the small patches of forest and closed woodland existing in southern Africa today are mere remnants of far more extensive communities which have now been replaced, through man's intervention with fire, by savannas and grasslands. Such an interpretation would also account for the surprising rarity of true swidden systems, such as the *chitemene*, in southern Africa today, as this pattern would have become redundant with the disappearance of forests. Fire is still used by small-scale farmers in order to prepare fields, but in a far less systematic manner than that employed by the Bemba. Thus the Zulu burn to remove troublesome trees: "When land covered with bush has to be cleared by the men for cultivation, the work is laborious... Fire is, however, usually used to remove the trunks of large trees" (Krige 1965). Junod (1962) has observed that Thonga farmers in southern Mozambique use similar methods, also drying out weeds and bushes and burning them on the fields, and, further to the north, BaVenda farmers also burn whatever cut grass and bush is available (Stayt 1931). There is no reason to suppose, however, that such agricultural systems have remained unchanged through the 1 500 yr of the Iron Age. The ancestors of today's farmers, faced with a high phytomass to remove before crop cultivation was possible, are likely to have made far more systematic use of fire in modifying the environment.

In considering man's intercession in forest and woodland communities an additional, more specialized use of fire must be mentioned. The use of fire as an adjunct to honey collecting has been a feature of both hunting/gathering and agricultural economies. Wild hives are usually smoked out, resulting in the introduction of fire deep in a woodland or forest, with the possibility of substantial accidental destruction (Phillips 1931; West 1965). It has also been suggested that there has been a coevolutionary relationship of considerable antiquity between flowering plants prolific in nectar and bees, with anthropogenic fire as an intermediate agency. Plant species such as *Julbernardia globiflora* (munondo), *J. paniculata* (large leaved munondo) and *Brachystegia* spp are dependent on early dry season fires for survival, and such fires have probably been systematically initiated by man for many millenia. The plants, once they have flowered, are important nectar sources for bees while honey is, in its turn, a traditional source of food among many human communities (Tinley 1977).

A number of other specialized forms of anthropogenic fires have been applied in southern Africa. These include, for example, the clearance of extensive areas of savanna and woodland in order to restrict the habitats of the trypanosome-carrying *Glossina* spp (tsetse fly). Swynnerton (1920) has recorded an example of such an operation which was carried out on a particularly large scale in 19th century Mozambique. Fire was also essential in the process of iron smelting – a clearly important technology in many Iron Age economies. Van der Merwe and Killick (1979) have assessed the impact that such activities could have had on forests in the eastern Transvaal and it has been suggested that the demand for iron in Zululand towards the end of the Iron Age may well have further accelerated the process of cutting woodlands (Hall 1980).

ANTHROPOGENIC FIRE REGIMES IN WIDER PERSPECTIVE

The conclusion that anthropogenic fire has been a factor of some antiquity in the ecosystems of southern Africa is in keeping with interpretations in other parts of the world, and it is useful to look briefly at this global situation so that local information may be placed in perspective.

The literature contains numerous accounts of the use of fire by hunting and gathering communities. Stokes, for instance, writing in 1846 of the voyages of H M S Beagle, records the following case from the Albany district of western Australia: "We met...natives engaged in burning the bush, which they do in sections every year. The dexterity with which they manage so proverbially a dangerous agent as fire is indeed astounding. Those to whom this duty is especially entrusted, and who guide or stop the running flame, are armed with large green boughs with which, if it moves in the wrong direction, they beat it out..." (Kayall 1974). There are parallel records from North America. Summarizing the evidence, Biswell (1974) concluded that "the Indians set burns to prepare feeding grounds for game and to make hunting easier; to facilitate collection of seeds, bulbs, berries and fibre plants, and to increase yield of useful plants". Such accounts are reminiscent of the description of southern African San (Bushmen) practice presented earlier in this chapter.

Interpretations of archaeological evidence in other parts of the world have also seen fire as an important agency employed by prehistoric man. Palynological evidence has suggested that, from about 10 000 BC onward, fires were recurrent in the arid savannas of Rajasthan, India. It has been suggested that these reflect the burning of grasslands by Mesolithic populations in order to improve grazing quality (Jacobson 1979). On the other side of the globe, Mesolithic populations have also been held responsible for the replacement of upland forests in Britain by more open vegetation (Simmons 1969).

The evidence for burning by farmers is equally widespread. As Conklin (1969) has pointed out, methods of shifting agriculture, invariably employing fire, are known from all over the world and are typical of vast areas of the tropics accounting, for instance, for a third of the total agricultural landuse of southeastern Asia. Indeed, it has been suggested that fire, employed by man, played a significant role in the emergence of agriculture itself in the Near East, acting selectively in favour of hard-grained grasses, accelerating rates of mutation and increasing the niche space of wild sheep and goats (Lewis 1972). Specific studies of the roles played by such anthropogenic fires have been carried out in a number of different areas. For example, it has been suggested that farmers began to destroy the subhumid climax forests of Cambodia some 2 000 yr ago. This was accentuated during the Khmer Empire, which flourished until the 15th century, when the northern plains were changed into a savanna created and maintained by fire (Wharton 1966). Writing of early man in New Zealand, Cumberland (1963) has observed that "there is now little doubt that their culture, economy and way of life depended on the use of fire. What is not fully appreciated is the extent of the disturbance of the ecosystem of New Zealand wrought, from the dawn of human settlement, by fires purposely and accidentally ignited by man". Cumberland estimated that by the early 17th century, some eight million acres of forest had been replaced by grassland and scrub while further extensive areas had been disturbed.

Thus it can be concluded that man has, through his use of fire, played a major role in many ecosystems. These include situations which parallel the environments of southern Africa. In his examination of the role of fire in the Mediterranean region, Naveh (1974a) concluded from evidence of Quaternary faunal assemblages that there had been progressive desiccation of habitats as a result of the impact of anthropogenic fire. In a different context Little (1974) has observed that the temperate forests of the northeastern United States were maintained as open mosaics by the Indian population. As Stewart (1956) has pointed out: "One may conclude that fire has been used by man to influence his geographic environment during his entire career as a human. Furthermore, it is impossible to understand clearly the distribution and history of vegetation of the earth's land surface without careful consideration of fire as a universal factor influencing the plant geography of the world".

Chapter 4 An Historical Review of Research on Fire in South Africa

J. D. SCOTT

INTRODUCTION

"While it is true that scientific writers have endeavoured to inform the public of the manifold evils following the wake of fire, it is equally true that but little scientific experimentation has been brought to bear upon the problems connected with the periodic fires that sweep through vast areas of Africa" (Phillips 1930). Even though this statement was made in 1930, the advent of fires in the landscape was by no means a new phenomenon. Fire had been a factor of ecological importance long before the colonization of the sub-continent (Hall, this volume, chapter 3). The records of the earliest European explorers testify to this. According to Sim (1907), Vasco de Gama named the southern African sub-continent "Terra de Fume" because of the pall of smoke which covered the land.

From the earliest days of European settlement, efforts were made to discourage veld burning and, after valuable wheat ricks had been destroyed as a result of fires sweeping from the veld through harvested wheat lands, various "placaats" (regulations) were issued to prevent the burning of veld altogether. The first of these was Placaat no 8 in 1658, the second was no 71 in 1661 and the third, no 215 in 1687 (Botha 1924). This legislation seems to have had very little effect as various travellers and writers described the frequent occurrence of veld burning and the ill effects of fire. While mostly they condemned the practice of veld burning, some favoured it as a means of improving the grazing. Brown, who was Colonial Botanist from 1863 to 1866, secured the prohibition of veld burning by further legislation. Some years later, the occurrence of a particularly damaging and disastrous fire in the Cape Colony caused Brown (1875) to conclude that had the veld been burnt regularly, such a fire would not have occurred. This point of view - the use of controlled burning to prevent disastrous fires - had not been previously expressed (Thompson 1936).

Perhaps this early recognition of the benefits of controlled burning contributed to the differences in objectives of fire research between South Africa on the one hand, and the United States of America and Australia on the other. In the USA the official attitude that burning was always harmful held sway till recent times. Burning was outlawed by legislation which was backed by an extremely effective propaganda campaign aimed at fire prevention. Only relatively recently did the research of Komarek and his co-workers reveal the association between fire and the disappearance of bobwhite quail *(Colinus virginianus)* and other wild life, and the replacement of softwood by hardwood forests at the Tall Timbers Research Station in Tallahassee, Florida (Komarek 1962a, b, 1965, 1966, 1976). This and other research has brought about a change in official attitude toward fire from anti-burning to controlled burning and then to fire management (Turcott 1976). In Australia too, the prevailing official viewpoint until fairly recently was that burning should be prevented at all cost. However, as a result of modern research which showed that continued protection from fire can be extremely detrimental through excessive accumulation of fuel, the advantages of controlled burning are now recognized.

The differences in attitude may well have had a bearing on the direction of fire research on the three continents. In South Africa fire research has for a long time had a strong agricultural bias and veld burning is seen as an important veld management practice in livestock production. Consequently the effect of fire on the vegetation has been a central theme of all veld burning investigations with emphasis being given to the effects of season and frequency of burning on the veld. Conversely in the USA and Australia, the occurrence of catastrophic wild fires that pose a very serious threat to life and property, greatly influenced the overall direction of fire research in these countries. Emphasis was rather given to fire behaviour studies aimed at the significant reduction of the serious wild-fire hazard. Thus until approximately a decade and a half ago knowledge about fire in South Africa revolved around the effects of season and frequency of burning on vegetation. Evidence for this is provided by the many publications by Scott (1947, 1955, 1971) on the effects and use of fire in veld management. Conversely, in the USA and Australia expertize was largely concentrated in the field of fire behaviour. Publications like "Forest Fire: Control and Use" edited by Davis (1959) in the USA and the numerous publications by McArthur (1962, 1966, 1967) on fire behaviour and fuel reduction burning in Australia, give a clear indication of the direction taken in fire research in these two countries at that time.

In recent years the situation has changed significantly through the catalytic effects of the Tall Timbers Fire Ecology Conferences organized by the Komarek family of Tallahassee, Florida. The conference held in 1971 on "Fire In Africa" served as a reminder to South African fire ecolgists that the effect of fire on the veld depends upon all the components of the fire regime viz season, frequency, intensity and type of burn. Thus in South Africa the field of fire behaviour is currently receiving serious attention and the effect of the intensity and the type of fire on the ecosystem is being monitored. A perusal of the proceedings of the Tall Timbers Fire Ecology Conferences and the First International Rangeland Congress held in 1978 indicate that fire research in the USA and Australia has also changed and become more broadly based.

EARLY INVESTIGATIONS

Mogg (1918) described an ecological investigation he had made of some stock diseases caused by certain plants which invaded grassveld when it was burned. Extensive veld burning at certain seasons had increased the population of poisonous plants and, in some "physiological formations", sweetveld had been made sour by indiscriminate burning.

Then Phillips (1919, 1920) reported on the veld burning experiments at Groenkloof, started in 1918. The effects of annual burning, mowing and complete protection on the development of plant succession and the formation of vernal aspect societies as well as on soil temperature and soil moisture in grassveld, were reported. These were the earliest recorded experiments with contrasting treatments laid out on a comparative basis.

In 1924 the South African Journal of Science contained a
number of papers delivered at a symposium on veld burning by
Botha, Levyns, Marloth and Pillans. Botha gave an excellent
summary on past legislation on veld burning. All condemned the
practice of burning the veld. Levyns, on the basis of newly
established field experiments, declared that fire was a menace to
the future of our country and, in the ensuing discussions, veld
burning in the Cape, the Orange Free State and the Transvaal was
generally condemned. Only Marloth, who blamed fire for the
extinction of species, increased runoff, diminished water
supplies and the reduction of the power of the mountains to capt-
ure moisture, made it clear that his remarks applied only to the
districts of the southwestern Cape. Marloth was one of the few
writers who did not make sweeping generalizations on the effects
of fire throughout the country on the basis of knowledge gained
only in the fynbos veld of the winter rainfall area of the
southwestern Cape.
    Early work gives the impression that it was assumed that fire
was always harmful and experiments were laid out to demonstrate
and measure the harmful effects. Later work seems to have had a
different approach. The effects of fire on vegetation, runoff,
water supplies, grazing for domestic and wild animals, soils and
other factors of the environment were studied rather to determine
whether they were harmful or beneficial to the land-use objective
and whether the effects differed according to time or season of
burning, fire intensity and purpose of burning. Most of the
early work concentrated on botanical changes in the vegetation
and this developed into a study of the effects of these changes
on water supplies, particularly where stock farming was not based
on the natural veld. In the grassland and savanna biomes economic aspects played an important part in the direction of research. These were the regions where stock farming played an
important role and the effects of burning, not only on the botanical composition but on veld production, were of utmost importance. The use of fire as a means of controlling unpalatable
plants in grassland and in preventing the dominance of bush in
savanna areas received more and more attention. No longer was
research on fire the field only of the botanist and the pasture
ecologist. The inclusion of soil scientists, agricultural
meteorologists, microbiologists, entomologists and hydrologists
has led to a holistic fire research approach which is a far cry
from the first experiments carried out.
    As more workers became interested in fire research the reali-
zation grew that the matter was complex and that the effects of
fire varied with climatic, physiographic and biotic factors. It
thus becomes more meaningful to deal with subsequent work on a
regional and, as far as possible, on a biome basis (Huntley, this
volume, chapter 1).

THE FYNBOS AND WESTERN CAPE FORESTS

    In the southwestern Cape Levyns (1927, 1929a,b, 1935a)
investigated the spread of *Elytropappus rhinocerotis* (renosterbos), an aggressive and unpalatable invader which ousted other

vegetation in areas subject to frequent fire. She showed that fire acted as a stimulus to seedling development. The results of burning Renosterbosveld at Riversdale differed, however, from those obtained at Stellenbosch where a series of successional changes took place and it took several years for the renosterbosveld to be re-established. In contrast, Bagshawe-Smith (1937) in the Grahamstown district showed that it was possible to control renosterbos in the eastern Province by judicious burning and grazing.

Phillips (1931) discussed preliminary results of fire effects in fynbos on soil pH and soil temperatures. He also described the effects of ground and crown fires on forest and the postfire succession.

In 1934 members of the Mountain Club tried unsuccessfully to ignite fires by means of broken bottles to determine whether veld fires could be started in this way (Anon 1934).

Adamson (1935) reported that a climax community on Table Mountain had returned to a condition similar but not identical to the original after 6 yr. The number of species showed a progressive increase during the post-fire recovery period.

Up to this time the accent in research had been on botanical changes in the fynbos - the effects on plants themselves and germination of seed. This was followed later by work on the effects of veld fires on certain geophytes (Bean 1962), on the distribution of Orchidaceae in relation to fire (Hall 1959) and on grasses in five veld types around Stellenbosch (van Rensburg 1962). Jordaan (1965) examined the effects of fire on the regeneration of four species of Protea and van der Merwe (1966a) undertook a survey of the flora of Swartkopskloof, Stellenbosch, with reference to the recovery of different species after fire. Van der Merwe and van der Merwe (1968) also did some interesting work on the dating of veld fires with the aid of *Protea repens* (sugarbush). Andrag (1977) worked on the effects of fire on the populations of *Widdringtonia cedarbergensis* (Clanwilliam cedar).

With the initiation of the hydrological research programme in the Jonkershoek area, a good deal of work has been done in the past 30 yr on the effects of fire on both vegetation and streamflow. Many reports have been published in this connection (Ryecroft 1947; Wicht 1948a,b; Banks 1964; Plathe and van der Zel 1969; Wicht and Kruger 1973; van der Zel 1974).

An interesting aspect of veld burning research has been that on forest danger rating which is described by King (1957), Vowinckel (1958) and Wicht and de Villiers (1963). Attention has also been paid to fire prevention with special reference to chemical methods of control (Sonntag 1960; le Roux 1969).

THE KAROO

Very little work on fire has been carried out in the karoo. In 1940 Scott and van Breda, working in the "Gebroke Karoo" near Worcester, showed fire to be extremely damaging. Not only were over 90% of the plants killed but the runoff on steep slopes caused very serious erosion.

THE SAVANNA

As early as 1926 Galpin had pointed out that the Springbok Flats were in the process of being transformed from open grazing plains to a closed *Acacia* woodland or thicket owing to the cessation of annual burning. He recommended that burning should be continued in plant communities on basalt but excluded from the sandveld areas.

Phillips (1930) pointed out that vast areas of southern and east Africa have had their vegetation kept in a "nonclimax" condition by periodic fires. Since then many workers have carried out research in bushveld and savanna areas. West (1952) recommended controlled burning at 4 yr intervals to suppress bush encroachment. Davidson (1953) reported on the effects of seasonal burning in sour/mixed bushveld in the Pretoria North area over the period 1939 to 1952. Van der Schyff (1958) described the experimental layout and procedure of research in connection with veld burning in the Kruger National Park. Experiments were laid out in the four most important veld types with 12 burning treatments in each. Preliminary observations in 1958 indicated that not only were different veld types affected differently by fire but that the time of the year in which the veld was burned was of the utmost importance. According to Brynard and Pienaar (1960) and Brynard (1964, 1971), further burning at intervals of 1, 2 and 3 yr was carried out at five different times of the year. Observations on vegetation changes, control of bush encroachment and grazing by game were carried out. Pienaar (1968) stated that definite trends had become evident as a result of different treatments and that it was possible to manipulate particular vegetation types according to the dictates of habitat selection, food preferences and seasonal migration of particular herbivores. The preservation of unique floristic areas or physiognomic aspects of the vegetation was thus also possible. Van Wyk (1971) showed how triennial burning was able to maintain the status quo of veld in the Kruger National Park. Kern (1978) analysed the effects of certain burning treatments on species composition, population density and species diversity of small animals in the Kruger National Park.

The problem of bush encroachment in the various savanna areas of South Africa has received a great deal of attention. Scott (1952a) showed how veld burning at different seasons in the thornveld of Natal affected and controlled the establishment of *Acacia* seedlings. Van der Schyff (1964) summarized and evaluated the research on bush control and eradication in South Africa up to that time. Since then various research programmes on the problem have been carried out (Downing 1974). Donaldson (1966, 1967) carried out much research on the potential use of fire in controlling *Acacia mellifera* subsp. *detinens* (blackthorn) in the Molopo area of the northwestern Cape. Du Toit (1972a) carried out an investigation in the eastern Cape sweetveld to determine the effect of frequency of burning, extended sparing and controlled grazing on the establishment of seedlings of *Acacia karroo* (sweet thorn). Fire, while not preventing establishment, did retard seedling development. Severe drought conditions prevailed during the course of this experiment, affecting the amount of grass to be burnt and hence the intensity of the fire. Trollope (1974) was of the opinion that it was the interaction of burning and browsing by wild animals that had played the major role in maintaining the original grasslands and preventing the encroachment of bush in the past. He showed that, after a controlled burn in dense sweet grassveld into which *A. karroo* and other bush species had encroached, most of the stems and branches had been killed but coppicing took place from the base of the stems. Stocking lightly with goats controlled the coppice growth with no detrimental effect on the grass, showing that a system of burning and browsing could be used to combat bush encroachment in certain situations. Trollope (1978a) also carried out a research programme on the behaviour of head and back fires under a variety of environmental conditions. The results demonstrated the value of a knowledge of fire behaviour in veld management.

THE TRUE GRASSLANDS

In the areas of summer rainfall Phillips (1920) was not only one of the earliest to investigate fire effects in field trials but he was also one of the first to introduce the grazing factor into experiments on veld burning. In the western Transvaal Theron (1932) laid out experiments to determine the effects of fire on the grassveld near Potchefstroom and he produced reports on this work in 1932, 1937 and 1946. Fire was found to be detrimental to the vegetation in all treatments. Burnt plots were more susceptible to damage in times of drought and the plant cover suffered as a result of burning both with and without grazing. Later, in 1956, Mostert and Donaldson described how winter burning, combined with light grazing by sheep in the central Orange Free State, resulted in deterioration of the grass cover and development of bare areas in the veld.

In 1933 Phillips opened an ecological research station at Frankenwald (Glover and van Rensburg 1938) and his research school contributed greatly to our knowledge of the effects of veld burning in different veld types over the next 40 yr. Experiments were laid out in grassland areas at Frankenwald, at Crescent Creek in the University grounds at Milner Park and on farms in the Bethal and Standerton districts. The results of these experiments have been described by various writers over the years (Cook 1938, 1939a,b; Glover and van Rensburg 1938; Davidson 1950, 1951a,b, 1952a,b, 1954; Daitz 1953b; Smit 1954; Jansen 1959a,b; Lowes 1963; Roux 1969; White and Grossman 1972). Cook (1939a) concluded from six years' experimental work that burning improved plant cover, that the best time for burning was late June or July and that burning should not be on an annual basis if grazing takes place. The advantages derived from burning good veld outweighed the disadvantages.

Davidson (1950, 1951a, 1952a,b) reported on the marked difference in species composition resulting from burns at different times, both at Frankenwald and on the highveld at Bethal and Standerton. He found that autumn burned veld (February and April) gave better grazing than October burned veld but the best yields and species composition were achieved with June and August burns. Complete protection of the veld resulted in deteriorated pastures.

In all this work, time of burning was found to be important and both Smit (1954) and Lowes (1963) reported on these effects in different veld types. Lowes found that these effects were influenced by soil moisture at the time of burning. While burning was done in specified months in most of the other experiments carried out on time of burning, Lowes investigated the effects of burning before and after rains, ie when the soil was dry or wet.

Just as veld burning has been blamed for the spread of renosterbos in the winter rainfall area, it was assumed that the encroaching weed *Stoebe vulgaris* was spreading due to the same cause. Cohen (1937) initiated experiments on the control of *S. vulgaris* by means of veld burning and these were reported on both by himself and Krupko (1961) and Krupko and Davidson (1954). They suggested that the curtailment of veld burning over the previous 20 yr had been partly responsible for the general increase of *S. vulgaris* and that its establishment could be prevented by spring burning of the grassland. Once established it was not eradicated by spring burning. Heavy burning without grazing reduced the amount of *S. vulgaris* but heavy grazing with burning eliminated it altogether.

Donaldson and Mostert (1958) conducted an experiment in the grasslands of the western Orange Free State on the control of another encroaching weed, *Chrysocoma tenuifolia* (bitterbos). Results revealed that burning in spring or mowing the veld once per year resulted in a significant decrease in *C. tenuifolia*. They pointed out, however, that burning in the sweetveld was detrimental to the grazing and could be recommended only under certain conditions.

In the sourveld of the eastern Transvaal Scott (1938) laid out comprehensive experiments on the effects of burning at different seasons with and without grazing at the Athole Research Station near Ermelo. Results from these experiments were discussed by Botha (1945, 1953) who indicated how burning was used in the main veld types to provide grazing throughout the year, often leading to veld deterioration and erosion. He showed how the results of these experiments could judiciously be introduced into farming systems to obviate veld retrogression.

Although a great deal of work was done in recording and comparing phenological changes in the vegetation under different treatments, research was not confined to these aspects of the effects of veld burning. Fantham (1924) had studied the effects of fire on protozoa in the soil long before much experimental work had been initiated. He found that a culture of soil from burnt veld yielded almost double the number of protozoa taken before burning. Cohen (1949) made the first survey of soil fungi in South Africa to discover whether or not prolonged burning and grazing had resulted in the establishment of distinct soil fungal floras. Burning and light grazing were found to produce a flora richer in the number of species and better balanced in the three main fungal groups than other treatments.

Daitz (1953a, 1954) investigated the relationship between CO_2 output by microorganisms in soil with different burning treatments and the carbohydrate content of roots to determine whether fluctuations in carbohydrate content of roots could explain the disappearance of *Themeda triandra* in plots burnt in October, but without success.

Mes (1958) investigated the effects of veld burning and mowing on the water, nitrogen and ash content of grasses and showed that, when plants were burnt in August or early September, the new leaves had a higher water, nitrogen and ash content than new leaves in undisturbed plants. Investigations into the effect of prolonged seasonal burning on soil fertility in *Trachypogon* veld (White and Grossman 1972) showed that after 38 yr of seasonal burning, losses of organic carbon and nitrogen were unexpectedly small but the losses of exchangeable bases (Ca, Mg, K and Na) in plant ash were large. The decrease in base saturation of the soil was greater after a spring burn and heavy rain than after a winter burn.

THE FALSE GRASSLANDS

Fire has always been an important factor of the environment in the sourveld and mixed false grassveld areas of Natal. Scott (1970) reported on the occurrence of fire, particularly in the mountainous areas, as a result of natural forces such as lightning. Much of the veld in these parts of Natal was burnt at frequent intervals but, just as in other parts of the country, there has always been much controversy as to whether fire is a legitimate tool or a serious malpractice which should be prohibited by law. As early as 1911, it was stated (Hall 1934) that veld burning experiments were being laid out at Cedara but it was not until 1926 that Staples reported on experiments laid out in 1921. In 1930 he gave a full report on these experiments from which he concluded that burning in the winter months encouraged the dominance of *Themeda triandra* but burning during the summer months was detrimental to the grazing. Gill, reported further on the same experiments in 1936. He stated that relative stability had been obtained in the reaction of the veld to the treatments applied. He recommended that veld should be burned before the early spring rains every second year to minimize erosion. Coetzee (1942) reported further on these experiments. He stated that leaving the veld unburnt and ungrazed for any length of time resulted in the disappearance of the better grazing grasses. Burning every second year in the dormant season encouraged the dominance of *Themeda triandra* and caused the density of the vegetal cover to increase. Burning during periods of active growth caused *T. triandra* to be replaced by the very unpalatable *Aristida junciformis*.

In 1936 Scott (1940a,b) laid out a very comprehensive series of experiments in the tall grassveld at Estcourt and in the highland sourveld at Tabamhlope. Complete protection from burning, grazing and mowing was compared with burning in winter, spring and autumn at intervals of 1, 2 and 3 yr. One difference between treatments in these experiments and those in other areas was that time of burning was not in specific months but according to the season, as determined by moisture and temperatures. Spring burns were applied only after the first spring rains whether they occurred in August or November. After these experiments, which included a study of botanical changes, soil temperatures and other soil factors, and the measurement of runoff and erosion, had run for 3 yr, the best treatments were applied in other experiments under selected grazing systems. Further reports on these experiments were given by West (1943), Scott (1952a,b, 1971), Edwards (1961, 1968) and le Roux (1968). Complete protection resulted in the vegetation becoming moribund and also gave the highest runoff of water with a minimum of erosion. Biennial burning in spring after rain gave the best results in both veld types from the aspect of both botanical make-up and runoff and erosion although a better basal cover was maintained with the mowing of the veld. Coutts (1945), working on soil samples from these experiments, showed that the influence of veld burning under field conditions upon the base exchange capacity of the soil was probably very small and transitory.

In 1950 Scott laid out a similar set of veld burning and mowing experiments in the southern tall grassveld at the Ukulinga Research Station near Pietermaritzburg. These were reported on by Rodel (1950), Routledge (1951), I'Ons (1960), Tainton (1963) and Tainton et al (1978). Effects were measured on soil temperatures, botanical composition, root development and dry matter production. Some observations here differed from those at Estcourt and at Bethal and Standerton (Davidson 1951a,b) possibly because this site was frost-free. Results from these experiments led to investigation of the effects of fire and clipping on apical bud development and seeding in the different grasses of the southern tall grassveld (Scott 1956; Booysen et al 1963; Tainton and Booysen 1963, 1965a,b; Tainton et al 1977).

The research on veld burning in Natal has, however, not been confined to veld used by domestic livestock. Firstly, burning in the catchment area of the Drakensberg has been examined in relation to its effect on the water balance (Nanni 1956, 1960; Granger 1976a). Secondly, as in the Kruger National Park (van der Schyff 1958; Brynard and Peinaar 1960; Brynard 1964, 1971; Pienaar 1968; van Wyk 1971; Kern 1978), fire in the Drakensberg has been examined and used as a tool in maintaining the spectrum of native species (Edwards 1969; Nanni 1969; Mentis et al 1974; Granger 1976a; Mentis and Rowe-Rowe 1979). Further, Ward (1962) reported on measures, including fire, to control scrub in the Hluhluwe Game Reserve. Thirdly, the use of fire in grassland to maintain populations of grassland francolins, which are prized by hunters for their sporting qualities, has been studied by Mentis and Bigalke (1973, 1979, 1981a).

In the eastern Cape, a good deal of work has been carried out to determine the effects of fire in controlling the encroachment of fynbos and other plants, in order to maintain the "false" grassland at a stage most suitable for grazing. The mountainous area of sour grassveld in the eastern Cape probably presents more problems in this connection than almost any other part of the country. As early as 1922, Schonland (1927) initiated an experiment which ran for 5 yr on veld infested with *Helichrysum argyrophyllum*. He showed that it was possible to destroy well-established *H. argyrophyllum* by burning at the end of winter and that it was possible to restore veld to its original *Themeda triandra* dominance within a period of 18 months.

Dyer (1932) described how, within 2 yr of burning veld infested with *Selago corymbosa* and *Helichrysum anomalum*, they had been eradicated and replaced by a 90% stand of *Themeda triandra*. Story (1951) concluded from his experiments that *Cliffortia linearifolia*, *C. paucistaminea* and *Erica brownleeae* had spread owing to the reduced incidence of veld fires and that it was impossible to maintain a grass sward in the highlands without the occasional use of fire.

In the Grahamstown Nature Reserve, Martin (1966) showed that the repeated burning of heath at short intervals led to a "grass/heath" complex while irregular occurrence of fires appeared to be essential for the maintenance of a diversified flora. Controlled burning of heath at average intervals of 8 to 20 yr would maintain all the components of the existing flora.

Trollope (1970, 1971, 1973, 1978b) carried out an extended programme on the use of fire to control fynbos vegetation (*Cliffortia linearifolia*, *C. paucistaminea* and *Erica brownleeae*) in the Amatola Mountains of the eastern Cape. As a result of these experiments he stated that burning could be used to maintain grassland in a vigorous and acceptable state for livestock and to control the encroachment of unpalatable woody vegetation. Burning, he maintained, had the economic advantage of being an indirect cost technique which gave it great applicability in solving certain rangeland problems in developing countries. Downing et al (1978) investigated the effects of burning and other treatments on the survival of different species. Basal cover of the different species was used as a criterion on which to base recommendations on veld burning management, whether this was aimed at water conservation or grazing.

CONCLUSION

The greatest impetus to veld burning research was due to the work of two schools in the grassland biome. Phillips, at the University of the Witwatersrand, followed up his work at Knysna (1931) and in east Africa (1930) by creating a grassland ecological research station at Frankenwald. Here many well-known ecologists were trained and their work on fire covered not only the Transvaal highveld but parts of east Africa as well. Much of this work concentrated on the botanical and ecological effects of veld burning.

Scott, who started with Phillips at Frankenwald, built up a research school with both an ecological and agricultural bias. The use of fire as a tool in livestock farming was investigated at Athole in the eastern Transvaal (Botha 1953), at the Estcourt and Tabamhlope Research Stations (Scott 1952a, 1971) and at the Ukulinga Research Station, attached to the Faculty of Agriculture at the University of Natal where many students were trained.

These two schools were followed in time by work in the savanna areas of the Kruger National Park, by that of Trollope on control of fynbos by fire and the use of browsing animals with fire in controlling bush encroachment. Wicht and others worked on water supplies at Jonkershoek and members of the Forestry Department and the Natal Parks Board have investigated veld burning problems in the Drakensberg.

Historical reviews have been written on the subject by Hall (1934), Thompson (1936), Phillips (1965), West (1965) and Tainton (1978).

Figures 1, 2 and 3 give some interesting information on the various publications cited in the text. Figure 1 shows the number of papers published per decade. As might be expected the number has risen steadily with the years except for the period of the second World War. Figure 2 shows the proportion of the papers devoted to the various biomes while Figure 3 indicates the proportion dealing with the different aspects of research.

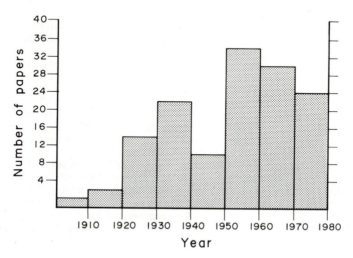

Figure 1   The number of papers published per decade on veld burning research.

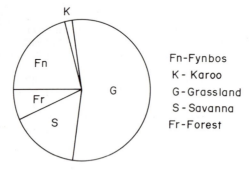

Figure 2   The proportion of papers on fire devoted to various biomes.

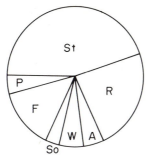

St-Structure
R-Fire regime
A-Plant adaptations
W-Water yield
So-Soil
F-Fauna
P-Production

Figure 3   The proportion of papers dealing with different aspects of fire research.

Whereas in earlier days, opinions expressed were mainly against burning - which was regarded as an unmitigated evil - today it is realized that such generalizations are dangerous. There are big differences in environmental conditions over the country as a whole and the objects of veld burning vary.   As Phillips (1971) pointed out at the Conference on Fire in Africa at Tallahassee, there is still a confusion of aims.   He stated: "the forester wants to achieve a particular objective and burns accordingly.   The pastoralist wants something different so he too burns, but differently.   The wildlife conservationist and manager [he must be a **manager** because as a conservationist alone, he understands only part of the story (Turcott 1976)] wants something in between.   We must clarify our concepts and our objectives."   While it is generally agreed that uncontrolled burning may be deleterious in some areas, it is also recognized that controlled burning may be absolutely essential in others and that it can be a very useful tool in the management of veld in many areas.

The research which has been carried out has shown where fire may be harmful.   It has also led to a change in farming practices and management of grazing in many areas.   As a result of research, management policy in the Game Parks has been improved. The treatment of mountain catchments has also received much attention in the light of work done but much more research is being planned and carried out because our knowledge in all these fields requires amplification.

The results of research too have led to improvements in past legislation and to new legislation on the practice of burning of firebreaks, plantation trash and grazing areas.

One of the most important features of all this research, however, has been the realization that the burning of vegetation is not a simple operation and that there are many facets to be investigated.   These can be fully understood only if an holistic view is taken of the ecosystem and the particular interests of the various specialist investigators are each seen in that perspective.

Chapter 5 Fire in Fynbos

F. J. KRUGER and R. C. BIGALKE

68

INTRODUCTION

Fires in fynbos are frequent, spectacular and alarming. They often cause considerable economic loss, as when 21 houses were lost in the Betty's Bay fire of 1970. Great fires, such as those in the region between Swellendam and Port Elizabeth in 1869, are cardinal in the history of land management in the zone and the lessons from them are embedded in the manager's lore. To the biologist the consequences of fire often seem disastrous. It is hard for an observer to imagine that the blackened waste to be seen after a fynbos fire is merely a stage in the cycle of regeneration and development of such rich and attractive communities.

The consequences of prevalent fire in the fynbos biome are varied, both ecological and economic. Costs include direct losses of assets such as timber plantations during fires, as well as the continuing costs of protecting those assets (Kruger 1979a). Indirect costs of unmanaged fire include those arising from invasions by exotic trees and shrubs – for instance, reduced catchment water yields, increased hazards of wild-fire, reduced ecological diversity, and loss of aesthetic values. Potential benefits of a managed fire regime include maintenance of natural biotas, cost-effective fire control, and enhanced water yields (Bands 1977; Kruger 1977a). The history of attitudes, ideas and policies regarding fire have been reviewed elsewhere (Wicht and Kruger 1973; Bands 1977). This chapter is a review of ecological studies and observations, as a step toward a basis for rational fire management of the fynbos biome.

All of the five Veld Types in the fynbos biome (Huntley, this volume, chapter 1) contain communities that are burnt periodically and recover subsequently, but they are not uniform with regard to the incidence of fire, nor in their responses to fire. Strandveld, for example, is likely to carry fire less often than the other types, because of the sparse canopy and the relative abundance of succulents. A comprehensive account of the ecological effects of fire in the biome is not possible, because our knowledge does not extend that far. This account centres on the mountain fynbos (Acocks's (1975) Veld Types 69 and 70), about which there is most information. Where possible, facts are adduced to show how the communities or biota of the other Veld Types resemble the mountain fynbos or differ from it, with regard to the ecological effects of fire.

CHARACTERISTICS OF FIRE REGIME AND FIRE BEHAVIOUR

FUELS, CLIMATE AND WEATHER

Fynbos communities can accumulate large quantities of fuel for fire. This fuel comprises well-dispersed, but nevertheless bulky, inflammable material in the intermingled herb and lower shrub strata sometimes up to 1,5 m above soil level but usually less than 0,75 m above soil level (Table 1). Emerging from this are taller shrubs (usually up to 3 to 5 m tall) whose crowns burn if conditions are suitable. In the herb and lower shrub layer fuel quantities of between 4 and 40 t ha^{-1} have been recorded (Kruger 1977b; van Wilgen 1982).

Table 1   Some physical characteristics of samples of fynbos
plants that provide flammable and less flammable
(*Leucadendron laureolum*) fuel, compared with a California chaparral dominant, *Adenostoma fasciculatum*
(from Countryman and Philpot 1970; le Maitre 1980).

Species	Physical properties of fuel				
	Mean height m	Mean crown volume m^3	Mean bio- mass g m^{-2}	Mean fuel dens- ity[a] g m^{-3}	% avail- able fuel[b]
Leptocarpus hyalinus	0,39	0,025	511	1546	100
Restio egregius	1,13	0,424	2166	1913	100
Sympieza articulata	0,66	0,054	642	1092	50
Leucadendron laureolum (male)	1,62	5,05	1399	868	30
L. laureolum (female)	2,15	4,13	2910	1296	23
Adenostoma fasciculatum	1,70	2,82	2220	1392	39

[a]Ratio of crown mass to crown volume.
[b]Arbitrarily determined as the proportion of crown mass in leaves
and in shoots with diameter less than 6 mm.

The physical and chemical characteristics of this fuel are
poorly known. Concentrations of secondary chemical products are
usually high, and many aromatic species are found. The essential
oils content of leaves in *Agathosma betulina* (round leaved buchu)
and *A. crenulata* (long-leaved buchu) (Rutaceae), for example,
ranges from 1,4 to 4,0% of oven-dry mass (Blommaert and Bartel
1976). The stems of restionaceous plants, an important fuel
component, are usually covered in a thick layer of cuticular
wax. The indications are, therefore, that the chemistry of
fynbos fuels favours combustion rate (King and Vines 1969). The
physical properties of the main fuel layer are determined by the
nature of the predominant narrow-sclerophyllous shrubs which have
leaves of widths and thicknesses of about 1 to 2 mm and fine,
much-branched shoots. Tufted and rhizomatous Restionaceae and
often various sedges and grasses add to the relatively fine text-
ured, highly combustible fuel mix. It is worth noting, however,
that most components of available fuel in fynbos have minimum
dimensions greater than about 1 to 2 mm, and are therefore coarser on average than those of grassland and savanna and this most
likely explains the normally lower rates of fire spread, despite
high fire intensities.

The amount and character of fuel varies considerably among vegetation types. Thus, in the restioid-ericoid zone (Taylor 1978) the fuel may consist almost entirely of about 4 to 6 t ha^{-1} of restioid material whereas in sclerophyllous scrub various life forms contribute (Table 2; Kruger 1977a). Naturally, fuel quantity varies also with succession after fire (Table 2 and Figure 6). Fires occur in 2 yr old vegetation under exceptional circumstances (Martin 1966). Four years' regrowth is usually necessary to sustain a spreading fire (Martin 1966; Kruger 1977a) and the vegetation must be somewhat older to burn readily under average summer conditions. Also important in determining the frequency of fire is the rate of accumulation of litter and standing dead material, which can comprise large proportions of above-ground biomass (Table 2). Martin (1966) has shown in field experiments that flammability of mature fynbos is largely due to the abundance of this dead component. In many fynbos communities litter and standing dead material begin to accumulate from the third year onwards, with death among 2 yr old shoots of Restionaceae that, unlike grasses and sedges, do not decompose readily. Other factors being equal, fire intensity increases with age of the vegetation as do height and depth of flame fronts. The large fires listed in Table 3 all occurred in very old vegetation (unburnt for 15 to 40 yr).

Table 2   Available fuel in fynbos stands of different ages and approximately similar sites at Jonkershoek[a] (from van Wilgen 1982).

| Biomass component | Above-ground biomass and available fuel, g m^{-2} | | | | | |
| | Vegetation age, yr 4[b] | | 21 | | 37 | |
	Biomass	Available fuel	Biomass	Available fuel	Biomass	Available fuel
Tall shrubs	0	0	3130	1050	1600	430
Low shrubs	73	73	115	72	557	305
Graminoid and restionaceous plants	468	468	112	112	41	41
Forbs	84	84	182	182	36	36
Litter and standing dead	43	43	1430	1250	5330	3500
Total	668	668	4969	2666	7564	4312

[a]Available fuel defined arbitrarily as leaves and shoots with diameter less than 6 mm.
[b]Average for two stands.

Table 3   Some properties of selected large fynbos fires (data from Bands 1977; Department of Forestry records).

Locality of fire	Area km^2	No. of ignition points	Date	Duration days	Predominant age of veld yr
Hottentots-Holland Mtns	112,0	2	Dec 1942	18	15-20
Hottentots-Holland Mtns	171,3	2	Jan 1958	16	ca 16
Du Toits Kloof Mtns[a]	180,0	5	Feb/Mar 1971	17	10-20
Krakadouwpoort, Cedarberg State Forest[a]	27,0	ca 5	Dec 1972	4	ca 38
Krakadouw-Groot Koupoort, Cedarberg State Forest	59,5	1	Feb 1975	5	ca 40
Kouga Mts Baviaanskloof State Forest	187,0	1	May 1975	10	20-30
Sneeuberg, Cedarberg State Forest	135,0	1	Dec 1975	6	15
Heksberg, Kouebokkeveld Mts	300,0	1	Feb 1976	10	30-35
Langeberg Mts Garcia State Forest[a]	26,8	9	Mar 1977	4	15-20
Middelberg-Boskloof Cedarberg State Forest	107,0	1	Jan 1979	8	ca 15

[a]Causes include lightning.

Fynbos fuels impose a certain character on the fire regime. They are coarser and more dispersed than grassland fuels, and therefore do not burn as fast or as frequently though productivity may be similar. On the other hand, compared with chaparral fuels in southern California, for example, where fine fuels are concentrated in the crowns of shrubs (Countryman and Philpot 1970), the fynbos fuel bed is evenly dispersed, and inclined to burn more frequently, mainly owing to the presence of persistent hemicryptophytes (grass, sedges and restionaceous plants).

The nature of fynbos fuels and the characteristic weather and climates combine to favour a fire regime unique in southern Africa. Pertinent features of weather and climate are the following:-

1   Southeasterly winds occur frequently in summer. These may blow for several successive days, are usually strong, gusting to 30 m s^{-1} or more in the lee of mountains, and averaging 12 m s^{-1} or more over 24 hr (Schulze 1965; Kruger 1974). They bring moisture in orographic clouds to certain montane locations but usually desiccate most surfaces traversed because the air is warmed and dried adiabatically as it descends. Major fires occur on "southeaster" days in the southwestern Cape, from the Peninsula northwards.

2   Fohnlike bergwinds often precede cyclonic weather systems, especially in winter. Dry subsiding air moves off the interior plateau of South Africa in response to strong coastward pressure gradients. Standing waves arise as the air is drawn across the coastal ranges, and strong downwash in their lee results in warm, turbulent winds where the waves reach the surface. Phillips (1931), Tyson (1964) and le Roux (1969) describe the pronounced anomalies in winter air temperatures and relative humidities associated with the onset of bergwinds. Wicht and de Villiers (1963) and le Roux (1969) have shown that major fires occur usually in winter during these conditions in the southern Cape, between Hermanus and Port Elizabeth. The devastating fires described by Brown (1875) occurred in summer but during bergwinds. The fire of May 1975 in the Kouga, for example (Table 3), spread largely under bergwind conditions, when air temperatures exceeded 30°C in spite of typical winter weather before and after the fire.

3   Summer heat favours conflagrations in fynbos of inland mountain ranges. Large fires in the Cedarberg in 1975 and 1979 (Table 3) occurred during periods of 7 to 10 days during which maximum air temperatures ranged from 35 to 45°C, minimum relative humidities between 5 and 20%, and turbulent, erratic winds prevailed (Kruger and Haynes 1978).

It is likely that weather conditions that favour large fires occur rather irregularly, perhaps only once or twice per year at a given place, and not necessarily in midsummer.

74

CAUSES OF IGNITION

Figure 1 depicts some data on the causes of fires in the fynbos zone. Most fires in areas close to population centres (as in
the case of the Cape Peninsula) are presently caused by human
activity. On the other hand natural causes of fire are important
in remote areas (see for example Table 4), no doubt because
these areas are less subjective to man-made fires. The Cedarberg
is subject to a relatively intensive fire protection system, and
is visited by only about 10 000 to 15 000 people annually, so
that fires owing to human agency are less likely and natural
fires more likely than for example on the Peninsula. Horne
(1981) reports a similar pattern in the Groot-Swartberge.

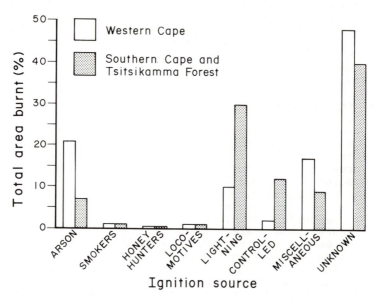

Figure 1   Classification of total area of unafforested State
Forest land burnt in 1966/67 to 1975/76 according to
ignition source (total area reported = 1 473 km²)
(Kruger 1979a).

It is difficult to determine the cause of a given fire. Nevertheless, there are documented eye-witness accounts of fires of
natural origin (Wicht 1945). Fires due to lightning strikes are
reported throughout the fynbos region, in spite of the relatively
low frequency of lightning storms (about five thunderstorms annually at typical Cape weather stations; Schulze 1965). Although
lightning is one-tenth as frequent or less in the western Cape as
it is in the areas prone to thunderstorm activity (Kroninger
1978), the flash density is nevertheless adequate to explain the
relatively high incidence of lightning fires reported in forestry

areas. An annual flash density of $1,0$ km^{-2} is equivalent to a record of 1 300 ground strikes within the 20 km range of a flash counter. This, at Citrusdal for example, is equivalent to about 400 strikes yr^{-1} which seems more than sufficient to cause a fire within the 1 300 km^2 area every few years.

Falling and rolling rocks arising from natural scarp retreat and earth tremors (which, according to Theron (1974), occurred in the southern Cape about 53 times over the past 50 yr) cause fires under suitable conditions of weather and fuel (Wicht 1945; van Wyk and Kent 1974).

FREQUENCY OF FIRES

Fire frequency can be expressed in terms of the number of years between fires at a site. The probability that the area will burn is the inverse of this return period. Thus, in a certain mountain range the vegetation on any given site may burn out once in 20 yr on average; the probability of fire is therefore $0,05$ yr^{-1}.

Some indication of low fire frequencies can be obtained from records for areas protected against fire. An analysis of fires recorded in the Cedarberg from 1957 to 1975 (from the map in Andrag 1977) showed that about 50% of the total area was burnt in 1957 to 1959, 11% during 1960 to 1969 and 30% during 1970 to 1975; about 17% escaped fire during this period. Roughly 30% of the total area burnt twice or more. Almost all burns were wild-fires. Records for the southerly slopes of the Groot-Swartberge indicate a frequency of natural fires of about once in 40 yr, though the actual frequency observed was once in 18 yr when fires of natural and human origin are considered jointly (Horne 1981). Frequencies on dry north aspects, transitional to karoo, were lower. Fire has been excluded for more than 30 yr from only relatively small areas such as Langrivier at Jonkershoek, and then usually by means of an elaborate firebreak system.

The frequency of fire in these protected areas can probably be taken as a lower limit for fynbos ecosystems under present conditions. Also, under past pre-colonial conditions, when fires, natural or otherwise, would have spread much more readily in the absence of manmade barriers, it is unlikely that such low fire frequencies occurred.

FIRE SEASON

The fine fuel component of fynbos communities includes dead material, the moisture content of which tends to follow that of ambient air. Thus, most mature fynbos will burn in warm, sunny conditions, whatever the season. It is not surprising therefore that wild-fires are reported in all seasons in any fynbos area (Figure 2). Nevertheless, most large fynbos fires occur in summer (Table 4) (Horne 1981), except that in the southern Cape coastal zone large fires occur frequently in winter (le Roux 1969). Martin (1966) refers to a fire of August 1955 as "... one of the most severe in the Grahamstown district".

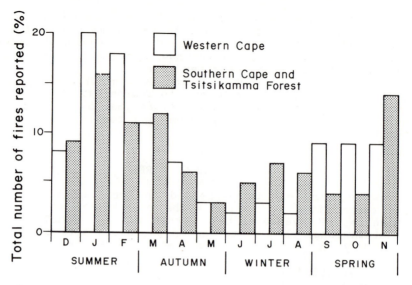

Figure 2   Seasonal incidence of fires on State Forest land in the fynbos biome during 1966/67 to 1975/76 (Kruger 1979a).

Table 4   Incidence and extent of wildfires in the Cedarberg State Forest (79 000 ha) during the period 1958 to 1974 inclusive (Andrag 1977).

Cause	Number of fires reported					Mean area per fire km^2	Proportion of total burnt area %
	summ.	aut.	win.	spr.	total		
Lightning	9	4	1	5	19	3,2	17
Rolling rocks	5	2	0	5	12	15,5	52
Escape from prescribed burn	0	0	1	3	4	8,8	10
From outside	0	3	0	1	4	1,7	2
Negligence of public	1	2	0	1	4	6,5	7
Honey hunters	0	1	0	0	1	18,2	5
Unknown	2	3	3	1	9	2,9	7
Total	17	15	5	16	53		
Mean area per fire (km^2)	10,9	7,5	1,8	3,2	6,8		
Proportion of total burnt area (%)	52	32	0	14			

The season of incidence of lightning fires could be a pointer to the possible seasonality of natural fires in fynbos. However, Department of Forestry reports for the 10 yr 1966/67 to 1975/76 show that while most large lightning fires occurred in summer, they occurred in all months but June and July (Horne 1981).

The relationship between season and frequency of fire is depicted hypothetically in Figure 3. This hypothetical model is no doubt an over simplication but probably reflects the essential trend.

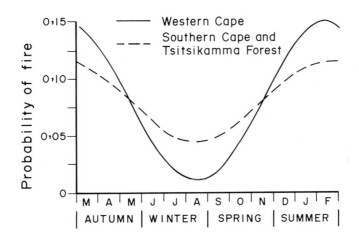

Figure 3   Hypothetical seasonal fire frequencies for the fynbos biome. Solid line represents a "western" fire regime and dashed lines, an "eastern" fire regime. Probability is calculated as the reciprocal of the interval in years between fires (Kruger 1979a).

FIRE INTENSITY AND BEHAVIOUR

There are few studies of fire intensity and behaviour in fynbos. Table 5 contains estimates of energy release rates from typical fynbos fires.

Fynbos fires are not exceptionally intense (though apparently more so than in grasslands), and have rates of advance rather slower than, for example, those in humid grassland with similar amounts of available fuel. Nevertheless, because the vegetation is tall and because of its structure as a fuel bed, flames tend to be rather high (2 to 5 m) and flame fronts deep (1 to 6 m). These fires are consequently difficult to control, especially in the prevailing rugged terrain.

Behaviour characteristics of very intense fires, such as powerful fire-whirls and long-range spotting, are not the rule in most fynbos fires. However, under hot windy conditions and highly combustible fuel loads, rapid rates of advance (over 4 km hr^{-1}) with moderate spotting (fires carried 200 m or more) have been

Table 5   Intensities for fynbos fires. Estimated values (from Bands 1977) for what are thought to be prevailing conditions. Observed values measured on plot trials in the Kogelberg (le Maitre 1980).

| | Intensity categories | | | |
	Low	Inter-mediate	High	Instantaneous maximum[a]
Estimated				
Available fuel				
(g m^{-2})	300	700	1 000	–
Rate of spread				
(m s^{-1})	0,07	0,38	1,11	–
Byram index (kJ s^{-1})	360	3 300	18 900	–
Observed on plots				
Available fuel				
(g m^{-2})	1 204	1 042	1 087	1 087
Rate of spread (m s^{-1})	0,22	0,35	0,47	2,0
Byram index (kJ s^{-1})	5 130	7 278	9 990	42 700

[a]Estimated on the basis of the maximum forward rate of spread on the plot ie 2,00 m s^{-1} as opposed to the average of 0,47 m s^{-1}.

reported. The large fynbos fires (such as those listed in Table 3) almost all occur under relatively rare, severe weather conditions (see above).

Temperature changes produced by fire near and in the ground have important effects on plant nutrients and soil microbial populations (Dunn and DeBano 1977) and, presumably, have consequent effects upon vegetation dynamics. However, there are few data for fynbos. Martin (1966) recorded subsurface and surface soil temperatures during experimental burns in small plots (5 x 5 m) in heathland near Grahamstown. The vegetation had an average height of about 0,6 m. Temperatures were measured by means of a thermocouple and small capillary tubes filled with various organic compounds of different melting points. The burn in a plot with undisturbed vegetation produced a maximum temperature of 550°C at the surface; high temperatures persisted only for about 10 s and were close to normal within 480 s. Sub-surface soil temperatures however did not rise greatly, and menthol (melting point 43°C) at a depth of 12,5 mm did not melt. A second plot when cleared of "dead brushwood" produced a maximum surface temperature of 350°C. Taylor and Kruger (1978) reported temperatures in a burn in 4 yr old fynbos, measured by means of pellets that melt at different temperatures. Maximum temperatures observed at the soil surface at 36 random locations ranged from 149 to 371°C, with the mode at 316°C. At two stations, temperatures were measured at 0,45 m and 0,90 m: a maximum of 316°C was recorded in all cases.

EFFECTS OF FIRE REGIME ON VEGETATION STRUCTURE AND DYNAMICS

SUCCESSION AFTER FIRE

Kruger's (1977b) account of plant succession serves as a basis for what follows. Development of fynbos communities after fire must vary considerably with differences in vegetation type and environmental variables. For example, Levyns (1935a) describes an unusual succession in coastal renosterveld where the vegetation was successively dominated by a different seeding species in each of the first three years after fire. A seeding species of *Aspalathus* dominated in the fifth year, but Levyns assumed this was likely to decline and to be replaced by *Elytropappus rhinocerotis* (renosterbos). Temporary dominance by pyrophytic perennials is found sometimes where *Aspalathus* spp proliferate after fire (Dahlgren 1963). On humid mountain slopes in the Jonkershoek area the post-fire community can comprise a nearly pure stand of a 1,5 m tall, robust grass, *Pentameris thuarii*, which is replaced by mixed fynbos after 4 to 6 yr (Kruger, 1982). However, successional changes in dominants seem to be exceptional. Field observations and information in Mitchell (1922), Levyns (1929b), Adamson (1935), Wicht (1948b), Martin (1966) and Taylor (1969a, 1978) indicate that most mountain fynbos communities follow an essentially similar course of succession after fire, although there clearly is variability within the mountain fynbos in terms of both floral properties and time scale. The major features abstracted from these sources are outlined below.

Immediate postfire phase

Although fire intensities in fynbos range widely, burns are seldom so intense as to kill sprouting species. Regeneration of all or most of these species occurs within the first twelve months after fire. Hemicryptophytes appear within days or weeks at most, and some are able to flower and set seed within this phase. Since hemicryptophytes are important in most communities, initial recovery is rapid. Fire lilies and almost all annuals reproduce in this phase.

It is also in the first 12 months after fire (ie usually in the first winter or spring) that successful germination and establishment occurs, apparently mainly from seed stored on the parent plants prior to the fire, or in the soil. Martin (1966) has suggested that seed of *Erica* spp is short-lived and must be imported to the site, and he, Adamson (1935) and Kruger (1972) have observed that germination and establishment of some *Erica* spp is delayed until more than 12 months after the fire. This may be due to the delay while seed is carried onto the site but could also be due to special requirements for germination that are met only after some development of the community. Time may be necessary for recovery of mycorrhizal associates of *Erica*, for example (Martin 1966). On the whole, it does not seem that immigration of species is an important process of postfire succession. Once established, young plants apparently suffer relatively little mortality (Martin 1966).

Youth phase (up to 4 to 5 yr)

Fynbos is quickly dominated by restionaceous and graminoid plants and sprouting shrubs (Figure 4), the herbaceous plants reaching a maximum biomass of up to 8 000 kg ha^{-1} in the first 4 to 5 yr. In this period, canopy cover reaches about 80% of pre-burn levels (Martin 1966, Figure 5). The remaining sprouting species attain reproductive maturity. Opportunistic shrubs, including succulent Mesembryanthemaceae (Adamson 1935), mature and die, but longer-lived shrubs begin to emerge from the canopy. The vegetation becomes flammable at about 4 yr.

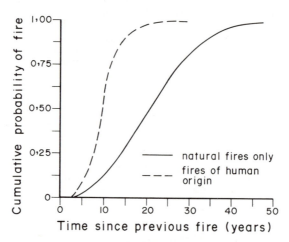

Figure 4   Hypothetical fire frequencies, expressed as cumulative probabilities of occurrence over any given area, as a function of time since previous fire (the burning rotation). Solid line represents a probability function for an area where fires of human origin are at a minimum, and broken line that for an area with many fires of human origin.

Transitional phase (up to about 10 yr)

Most plant species attain reproductive maturity in this phase. Tall shrubs emerge from the canopy and adopt the ascending branch habit.

Mature phase (up to 30 yr)

Tall shrubs attain maximum height and full, rounded form, with maximum flowering activity. Seeding low shrubs (eg *Erica* spp) begin to die, litter accumulates more rapidly and lower herbaceous strata are reduced in importance and negligible establishment of germinules occurs. Although germination may be quite prolific in winter, few or no seedlings survive (Wicht 1948b).

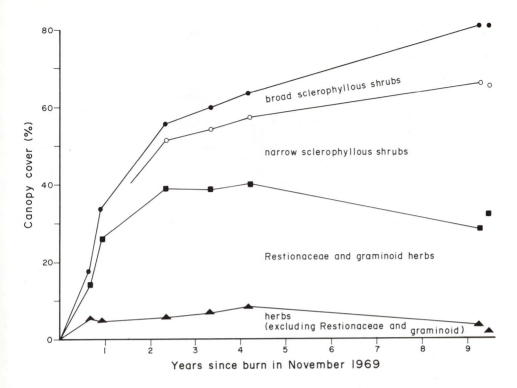

Figure 5   Change   in   vegetation   cover   after   fire   in   a
broad-sclerophyllous   open   scrub   at   Jakkalsrivier,
Grabouw.   Data points at extreme right represent cover
before the burn, at age 11 yr (Kruger 1982).

Senescent phase

Mortality among seed-regenerating shrubs accelerates, foliage
on survivors is reduced to tufts at tips of branches, and crowns
become open.   With the opening of the canopy, some seed regeneration may occur.   Litter and dead shoots continue to accumulate.
On special, limited sites that are both fertile and have moist
soils, immigration of forest precursors may occur.
    Thus, postfire succession in most fynbos communities is not-
able for rapid initial recovery owing mainly to growth of perennial graminoid herbs and sprouting shrubs.   Although germination
after fire may be delayed in some instances, species richness in
the plant community is at a maximum in the immediate postfire
phase and after.   Adamson's data suggest some turnover in species
in the first few years, but thereafter there is a steady reduction in diversity, particularly in the moist sites.   Dominance
concentration, perhaps initially intermediate, falls in the late
youth phase when species are roughly equal in height, and then
increases to a maximum in the mature phase.
    Postfire growth rates of different fynbos communities vary
widely (Figure 6).   Initial growth rates are highest on moist

sites, lowest on dry (Kruger 1977a) but above-ground biomass
attained at maturity seems to depend on whether or not tall,
long-lived shrubs (*Protea* spp, *Leucadendron* spp) are present; if
so, biomass continues to accumulate fairly rapidly for 30 yr or
more and may reach 75 t ha^{-1} (van Wilgen 1982). Live biomass
reaches a maximum at about 20 yr in the *Protea* scrub at Jonkershoek; older stands comprise 54 t ha^{-1} of dead material of the
total 75 t ha^{-1} (van Wilgen 1982). Low heathlands on dry aspects, by contrast, accumulate only about 10 to 15 t ha^{-1} (Kruger
1977a). These differences in postfire growth rates also indicate
probable differences in successional patterns, such as different
rates of recovery to the prefire condition, and rates at which
species composition will change.

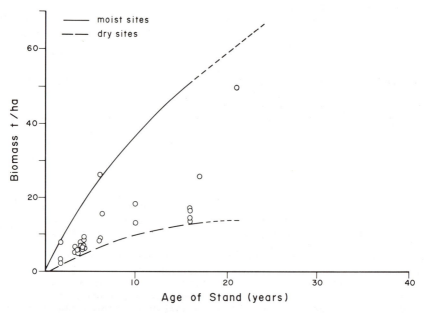

Figure 6   Change in above-ground plant biomass with succession
            after fire in fynbos communities. Biomass as total
            standing crop ie live plants, standing dead and litter
            (Kruger 1982).

EFFECTS OF FIRE INTENSITY

Studies on the effects of fire regime on vegetation structure
and dynamics have so far focused on the effects of rotation and
season, with scant attention to intensity effects. That extreme
intensities have important effects is confirmed by field experience and the few extant studies available. On humid, cool
sites, for example, field observation indicates that light burns
fail to consume sufficient litter and vegetation to create a
satisfactory seedbed for good germination and establishment.

Observations show that young *Mimetes hottentoticus* plants are established only in mineral seedbeds, and fail on peaty surfaces especially if littered (Kruger and Lamb 1978). This is possibly related to water repellency on organic and humic soils as Bond (1980) has reported that high intensity burns are necessary to oxidize and volatilize the organic compounds which cause repellency and maintain an unfavourable moisture balance. Elsewhere, growth of shrubs regenerated from seed has been seen to respond strongly where soils had previously been oxidized by very intense burns which is presumably analogous to the "ashbed" effect reported in *Eucalyptus* forests (Humphreys and Craig 1981). Other effects of high intensity burns could be seen after the unusually hot fire in the Cedarberg in January 1975 (Kruger and Haynes 1978). This fire, which was hot enough to cause considerable flaking and cracking of quartzite boulders, consumed the organic soil layers of bogs and seeps, virtually eliminating plant life from such sites. On other sites most sprouting herbs such as Restionaceae and Gramineae were killed, although mortality among adults of sprouting woody plants such as *Protea nitida* (1 to 3,5%) (Haynes 1976) was relatively low. Recovery was marked by abundant regeneration from seed among most taxa, so that the vegetation was initially dominated by seeding grasses (eg *Ehrharta ramosa)* and shrubs and semi-shrubs in the Asteraceae, and local colonies of hard-seeded *Aspalathus* spp. Re-establishment from seed of species of Restionaceae indicated that communities would return approximately to their original composition, though their initial growth was slow. This sequence of events, unusual in fynbos, seems to be due mainly to this exceptionally intense burn.

Fire intensity as a factor influencing vegetation structure and dynamics could perhaps be viewed as follows. High intensities will have several important effects. Abnormally high mortality among sprouting plants is likely (eg Trollope (1973) reports reduced grass basal cover due to "hot" fires), to the advantage of seeding species. Also, germination of hard-seeded species will be favoured. Growth of all plants will be favoured by the ashbed effect, but the net consequence of abnormally high intensities would be a change in composition toward an increased woody plant component, especially seeding shrubs. Abnormally low intensities will apparently have an opposite effect, favouring graminoid and restioid herbs over woody elements. The effects of average intensity fire would be intermediate between these two extremes.

EFFECTS OF FIRE FREQUENCY

The gross effects of fire frequency are usually the most easily seen and most frequently commented upon of regime effects. The marked contrast between vegetation at Jonkershoek subject to 6 yr burning and that subject to fires once in about 15 to 20 yr has been reported by van Wilgen (1981b, 1982). The 6 yr regime changed structure profoundly from a tall shrubland with aboveground biomass of about 50 t ha^{-1} to a low herbaceous shrubland with biomass of around 6 to 8 t ha^{-1}.

Most fynbos retains relatively abundant, mainly sprouting shrubs whatever the fire frequency, but in marginal fynbos zones, burning frequency can be a critical determinant of vegetation composition. Trollope (1973) and Downing et al (1978) have shown this in the case of grassland in the Dohne Sourveld of the Amatole Mountains invaded by "macchia," ie scrub of fynbos species in the genera *Clifffortia* and *Erica*. The shrubs are easily reduced and some finally eliminated by repeated burning at short intervals of 2 to 4 yr. Martin (1966) also noted that certain fynbos communities near Grahamstown could be converted to perennial grassland by frequent fires. Trollope (1970) has reviewed the general problem of invasion of grasslands along the margin of the winter and all-year rainfall zones by "macchia" elements, ie mainly shrubs of genera such as *Clifffortia* (Rosaceae), *Erica*, and *Euryops* and other Asteraceae, and how these may be checked by burning on a short rotation. Similarly, where marginal grassland and grassy fynbos types have become altered and dominated by *Elytropappus rhinocerotis* through certain grazing and burning regimes the original grassland, often dominated by *Themeda triandra*, can be regained successfully in many cases if the veld is rested from grazing and burnt at intervals of about 4 yr and less (Levyns 1956; Moffett and Deacon 1977).

The influence of low-frequency burning as such has not been studied. Campbell and van der Meulen (1980) and van Wilgen (1981b, 1982), however, have reported effects of prolonged deferral of fire. In fynbos protected for 37 yr tall *Protea* shrubs were reduced in cover and abundance owing to high mortality with senescence and low seedling recruitment, as opposed to their dominance in 20 yr stands. The opening of the stand was apparently accompanied by a recovery among undergrowth species, including rhizomatous restionaceous plants, sedges and grasses. These graminoids are considerably reduced in old vegetation dominated by tall shrubs, relative to their condition in frequently burnt vegetation. Thus, in the Langeberg foothills at Swellendam, Haynes and Kruger (1972) reported a marked reduction in basal cover of graminoid and restionaceous plants in 47 yr old stands, relative to that in 4 yr old vegetation of firebreaks burnt on a 6 yr rotation (Table 6). Bond (1980) reported similar effects.

Fynbos communities are complex in their life form composition and, as already shown, in the range of plant responses to fire regime. Generally, fire frequency effects relate to the following:-

1   The demographies - especially primary juvenile periods, age-specific seed productions, and life spans - of the dominant seeding shrubs (Jordaan 1949). Many of these shrub species are precocious - *Protea repens* (sugar bush) flowers within 3 to 4 yr. Nevertheless the numbers of *P. repens* and *P. neriifolia* (oleander-leaved protea) are severely reduced by burning at average intervals of 6 yr (van Wilgen 1981b). Therefore, reproductive potential may be limited at early maturity because of delayed ripening of seed (Jordaan 1949) or similar factors. Seeding shrubs of a smaller stature,

Table 6   Comparison between basal cover of vegetation protected
           from fire for 47 yr and that of 4 yr old vegetation in
           a firebreak burnt on a 6 yr rotation on the Swellendam
           State Forest.   Statistics from a paired sample of
           10 line transects, located in a physiographically
           uniform area (Haynes and Kruger 1972).

	Mean basal cover, % (with standard error)	
	Firebreak	Protected vegetation
Total	$6,59 \pm 0,70$	$3,39 \pm 0,95$
t	$2,75$ (P $\leq$ 0,05)	
sprouters only	$6,30 \pm 0,70$	$2,76 \pm 0,89$
t	$3,09$ (P $\leq$ 0,05)	
Graminoid and restionaceous plants[a],[b]	$4,09 \pm 0,39$	$2,29 \pm 0,90$
t	$5,34$ (P $\leq$ 0,01)	

[a]Two transect pairs that fell on open patches in the protected
  vegetation, dominated by Cyperaceae, omitted from the analysis.
[b]Includes sprouting plants.

such as *Erica* and *Cliffortia*, are less readily decimated by
frequent fire (van Wilgen 1981b).
    Few data are available on age-specific reproductive
potential. Lombaard (1971) has shown that *P. repens*, for
example, carries sufficient viable seed per individual at age
10 to 12 yr to replace the parent population.   With
senescence (at about 25 to 50 yr in tall *Protea* spp) the
number of reproductive individuals in the population declines
markedly. Bond (1980) showed how, after the same fire, seedling densities in 40 to 45 yr old stands of Proteaceae are
much less than in 20 yr old stands, because populations have
declined more than the individual fecundities have increased
with age and though these Proteaceae retain viable seed on
the plant it is short-lived when released.   It is not clear
when reproductive effort and success per individual culmi-
nates and this problem requires further study.

2   Extreme frequencies may have nonreversible effects on
vegetation and result in new stable vegetation equilibria.
For example, high frequencies may cause local extinction as
in the case of *Erica* spp and *Cliffortia* spp in the Amatole
Mountains (Downing et al 1978).   On the other hand, long
periods between fire, in excess of 50 to 100 yr, could allow
establishment of forest precursors such as *Kiggelaria
africana* (wild peach) (van Wilgen 1981b), although such
communities are rarely observed except on sites unusually
favourable in fertility and moisture status (McKenzie et al
1977; van Wilgen 1981b).   In most cases it seems that

variations in frequency will instead govern the relative abundance of different plant forms. This is illustrated hypothetically for the case of seeding and sprouting species in Figure 7. High frequencies favour sprouters, especially graminoid plants, as discussed earlier. Intermediate frequencies allow succession to proceed to a stage dominated by tall shrubs, to the long-term disadvantage of sprouters. Low frequencies allow succession repeatedly to proceed beyond the onset of senescence among seeding shrubs and there is an equilibration of postfire recruitment at relatively low densities because of declining reproductive potential of parent populations as discussed. Sprouters persist in the more open vegetation, but their composition no doubt changes from an assemblage characterized by species adapted to frequent defoliation to one where dominant species are those which survive and grow under a regime of infrequent defoliation. Thus, the spectrum of species is retained but the relative abundances change.

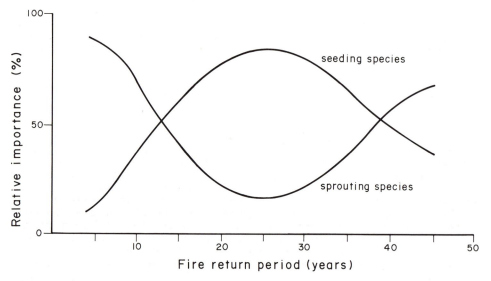

Figure 7   Hypothetical illustration of different proportions of community biomass in sprouting and seeding plants that may result under different average fire frequencies.

3   The effect of fire frequency is governed by feedback controls among frequency, rates of accumulation of biomass and fire intensity. Fires in short succession have low intensities and spread slowly because insufficient time elapses for vegetation to grow and accumulate the fuel necessary for intense fires. Thus ignition probabilities decline, fires that do occur are less intense and smaller than otherwise and the average fire frequency will tend to decrease.

4   Habitat patchiness, especially in the rocky mountain fynbos
     landscapes, causes spatial heterogeneity in distribution of
     fire and a pattern that includes patches where fire tends to
     occur less frequently, allowing existence of species that
     would not tolerate the mean fire frequencies experienced on
     the prevailing landscape elements. Even where the landscape
     is uniform and fires intense, patches are often left unburnt
     more or less at random (Martin 1966). Where frequencies are
     high this effect is more pronounced and will allow survival
     in refuges of species that are exterminated elsewhere. Re-
     colonization from such refuges would be more rapid than from
     outside the area experiencing high frequencies.

5   Current views hold that maximum species diversity would be
     found under intermediate burning frequencies (Connell 1978;
     Huston 1979). Van Wilgen (1981b) found most plant species
     per sample quadrat in fynbos burnt once in 6 yr, lowest in
     that burnt once in 20 yr, and intermediate in that protected
     from fire. As he pointed out, however, many species in the
     20 yr vegetation are dormant, as seed or underground organs,
     for example, and the full richness can only be measured over
     time. Pyric succession must be accounted for in assessing
     the role of fire frequency on diversity, and highest richness
     would exist, hypothetically, at intermediate frequencies.
     The relatively high richness observed in very old stands was
     due to immigration of species including forest precursors and
     appears to represent a special case.

EFFECTS OF FIRE SEASON

The influence of season of burn is related to the seasonality
of growth and reproduction in species of any given plant community, as illustrated by examples described above. Phenology of
fynbos communities is complex (Kruger 1981) so that a uniform
response among species in any given community is not to be expected. Nevertheless, burns in late summer or autumn (February to
April) are considered to be "natural" in the fynbos environment,
so that vegetation subject to burns in this season should remain
relatively stable (Jordaan 1949, 1965). This is because sprouting plants are dormant or nearly so at the height of the summer
drought, and because dormant viable propagules are then available
on site.

Out-of-season burns could have many effects on composition
and structure. First, where veld is burnt when certain species
are in active growth, survival and regrowth of resprouters could
be reduced because they are defoliated when reserves are depleted
and these are drained further by resprouting: there is some
evidence of this effect in *Watsonia pyramidata*, for example
(Kruger 1977b, 1978). Because species differ phenologically,
response to season of burn will vary interspecifically and this
could lead to compositional changes. For example, temperate
grasses, which tend to grow in autumn through to spring, could be
favoured over tropical grasses by autumn burns, and vice versa
with spring burns. Restionaceae and Cyperaceae, which grow

predominantly in spring, would also be favoured by early spring burns because even if emerging shoots and leaves are scorched, regrowth from intercalary meristems is immediate and rapid, and ought to have the advantage of exploiting resources under conditions of low competition. Presumably, the same advantages would accrue to sprouting shrubs. These advantages would be greater the earlier the burn because of the relatively small effect on energy and nutrient reserves.

Secondly, insofar as fire permits or induces germination and subsequent establishment, season of burn can have pronounced effects on populations regenerated from seed. Most successful germination and establishment apparently occurs in winter through to early spring, and this is favoured by summer and autumn burns. Germination does occur after early spring burns, but establishment can be severely hampered by ensuing summer drought and by pathogens favoured by warm, moist spring conditions, leading for example to losses through damping off. Other seasonal effects could arise from differences in microclimatic change and exposure to weather, especially the effect of strong winds in removing ashed nutrients and in shifting soil.

Whatever the case, both Jordaan (1965) and Bond (1980) have indicated how "unseasonal" fires can have a profound influence on populations of Proteaceae. Bond showed that other dicotyledons responded similarly, and, clearly, other strong seasonal effects must be expected. Thus, repeated late summer or autumn burns ought to favour vegetation dominated by seeding shrubs, while repeated spring burns would favour vegetation where graminoid and restionaceous plants and sprouting shrubs are more prominent. Species whose phenology is closely attuned to survival of summer drought through dormancy and rapid exploitation of moist conditions in autumn and early winter would also be favoured by late summer and autumn burns. Thus Levyns (1929b) reported that petaloid monocotyledons were favoured over grasses by an April burn. Also important is the fact that geographic variation in vegetation and phenology may play a subtle role in the interaction between fire season and vegetation structure and dynamics. Thus Williams (1972) has noted differences in flowering phenology between western and eastern species of *Leucadendron*, which ought to be reflected in different reproductive responses to fire in different seasons.

INVASIVE PLANTS AND THE EFFECT OF FIRE REGIME

The fynbos biome is characteristically prone to invasion by exotic shrubs and trees of species that are preadapted to the local environment and to fynbos fire regimes. This is probably the most pressing environmental problem at present. Of 23 terrestrial plant species listed by Hall and Boucher (1977) as alien weeds in the fynbos biome just four are sprouting shrubs. Of the remainder, 16 are trees or shrubs that rely on seed for regeneration and reproduction. Their life cycles reflect adaptations to fire regime that are important in considering problems of control (Roux and Middlemiss 1963; Taylor 1969b; Kruger 1977b; Fugler 1979; Milton 1980). In every case, long-range seed dispersal to safe sites in more or less undisturbed fynbos (by birds and other animals in aril-bearing *Acacia* spp such as *A. cyclops* (rooikrans) and *A. melanoxylon* (blackwood), and by wind in the case of *Hakea* spp (episodically after bradysporous parent plants have been killed) and *Pinus* spp (usually seasonally)) marks the initial phase of establishment of a sparse population, as in the case of *Pinus taeda* in the southeastern United States (Spring et al 1974). When the initiating population matures, numbers proliferate in response to repeated fire until the natural vegetation has been replaced or nearly so. On the other hand, fire is successfully employed in efforts to control these plants.

Three models seem appropriate in analysing the role of fire in this problem. Firstly, precocious bradysporous *Hakea* spp are relatively easily controlled by a combination of clearing (or killing by other means) and burning. Seed once released from follicles remains dormant until moisture is taken up but germinates or dies thereafter. Seeds and young plants up to ca 24 months are heat-sensitive. Hence, seed released when parents are killed, or the seedlings and young plants, or both, are readily eliminated or reduced several orders of magnitude in density by a burn within 24, but preferably 12 months. Managers prefer to defer burning until seed has germinated because young plants are more sensitive to the heat of a fire than is seed. Any further deferral of fire and any accidental fire before clearing operations would negate control efforts (Taylor 1969b; Fenn 1980).

Secondly, less precocious pine species offer somewhat more flexible approaches. Primary youth periods are 6 yr or longer and young saplings are susceptible to fire, though most adults survive moderate fires. Thus, frequent fire must be used near sources of seed to prevent spread by killing immature plants (Kruger 1977b). However, fire does not effectively eliminate adult populations which must be killed by other means for proper control.

Finally, hard-seeded *Acacia* and other leguminous species require other methods. They are often extremely precocious, with primary youth periods of as little as 24 months and once established, are virtually immune to fire. Fires simply stimulate germination of soil-stored seed. No fire recurs soon enough to kill plants before maturity and, in any event, not all seed germinates after fire, some persisting until the next opportunity. Thus, the postfire seedling population must be killed repeatedly with herbicides and the soil seedbank eventually depleted in this manner.

Coastal Renosterveld communities, on nearly neutral, heavy-textured soils of shales and granites, are prone to invasion by Mediterranean herbs after fire or other disturbance, and these species, which include *Anagallis arvenis* (scarlet pimpernel), *Avena fatua*, *Briza maxima*, *B. minor*, *Koeleria cristata* and *Vulpia bromoides* (Levyns 1929b), are often also invasive in other mediterranean-type ecosystems (Gulmon 1977). Levyns (1929b) has shown how these species, absent from the undisturbed community, become abundant after fire. On the whole, responses of herbaceous invaders to fire have not received attention because they have not yet presented any great management problem.

EFFECTS OF FIRE REGIME ON FORAGE PRODUCTION AND QUALITY

It seems that fire has been used by pastoralists to improve forage in fynbos (Wicht and Kruger 1973; Bands 1977) since their advent some 1 500 or more years ago (Schweitzer and Scott 1973). Grazing with burning is still practised through much of the fynbos biome, both in the mountains and on the coast. This is typified by the practice of patch-burning, where the herder or his overseer sets fire to any patches of vegetation that will burn. This is usually done toward the end of the wet season and prior to the introduction of the livestock. Because of the mosaic pattern produced and because of the experience of the practitioner in judging weather and fuel conditions, no single fire spreads far. The veld is thus patterned in a fine-grained, very irregular mosaic, and any stand of vegetation is burnt once in about 4 to 8 yr. This practice was almost invariably (and is occasionally still) associated with transhumance, stock being alternated seasonally between fynbos and other pastures (karoo or stubble fields and ley pastures on wheatlands). This is probably owing mainly to climatic influences, but also possibly to calcium and other nutrient deficiencies in fynbos forage (Louw 1969).

The principal value of fire in the context of pasturage lies in its effect in making relatively high quality material more readily available by removing the obstructive bed of unpalatable material and stimulating new growth. Fresh young growth even of Restionaceae is palatable, but only for a few seasons after fire. These direct effects of fire on forage production and quality and their variability have nowhere been measured. Fire regime can be manipulated to change the structure and composition of certain fynbos types to induce a more or less permanent change to more productive pasture, especially in marginal fynbos in the year-round and summer rainfall zones. Van Rensburg (1962) has indicated how short-rotation burning can induce a vigorous grass cover. The stands of *Themeda triandra* in firebreaks at Jonkershoek further attest to this. Nonetheless, fire-induced grassland or mixed grassland, which may at one time have been the predominant formation on the coastal forelands (Acocks 1975), can be obtained only under particular combinations of climate and soil such as in renosterveld in the lowlands and certain Waboomveld in the uplands, and are not found on the extremely acid substrates of the prevailing forms of mountain fynbos. Here, the most that is obtained is the elimination of tall shrubs and a predominance of low shrubs with Restionaceae, Cyperaceae and sclerophyllous grasses.

EFFECTS OF FIRE REGIME ON FAUNAL STRUCTURE AND DYNAMICS

The changes in structure and composition induced by fire profoundly affect fynbos vegetation as a habitat for animals. As already indicated, a series of very marked successional stages follow one another rather slowly. Corresponding faunal changes have been little studied and can be discussed only in broad terms, mainly with reference to birds and mammals.

IMMEDIATE POSTFIRE EFFECTS

Although there is little evidence for dramatic animal mortality during a fire, dramatic changes in the faunal component occur as a consequence of the fire. Some species flee the fire and do not return to the unfavourable habitat while others disappear soon afterwards because they are unable to adjust to the change in resources. Forms which depend on the later stages of plant succession are particularly seriously affected. They are instantaneously deprived of habitable environment by fire. Sugar bird *(Promerops cafer)* is an example. It relies on elevated inflorescences of Proteaceae for nectar and insects (Mostert et al 1980) and because dominant shrubs of this kind are usually seeders, no resources are available to sugar birds for the first 4 to 8 yr after fire in most cases. More important, however, are their nest-site requirements which include a sheltering canopy (Burger et al 1976), not available until the stand is well developed, ie from about 8 yr onwards (and unavailable again when shrubs open up with senescence).

There are, on the other hand, examples of almost immediate postfire immigration. Some may be passive, as in the case of parachute spiders. However, reports of immigration for exploitation of ephemeral food resources in the postfire environment are common. Levyns (1929b) discusses foraging on recently burnt plots by various animals. Among those observed were "...buck, a hare, and several tortoises...". She also noted selective foraging patterns on the regrowth. *Anthospermum aethiopicum* seedlings, for example, were preferred and *Elytropappus rhinocerotis* seedlings were avoided. Especially nutritious food resources such as seed released from plants, corms, cormlets and other structures among geophytes, and sprouts are used by a wide variety of transients including genera of birds such as *Francolinus*, *Serinus* and *Streptopelia* and others discussed below. Baboons have been found to forage over a new burn (R C Bigalke, personal observation, 1974). However, it is not clear whether these immigrants are responding to increased productivity, or whether it is simply the open habitat that favours certain foraging strategies. Martin (1966) for example noted "...a minute spider, spinning threads from tip to tip of ...burnt stalks..." to occur commonly on the site of a recent wild-fire, also on cleared areas along pathways though it was absent from undisturbed vegetation. Species able to make effective use of resources which increase in abundance after a fire include rodent moles. Levyns (1929b) found activity of *Georychus capensis* to increase markedly on burnt plots and suggested that this was due to greater availability of underground storage organs of geophytes. Whether the resource did in fact increase in abundance or in quality, or simply became more accessible, was not clear (Wicht 1948b).

EFFECTS OF FIRE SEASON

Most major fynbos fires tend to occur in summer and autumn in the west, and in winter in the southern coastal zone. Comparative effects of fire on fauna in these and other seasons have not been studied. Late summer and autumn fires probably do not disrupt nesting or the birth and rearing of young in at least many bird and mammal species. Those in spring may be expected to do so, perhaps affecting animal density and even species composition, if repeated regularly. On the other hand the establishment of territories in winter, for example by greywing francolin (*Francolinus africanus*) (R C Bigalke, personal observation, 1974), precedes nesting by several months and could be affected by loss of cover following autumn fires.

Herbivore food supplies may be improved more by repeated spring burns, favouring restionaceous and graminoid plants (including tropical grasses) and sprouting shrubs, than by fires in summer and autumn. The timing of patch burning to improve pasturage for livestock - it is usually carried out towards the end of the wet season - perhaps results from recognition of this fact.

Since intervals between fires are usually much longer in fynbos than in other vegetation types, the long-term effects on fauna of burning in a particular season can perhaps be expected to be less marked than elsewhere.

EFFECTS OF FIRE FREQUENCY

Limited data, mainly from trapping studies on small mammals, are available. Habitats of 12 different aged stands (0 to 38 yr) have been sampled in various areas of montane fynbos, mostly at Jonkershoek State Forest, some of them by more than one worker (Toes 1972; Lewis 1978; Willan and Bigalke 1982). Their combined results (Table 7) summarize species composition in newly burnt (less than 1 yr old), young (2 to 6 yr), mature (10 to 17 yr) and senescent (30 to 38 yr) habitats. No sampling was undertaken in vegetation of intervening ages. Species richness is lowest in newly burnt sites, attains a peak in 2 to 6 yr old fynbos (youth phase, start of transitional phase again, declines in mature stands and is again higher in senescent vegetation (30 to 36 yr old)).

A similar trend is evident in the results (Table 8) from the first few years of a long-term trapping study in transitional coastal renosterveld at the Duthie Reserve, Stellenbosch (Bigalke and Pepler 1979). Although the reserve represents a small "island" habitat surrounded by seriously disturbed vegetation and probably has abnormally dense mammal populations as a result (Halpin and Sullivan 1978), succession is likely to resemble that in other fynbos communities. A single pioneer species appeared in the first year while in the second four were present. There were six or seven in each of the succeeding five years, with some changes in species composition. These are discussed further below. In terms of abundance, a slow increase leads to peak values

Table 7   Small mammal species present in relation to postfire age of southwestern Cape mountain fynbos (* indicates presence) (data from Toes 1972; Lewis 1978; Willan and Bigalke 1982).

SPECIES	Postfire age of vegetation (yr)			
	Newly burnt (< 1)	Young (2-6)	Mature (10-17)	Senescent (30-38)
Otomys spp		*	*	*
Rhabdomys pumilio		*	*	*
Mus minutoides	*	*		
Dendromus melanotis		*		
Dendromus mesomelas			*	*
Aethomys namaquensis		*	*	*
Acomys subspinosus	*	*	*	*
Praomys verreauxi				*
Crocidura flavescens		*		
Crocidura cyanea		*		
Myosorex varius		*	*	*
Totals	2	9	6	8

Table 8   Small mammal species presence and abundance (% trap success) in Duthie Reserve, Stellenbosch, in relation to postfire age of the vegetation (* indicates presence) (Bigalke and Pepler 1979).

SPECIES	Postfire age of vegetation (yr)						
	1	1-2	2-3	3-4	4-5	5-6	6
Otomys spp			*	*	*	*	*
Rhabdomys pumilio	*	*	*	*	*	*	*
Acomys subspinosus		*					
Mus minutoides		*	*	*	*	*	*
Dendromus melanotis			*	*	*	*	*
Rattus norvegicus			*	*		*	
Crocidura flavescens					*	*	*
Myosorex varius		*	*	*	*	*	*
Totals	1	4	6	6	6	7	6
Abundance (% trap success)		3,6	16,7	50,4	22,6	25,7	

Table 9   Relative abundance (% trap success station-night^{-1}) and biomass (g station-night^{-1}) of small mammals in south-western Cape mountain fynbos in relation to postfire age of the vegetation. Absolute numbers trapped are given in brackets (Willan and Bigalke 1982).

SPECIES	Postfire age of vegetation (yr)				
	2	4	10	14	38
Otomys spp	0,7 (1)	14,4 (62)	7,3(22)	8,3(15)	8,3(15)
R. pumilio	8,6(18)	8,4 (36)		1,7 (3)	8,3(15)
M. minutoides	4,3 (9)				
D. melanotis	2,9 (6)				
D. mesomelas			2,7 (8)		1,7 (3)
A. namaquensis	10,7(23)	0,9 (2)	0,7 (5)		1,7 (2)
A. subspinosus		2,8 (12)	1,7 (5)		1,7 (2)
C. flavescens		0,2 (1)			
C. cyanea		0,2 (1)			
M. varius		0,7 (3)	5,3(16)	6,7(12)	15,0(27)
Totals	27,2(57)	27,6(117)	17,7(56)	16,7(30)	36,7(64)
Biomass (g station-night^{-1})[a]	9,9	19,0	9,1	9,7	14,3

[a]Calculated from mean masses for each species

in the fourth year after the fire and to subsequent stabilization at lower levels.

Changes in population density are shown Table 9 by samples trapped in montane fynbos of postfire ages 2, 4, 10, 14 and 38 yr (Willan and Bigalke 1982). Total abundance was higher in young (2 and 4 yr) than in mature (10 and 14 yr) habitats, but was highest in old (38 yr) fynbos. However total biomass is highest in the 4 yr old community, then declines and rises to a second, lower peak in senescent fynbos (Table 9).

To summarize, small mammal populations are disrupted by fire but small numbers of a few pioneer species are encountered within the first or second years. Peak density, biomass and diversity appear to develop during the youth phase when canopy cover is rapidly increasing and herb biomass reaches a maximum. Then when the vegetation is in the transitional and early mature phases these parameters decline. Finally, senescent fynbos seems to support more species and a higher total density than the preceding successional stages although biomass may not be as high as in the youth phase.

The generality of these trends remains to be tested and detailed explanations await further work. Geographic and altitudinal differences are to be expected in the timing, nature and magnitude of successional processes. A study by Bond et al (1980) in the southern Cape suggests that at least rodent species diversity (H), an index measuring both the number of species and equality of representation of the individuals of each species, may depend largely on vegetation structure. They found an inverse relationship between species diversity (but not population size and specific composition) and the proportion of foliage in the 0,4 to 0,6 m layer above the ground. Two tentative hypotheses are proposed: that the vertical distribution of plant material, irrespective of its form or nature, is significant in rodent niche partitioning and that rodent species diversity can be predicted from foliage profiles.

These authors go on to predict low diversity, associated with a high proportion of total foliage below 0,6 m, in young fynbos after fire. This should increase as upper layers develop and perhaps decrease with senescence of the plant community many years after the fire. The data in Tables 9 and 10 partly confirm these expectations but the high species richness, density and biomass in senescent stands do not fit the pattern.

Habitat preferences of some species can be invoked to explain their appearance at particular stages in the postfire succession. Thus *Rhabdomys pumilio* (four-striped field mouse) is omnivorous and therefore fitted for a pioneering role. Its early presence can also be related to its preference for "grassy" ground cover, which includes Gramineae as well as Cyperaceae and Restionaceae (Bond et al 1980). These authors found numbers of *Otomys* spp, specialized herbivores, correlated with dense, shrubby vegetation. This factor presumably explains its absence from young postburn vegetation where one would expect it to find adequate nutritious plant material. Insectivorous shrews of the genera *Myosorex* and *Crocidura* also seem to require well-developed vegetation cover. Thus *Crocidura* was first trapped in the fifth year after the fire at Duthie. This may depend on the accumulation of sufficient litter to support a good invertebrate fauna, as well as on microclimatic factors and cover preferences.

Further data on mammals are restricted to general observations on medium-sized herbivores. Many are attracted to young fynbos. Thus grey rhebuck *(Pelea capreolus)* and - near rocky sites - klipspringer *(Oreotragus oreotragus)* are commonly seen on burns. In the eastern parts of the fynbos region, within their geographic range, mountain reedbuck *(Redunca fulvorufula)* are similarly attracted and mountain zebra *(Equus zebra)* are thought to respond in the same way. Antelope probably migrate over fair distances to reach fresh burns but the extent of these movements is unknown. The improved accessibility and enhanced nutritive value of vegetation on young burns may stimulate reproduction and enhance survival and so affect population densities.

The dependence of some birds on mature fynbos for food and especially for nesting sites has already been mentioned. Cody (1975) found bird species richness in fynbos to be directly related to structural diversity of the vegetation. Casual observation shows birds to be rare on recently burnt sites and successional changes in the avifauna must be expected to parallel development of increasingly complex vegetation structure. There may be a decline in species richness as well as in density in mature or senescent stands. Winterbottom (1972) found that "Dense Protea" (apparently late mature or early senescent fynbos) had only 6 dominant bird species while in "Fynbos" there were 12.

Maintenance of a range of different aged stands of fynbos would seem to be necessary to maintain a complete spectrum of animal species, population densities and biomasses.

ADAPTIVE RESPONSE OF ORGANISMS TO FIRE

It is difficult from observations of responses of modern biota to fire to determine which responses indicate adaptation to the fire environment and which are in fact preadaptive (Frost, this volume, chapter 13). In this chapter the characters of several species are described to indicate how these favour survival and growth in the fynbos fire environment, not distinguishing between preadaptations and adaptations except to draw attention to characters which could have emerged solely as responses to the particular fynbos fire regime. In the case of vascular plants, floras are analysed to give some indication of the relative importance of certain response types in the species assemblages of different forms of fynbos.

MICROORGANISMS

We are not aware of any studies which provide information immediately relevant to the question of responses among microorganisms to fynbos fires. This is a considerable problem. Firstly, it is clear that microorganisms play a crucial role in nutrient cycling and nutrition, especially in nutrient deficient, impoverished soils where mutualistic relations between microorganisms and higher plants are apparently fundamental to nutrient uptake from the soil (Lamont 1981; Malajczuk and Lamont 1981). It is therefore vital to understand how fire influences the activity of microorganisms (Dunn and DeBano 1977). Secondly, higher plant population dynamics are at least partly influenced by the immediate effects of fire on community composition of and postfire succession in pathogens such as the soil root-rotting fungus *Phytophthora* spp (Parmeter 1977; Malajczuk and Glenn 1981). Thirdly, there clearly are characteristic fire-response patterns among microorganisms which must be studied for any worthwhile understanding of fire-related aspects of ecosystem function (Dunn and DeBano 1977). Finally, since there are large net losses of nitrogen from the ecosystem in any fire it is particularly important to know the responses of nitrogen-fixing organisms, free-living or otherwise, to fire and the postfire environment.

HIGHER PLANTS

Many fynbos areas support abundant mosses and lichens on the ground or on rocks and on stems of woody perennials. This component of the flora is known to respond strongly to fire elsewhere (Gimingham 1972) and field observations suggest there are local parallels. No information is available for fynbos, however, and the account which follows, drawn largely from Kruger (1977b), is confined to vascular plants.

Species traits and responses to fire

Scorching avoidance

Individuals of a few species of erect shrubs survive fire with all or most of their crowns intact while those of others around them are killed or obliged to sprout. In some cases, shoots and foliage are possibly protected by the shape of the crown, which apparently deflects the heat of the fire, while cambium is protected by thick bark (eg *Protea laurifolia* (laurel protea), *Leucadendron argenteum* (silver tree), *Leucospermum conocarpodendron* (tree pincushions)) (Wicht 1945). Rourke (1972) discusses this habit in tree pinchushions, but states that "...regeneration takes place from the apical branchlets...". Wicht (1945) implies the same. This is slightly misleading since individuals that survive fire are those in which at least some apical meristems survive to produce the new shoots of the coming season; strictly, regeneration does not occur. Some low, spreading shrubs with dense, matted crowns, such as *Protea effusa* and *Leucadendron glaberrimum* also survive. Although the perimeters of their crowns may be scorched, the foliage and shoots are relatively nonflammable and few plants burn out. These species do not have the capacity for vegetative regeneration, a proportion of each population is killed in every fire, and populations therefore usually consist of several cohorts. They do not survive very intense fires except through seed regeneration. Consequently, they are favoured by factors that maintain above-ground biomass and thus fuel at moderate levels, and respond well to fairly frequent, light fires.

Seed production

Species that rely entirely on seed for survival are found mainly among shrubs (trees are almost exclusively sprouters, with the notable exceptions of *Widdringtonia cedarbergensis* (Clanwilliam cedar) and *W. schwarzii* (Willowmore cedar)). Some hemicryptophytes, eg *Chondropetalum hookeranum* (Restionaceae) and *Ehrharta ramosa* (Gramineae), are killed by fire, so that with the limited number of annuals, there are also a few herbs which return through germination. Thus, although fynbos floras are dominated by species which sprout, there is a significant proportion of seeders (Mitchell 1922; Wicht 1945; van der Merwe 1966b) (Table 10).

Survival among seeders is enhanced by a variety of mechanisms. Among these is bradyspory, the retention of seed on the plant for release when the parent dies (Wicht 1945). In *Leucadendron*, 49 of 82 fynbos species retain seed in conelike fruiting heads up to at least 8 yr in some species (Williams 1972), and a similar feature is found among many species of *Protea*. Here seed is released from dormancy when the plant or the organ dies, as after fire, and germination follows soon after. This mechanism seems to protect effectively protein- and energy-rich seed against the heavy predation experienced on the ground in mature vegetation (Bond 1980). Other species, in

Table 10   Two fynbos floras classified by Raunkiaer life form and mode of regeneration after fire.

Life form	Swartboskloof[a]		Jakkalsrivier[b]	
	No of spp in class		No of spp in class	
	Vegetative regener- ation	Regener- ation from seed only	Vegetative regener- ation	Regener- ation from seed only
Phanerophyte	84	67	43	110
Chamaephyte	76	63	33	50
Hemicryptophyte	70	1	128	11
Geophyte	67	0	111	0
Therophyte	0	16	0	7
Unclassified	1	3	6	9
Total:	298	150	321	187

[a]From van der Merwe (1966b).
[b]From unpublished Directorate of Forestry records.

Proteaceae, Rutaceae, *Cliffortia*, *Aspalathus* and other taxa release seed or fruit on ripening, and these have biochemical inhibitors or hard testas or pericarps which promote dormancy and longevity (van Staden 1966; Brown and van Staden 1971, 1973; van Staden and Brown 1972, 1973; Williams 1972). Circumstantial evidence shows that this seed can remain viable on or in the soil for about 15 yr or longer (Boucher and McCann 1975; Rourke 1976). These often require heat as a scarification mechanism (Blommaert 1972; Williams 1972). Many species, as in Ericaceae and Asteraceae, produce a superabundance of small seeds, some at least of which (eg *Elytropappus glandulosus*) (Levyns 1935b) are moderately long-lived in the soil. Laboratory studies showed a life of 7 yr. Percentage survival and germination among such seeds needs to be relatively small to replace parent populat- ions. Whether or not species rely on postburn dispersal of seed to the site from outside has a strong bearing on how communities are maintained in a fire environment. Levyns (1929b) reports cases where circumstantial evidence in her experiments indicated germination from soil-stored seed. Wicht (1948b), from his experience in a detailed replicated burning trial, inferred that most seeds that germinated on burnt plots "...were not derived from adjacent unburnt areas". Bond (1980) has noted how Proteaceae seed fails to disperse beyond the boundaries of a burn. Short-distance dispersal seems the prevalent pattern in species with large long-lived seed, and in any species with isolated subpopulations. However, Martin (1966), for example, has suggested that some *Erica* spp rely on dispersal to the site after fire. This important question requires further investigat- ion.

Vegetative regeneration

The full array of vegetative regeneration modes in mediterranean-type fire environments is found also in fynbos communities. It includes the following: (i) epicormic sprouting for
dormant buds protected by thick bark of the stem (Figure 8), in a
few species like *Protea nitida*, *Maytenus oleoides* (mountain
maytenus) and *Heeria argentea* (rockwood) (Wicht 1945); (ii)
sprouting from dormant buds in lignotubers or similar organs at
or below the soil surface, which is perhaps the most common mode
among shrubs and is associated with typical, multi-stemmed growth
forms like Australian mallee (Mitchell 1922; Wicht 1945; Martin
1966); (iii) sprouting from rhizomes at or near the soil surface,
as in most grasses, sedges and restionaceous plants such as
Pentaschistis, *Tetraria* and *Restio* spp, but also in a few dwarf
shrubs, eg *Protea acaulos* (Rourke 1980), and (iv) survival and

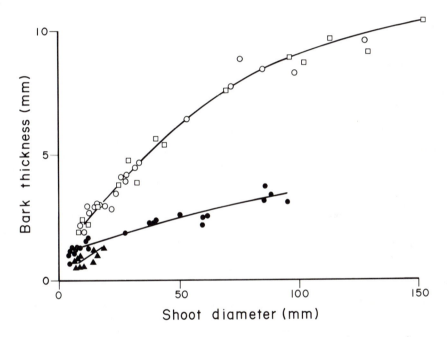

Figure 8   Bark thickness in relation to shoot diameter in various fynbos Proteaceae. Dots represent values for
Protea repens (sugar bush), a species where individuals are killed by fire, and triangles, *Leucadendron
salignum* (geelbos), where the shoots are killed and
plants sprout from lignotubers. In *Protea nitida*
(squares) and *Leucospermum conocarpodendron* (tree pincushions) (circles) shoot systems tend to survive
fire; the former regenerates by epicormic shoots, the
latter does not. Data from populations sampled at
Jonkershoek (Kruger 1982).

growth from dormant buds on underground storage organs (geophytes), as in Liliaceae, Haemodoraceae, Iridaceae, Orchidaceae, *Drosera*, *Oxalis* and various Asteraceae *(Berkheya, Gerbera, Osteospermum)* (Mitchell 1922; Levyns 1929b; Adamson 1935; Wicht 1945, 1948b; Martin 1966).

Flowering responses

Martin (1966) has classified plants regenerating after fire according to their flowering responses, as follows: (i) species that flower shortly after fire and rarely or not at other times, including typical "fire lilies" in the Haemodoraceae *(Cyrtanthus contractus* (fire lily), *Haemanthus canaliculatus)*, Liliaceae *(Androcymbium leucanthum)*, Iridaceae *(Moraea ramosissima* (geeltulp)), Orchidaceae and other families (Mitchell 1922; Levyns 1929b, 1966a; Wicht 1945, 1948b; Hall 1959); (ii) species that flower in abundance shortly after fire, less frequently afterwards, for which Martin notes a graded series in the intensity of responses; *Watsonia pyramidata* is an example (see below); (iii) species in which flowering does not occur immediately after burning, but is enhanced relative to unburnt stands in the second and third years *(Themeda triandra, Restio triticeus)*; (iv) species in which flowering is depressed after fire and normal in subsequent years *(Phylica axillaris)* and (v) species that are neutral to fire *(Dierama pendulum, Leonotis leonurus* (wild dagga)). Thus, in some cases the fire response may well be adaptive (as in "fire lilies") while in others, especially shrubs, the response appears to reflect increased vigour as a response to defoliation and/or removal of senescent tissue that is costly to maintain, as in *Protea scabra, P. speciosa* and other *Protea* spp (Rourke 1980), and very likely in most sprouting shrubs (except, for example, *Asparagus* spp). Among many monocotyledons (eg *Watsonia pyramidata)* and some dicotyledonous shrubs (eg *Cliffortia linearifolia)* (Martin 1966) vegetative reproduction is also enhanced by fire. In some cases, at least among geophytes, it has been suggested that flowering but not vegetative activity responds to burning (Wicht 1948b), but observations by Levyns (1929b) agree with the general field experience that most sprouting plants grow more luxuriantly on burnt than on unburnt sites.

Interestingly, annuals appear to respond similarly to clearing and to burning, at least in the study reported by Levyns (1929b), though few or none grow and reproduce in unburnt vegetation. Levyns (1929b), comparing cleared and burnt plots, showed that the flowering responses among geophytic monocotyledons were owing to fire effects rather than simple clearing. Unfortunately she could report no results from ash and fertilizer trials. Martin (1966) discounted the direct effects of fire on plant reproductive effort, as opposed to clearing, but his experiment confounded burning and clearing.

In some instances, fire may induce much earlier flowering (eg *Asparagus capensis* and *Cyrtanthus contractus)* although flowering seasonality in most species is not affected (Mitchell 1922; Martin 1966). On the other hand, there is evidence that the nature and intensity of the responses depend partly on the season of the burn (eg *Watsonia pyramidata*, see below).

Juvenile periods

The time required for plants to reach reproductive maturity after regeneration following fire varies from about 1 to 10 yr (Table 11). Species which sprout, including some shrubs, often flower within 12 months (this is the secondary juvenile period), though others may require up to 24 months *(Rhus lucida, Hibiscus aethiopicus, Leucadendron salignum* (geelbos), *Podalyria myrtillifolia* and others) (Mitchell 1922; Wicht 1948b; Martin 1966) and sometimes 36 months (eg *Brunia stokoei)* (Kruger and Lamb 1978). Primary juvenile periods (time elapsed between germination and flowering), at least among shrubs, are more variable but most species reach reproductive maturity within 8 yr (Kruger 1979b). Some species are precocious, as in *Anthospermum aethiopicum,* reported as flowering in the second year after fire (Martin 1966), and *Erica mauretanica,* flowering after 30 months (Mitchell 1922). Van der Merwe (1966b) reports that some *Protea repens* individuals flowered in the third year. Rourke (1980) presents observations on the age at first flowering in cultivation among members of *Protea* (Figure 9). The median juvenile period among 42 seeding fynbos species is 4 yr. Species that required 6 yr or more to flower were among those that are usually slow-growing and occur in special habitats with a degree of protection from fire, eg rock outcrops and ledges *(P. magnifica* (bearded protea) – 6 yr), cool, moist upper montane sites *(P. stokoei* – 5 to 12 yr), extremely arid localities *(P. glabra* (Clanwilliam protea) – 10 yr) or crest ridges of high peaks *(P. rupicola* – 16 yr).

There is usually a lag between the age at which the first plants flower and the majority flower. In *P. eximia* (broad-leaved protea), for example, precocious individuals flower at 2 yr but most flower after 3 yr. Observations on cultivated plants may not reflect performance in the field; nevertheless, Williams (1972) and Taylor (1977) report field observations on some species of *Leucadendron* and these show that juvenile periods

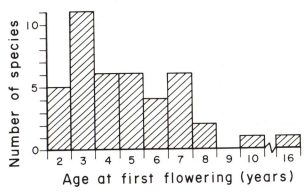

Figure 9   Frequency distribution of youth periods in cultivated fynbos *Protea* spp (Rourke 1980).

Table 11   Primary juvenile periods of some seed-regenerating fynbos species: percentage of population at given age with ripe seed (Kruger 1978).

Species	Age of sample (yr)							
	1	2	3	4	5	6	7	8
Erica sessiliflora	0	0	0	0	1,0	21,0	–	–
Leucadendron concavum	0	0	0	0	37,5	–	–	–
L. salicifolium	0	0	0	0	1,0	64,0	100,0	–
L. xanthoconus	0	0	0	0	0	5,0	45,0	–
Protea lacticolor (moist site)	0	0	0	1,0	6,0	19,0	85,0	–
P. lacticolor (dry site)	0	0	0	0	0	1,0	28,0	–
P. mundii	0	0	0	0	0	1,0	7,0	–
P. stokoei	0	0	0	0	0	0,8	14,2	–
Roridula gorgonias	0	0	0	0	17,0	73,0	–	–

under field conditions are not markedly longer than in cultivation. Their field observations for *Leucadendron* indicate juvenile periods of 3 yr *(L. floridum, L. macowanii)*, 4 yr *(L. platysper-mum)* and 6 yr *(L. muirii)*.

The balance of evidence, therefore, shows that seeding fynbos shrubs of habitats exposed to frequent fire are highly precocious except where individuals have the capacity to survive fire *(Leucadendron argenteum, Leucospermum conocarpodendron)* or where moist conditions or sparseness of vegetation due to rockiness or aridity makes for infrequent fire, at least locally *(Protea glabra, P. magnifica, P. stokoei, Leucadendron praemorsum)*.

Many Proteaceae and other taxa require up to 12 months after flowering for seed to ripen. Thus, if the production of viable seed rather than flowering is viewed as marking the end of the juvenile phase then 1 yr should be added to the figures quoted above.

Features of life cycles in relation to fire

There are no comprehensive and detailed studies on the life cycles of representative fynbos species which would serve to illustrate possible adaptive groups, but information assembled mainly from unpublished sources provide a useful picture. The account that follows is drawn largely from Kruger (1977b).

Herbaceous plants whose responses are most often noted are the geophytes. The extreme instance is the so-called "fire lily" type noted above. Hall (1959) showed that the incidence of geophytic Orchidaceae was strongly associated with recent fire. Tagged samples of 10 species were all most abundant and active in the first one to four spring seasons after a burn, and virtually absent thereafter.

Some information on *Watsonia pyramidata* (Kruger 1977b, 1978) illustrates geophyte life cycles and responses to fire. In this species, corm discs are produced annually, are highly resistant to decay and remain in chronological sequence in the soil. Two new corms are almost invariably produced when a ramet flowers. It is therefore possible to excavate clones and examine their genealogy with some accuracy. Clones have a great longevity, several older than a century being found in random samples. Individual ramets are also long-lived, with a maximum observed age (before first flowering and clonal reproduction) of about 35 yr. In unburnt populations, about 5% or less of all ramets flower annually. If burnt in autumn (and possibly also in late summer), populations respond strongly, at least half of all ramets producing inflorescences. Populations burnt in spring do not respond. Since each inflorescence produces about 700 seeds and flowering induces vegetative reproduction, fires in the "right" season obviously have a strong impact on *Watsonia* populations. Seedlings germinate freely in the following winter and spring, and contractile roots draw the new corm to an average of 26 mm below the soil surface within 12 months. Corms apparently grow for 4 to 8 yr or more before first flowering. Thus *W. pyramidata* has various adaptive features of survival value in an environment subject to fire, although fire may well not have been the key factor in the natural selection process. Long-lived clones with deeply buried meristems enable continued occupation of a site in the variable, sometimes long, interval between fires. Reproduction in the favourable postfire environment is enhanced by synchronous and marked population responses, a behaviour that probably also favours pollination, and relatively low predation on fruit and seeds. Contractile roots ensure burial and good protection of the perennating bud against climate, predators and fire.

There is little information on short-lived opportunistic shrubs which are often conspicuous after fire, disappearing or becoming rare thereafter (Levyns 1929b; Adamson 1935; van der Merwe 1966b). Some have hard, apparently long-lived seed (eg *Aspalathus chenopoda* and *Chrysanthemoides monilifera)* but many, especially the Asteraceae such as *Euryops abrotanifolius* and *Othonna quinquedentata,* have small seed that may be highly dispersible and short-lived. Levyns (1929b), discussing this characteristic among *Pelargonium* spp, notes seed burial mechanisms and suggests linkage with dormancy and longevity as adaptive.

The *Protea repens* and some allied species serve as examples of seeding shrubs with longer life cycles. *P. repens* itself is easily killed by fire but seeds germinate readily and there is usually little mortality among young plants. Plants require about 4 to 8 yr to reach reproductive maturity after establishment (Jordaan 1949; van der Merwe 1966b), and bradysporous capitula retain a reasonable supply of viable seed. In a 19 yr old stand at Jonkershoek, for example, all plants carried capitula 2 yr old and older, and most had retained seed for at least 4 yr (Kruger 1978). Lombaard (1971) has shown in stands about 10 to 12 yr old that current seed production amounted to about 900 to 1 300 seed per shrub, of which about 9% was viable. Jordaan (1949) has drawn attention to the significance of the length of the juvenile period in determining whether or not the species would survive a given fire regime. He suggested on the grounds of embryology and phenology that populations were liable to be exterminated if burnt during the period July to December, less so if burnt in April to June, but would regenerate in the period January to March because ripe seed was freely available in that season. Later he showed that *P. repens* had been eliminated in a June burn on Paarlberg. His observation seems to have limited generality, since *P. repens* elsewhere survives winter burns because of bradyspory, but he drew attention to important interactions between fire regime and phenology (Jordaan 1965).

Dominant seed-regenerating shrubs reach ages of about 20 to 50 yr, low shrubs such as *Erica* spp having, on the whole, shorter life spans than tall shrubs. There is little or no establishment of young plants in vigorous stands, but some seed regeneration occurs when adults begin to die out.

The only species of sprouting shrub about which there is some information is *Protea nitida* (Haynes 1976). This species does not have bradysporous capitula, but flowering and seed release occur somewhat irregularly through the seasons with maximum in winter and spring, and germination is usually abundant after fire and rare at other times. Young plants soon develop lignotubers. In the nursery, this occurs within 12 months after germination. These plants seldom reach maturity before being burnt for the first time, upon which they adopt a low, multistemmed habit. This habit is seemingly retained for many years until one of the shoots gains dominance and the plant takes on the form of an erect if crooked shrub, attains maturity and grows in height. At this stage, individuals are able to resprout from epicormic buds in the branches and stem or from the base after even the most intense fires (Haynes 1976).

Animals

Frost (this volume, chapter 13) provides a detailed review of this topic that covers many of the known responses among fynbos animals. It seems that animal responses in fynbos should show peculiarities owing to the following circumstances:-

1   Plant sclerophylly, the widespread occurrence of secondary compounds which apparently reduce palatability, and low nutrient concentrations in plant parts in general, as well as the scarcity of palatable grasses, make for "poor" forage. Herbivores must either accommodate to these conditions, adapt to seasonal "herbivore windows" such as the temporary palatabil-

ity of expanding leaves, relatively rich in protein and not yet hardened, or search for unusually nutritious resources such as nectar, fruit and seeds. Others may simply avoid the plant assemblage so characterized and immigrate only at certain successional stages when the vegetation is mostly palatable. These features may be intensified by the fine-grained nature of resources in fynbos with its mixture of plant growth forms.

2   The successional changes in fynbos are very marked, proceeding from "bare" ground through a (structurally) grasslandlike stage and mixed herb/shrubland to shrubland. These changes are relatively greater than in grassland or savanna. They would seem therefore to provide opportunity for greater packing of annual species through temporal partitioning of resources than in other ecosystems and responses to firedriven plant succession might be expected to be more diverse. However, richness in annual species does not appear to be particularly great and there are also few endemics (Bigalke 1979).

3   Fynbos fires release more energy, move more slowly and have taller flames and deeper flame fronts than grassland or savanna fires and these features should present special problems of survival to animals.

4   Relatively low fire frequencies in fynbos may favour stratagems that allow low rates of animal survival in situ and show population growth thereafter. In addition, where species are exterminated locally re-establishment through slower immigration than elsewhere would be feasible.

5   Fire seasonality is coupled with hot, dry summers during which many plants are dormant and forage may be scarce.
        Survival in situ seems quite feasible in many arthropods. Subterranean forms have not been studied in relation to fire, but Endrody Younga (1978), for example, describes litter and soil insects with Gondwana origins. They must be presumed to have evolved under conditions when fire was rare, and yet have survived in the fire environment of the fynbos. Ants, termites and earthworms generally, though perhaps variably, survive in situ and are active shortly after fire in most places (Martin 1966; Kruger 1980). Specialized life cycles enable some insects to be little affected by fire. For example, various species of scarab beetle, which forage mainly on *Protea* inflorescences, pupate under termitaria of *Amitermes hastatus* (Kruger 1980). Pupation occurs during late summer and autumn, the height of the fire season, and adults emerge not simultaneously but at different times over weeks. These properties would seem to favour survival even if the adults must fly some distance to reach unburnt vegetation.
        There are no doubt other examples of survival by particular stages in the life cycle, as well as by use of refuges or by escape. As Tainton and Mentis (this volume,

chapter 6) point out, invertebrates are generally fecund enough for populations to recover rapidly. The means whereby the various species of land snails found in fynbos habitats maintain themselves poses an intriguing problem.

The effects of fire on fynbos amphibians have not been studied but are probably similar to those suggested for grassland species (Tainton and Mentis, this volume, chapter 6). For reptiles too it is likely that refuge habitats are probably important. *Psammobates geometricus* (the geometric tortoise) is an especially interesting case. It is a species of lowland fynbos ecosystems which has a life cycle seasonality and exploits soil insulation in a fashion that suggests adaptation to a fynbos fire regime (J C Greig, personal communication, 1980). Eggs are laid in spring and buried about 100 mm below the soil surface. Incubation lasts about 4 to 6 months and hatchlings emerge in April and May, when exposure to fire is unlikely. Winter and spring are seasons with the best forage and maximum growth rates, and juveniles are well established by the first summer. They reach reproductive maturity at 7 to 8 yr, live till about 30 yr and may attain peak fecundity at about 15 yr. The tortoises avoid the closed habitats of mature vegetation. Thus juveniles are able to grow rapidly in the relatively productive postfire environment and reach reproductive maturity before the probability of fire reaches its maximum. Adults are able to survive some fires, but eggs and hatchlings are seldom if at all exposed.

There would seem to be no reason to expect that birds, by virtue of their mobility, are less able to survive fires in fynbos than in any other vegetation type (Tainton and Mentis, this volume, chapter 6). Though nests are vulnerable, Winterbottom (1963) shows that the incidence of nesting among birds in the winter rainfall region of the southwestern Cape reaches a peak in September (spring) when the wet season has passed and temperatures begin to rise. Although his data may be biased by the inclusion of records from farm and garden birds, it seems that the probability of significant nest loss from fire in fynbos is usually not very great.

Among small mammals, fossorial species are probably least affected by fire as their effective survival has been readily observed (eg Levyns 1929b for rodent moles). Others are likely to survive fire in underground refuges (Delany 1972), under rocks or in unburnt islands of vegetation, although nonburrowing taxa (eg *Otomys* spp, *Rhabdomys pumilio, Dendromus mesomelas*) may be especially vulnerable. Willan and Bigalke (1982) report that all of the 11 species listed in Table 7 were found to occur in mesic refuge habitats (Vesey-Fitzgerald 1966; Stewart 1972) unrepresentative of typical fynbos. Trapping on rocky outcrops, usually also regarded as refuge habitats, showed only *Aethomys namaquensis*, *Elephantulus edwardii* (Cape elephant-shrew) and a single specimen of *Mus minutoides* to be present. No dead or injured small mammals were noted after a prescribed burn in the Jakkalsrivier catchment, Lebanon State Forest (Willan and Bigalke 1982).

Mobility probably enables hares, carnivores, bovids and baboons to escape all but very large, intense conflagrations, although anecdotal accounts of small antelope such as Cape grysbok *(Raphicerus melanotis)* burning to death are not uncommon. Dependent young are more likely to perish but in some species (Cape grysbok, grey duiker *(Sylvicapra grimmia))* births may be concentrated in spring (Manson 1974) when fire incidence is low.

Variation in survival rate with variation in fire intensity is expected for at least some species but has not yet been investigated. This brief description of possible patterns of adaptation to the fynbos fire regime indicates an intriguing array of responses well worth investigation.

EFFECTS OF FIRE REGIME ON MICROCLIMATE, SOILS AND HYDROLOGY

Few microclimate studies have been reported for fynbos ecosystems. The immediate, ephemeral effects of fire on microclimate and hence on the ecosystem are seemingly drastic (high temperatures, great turbulence, etc). Apart from the fact that vegetation is razed, the effects are poorly known and perhaps too short-lived to be important in the long run. Nevertheless, cases such as the reported stimulation by ethylene in smoke of flowering of *Xanthorrhoea australis* in Australian heathland (Gill and Ingwerson 1976) suggest that it is important to understand these effects to know the overall ecological role of fire.

Mountain fynbos communities are usually at least 0,75 to 1,0 m tall, with cover normally exceeding 70%. Fire through these stands nearly eliminates or at least severely reduces the vegetal cover. This would immediately change microclimatic lapse rates near the ground and markedly affect wind profiles. Furthermore, the reflective properties of the surface change dramatically. Infiltration capacity of the soil is apparently not changed in many cases (but see below). It is possible to explore the likely effects of fire on the energy balance, evapotranspiration, and wind near the ground by means of established microclimate models, but the likely influences may be summarized as follows:-

1   The uppermost layer of the soil, ca 300 mm deep in sands, deeper in sandy loams, is subject to drying through direct evaporation and when exposed by fire, losses through evaporation are greater and so the surface layers of the soil become drier. However, removal of the vegetative cover drastically reduces losses through transpiration and the subsurface layers may well be moister after fire. The precise nature of the soil profile and the rooting characteristics of the vegetation will determine the net effect on evapotranspiration.

Levyns (1929b) sampled the upper 150 mm of a granitic soil through a full year and found little difference between the moisture contents of soils of burnt and unburnt sites. Wicht (1948b) sampled soils, also granitic, from replicated plots at depths of 0 to 150 and 610 mm at the end of summer.

No statistically significant differences were found between soil moisture of sites burnt 44 days before and that of unburnt sites, although the former were all moister at 610 mm depth. These observations are too few for a proper test of predictions concerning the effect of fire on local soil moisture regimes.

2   Upper soil layers exposed after fire will profoundly influence temperatures of air near the ground, especially since most soils are sands. Surface temperatures will fluctuate more widely, and will be likely to exceed 50°C often in summer. This effect will probably be confined to the upper 50 mm in sands (Geiger 1957). Local variations owing, for example, to variations in soil moisture, aspect differences and different organic matter contents must play a profound role in plant germination and establishment and in determining distribution of plant species, through, among other things, the effect of temperature fluctuations on dormant seed and on relative survival of seedlings. Effects on microorganisms and hence, for example, on mineralization processes would be equally profound.

Levyns (1929b) was apparently the earliest to attempt studies on responses of soil temperatures to burning, without much success. Martin (1966) made a more comprehensive study, but also with limited results. He found little difference in spring between recently burnt and unburnt soils though the former were warmer by about 2°C at 100 mm depth. Differences at 50 mm were small. On a cloudy day in summer, temperatures at 50 mm ranged from 15 to 18°C diurnally and exceeded maximum temperatures of air at 1,2 m (24°C) and of unburnt soil (23°C) by 8 to 9°C.

3   Sands, both in mountain and in coastal fynbos, are sometimes subject to deflation after fire (Walsh 1968; Bond 1979). Wind erosion is apparently not a great problem unless burning is accompanied by grazing with domestic stock, but ecological effects of deflation could be significant. Wind and saltating soil particles will erode or damage young plants, and drift of soil and seed could cause small-scale vegetation patterns.

4   After fire, soil is exposed to raindrops and moved accordingly. This causes patterning through pedestalling, debris dams and large-scale soil transport (Specht et al 1958).

5   At elevations exceeding about 1 500 m and in other frost-prone zones, frost action after fire could become important in determining plant establishment patterns.

6   The effects will be ameliorated gradually as vegetation recovers, but initial microclimatic controls or regeneration will influence the composition of a stand throughout its successional history.

Certain prominent features of the mountain fynbos landscape dominate the effects of fire regime on soils and on the hydrological cycle. First, the steep and rugged topography is in fact relatively old and stable. Frequent rock outcroppings provide local erosional base-levels. Soils derived from the dominant sandstone formations are coarse, structureless and highly permeable and the underlying material coarsely weathered. Deep colluvial and alluvial material is prominent in certain landscapes. Underlying rock is often heavily cracked and jointed. Rainfall intensities are seldom excessive. The highest 15 minute intensity recorded at Jonkershoek in 20 yr was around 60 mm hr^{-1} (Wicht et al 1969) and largest 1 hr storms reported amounted to 50 and 75 mm (Wicht 1943). Consequently, surface runoff as overland flow is exceptional even in the heaviest storms (Versfeld 1981). Most water during storms leaves catchments through rapid lateral drainage (quick seepage) and channel flow, except in zones of saturation near streamlines or below pronounced breaks in the slope. Stream levels respond rapidly and markedly to rainstorms (Wicht 1943) though such stormflow is a small part of annual flow, relative to baseflow (Bosch et al, this volume, chapter 15). Mountain streams usually have very low silt loads, and the major erosional process is apparently in the form of soil slips and subsequent gully erosion during exceptional storms of less than annual frequency (Wicht 1943).

With such physiography and hydrology it is not surprising that the prevailing fire regime has a relatively small effect. Soil structure is apparently not much affected. In a runoff plot study on a sandy loam on granite at Jonkershoek, cover types monitored included a pine stand, a protected fynbos stand and a hoed and a burnt fynbos site. Surface runoff as overland flow collected from these plots was negligible or zero irrespective of treatment, in spite of one of the heaviest storms on record having occurred shortly after hoeing and burning (Versfeld 1981). Clearly, there are many situations where infiltration capacities of soils are greatly in excess of maximum rainfall rates and unlikely to be sufficiently affected by burning so that noticeable reductions in infiltration rates are likely. However, Bond (1980) has reported water repellency in certain fynbos soils, especially humic and organic soils, of the southern Cape, and shown from laboratory studies that the heat from fire is likely to increase repellency, as in chaparral fires of the mountains of southern California (DeBano 1981). The extent of this phenomenon and its importance in erosion and hydrology have yet to be evaluated, but the catastrophic floods and debris flows which follow so many chaparral fires are not a feature of the mountain fynbos.

Field observation indicates also that extremely intense fires which oxidize the organic material of surface soil horizons, drastically modifying physical properties, lead to accelerated erosion after fire, both because soil particles are more mobile and because the site is denuded of vigorous resprouting herbs.

Few studies have been completed of fire's effects on soil chemistry and fertility. Martin (1966) measured pH of soils on burnt and unburnt sites over several months and could find no consistent difference. This contradicts experience elsewhere and merits further investigation. He also looked for responses in nitrification to burning and could find none. Regarding overall fertility, Schutte (1960) pointed to chlorosis in certain fynbos plants as indicative of deficiencies in the trace elements magnesium, manganese and zinc and used simple field trials to confirm the diagnosis. He suggested that plants in nutrient-deficient environments would be adapted to such conditions, and that an evident deficiency syndrome must therefore be due to soil impoverishment because of "clearing and burning".

The removal of vegetation by fire changes the hydrological regime, but these hydrological effects of fire are not straight-forward and require further study. Rycroft (1947) reported increased spateflow rates from a catchment in Jonkershoek after an autumn burn, but this effect had disappeared by the second winter (Banks 1964). Conversely, van der Zel and Kruger (1975) showed in a similar catchment study in Langrivier, Jonkershoek, how streamflow declined with time since burning and ascribed this to steadily increasing evapotranspiration through interception and transpiration losses. Later, van Wyk (1977) analysed results of the same experiment, using additional records, and found a smaller streamflow response (decreases of about 16 mm yr^{-1} of protection on average, as opposed to 20 mm yr^{-1}) that did not persist beyond about the first two decades. Streamflow from catchments nearby, with lower rainfall and shorter vegetation, did not show a declining trend with protection of fynbos against fire. At Zachariashoek, also with low fynbos communities, burning the vegetation produced slight increases in streamflow that were not detectable beyond the first winter after fire (van Wyk 1982).

Van Wyk (1982) has studied aspects of the mineral nutrient balance of fynbos catchments near Zachariashoek, Paarl, and the effects of fire on it by monitoring atmospheric inputs and losses in streams. Concentrations of nitrogen and phosphorus were too low for detection by the analytic techniques used (thresholds for NH_4-N, NO_3-N, and PO_4 were 0,1, 0,05 and 0,02 mg l^{-1}, respectively) and it seems that quantities of these compounds moving through the ecosystem in water are negligible, even after fire. Ion export, estimated from water conductivity records, rose by 8% of preburn levels (on an annual basis) after fire. The increased rate of outflow persisted only for about 10 months. Most net losses occurred in the first two spates after the fire, when ionic concentrations increased briefly to averages double the pre-burn levels. All ions normally detectable (Na^+, K^+, Ca^{++}, Mg^{++}, $SO_4^=$ and $CO_3^=$) increased in concentration during these spates, but estimated net mass losses were negligible compared to normal inputs and outputs. Suspended sediments behaved similarly, and net yields were 0,2 kg ha^{-1} and about 1,0 kg ha^{-1} for the two burnt catchments. Mineral losses in this form were therefore also negligible. Van Wyk also reported preliminary results for a burning experiment in a nearby catchment with different fynbos communities (more phreatic vegetation, higher average biomass). Here, increases in ionic concentration were greater though also short-lived. The pH in these "black waters" increased from about 3,5 to about 4,5 immediately after burning, but the effect did not persist.

PRESCRIBED BURNING IN CONSERVATION AND MANAGEMENT
OF FYNBOS ECOSYSTEMS

Fire is applied by managers in almost all natural or near-natural fynbos vegetation. The objectives vary. On the lowlands as in the mountains, patch-burning is often used to provide seasonal grazing, as described above, and this practice was previously widespread as shown by air photographic records. Timing of burns varies according to local custom as dictated, apparently, by local climatic conditions. Thus in the southwest burns are applied in early spring, with favourable weather at the change of the season. Stock is also brought onto the land at this time, but the animals would of course first graze the burns of the previous and earlier springs, and later that of the current spring. In the south, for example around Bredasdorp, the practice has been to burn in late summer, around February, as winds are then steady, bergwinds few, and relative humidities high. Stock is brought onto the burns for about 2 spring seasons, and not thereafter. Burns are repeated on a cycle of about 6 yr.

Fire has been and is also applied to increase or regulate the yield of veld products. Thus in the Cedarberg and southwards veld from which *Agathosma betulina* and *A. crenulata* are harvested is burnt by farmers in late summer or autumn, on about a 6 to 8 yr cycle, after the last of two or three biennial harvests. Experience has shown that such burns are required to rejuvenate the sprouting shoots and maintain yields, while also favouring recruitment from seed (Bands 1980). In the south, especially on coastal lowlands where flowers and florists' material are harvested from for example short-lived *Helichrysum* spp and Restionaceae, there is a tendency among some producers to burn on short rotations to increase yields.

Burning fynbos for fire control and safety of humans, livestock and property is seldom an explicitly stated goal among private landowners and seems to have been implicitly accepted as important.

Prescribed burning also has a place in conservation areas. It is instructive to examine the policies and practices applied on State forests, since these are the largest conservation areas in mountain fynbos ecosystems. These areas are managed with several objects in view including the following:-

1   Maintenance of maximum yields of silt-free water.

2   Nature conservation, principally the maintenance of species diversity and the control and eradication of invasive plants.

3   Provision of outdoor recreation opportunities compatible with 1 and 2.

4   Control of wildfires by creating a mosaic of veld of different ages and hence discontinuous fuels of low average flammability.

Ecological and managerial considerations led to a management policy that includes prescribed burning and in 1970 replaced a policy of complete protection against fire (Garnett 1973; Bands 1977). This policy includes the following:-

1   "Dry" catchment areas, high peaks, forest kloofs and "...areas in which springs occur..." will not be burnt.

2   Burning will be applied at a frequency of about once in 12 yr, although the frequency would be adjusted according to the conditions and management objectives specific to a certain area.

3   Burns shall be applied in late summer, in simulation of a "natural" regime, but burns at safer times will be used where necessary because in the initial stages of implementing the policy much of the country would be covered in old vegetation and burning conditions would be hazardous.

The framework for management is provided by a compartment system where each reserve is subdivided into natural units of some 500 to 1 500 ha, each of which receives a uniform treatment. Weed control is sought principally by a judicious combination of clearing and burning (Fenn 1980).

Wicht (1945) and Wicht and Kruger (1973) have reviewed the history of controversy surrounding the ecological role of fire and use of prescribed burning in fynbos, and Bands (1977) and Kruger (1977b, 1979a) set out the rationale of the policy and the elements of practice. Policies have now been laid down for several mountain fynbos ecosystems, and the practice that emerges has the following features. Firstly, weed control takes priority where necessary, and management is adjusted accordingly (Fenn 1980). Secondly, burning cycles prescribed range from 9 to 15 yr, depending on how planners interpret vegetation dynamics. In several cases, a "natural" fire regime has been prescribed especially in the case of dry north slopes in karoo mountains. Here, burns may be used initially to create a compartment mosaic of different veld ages but thereafter individual compartments would be allowed to burn if a fire does occur and on condition that the vegetation is older than a stated minimum age and contains no invasive plant species, with the proviso that the fire is to be contained within compartment boundaries. Thirdly, burns are proscribed for the period from the end of April until the end of August. Field managers are encouraged to burn in late summer and autumn.

Management of reserves of this kind is constrained by various factors, including legal requirements and developments outside the reserves. The Forest Act makes the landowner responsible for reasonable precautions against spread of fire to adjoining properties, for example. Specific management objectives within the reserve are often an expression of imperfect scientific knowledge that must be incorporated in policy and practice by the planner. Parallel objectives, pursued simultaneously on the same site, often contain a greater or lesser measure of conflict and the need for fire control in nature conservation is an example. Certain options are also closed. Thus, presence of invasive plants dictates the controlled use of fire. Consequently, the final prescription of a fire regime is the best possible compromise using current methods selected from limited options and criticisms of policy must take this into account to be effective.

Focusing for the present on policies for State forests, it would seem that criticism to date has not yet contributed to constructive evaluation of the problem of determining appropriate prescriptions. Thus Moll et al (1980) propose much longer (40 yr) burning cycles than are presently employed, on the grounds that shrub species with relatively long primary youth periods will not survive the cycles presently favoured, but fail to accommodate the alternative mechanisms and conditions that allow persistence of such species and neglect to consider the effects of senescence like those reported by Bond (1980). We feel that the problems that require attention for development of appropriate polices are as follows:-

1   The constraints outlined above and goals of individual owners (eg production of *Helichrysum* flowers) tend to favour shorter rather than longer burning cycles. Methods of simulating the consequences of such shifts and hence of selecting among alternatives are urgently required.

2   Field managers have legal obligations and tend to burn in safe seasons, for example in spring in the southwest (van Wilgen 1981a). The means to proper fire management, including fire hazard and behaviour prediction systems, are required to enable safe burning operations in the desirable season.

3   Successional depletion of plant populations through senescence and decay of seedbanks are processes poorly understood yet central to considerations affecting choice of fire frequency.

4   Fire intensity is an important but poorly understood factor governing the nature of the postfire community. Management will tend to favour low to moderate intensities and this may have important consequences which must be urgently identified.

5   Some evidence of the importance of variance in the regime experienced by the community at any given site indicates that this aspect requires evaluation for possible incorporation in management systems.

6   The likely depletion of nutrient pools and enhancement of erosion rates by relatively frequent burning could severely constrain management options, especially where water conservation is a primary aim, and this question must be urgently resolved.

7   Effects of compartment size, frequency, season and intensity of burn on faunal composition and dynamics require investigation, particularly in relation to the roles that animals play either as pollinators or dispersers of plants.

8 No attention has been given to the effects of burning regimes on recreational use of fynbos reserves.

CONCLUSION

The view of fire in fynbos presented here focuses largely on its role as an agent in community succession. This perhaps reflects the immediate need to understand pyric succession to manage fynbos ecosystems, and its importance as a very pervasive process in the fynbos landscape. The demographic and morphological responses to fire and consequences of changes in fire regime have been touched on but this is clearly an area where much work is necessary for an understanding of the likely long-term effects of man's influence in this environment. It seems particularly relevant to study the population biology of representative fynbos organisms in relation to burning. The rich array of life strategies evident in the biota promises to reward further study.

Aside from pioneering work by forest hydrologists there has been little study of fire in the ecosystem context and it is clearly imperative to expand our knowledge of the influence of fire regime on the hydrological cycle and nutrient balance. This would require carefully targeted studies of ecosystem processes and the ecophysiology of nutrient transfer between the plant and soil as they are affected by burning. A central question here is how fire regime could play a role in releasing nutrients accumulated in standing biomass and litter to the active pools, and how this reflects on possible adaptations of plants to a fire environment under nutrient-poor conditions. Furthermore, the ecological role of fire in the longer term and on a geographic scale requires closer attention. Thus, major patterns of vegetation such as those of rain forest, eucalypt forest and shrublands in Australia and Tasmania have been linked with patterns in fire regime and this view must clearly be tested in the fynbos environment, for example as a possible explanation of the relationships between fynbos and forest.

In spite of the major gaps in our knowledge it seems that a coherent account of certain features of the ecological role of fire can be presented. Firstly, fire regime should be viewed as a stochastic process, varying temporally and spatially within certain wide limits (Martin 1966). It is partly this variability that permits the existence of so large a number of species in the fynbos biome, diverse in form, phenology and life history. Secondly, the process of pyric succession itself allows coexistence of plant and animal species by preventing final dominance of the plant community by one or a few species and by allowing dynamic local migrations. If these relationships between fire regime and species' biology can be explicitly elucidated much of the knowledge required for rational management of fynbos will be made available. However, a knowledge of fire behaviour in relation to climate, weather and vegetation type is an essential prerequisite for management. Without this understanding field practitioners using fire or seeking to control fire regimes will not achieve their goals economically. This is a priority requirement, because without fire control and management, protection of fynbos ecosystems against deleterious effects such as invasive weeds is impossible.

Chapter 6 Fire in Grassland

N. M. TAINTON and M. T. MENTIS

116

INTRODUCTION

That fire has been an important ecological factor in the grassland biome of South Africa long before colonial times has been well documented (Hall, this volume, chapter 3). Both natural (other than those caused by man) and anthropogenic fires have occurred widely and for many hundreds of centuries in the grasslands and have had an important influence in shaping these grasslands as we know them today. With intensification of rural settlement since colonization, anthropogenic fires became first a common feature of the grassland landscape and then a tool well entrenched in the management options of the grazier. Thus much research on fire in grassland in recent times has had a strong management orientation which accounts for the management emphasis evident in this chapter.

As defined by Huntley (this volume, chapter 1) the grassland biome includes both "true" or natural grasslands and the "false" grasslands of the higher rainfall areas. Acocks (1975) referred to the former as "pure" or climatic climax grassveld types and defined them as veld types in which either low rainfall or low temperature arrested succession in the grassland stage. The "false" grasslands he saw as occurring in high rainfall areas where the climate was suitable for progression of succession beyond the grassland stage but where grazing or fire retained the vegetation in the grassland condition and prevented the development of a woody climax. As is indicated by Huntley (this volume, chapter 1) a significant distinction between the "true" and "false" grasslands is the difference in the acceptability and quality of the forage they offer to livestock through the year. The "true" grasslands are predominantly "sweet" and tall while the "false" grasslands are for the most part "sour" and short. This difference in acceptability of the grazing in winter has important consequences on the animal, on grazing management and also on the role of fire as a natural factor and as a management tool.

The purpose of this chapter is to synthesize current knowledge concerning fire in the grassland biome. The considerable variation in the grassland biome, the fragmentary nature of the research on fire in grassland and the strong management bias of this work inevitably make this record incomplete. However, sufficient is known to reveal a broad understanding of the nature of fire as an ecological factor in grasslands. At the same time the record will clearly reveal the gaps in knowledge which need to be investigated by future studies.

CHARACTERISTICS OF FIRE REGIMES AND FIRE BEHAVIOUR

The characterization of grassland fires and investigation of the influence of different kinds of fire on grassland structure, stability and productivity have received scant attention by researchers. Only recently has attention been focused on fire characterization, in the form of a description of the characteristics of fires which are applied to experimental plots rather than an investigation of the effects of different fires per se on the performance of grassland. Such data have limited value, but they may prove useful at some future date to interpret the response of grassland to the fires currently being applied to experimental plots.

In recent years fire characterization has been adopted as a standard procedure in fire research by Dillon (1979) in the Tall Grassveld of Natal and by C S Everson (personal communication, 1979), Granger (1980) and Smith (1982) in the mountain catchments of the Drakensberg. Everson's records apply to fires in the grassland, whereas Smith has derived data from pioneer scrub communities of the postfire climax. Some of the data derived by Dillon (1979) are presented in Table 1 and give some indication of the types of fire which can be expected in these communities.

Table 1   Some examples of fire intensities found in the Tall Grassveld of Natal (Dillon 1979).

Fuel[a] load kg m^{-2}	Fuel moisture %	Relative humidity %	Wind speed m s^{-1}	Type of burn	Fire intensity J m^{-1} s^{-1}
0,038	32	37	1,25	Back fire	0,78 x 10^4
0,270	31	25	0,70	Head fire	2,12 x 10^4
0,171	13	34	8,21	Back fire	5,90 x 10^4
0,122	29	60	6,60	Head fire	10,34 x 10^4
0,196	14	65	4,01	Head fire	36,00 x 10^4
0,134	19	52	6,04	Head fire	82,88 x 10^4

[a]Energy value of fuel, based on 60 independent samples, was 37 515 ± 606 k cal^{-1} t (15,7 x 10^7 ± 0,25 x 10^7 J t^{-1}).

EFFECTS OF FIRE REGIME ON VEGETATION STRUCTURE AND DYNAMICS

The influence of fire on the structure and dynamics of plant communities within the grassland zone is largely dependent on the successional status of the grassland at any particular site. Where rainfall is low, so that grassland is climax, the role of fire is different from that in areas which have a high rainfall and where grassland is successional to scrub or forest. It is necessary therefore to subdivide the grassland region into categories based on the successional status of the grassland, and to examine each separately. It is convenient to recognize five categories of grassland in this context, of which the first four would be included in Huntley's (this volume, chapter 1) "false" grassland and the last in his "true" or climatic climax grassland.

AFRO-ALPINE GRASS-HEATH COMMUNITIES

These communities occur at high altitude along the Drakensberg and other mountains where rainfall is high but winter temperatures are low and snow may lie for several months of the year. While rainfall is generally adequate for successional development to scrub and forest, such development is prevented by low winter temperatures in all but well-protected sites, and here species of heath often dominate communities transitional to forest. No formal research work on fire has been undertaken in these regions, but it appears that fire may play an important role in maintaining open grassland communities. Killick (1963) has described an *Erica-Helichrysum* heath as the climax community of this community in Natal, and has suggested that, but for fire, heath would probably occupy greater areas than it does at present. In fact, Edwards (1963) has ascribed the relative abundance of patches of this community to the reduced incidence of fire, and its patchy character in these high altitude areas to patch burning.

MONTANE FOREST/GRASSLAND COMMUNITIES

This region of high rainfall and moderate temperatures is well suited to successional advance beyond the grassland stage to scrub and forest, and here fire plays a major role in maintaining open grassland (Schelpe 1946). In such areas woody plants are typically confined only to refuge sites where fires are absent, infrequent, or burn at low intensity (Mentis et al 1974). Over much of the area frequent and often intense grassland fires have either led to the destruction of communities which are ecologically more advanced than grassland, or have never permitted the development of such communities. Because of this, all but a small proportion of this region is today open grassland, and it is on these grassland communities that much of the research into the effects of fire has been undertaken. In particular, the work reported by Scott (1952a) and Edwards (1968) at Tabamhlope, by Staples (1926, 1930) at Cedara and the report by Killick (1963) on the ecology of the Cathedral Peak area confirm that frequent and moderately intense defoliation is essential to the maintenance of a vigorous and dense grassland sward. Staples (1926, 1930) showed, for example, that infrequent defoliation led to the replacement of the dominant *Themeda triandra* initially by *Trachypogon spicatus*, and later by shrubs such as *Athenasia acerosa* (Curry's Post weed). He suggested that the grassland should be burned every second year in order to maintain it in its most productive condition, and that such burning should be applied in winter to encourage the dominance of *Themeda triandra*. Summer burning led to a decline in the density of the grassland community and a replacement of *T. triandra* by the wiry *Diheteropogon filifolius* and *Aristida junciformis*.

At Tabamhlope, Scott (1952a) and Edwards (1968) reported that, in the absence of any other form of defoliation, annual burning proved more effective than both biennial and triennial burning in maintaining a dense productive grassland, while

C S Everson (personal communication, 1979) has found no difference in the condition of firebreak areas which are burnt annually in early winter and the catchment areas burnt biennially in spring in the Cathedral Peak Forest Reserve. Frequent burning resulted in the dominance of *Themeda triandra*, *Heteropogon contortus* and *Trachypogon spicatus*, while infrequent burning led to their replacement by *Tristachya leucothrix*, *Alloteropsis semialata* and *Harpechloa falx*. With any appreciable period of protection, the grassland degenerates, to be replaced eventually by shrubs, and particularly by *Pteridium aquilinum* (braken fern), *Leucosidea sericea* (ouhout), *Buddleia salviifolia* (sagewood), *Philippia evansii* and *Widdringtonia nodiflora* (mountain cedar), although the changes which do occur vary widely from place to place. Granger (1976a) has described differences in the communities which have developed under protection in the now well-known Catchment IX in the Cathedral Peak Forest Reserve. On the southern aspect, *Philippia evansii* has invaded, communities of *P. aquilinum* and *L. sericea* have expanded, and *Andropogon appendiculatus* has largely replaced *Themeda triandra*. The vegetation of the north-facing slopes has, however, changed much less than that of the southern slopes. Here *P. aquilinum* has expanded, while *Alloteropsis semialata*, *Diheteropogon filifolius*, *Elyonurus argenteus*, *Erica woodii* and *Helichrysum aureo-nitens* have increased in abundance. Shrubs have not invaded these slopes to any appreciable extent. Burning for grassland maintenance should, however, be restricted to the dormant winter or early spring period. Burning in late spring, after active growth has commenced, has been shown in a series of trials at Nottingham Road and Underberg in Natal to lead to severe damage to the grass cover and to *T. triandra* in particular. These trials have shown that the more nearly the time of the burn coincides with the start of active spring growth, the more rapid is the recovery of the grassveld. However, early burning, before growth commences, is preferable to burning after the commencement of active growth.

Further south, in the Amatole Mountains of the eastern Cape, Trollope (1973) has reported the possible role of fire in the conversion of fynbos-dominated communities to grassland, and its role in maintaining such open grassland communities. In both a lowland fynbos community dominated by *Cliffortia linearifolia* and in an upland fynbos community dominated by *Erica brownleeae* and *Cliffortia paucistaminea*, fire has proved an effective means of eliminating the shrub species and promoting the development of a grassland community. Frequent application of fire also proved effective in preventing the re-establishment of the fynbos communities (Trollope 1973).

There can be no doubt that fire has played a major role in the development and maintenance of grassland communities in the humid montane forest/grassland regions of South Africa. Without fire, grassland is replaced by ecologically more advanced communities and succession may proceed through to forest in moist sites, and particularly on southern slopes, where fire is excluded.

GRASSLAND COMMUNITIES OF POTENTIAL SAVANNA AREAS

These communities generally occupy regions of intermediate rainfall where, in the absence of fire or some alternative defoliating agent, a community of tall grasses (species of *Hyparrhenia* and *Cymbopogon*), vernal aspect herbs *Erigeron*, *Helichrysum*, *Senecio* and others) and dwarf shrubs develops, to be replaced in the continued absence of defoliation by a community of scattered trees in a sparse moribund grassland. The absence of fire permits fire-intolerant woody species to invade a grassland which comprises largely dead and dying grass plants, but in practice such areas are inevitably subject to occasional high-intensity wild fires, which will kill the woody species. Here annual burning assures the retention of a dense grass cover where rainfall is moderately high (ca 650 mm), but where rainfall is low, or during a cycle of dry years, annual burning may lead to plant death and so a reduction in the density of the community.

Long-term burning trials at Ukulinga, in the Tall Grassveld of Natal (average annual rainfall > 700 mm) have shown that in the absence of any other form of defoliation, annual burning produces a denser cover (15,3%) and higher veld condition score (80%) than biennial (8,9% and 60%) and triennial (6,1% and 45%) burning. However, where the grassland is mown for hay in summer the frequency of burning has had no influence on basal cover, but it has affected species composition and so veld condition. Where burning is frequent, *T. triandra* makes up a greater proportion of the cover than when mowing is the defoliating agent instead of fire. Here *Tristachya leucothrix* replaces *T. triandra* even though defoliation by mowing is frequent (three times each season; Dillon 1979). Also, burning annually and mowing twice for hay in summer produces a denser cover, and a greater dominance of *T. triandra*, than does annual burning without summer hay cutting. Clearly, therefore, *T. triandra* is adapted to frequent and intense defoliation compared to many of its associates in the fire-climax community of this area, although it is possible to eliminate it from the sward when defoliation is too intense, as by overgrazing with sheep.

Once it is recognized that the fire-climax sward of the Tall Grassveld is adapted to frequent defoliation, which if not applied by mowing or grazing must be applied by burning, it is necessary to determine the most appropriate time to burn such veld for the maintenance of productive grassland. Twenty-eight years of scheduled annual, biennial and triennial burns at Ukulinga have failed to show any major difference in cover between veld burnt either in autumn (usually in April), late winter (first week in August) or after the first significant spring rains (15 mm of rain in 24 hours), usually in September. However, veld can be burnt in autumn only if it is protected long enough to allow dry material to accumulate, which will burn at this time. To achieve this veld must rest from the spring of one season to the autumn of the next (two full summer seasons and one winter). This in itself leads to veld degradation in autumn-burnt plots where the cover of the veld declines to about half that of frequently burnt plots, but it applies equally to August and spring-burnt veld which is not cut for hay and to which burning is applied with equivalent frequency. The detrimental effect of autumn burning (in the absence of grazing animals) on cover is not, therefore, due to the autumn burn per se, but to the required period of herbage accumulation which must necessarily precede it. Differences in species composition are, however, apparent between autumn-burnt plots and those burnt later in the dormant period. The former plots are dominated largely by post fire-climax species, principally *Tristachya leucothrix*, but this trend is less evident in the August and spring-burnt plots, presumably because of the greater intensity of the fires applied at this time. Therefore fire-climax species (*T. triandra, Heteropogon contortus* and others) have remained important components of the winter- (early August) and spring- (September-October) burnt community (46%), whereas in the autumn- (April) burnt plots they have not survived in any great quantity (19%).

VLEI COMMUNITIES

Although vleis are extensive in certain ecological regions, only Downing (1966) has directly examined the effects of fire on these wetland communities. In a study of the ecology of vlei vegetation at the Tabamhlope Research Station he reported that fire, by increasing the extent to which the soil is exposed, promotes a less hydrophytic environment. Frequent fires therefore hasten the successional change from hydrophytic reed-swamp communities to what he has termed the vlei-grassland stage, which he considers is maintained as the climax by fire. In its absence, woody shrubs invade and the vlei will eventually be occupied by hydrophytic woodland communities.

ARID AND SEMI-ARID GRASSLAND COMMUNITIES

Relatively little recent research work on veld burning has been done in the drier grassland regions, and it has generally been assumed that fire should be excluded from this type of grassland. Early work reported by Theron (1937) showed that 3 yr of protection almost doubled the contribution of *T. triandra* to the cover of veld at Potchefstroom, but that longer periods of protection led to the replacement of *T. triandra* by the unpalatable *Cymbopogon plurinodis* and *Elyonurus argenteus*. Under annual burning the stand produced appeared stunted, the perennial species died out and the cover declined. It became apparent that, in these relatively arid regions, burning should be excluded or at best applied only infrequently. Mostert et al (1971) also suggested that burning should be excluded from the more arid grasslands of the central and western Orange Free State.

More recently Trollope (1978b) has examined the possible role of fire in the arid grasslands of the eastern Cape, and has suggested that it may be used in conjunction with browsing animals to reduce the density or prevent the encroachment of woody savanna species and karoo pioneers, particularly *Chrysocoma tenuifolia* (bitterbos). However, in the Karoo mountains, fire has a definite role in livestock production. Here it is used widely to stimulate forage production in a vegetation dominated by coarse grass and woody shrubs. As in the sour grassveld of the more humid areas, it is used to remove accumulated rank growth of little forage value and rejuvenate moribund grass tufts, but in coarse grass-woody shrub vegetation it is also used to increase production in the herb layer and to make this material more accessible to livestock by reducing canopy density in the shrub layer. However, there are indications that in at least some of this mountain veld the low successional stages produce more nutritious forage than the climax stage. Fire may therefore be used in conjunction with grazing to maintain the low successional status of some of these communities (Roux and Smart 1980).

EFFECTS OF FIRE REGIME ON HERBAGE PRODUCTION AND QUALITY

HERBAGE PRODUCTION

Short-term effects

Yield measurements have seldom been taken in veld burning experiments and most assessments of the effects of burning have been based on visual ratings. One exception to this is the Ukulinga trial, where yields were measured annually for the first 18 yr of the experiment (1950/51 to 1968/69) and thereafter at 6 yr intervals. In this trial, late winter (August) and spring (September to October) burning have been compared with mowing treatments applied at the same time, and here it has been shown repeatedly that the immediate effect of burning is to reduce yield, relative to veld which is mown at the same time, by between 50 and 70% when yields are recorded in mid-December, and by between 5 and 35% in veld which is allowed to grow out until March (Anon 1974). A more detailed description of the recovery rate of burnt veld relative to mown veld has been provided by Tainton et al (1977), who have shown a yield advantage in mown veld compared with burnt veld throughout the spring period. They showed that this effect resulted from a destruction of tillers by fire, at least in the dominant *Themeda triandra*. In particular, those tillers destined to flower in the spring (October, November) immediately following the fire are almost completely destroyed, eliminating the rapid phase of tiller growth which accompanies stem growth prior to flowering. The *T. triandra* plant responds to such treatment by producing large numbers of new lateral tillers but, as Drewes (1979) has shown, fewer of these tillers survive than in mown veld where the development of new tillers through spring is more gradual. Plants of *T. triandra* which are mown in late winter (August) or early spring (September, October) carry, on average, more tillers into midsummer than do plants which are burnt.

The effect of fire on the recovery rate of veld in the Tall Grassveld of Natal is, however, greatly influenced by the time at which the burn is applied. The dominant *T. triandra* is intolerant of fire once growth has commenced in spring, and a late spring burn considerably reduces the yield of this species. As shown in Table 2, it is the reduction in the yield of this

Table 2　Effect of time of burn on growth rate of Tall Grassveld (Dillon 1979).

	Recorded on 11/1/78					Recorded on 1/8/79				
	Early[1] burn	Burn[2] with spring rains	Late[3] burn	Mow[4] with spring rains	SE	Early[1] burn	Burn[2] with spring rains	Late[3] burn	Mow[4] with spring rains	SE
Total yield (t ha^{-1})	1,75^{a,b}	1,56^{b}	0,95^{c}	2,15^{a}	0,17	2,56^{Y}	2,50^{Y}	1,54^{z}	2,95^{x}	0,06
Yield *T. triandra* (t ha^{-1})	1,09^{b}	0,93^{b}	0,20^{c}	1,37^{a}	0,07	1,71^{Y}	1,69^{Y}	0,53^{z}	2,33^{x}	0,03
Yield other grasses (t ha^{-1})	0,50^{a}	0,44^{a}	0,48^{a}	0,67^{a}	0,05	0,85^{x,Y}	0,77^{x,Y}	0,99^{x}	0,61^{Y}	0,06
Mean mass *T. triandra*	0,21^{b}	0,23^{b}	0,11^{c}	0,29^{a}	0,09	0,43^{x}	0,40^{x,Y}	0,33^{Y}	0,35^{x,Y}	0,02

a,b and c)　any two treatments which do not have the same symbol are significantly
x,y and z)　different at the 5% level

1 = 4/8/78
2 = 28/8/78
3 = 28/9/78
4 = 28/8/78

First spring rains fell on the three days preceding the burn and mow on 28/8/78.

species which is responsible for the reduced yield of the veld as a whole with late burning. A more detailed analysis of the effect of a late burn on *T. triandra* has shown that it results from both a reduction in tiller size and number (Table 3) but that its effect on tiller size arises through the delayed inception of tiller growth on plants burnt late, and not from any difference in tiller growth rate of individual tillers on early and late burnt plants subsequent to the fire (Table 3). When these tillers were measured 50 days after the fire in early and late burnt plants, no differences in size were apparent (Dillon 1979). These data show the high mortality of tillers of *T. triandra* due to late winter or early spring fire, but also that more new tillers are subsequently formed on early than late burnt plants.

Table 3   Effect of early (23/8/79) and late (26/9/79) burning on the spring recovery of *T. triandra* in the Tall grass-veld (first spring rains fell on 17/8/79) (Dillon 1979).

Treatment	Tiller no. at time of burn	No. of newly initiated tillers as % preburn no.		Size of newly initiated tillers (gm)		Survival of parent tillers (%)	
		A	B	A	B	A	B
Early burn	17,2	122,8	138,2	0,052	0,102	8,2	7,4
Late burn	16,0	58,0	58,0	0,048	0,048	0	0
Early-late	1,2	64,8	80,2	0,004	0,054	8,2	7,4
SE of difference		9,0	9,6	0,004	0,008		

A = 50 days after the respective burn
B = at the same time in spring (14/11/47) when sufficiently recovered for grazing.

The results from research undertaken in the Tall grassveld at Ukulinga are substantiated by other work at a number of sites throughout the Natal Midlands. Three trials in the highland sourveld in the Nottingham Road district and two in the Underberg district have shown that recovery growth after a burn is most rapid when the burn is applied in late August or early September, and complementary data have shown that this coincides with the time at which soil temperatures begin to rise. Where burning is earlier than this, yields are reduced but the effect is not pronounced, at least in veld burnt after mid-July. However, where veld is burnt later than this, and particularly where soil moisture has been adequate for growth prior to the burn, yields are greatly reduced.

The overall picture suggests, therefore, that if sufficient ungrazeable material accumulates to warrant burning, then the veld should be burnt prior to the rise of soil temperatures in the spring, particularly if the soil is moist. Over a range of altitudes in Natal, it appears that the veld should be burnt in late August or early September. Such treatment will reduce spring yields below those which can be expected from unburnt but previously mown or grazed veld, whether this mowing or grazing is applied in the previous autumn (Anon 1974) or in the winter (Drewes 1979).

Long-term effects

Long-term effects of burning on yield have been recorded on the Ukulinga trial by applying a standard harvesting procedure (a spring mow followed by two hay cuts) to all treatments except the control, at 7 yr intervals from the 18th season onwards. These data provide information on the long-term effects of fire on the grassland free from any short-term confounding with the different treatments.

After 26 yr of treatment, the only significant result to come out of the analysis of yields of previously burnt and mown plots was that the former treatments, whether applied in late winter or with the rains in spring, produced more herbage than the mown treatments. Therefore, the reduced yields which are recorded in the season which immediately follows a burn are temporary and not a permanent effect of fire on grassland. This effect is illustrated also in Figure 1 where the yield of annually mown veld is

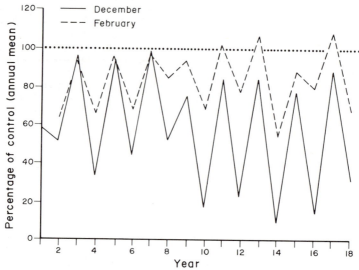

Figure 1 Yields recorded in early (December) and late (February) summer, from veld burnt and mown in alternate years after the first spring rains and expressed as a percentage of the control (mown plots). Veld burnt in even years.

compared with that of veld which was alternately mown and burnt in spring. The mown veld outyields the burnt veld only in those seasons in which the burn is applied. In alternate years, when both treatments are mown, no appreciable yield differences are apparent. Also apparent in Figure 1 is the extent to which yield differences decline as the season progresses, an effect which was also shown by Drewes (1979).

Frequent fire in the humid grasslands would seem, therefore, to have no long-term detrimental effect on grassland, a result which is to be expected in view of the long history of fire in this vegetation type. However, in the more arid regions, frequent fires detrimentally affect the grassland community. At Potchefstroom, Theron (1937), showed that grass plants were stunted and perennial species died when veld was burnt annually.

HERBAGE QUALITY

Short-term effects

Mes (1958) reported that on Transvaal highveld burnt in August, the nitrogen and ash content of recovery growth of *Hyparrhenia hirta*, *Themeda triandra* and *Eragrostis atherstonei* exceeded that of new growth of unburnt plants through September. The differences had disappeared by the end of October. She attributed this effect to the absence of competition to the new developing growth by the older leaves and stems in burnt plants, and to the earlier root growth in these plants resulting from higher soil temperatures on burnt than on unburnt veld.

At Ukulinga, the crude protein content of the recovery growth of spring-burnt veld averages approximately 9% through November, compared with an average of only 6,5% in veld mown at the same time. In both burnt and unburnt veld the crude protein content of the new season's growth declined as the season progressed, to 5,2% on burnt veld and 4,7% on mown veld in late December and to approximately 4% in both burnt and unburnt veld in February (Tainton et al 1977). This improved early season quality of spring-burnt compared with unburnt veld has been shown by Lyle and Brockett (1974) to result in substantially improved animal performance on burnt veld. This effect may result not only from improved quality of diet, but also from a higher intake of more nutritious material.

Long-term effects

In the long term fire improves the quality of the grazing by assisting in the maintenance of fire climax grassland in the humid grasslands. In these areas the postfire climax species are invariably of lower acceptability to animals than those of the fire climax grassland, and so animal performance declines in veld which is permitted to advance beyond the fire climax community. While it is true that such successional advance may be prevented by using other methods of defoliation (mowing or grazing), in practice fire is the method which is most widely adopted because of its ease of application and the low costs.

In the more arid grassland regions, fire may lead to a reduction in the quality of grazing if it is frequent enough to promote a die-out of the perennial climax species and an invasion of pioneers. Occasional fires, however, may improve the quality of the grazing if they are instrumental in maintaining the grassland climax (as during a cycle of above average rainfall) or if they effectively destroy encroaching plants and permit the re-establishment of a grass cover, as in the false karoo (Trollope 1978b).

EFFECTS OF FIRE REGIME ON FAUNAL STRUCTURE AND DYNAMICS

VERTEBRATES

There have been no specific studies in the South African grassland biome on the effects of fire on aquatic vertebrates. However, possible factors, mediated by changes in the vegetation and other features of the catchment, include the quality and quantity of runoff, water temperature, physical shelter and food availability. Similarly, there is a lack of information on many likely effects of the incidence, absence and frequency of fire on the herpetofauna.

Turning to warm-blooded vertebrates, in the Natal Drakensberg the abundance and species richness of francolins, small mammals and antelope are related to the time elapsed since the last fire (Mentis and Rowe-Rowe 1979). Greatest abundance and species richness occurs up to 3 yr after fire, and on areas never or rarely burnt. Under an intermediate frequency of fire the numbers of both species and individuals are low. This bimodal distribution of faunal abundance and species richness in relation to fire frequency reflects a separation of the animals into those of the fire climax and those of the postfire climax, with few occupying the moribund sward between the two ecological stages. This pattern would be unlikely had the biota not been exposed to frequent fire in fire-accessible areas, and to infrequent or no fire on fire-inaccessible areas during recent geological time. An implication is that the biota of the fire-accessible areas is not one which, although now extensive, formerly was necessarily confined to small areas, or invaded from the adjoining climatic climax grasslands. This interpretation conflicts with that of Acocks (1975: map 1) who indicated the eastern and southern portions of the present grassland biome to have been forest or scrub forest as recently as 600 BP. The boundaries of vegetation types have indeed changed in recent geological time. These changes, apparently caused by climatic fluctuations (van Zinderen Bakker 1978), explain the otherwise puzzling distribution of some of the biota (Bigalke 1978). However, while Acocks's map 1 might estimate the potential vegetation (the climatic climax including the associated fauna), it does not necessarily follow that the predominance of the fire-climax grassland (and its associated fauna) is a very recent phenomenon. As already explained the biota of the fire-accessible areas appears to be adapted to frequent (annual and biennial) fire. It is therefore unreasonable to suppose that the tolerance to such frequent fire has developed in the span of a few centuries. Also, judging from the relatively infrequent ignition of vegetation by natural means (eg lightning, rock falls, etc) small glades of grassland scattered within large areas of forest or scrub forest are unlikely to have been exposed to frequent fire. Taking a different line, it is remarkable that a typical grassland animal like redwing francolin *(Francolinus levaillantii)* has its distribution centred on the area indicated by Acocks (1975) to have been forest or scrub forest a mere 600 yr ago. Finally, remains of typically grassland animals occur in the excavated floor deposits of caves of inland Natal, and these remains come from several layers, the oldest dating back to nearly 8 000 yr BP (Maggs and Ward, 1980; Cable et al 1980).

In the Cathedral Peak area of the Natal Drakensberg, the number of small mammal species in biennially burnt grassland at low (1 430 m asl), intermediate (1 890 m asl) and high (2 440 to 2 740 m asl) elevations was recorded as four, six and six respectively (Mentis and Rowe-Rowe 1979). In grassland not burnt for 5 yr there were only two species, and in fire-protected grassland there were three species. At all three elevations the number of individuals and species was low shortly after the incidence of fire, when only nocturnal omnivores and insectivores *(Praomys natalensis* (multimammate mouse) and/or *Myosorex varius)* were recorded. After about 12 months there appeared to be sufficient food and cover for diurnal and crepuscular granivorous and graminivorous species *(Rhabdomys pumilio* (four-striped field mouse) and *Otomys irroratus* (vlei rat)). Relatively rare species *(Dendromus melanotis, Mus minutoides* and *Crocidura flavescens)* were generally recorded only 18 to 24 months after burning. Trapping success and species richness were poorest in grassland at low elevations which had not been burnt for 5 yr. Here the vegetation was rank and moribund. Trapping success and species richness at the low and intermediate elevations reached maxima about a year after burning, but at the high elevations these maxima were attained between 18 and 24 months after fire. The implication is that primary productivity generally declines with increasing elevation in the Natal Drakensberg and that it is the rate of accumulation of plant material which firstly re-establishes an optimal habitat and secondly renders grassland, in the 3 to 10 yr absence of fire, moribund and poorly habitable to small mammals. Much the same results have been obtained in Giant's Castle Game Reserve, as well as the Natal Drakensburg (Rowe-Rowe 1980). In biennially burnt grassland peak trapping success occurred about 12 months after fire at low (1 600 m asl) and intermediate (1 900 m asl) elevations. At high elevations (2 200 m asl) the peak occurred 20 months after burning. Both in the Giant's Castle and Cathedral Peak areas *Protea* woodland was the most depopulated of the habitats sampled, and this was so both shortly after (Giant's Castle) and 5 yr after (Cathedral Peak) fire. Recovery of the small mammal populations occurred most rapidly where conditions had prevented fires from burning cleanly, and where in addition to any unburnt grass a certain amount of cover remained after the burn (eg in boulder-strewn country).

In the Natal Drakensberg, greywing *(Francolinus africanus)* and redwing francolins rarely occur on large expanses of cleanly burnt grassland (Mentis 1973; Mentis and Bigalke 1979, 1981b; Mentis and Rowe-Rowe 1979). The birds apparently require a certain minimum grass cover for escape from predators and for shelter from extremes of weather. Population densities recover during the first or second years after fire but decline in its long-term absence and with the accumulation of vegetal material. This decline is thought to result from (a) the increased difficulty the essentially terrestrial birds experience in forcing their way through matted, moribund grass, (b) reduced detectability of the aerial portions of geophytes, which the birds use in their search for the underground storage organs which make up most of their diet, and (c) a suppression of the flowering and leaf production of grassland geophytes by the accumulating top hamper. For a few months after fire the birds select strongly for unburnt grass, but within six to nine months this selection is reversed and strongly in favour of the most recently burnt areas.

The optimal frequency of fire for greywing and redwing francolins varies inversely with elevation, suggesting again that it is the rate of accumulation of plant material (which itself is apparently inversely related to elevation in the Natal Drakensberg) which determines how soon after burning the habitat for grassland francolins degenerates.

Greywing and redwing francolins undergo an annual fluctuation in population density typical of phasianids, with the maximum in autumn and the minimum in late spring. The autumn-spring decline averages about 50% of the autumn population and is apparently socially induced. However, spring densities are lower when fire is applied than when not applied. Since the birds are of localized habit it was hypothesized that developing a fine-scale fire mosaic would maintain a higher population density than would the normal large-scale mosaic currently developed over most of the Natal Drakensberg. This hypothesis was tested in a field experiment in Highmoor State Forest and not refuted. A similar mosaic developed by Mr G H Mitchell-Innes on the Biggarsberg in northern Natal maintained redwing at a high density (1 bird 7 ha^{-1} in autumn), well above the average on farmland in the Highland Sourveld. The same practice applied on a 400 ha farm near Howick in Natal apparently raised the local redwing population from 3 or 4 coveys of 3 to 4 birds each, to 6 or 7 coveys of 6 to 7 birds each (H Tully, personal communication, 1979).

While greywing and redwing francolins in Natal may be classed as "decreasers," as defined by Foran et al (1978), rednecked francolin *(Francolinus afer)* is an "increaser I." Despite hundreds of hours of sampling in the Natal Drakensberg, the rednecked francolin has never been observed far from forest margins, scrub patches and copses or plantations of alien trees (Mentis 1973; Mentis and Rowe-Rowe 1979). Interestingly, the rednecked francolin occurs on the plots protected for about 25 yr from fire at de Hoek near Estcourt and in the early stages of the cycle in alien tree plantations at Weza in southern Natal.

Other birds which respond to the changes in the vegetation following fire are common quail *(Coturnix coturnix)* and helmeted guineafowl *(Numida meleagris)*. In summer in the Natal Drakensberg quail occur at higher densities in recently burnt than unburnt grassland (Mentis 1972a). While guineafowl often nest in ungrazed, untrampled and unburnt veld, protection from defoliation for 2 or more yr renders the veld unattractive for nesting (Mentis 1972b).

It has been claimed that predation by jackal *(Canis mesomelas)* has caused a population decline in mountain reedbuck *(Redunca fulvorufula)*, grey rhebuck *(Pelea capreolus)* and oribi *(Ourebia ourebi)* in the Natal Drakensberg. While the basis of this claim has not been published, and the role of the jackal remains conjectural, the effects of fire alone may account for the alleged decline. The small antelope select strongly for the green flush of grass shortly following fire (Oliver et al 1978; Rowe-Rowe 1980). The crude protein and phosphorous contents of this young regrowth are higher than in unburnt grass (Mentis 1978; Scotcher et al 1980b). Mortality among small antelopes is highest from August to October, shortly following the coldest, driest time of the year when food quality is lowest (Mentis 1978; Oliver et al 1978). The development of a fine-scale mosaic of spring burnt and unburnt grassland with a network of firebreaks prepared annually in winter apparently increased the population densities of grey rhebuck and oribi (Mentis 1978). Thus the availability of green grass for the antelopes appears important. In Giant's Castle Game Reserve most fires between 1907 and 1955 were applied in autumn, but since 1956 and for the period during which the antelope populations allegedly have declined, most fires have occurred in spring (Scotcher et al 1979). The effect of this change in burning policy is likely to have reduced the amount of young green grass for the antelopes in winter. This is consistent with the observation of a high density of oribi (10 ha per oribi) on the farm "Strathcona" near Vryheid where the owner, Mr A Frield, applies fire in autumn (R F H Collinson, personal communication, 1979). This density is much higher than that (47 to 137 ha per oribi) observed in biennially spring-burnt veld in the Natal Drakensberg (Mentis 1978; Oliver et al 1978).

It has been suggested also that the increase in frequency of dry season fires in Giant's Castle Game Reserve has so changed or reduced the scrub and forest-margin communities that Cape grysbok *(Raphicerus melanotis)* has been locally exterminated (Mentis et al 1974).

On the van Riebeeck Nature Reserve in the central variation of the Bankenveld, grazing blesbok *(Damaliscus dorcas phillipsi)* selected strongly for firebreaks and, before burning was applied as standard management, created a fine-scale overgrazing-under-grazing mosaic (du Plessis 1972). After regular burning was adopted in the reserve the blesbok preferred the recently burnt grassland and their diet preferences differed between burnt and unburnt grassland. In Giant's Castle Game Reserve, those blesbok observed on unburnt grassland in close proximity to burnt grass-land were mostly territorial males standing or lying in their dung patches (Rowe-Rowe 1980). On Coleford Nature Reserve in the

Highland Sourveld near Underberg, burning the two halves of game enclosures in alternate springs, and stocking modestly with one blesbok per 3 ha, led to extreme and destructive selective grazing and severe mortality of the blesbok, probably from malnutrition (Mentis 1979a). Apparently biennial and even annual spring burning of blesbok range is inadequate, at least in the highland sourveld, to maintain veld condition in the long term and to support blesbok productivity in the short term. Increasing the stocking rate of blesbok to prevent the accumulation of low quality material has resulted in veld deterioration. It therefore appears that in the interests of maintaining both veld condition and populations of small gregarious antelopes like blesbok, biennial spring burning must be supplemented by two or three summer defoliations by grazing with bulk grazers like domestic cattle, or by mowing.

Cape eland *(Taurotragus oryx)* differ from other antelope of the grassland biome in that in the Natal Drakensberg they summer on recently burnt veld but in winter divert their attention to forest, scrub and fynbos (Mentis and Rowe-Rowe 1979).

Despite the few studies of the responses of vertebrates of the grassland biome to fire it may be concluded that for typical grassland animals recurrent fire is necessary to maintain the fire climax to which the animals are adapted, although it temporarily lowers the habitability of the veld and in cases causes mortality.

INVERTEBRATES

In an exploratory study of the population dynamics and composition of the above-ground insect fauna on the veld burning experiment at Ukulinga, little significant information was obtained. This probably reflects the high mobility of the insects relative to the size of the plots (Huleatt-James 1979).

In the apparent absence of additional local studies a summary of the review of Lamotte (1975) for tropical African savannas is provided. There are several immediate effects of fire on insects. Firstly, strong flying groups disappear, indicating dispersal or mortality. Secondly, fire has a weak effect on the fauna of the soil surface, probably because of the relatively low temperatures at and below the soil surface. Thirdly, the mean size of the individual decreases, indicating that large animals are more vulnerable to fire than are small ones, or that large ones disperse. The immediate effect of fire on the habitat of grassland arthropods is to reduce the diversity of niches. For example, several strata are reduced to one. Shelter, providing protection from extremes of weather and facilitating escape from predators, is removed. Detritus is eliminated. In accordance with these dramatic changes to the microhabitat, the arthropod fauna alters in composition in the month following fire, and about 60% of the fauna disappears. Strong flying insects leave unburnt refuges to recolonize the new environment, and the fauna of the bottom stratum of the formerly unburnt grassland disappears, either by dispersal or by mortality. In the long term, burnt tropical savannas support only about 30% of the fauna of unburnt savannas. In the absence of fire the fauna develops into one composed largely of moisture-loving arthropods, while frequently burnt areas have high proportions of orthopterans.

The situation in the grassland biome of South Africa may well be more complex than in the tropical savannas. In the former, seasons, which have a strong effect on arthropods, are distinct, so that the influence of fire must depend not only on frequency but also on the season of occurrence.

ADAPTIVE RESPONSES OF ORGANISMS TO FIRE REGIMES

FLORA

Microflora

Only those microorganisms which live at or near the soil surface will be directly affected by grassland fires and here a tolerance to high temperatures will serve as a useful adaptive mechanism. In this respect the spore-forming organisms, particularly the endospore-producing bacteria, appear to have a distinct advantage (F M Wallis, personal communication, 1979), for the spores survive relatively high, dry heat and their germination might be stimulated by the rapid heating of the upper soil layers after a fire. These spore-forming organisms are therefore likely to be well adapted to a fire regime. For the most part, in the relatively litter-free situation typical of grasslands, the microorganisms live at a soil depth which permits them to escape the direct effects of fire, although they may in the long term be influenced by the nature of the fire regime through its effect on the vegetation.

Macroflora

The grass plant

Most grass plants are structured so that they are able to tolerate periodic almost complete removal of aerial structures. Some of the grasses survive such drastic defoliation by producing underground rhizomes or stolons at or close to the surface. Such structures possess tiller initials, some of which may develop into tillers in the absence of defoliation. However, removal of a proportion of the aerial growth invariably stimulates tiller development (Booysen et al 1963), so that the plant is able to recover fairly rapidly after such treatment. Such resistance is further strengthened by the tendency for the meristematic apex of the grass stem to remain close to the soil surface during the vegetative stages of tiller development. As nodes develop, the internodes remain short so that the leaf-bearing stem remains compact. Hence the leaf bases are also situated near the soil surface (Figure 2). Defoliation at this time will therefore largely or entirely involve the removal of leaf blades of already mature or nearly mature leaves. The leaf initials situated on

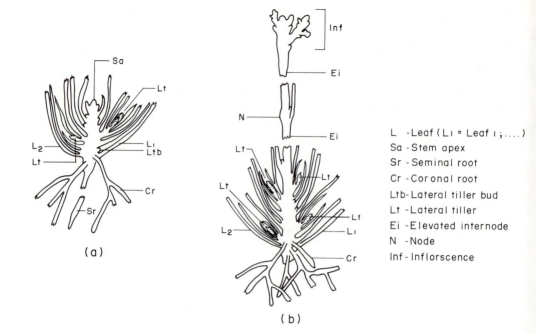

Figure 2   Stages in the growth of a grass tiller: (a) late vegetative stage and (b) early flowering stage (after Tainton 1981).

the flanks of the apical meristematic region are normally sufficiently close to the soil surface to survive all but the most intense defoliation treatments and at least in some species they may be totally protected against destruction by defoliating agents.

Among the tufted species which largely dominate South African grasslands, the protection of the meristematic stem apex is not as complete as in the sod-forming species, but with few exceptions, their apices remain sufficiently close to the soil surface during the vegetative growth stage to survive even intense defoliation.   In addition, the apex is completely surrounded by the often succulent sheath bases of earlier formed leaves of the tiller and it is therefore well-insulated against temperature extremes.   While in this condition the apices will normally survive unscathed the heat of all but the most intense grassland fires.   Only when the tillers are young and have not yet developed the protective covering of leaf sheaths around their apex are they subject to large-scale damage by fire.

At some stage in the development of the tillers of most grass species, the vegetative leaf-producing stage of the tiller is terminated by a transformation from vegetative to reproductive growth.   This transformation is usually accompanied by a rapid elongation of the internodes of the stem and a rapid lengthening of the stem. The meristematic and now reproductive apex is elevated to some distance above the soil surface, where it is extremely vulnerable to any form of defoliation. During this process it also loses its protective sheath covering and so is also more vulnerable to changes in temperature. However, the removal of the apex at this time will do little more than prevent the formation of flowers and seed, for it is usually accompanied by the development of the next generation of tillers from basal stem node positions, at least in perennial plants.

From the above discussion it would seem logical to assume that sod-forming species would be more resistant to frequent and intense defoliation than would tufted species. However, this would appear not to be so since the tufted *Themeda triandra*, *Heteropogon contortus* and *Trachypogon spicatus* dominate frequently burnt grassland, whereas species which produce tillers from nodes situated below the soil surface, such as *Tristachya leucothrix*, *Alloteropsis semialata* and *Harpochloa falx*, dominate grassland which is burnt infrequently (Dillon 1979; C S Everson, personal communication, 1979). This response would appear to arise, however, not from the lack of resistance of the latter species to fire, but from the inability of the former tufted types to survive where the canopy remains dense for any length of time. In these tufted species, new tillers will not develop from the heavily shaded basal nodes, but from elevated node positions. These tillers do not develop effective roots and die before reaching reproductive maturity. In contrast, however, those species which produce tillers from nodes situated below the soil surface are apparently relatively unaffected by dense base shading. They are incapable of producing aerial tillers and although new basal tillers may develop only slowly, they persist in sufficient numbers to ensure the survival and even spread of the plant.

The dominance of the tufted perennial grass species over much of the grassland region of South Africa, and the replacement of such species by the shade-tolerant sod-forming species when defoliation frequency is low, suggests that frequent fire has long been a part of the grassland habitat.

The vernal aspect geophytes

These broad-leaved spring flowering plants of the grassland depend on regular grassland fire for their survival. Many possess underground storage organs capable of providing sufficient moisture to trigger growth before the spring rains. Growth in these plants is apparently determined by soil temperature rather than by the moisture status of the soil, so that the increased soil temperatures which follow the burning of veld (see later) promote early growth in these species. They are often capable of reaching reproductive maturity before the grasses have recovered sufficiently after rain to afford much competition, whereafter their aerial portions die back.

In the absence of frequent fires, the vernal aspect plants develop poorly or not at all and few if any will reach reproductive maturity and produce seed. The underground storage organs will survive for a number of years, but if the grass canopy is not removed for an extended period of time, they will eventually die (Schelpe 1946; Bayer 1955). They are usually absent, therefore, from dense grassland which is not intensively grazed or burnt at frequent intervals.

The autumnal aspect plants

These often tall and late-summer flowering herbaceous plants are intolerant of fire and survive only in fire-protected areas (Schelpe 1946; Bayer 1955). Their distribution is therefore often restricted to moist southern slopes or to bottomland sites, particularly in the forest margin or vlei type community. They will, however, invade any moist grassland community which remains sparsely utilized for any length of time.

The woody invaders of grassland

The large-scale absence of woody species from all but protected sites within the grassland region bears testimony to their general lack of resistance to fire. Certain species with a thick corky bark are able to resist fire once they are well established and therefore survive as open communities in grassland eg *Erythrina latissima* (broad-leaved erythrina), *Acacia sieberana* (paperbark acacia) and *Cussonia spicata* (cabbage tree). In other species the bark, while not corky, still provides considerable protection to the cambium layers of the stem eg *Protea multibracteata* (Natal protea) and *P. roupelliae* (silver protea). However, these species require protection from fire when young and therefore are usually found only where the grassland is sparse, particularly in rocky sites. Other species are able to form coppice shoots if the aerial growth is killed by fire (*Leucosidea sericea, Buddleia salviifolia, P. dracomontana* and *Widdringtonia nodiflora* and are therefore able to survive occasional fires. *L. sericea* and some *Protea* spp produce lignotubers, from which coppice shoots may develop in large numbers.

These species, except for *P. dracomontana* which often occupies short grassland on shallow soils, are largely confined to moist sites where fire is infrequent. Here they often form pioneer communities to forest. Yet other species are completely intolerant of fire but such treatment apparently stimulates seed germination so that stands which are killed by fire are able to regenerate rapidly eg *Philippia evansii* (Smith 1982).

FAUNA

There has been little specific study of the characteristics of animals enabling them to survive fire in the grassland biome of South Africa. Reviewing only such specific study would consequently provide a hazy picture. The approach taken has therefore been to outline the apparently relevant aspects of the life styles of the animals of the grassland biome. Naturally this is easier to do for the vertebrates than for the invertebrates. Further, in mentioning apparently fire-evasive or fire-resilient properties of grassland species it is not implied that the characteristics are necessarily specific adaptations to fire. Indeed, in many cases the characteristics of the fauna are more conspicuously adaptations to the habitat created by recurrent fire, rather than to fire itself.

Vertebrates

Like fishes, the two almost purely aquatic anurans, *Xenopus laevis* (platanna) and *Rana vertebralis* (aquatic river frog), are not exposed to fire. The *Breviceps* spp (terrestrial rainfrogs) lay eggs in burrows in which the larval stage is passed (Poynton 1964), so that the reproductive phase is sheltered from fire. All other grassland anurans lay eggs in water or near to it under moist conditions (when fire is unlikely) (Poynton and Broadley 1978) so that they too are sheltered from fire. While the majority of anurans are amphibious in the adult stage, terrestrial activity occurs under conditions of high atmospheric humidity when fire is unlikely. Under dry conditions, when fire is likely, the animals are normally in water, burrows or crevices, or under stones.

Terrapins may similarly be considered to live in a fire-sheltered environment, but at the Weenen Nature Reserve in inland Natal, about 25, apparently basking in the sun at the edge of a dam, were killed by an unscheduled fire on 19 June 1976 (O Bourquin, personal communication, 1979). There are a few records of tortoises in the grassland biome. *Geochelone pardalis* occurs marginally in the south and west, *Psammobates oculifer* marginally in the north-west, *P. tentorius* and *Hormopus femoralis* in the south-west, and *Kinixys belliana* marginally in the north (Greig and Burdett 1976). A scarcity of these slow-moving, medium-sized reptiles in the grassland biome may be due partly to there being little or no possibility of them finding shelter when fire burns through a dry, dense sward. Snakes and lizards of the grassland biome doubtless evade fire to a greater or lesser extent by taking refuge or aestivating in the cold dry season in holes of many descriptions, under stones, up trees and in water. Oviparous species lay their eggs in holes or hollows in the ground, in trees and under stones, but it is not known to what extent the survival of eggs, despite mortality by fire of hatched individuals, might permit population maintenance.

With the exception of ostrich *(Struthio camelus)*, a large, fleet-footed terrestrial bird occurring marginally in the grassland biome, adult birds generally evade fire simply by flying. Many species nest on cliffs or in trees, in association with aquatic habitats, in other refuge sites, and generally after the main fire hazard season, so that the direct effects of fire are minimal. However, the typical grassland birds, such as some of the francolins, quails, bustards, larks, cisticolas, pipits, longclaws and widow birds, nest between August and April on or close to the ground, often in places where they are vulnerable to fire (McLachlan and Liversidge 1957). Nevertheless, the main nesting season is from November to January, after the most fire-hazardous season. Phasianids generally renest, conditions permitting, if a clutch is destroyed. Greywing and redwing francolins have above average fecundity for phasianids, by virtue of the long breeding season (August to March), the possibility of adults raising more than one clutch per season, and the rapid growth of young which may breed in their first summer (Mentis 1973; Mentis and Bigalke 1980). Such fecundity would aid in population recovery following the heavy mortality caused directly or indirectly by fire.

Among small terrestrial mammals such as shrews (*Crocidura flavescens* and *Myosorex varius*) and rodents (*Dendromus melanotis, Mus minutoides, Otomys irroratus, Praomys natalensis* and *Rhabdomys pumilio*), some resort to crevices, burrows and other refuges when fire occurs, but population densities are low immediately after fire which directly or indirectly causes considerable mortality (Mentis and Rowe-Rowe 1979). However, these animals are characteristically fecund, permitting rapid population recovery from the small nucleus surviving fire. Bats, like most birds, are exposed to fire only to a limited extent because of their flying ability and their use of the depths of caves, cave mouths, crevices, trees and tree hollows for roosting. Slow-moving, medium-sized mammals appear also to use refuges to escape fire (eg porcupine (*Hystrix africaeaustralis*) occupies burrows by day (Bigalke 1978) and Cape clawless otter (*Aonyx capensis*) is associated with aquatic habitats and uses burrows and tunnels caused by subsurface erosion). However, cane rat (*Thryonomys swinderianus*), which shelters in dense, matted vegetation (Bigalke 1978), is vulnerable to fire, perhaps one reason for its limited occurrence in the grassland biome. Red rock hare (*Pronolagus crassicaudatus*), spring hare (*Pedetes capensis*), some of the viverrids (eg yellow mongoose (*Cynictis penicillata*) and suricate (*Suricata suricatta*)) and the moles and mole rats make greater or lesser use of burrows, thus being relatively immune to fire. Rock hyrax (*Procavia capensis*) and klipspringer (*Oreotragus oreotragus*) live on screes, tumbled boulders and krantzes naturally sheltered from fire. Except for lion (*Panthera leo*), now extinct in the grassland biome, the canids, hyaenids and felids use some or other retreat, generally sheltered from fire, for daytime resting and for raising young. Adult scrub hares (*Lepus* spp) and adult common reedbuck (*Redunca arundinum*), mountain reedbuck, grey rhebuck, oribi and steenbok (*Raphicerus campestris*) may be expected to escape most fires readily. However, the young, for which there is a "lying-out" period (Leuthold 1977), are vulnerable to fire. Typically the young during the early lying-out period respond to disturbance by lying still rather than running away. Nevertheless, parturition is not highly synchronized (Mentis 1972c) and in at least some of the species most births occur after the most fire-hazardous season (Olivier et al 1978) so that the probability of many of the young surviving fire is high. Other antelope such as bushbuck (*Tragelaphus scriptus*), grey duiker (*Sylvicapra grimmia*), red duiker (*Cephalophus natalensis*), blue duiker

(C. monticola) and Cape grysbok occupy forest, scrub or bush habitats more or less sheltered from fire. However, the young "lie-out" and are vulnerable to fire, and occasionally have been "rescued" from or burnt by fire. The gregarious antelope of the grassland biome ie eland, blesbok, black wildebeest *(Connochaetes gnou)* and red hartebeest *(Alcelaphus buselaphus)* typically give birth to precocious young for which there is a brief or no lying-out period so that escape by the young from fire is likely. Among these antelope births are highly synchronized, and in blesbok and black wildebeest parturition occurs in November and December, after the annual peak in the fire hazard season. However, despite some natural abilities which grassland antelope possess to evade fire, they should not be enclosed within relatively small areas without precautions taken to ensure their safety in the event of fire. Within the grassland biome vervet monkey *(Cercopithecus aethiops)* is associated with forest, scrub on hillsides and along watercourses and plantations, so is only marginally exposed to fire. Samango monkey *(C. mitis)* is strictly a forest animal and occurs in such habitat marginally within the grassland biome. Chacma baboon *(Papio ursinus)*, the most terrestrial of South African primates, does range far from its forest, scrub and krantz refuges, to which it doubtless resorts in the event of fire.

Invertebrates

While the soil fauna is protected to a degree from fire itself, there may well be profound indirect effects involving smoke and altered ground surface temperatures, moisture regimes, and the nutrient status and physical properties of the soil. However, this appears to be an unstudied field in the South African grassland biome, and the characteristics of the fauna in enduring the effects of fire can only be speculated upon.

Regarding the above-ground invertebrates, a wide variety of characteristics may be expected to enable members of this very diverse group to escape from fire or survive in its wake. It is well known that fire or smoke alarms insects and other arthropods, some of which take wing and so attract insectivorous and scavenging birds. Slow-moving or relatively immobile animals, such as stick and leaf insects, are, without any special fire-evasive characteristics, vulnerable to fire. Ticks respond to smoke by crawling down or dropping from grass stems to the soil surface where protection from fire is sought in cracks and crevices in the soil surface (T Bosman, personal communication, 1979). Interestingly, ticks bred in the laboratory for several generations may not respond to smoke. It is not known whether this arises from habituation, deficient behavioural development in an artificial environment, or relaxation of selection for a fire-evasive strategy. Those invertebrates such as locusts, grasshoppers and dung beetles, which live above ground but bury their eggs below ground, are able to persist and recover rapidly, even if fire directly or indirectly kills most or all of the larval and adult instars. Many invertebrates with limited or no flying abilities (eg termites, ants, crickets, spiders and scorpions) occupy, to a greater or lesser degree, burrows and other sheltered sites which provide refuge from fire. Other animals adept at flying, such as bees and wasps, have hives or nests in hollows of trees, in recesses on krantzes or in the ground, or on large rocks and other objects more or less remote from grass fires. Many invertebrates are characteristically fecund so that even though fire may cause high mortality, only a nucleus of sur- vivors is necessary for rapid recovery of populations. For the mobile groups individuals surviving in small unburnt islands later recolonize the burnt areas.

Despite the paucity of specific studies, it may be expected that animal mortality caused by fire is related to its intensity and the extent of the area over which it burns.

EFFECTS OF FIRE REGIME ON SOIL PROPERTIES AND MICROCLIMATE

PHYSICAL AND CHEMICAL PROPERTIES OF SOIL

Soil pH

After 6 yr of burning Transvaal highveld, no apparent change in pH was noted by Cook (1939b), nor were changes noted by White and Grossman (1972) after 37 yr of burning the same type of veld, but after 28 yr of burning at Ukulinga in Natal, significant differences (P = 0,01) have emerged within the 0 to 5 cm soil layer between plots in which the only form of defoliation is burning (pH 5) and those which have been neither burnt nor mown (pH 4,8), mown 3 times a season and the material removed as hay or bedding (pH 4,6) and those which have been mown twice for hay each season and burnt in late winter or spring (pH 4,75). It would appear, therefore, that burning does increase pH, although the effect is certainly not dramatic (Cass and Collins 1983).

Mineral salts

No evidence of any effect of fire on the phosphorus, potass- ium, calcium, magnesium, sodium or aluminium content of soils has been recorded after 28 yr of veld burning at Ukulinga (Cass and Collins 1983). Similarly, Cook (1939b) noted no change in the concentration of soluble salts in the soil of veld burnt annually in the Transvaal for 6 yr, but White and Grossman (1972) have reported a decline in calcium, magnesium, potassium and sodium concentration and in the base saturation of soils in which the grassland was burnt annually for 37 yr. No differences in miner- al concentration were recorded between soils in veld burnt in different months of the year, although base saturation did dec- line as the time of burning was delayed through the winter and into the spring. Percent base saturation on burnt plots was, in fact, inversely correlated with the rainfall in the month which followed the burn, suggesting that nutrients were removed from the system by water.

Nitrogen

Almost all the nitrogen contained in the fraction of the plant which is burnt is lost in grassland fires, but where combustion is incomplete, some organic nitrogen remains in the residue (Raison 1979). This aspect is discussed more fully in chapter 14. According to West (1965), however, the amount lost is small and perhaps negligible, but data from Ukulinga suggest that it may be as much as 18 kg ha^{-1} yr^{-1}. This grassveld yields about 3 t DM ha^{-1} in one season, and in late winter this material contains about 0,6% N. However, since there is no evidence that yield declines with continued annual burning, this amount is apparently replaced each year, even though Meicklejohn (1955) has reported that burning may adversely affect the ability of the soil to replace nitrogen through its effect on the aerobic nitrogen-fixing organisms at the soil surface. He has reported, however, that fire has no detrimental effect on the anaerobic nitrogen-fixing organisms. Data published by White and Grossman (1972) do suggest, however, that annual burning over an extended period of time does reduce the concentration of nitrogen in soils (from 0,066% to 0,059% after 37 yr of annual burning).

Base exchange capacity

There is little evidence that fire affects the base exchange capacity of soils, even when soil temperatures increase to as much as 250°C (Coutts 1945). White and Grossman (1972) have, however, noted a reduction in the cation exchange capacity of highveld soils with annual burning for 37 yr.

Organic matter content

Reports on the effects of grassland fires on the organic matter content of soils are inconsistent, but South African work to date suggests that the effect is negligible. Cook (1939b) could establish no difference in the organic matter content of soils on unburnt plots and those burnt annually for 6 yr. Similarly, data derived by Cass and Collins (1983) indicated no difference between the carbon content of soils of veld burnt annually for 28 yr and of veld completely protected for the equivalent length of time. White and Grossman (1972) have, however, reported a reduction in carbon content of soils due to burning, but they could not detect a change in the carbon:nitrogen ratio in these soils, while Edwards (1961) measured a higher organic matter content in soils of mown plots than in those of burnt plots, both of which were higher than in protected plots. However, these differences were not significant and therefore the effect of fire on the organic matter content of the soil, even after 24 yr of applying treatments, was inconclusive.

Bulk density of surface soil

Cass and Collins (1983) has shown a lower bulk density in the 0 to 50 mm soil layer on protected grassland (1 359 ± 186 kg m^{-3}) than on unprotected grassland (1 505 ± 178 kg m^{-3}) at Ukulinga, but they could find no difference in bulk density within the 50 to 150 mm soil layer and there was no apparent difference between soils which were burnt and mown at different frequencies.

Other physical characteristics of soils

In a comprehensive survey of the size of water stable aggregates in the 0 to 5; 5 to 10; 10 to 20 and 20 to 50 mm layers of soil from grassland protected for 28 yr and adjacent grassland burnt annually in spring and mown twice for hay each summer, Cass and Collins (1983) could establish no significant treatment effects. However, Edwards (1961) did record a significantly greater percentage of water stable aggregates in soils of mown plots (76%) as against those of protected plots (64%) in the Tall Grassveld at Escourt after 24 yr of treatment. The aggregates from mown plots (76%) were also more stable than those from burnt plots (72%), but not significantly so. Also, Cass and Collins (1983) were unable to establish differences in the modulus of rupture of the surface of the soil on plots subjected to annual burning and complete protection or in the matric potential of the soil in the 0 to 50 mm soil layer on plots burnt and mown at different frequencies.

SOIL MICROORGANISMS

Any analysis of the response among populations of soil microorganisms to fire is complicated by the large range in species density which accompanies the wide spatial and temporal range in the microenvironment within any grassland community. Analytical techniques are tedious in the extreme, so that any comprehensive analysis of treatment effects is laborious and time consuming. It is no wonder, therefore, that little work has been undertaken in this field.

F M Wallis (personal communication, 1979) and W J Price (personal communication, 1979) have recently examined the effects of grassland fires on the populations of microorganisms at Ukulinga. Although this work is as yet incomplete, they have been able to show some differences in the populations of these organisms under different fire regimes. For example, they have established that the behaviour patterns of the fungi are very different from those of the bacteria and the actinomycetes. Treatments which greatly affect the fungal populations may have little effect on the bacteria and actinomycetes and vice versa. Generally, however, they have shown that grassland fires have little effect on the population of microorganisms in the upper soil layers (Table 4). Differences were apparent in certain treatments but were inconsistent and may have been related to the intensity of the fire at the specific sites sampled. These

Table 4   Numbers of fungi and of bacteria and actinomycetes in the upper soil layers on plots subjected to different burning and mowing treatments for 28 yr. Plots sampled in March 1979 (F M Wallis and W J Price, personal communications 1979).

Treatment	Numbers of organisms g^{-1} dry soil	
	Fungi ($\times 10^3$)	Bacteria and actinomycetes ($\times 10^5$)
Complete protection	55 ± 12	40 ± 12
Burnt annually in spring	41 ± 5	33 ± 14
Mown annually in spring	57 ± 7	26 ± 3
Burnt annually in spring and mown twice for hay in summer	40 ± 5	41 ± 15
Burnt triennially in spring	65 ± 11	31 ± 5
Burnt triennially in autumn	81 ± 6	24 ± 5
[a]Burnt triennially in spring and mown twice for hay in summer	29 ± 13	85 ± 29

[a]Plots were mown in spring in those years in which burning treatments were not scheduled.

authors also sampled a wide range of treatments in March 1979 to determine the long-term effect of fire on microbial populations not subject to recent burning treatments. Plots previously burnt were sampled near the end of the following growing season when, it was assumed, the recorded populations would reflect the suitability of the habitat created by the different burning treatments for microorganisms. These data are presented in Table 5. Once again results were inconsistent and surprisingly, the substantial accumulation of surface litter on grassland protected for 28 yr has not led to a substantial increase in the numbers of organisms found in the upper layers of the soil. This result contrasts, however, with those recorded by F M Wallis (personal communication, 1979) under high altitude conditions at Cathedral Peak, where there was a greater incorporation of organic matter into the surface soil layers on protected plots compared with frequently burnt plots, so that soil microbial populations were higher in protected than in frequently burnt grassland.

Table 5   Numbers of fungi and of bacteria and actinomycetes in the upper soil layers immediately before and immediately after fire (F M Wallis and W J Price, personal communications, 1979).

	Numbers of organisms g^{-1} dry soil			
Month	Fungi (x 10^3)		Bacteria and actinomycetes (x 10^5)	
	Before fire	After fire	Before fire	After fire
MAY	41 ± 10	58 ± 16	56 ± 6	60 ± 10
	27 ± 10	29 ± 2	91 ± 17	144 ± 34
	31 ± 4	44 ± 5	20 ± 5	39 ± 12
AUGUST	19 ± 4	22 ± 2	17 ± 2	21 ± 2
	40 ± 10	37 ± 7	70 ± 6	42 ± 7
	32 ± 5	31 ± 4	19 ± 3	12 ± 1
	12 ± 2	35 ± 12	24 ± 12	24 ± 5
	36 ± 7	54 ± 5	171 ± 45	172 ± 22
	35 ± 3	30 ± 12	165 ± 6	126 ± 10
	53 ± 14	41 ± 5	93 ± 10	110 ± 21
	49 ± 6	69 ± 9	100 ± 8	120 ± 13
	110 ± 31	90 ± 7	398 ± 160	258 ± 7

MICROCLIMATE

Temperature

During the fire

. No data are available on the rise in air temperature associated with fires within the grassland biome, and only Cook (1939) has reported on changes in soil temperatures at this time. In common with data from both Australia (Norton and McGarity 1965) and the USA (Heyward 1938; Bentley and Fenner 1958), Cook (1939) established that grassland fires had little effect on soil temperature, even at a depth of 50 mm.

After the fire

Phillips (1919, 1930) reported large differences in soil temperatures between burnt and unburnt grassland during the period of recovery following a burn. He reported that soil surface temperatures on burnt veld may rise twice as high during the day as they do on unburnt veld, and that they may drop several degrees lower on cold nights. Even at a depth of 150 mm large differences in temperature may still be apparent. During six days of mild weather in May 1974, cleanly burnt grassland at 2 140 m above sea level in the Natal Drakensberg experienced higher daily maximum and minimum temperatures and a greater diurnal temperature range than nearby unburnt grassland (Mentis and Bigalke 1979). In more recent work, Cass and Savage have shown that soil temperatures at a depth of 50 mm on burnt veld increase considerably more during the day than they do on unburnt veld. They remained higher throughout a 3 day monitoring period which commenced 13 days after a burn on 18 April 1979. The diurnal temperature range was also higher on burnt veld (ca 6,0°C) than on unburnt veld (ca 2,5°C).

Savage (1980) has also established differences in net radiant flux density (R net) and in the reflection coefficient between burnt and unburnt grassland. Maximum R net values were higher for burnt than unburnt grassland because of the higher reflection coefficient for the unburnt grassland. Net long-wave radiant flux density was also generally greater for the burnt than for the unburnt site, except in the afternoon, as was the long-wave radiant flux density because of the higher soil surface temperatures.

At night, however, R net was lower on burnt than on unburnt sites because of the higher surface temperature of the burnt plots, and therefore the greater long-wave radiant flux density.

In general, therefore, burning appears to increase the net radiant flux density, decrease the reflection coefficient and increase the temperature of the soil. It should, therefore, stimulate growth in early spring when temperatures may limit growth, provided that there is available water. In a water-stressed sward, complete defoliation by burning may allow plants to use a limited store of soil water at a higher leaf water potential, leading to growth when little or none occurs in a comparable unburnt sward (Fisher 1978). However, the overall effect of fire on soil temperatures will inevitably depend on its frequency and the season in which it is applied. The seasonal effect is associated with the rate at which the canopy redevelops after the fire, and therefore on the length of the period of soil exposure. Where, for example, grassland is burnt at the start of the dry season, the redevelopment of a canopy will be delayed over many months and the impact of the fire on soil temperatures will be considerably greater than where fire is applied early in the wet season.

MOISTURE RELATIONSHIPS

The effect of veld burning on the moisture status of the soil depends on so many factors that generalizations can be extremely dangerous. In unburnt grassland, the canopy may intercept a considerable proportion of low intensity rain which may therefore never reach the soil. Also, after extended periods of protection the grass tufts may "thatch" over, so that rainwater is concentrated between the tufts, and a greater proportion will be lost as runoff. Both these factors mean that less rainwater will penetrate the soil, in spite of the greater infiltration capacity of soil in grassland which has been protected for a number of years compared to that of grassland which is regularly burnt and mown (Table 6) (Cass and Collins 1983). However, the rainwater that

Table 6   Infiltration capacity of soils of grassland burnt and
           mown at different frequencies for 28 yr (Cass and
           Collins 1983).

Treatment	Infiltration rate (m day^{-1})
Complete protection	36,36 ± 26,41
Burnt triennially in spring	3,25 ± 1,64
Burnt biennially in spring	4,55 ± 3,54
Burnt annually in spring	1,31 ± 1,58
Burnt annually in spring and mown twice for hay each summer	3,38 ± 2,23
Mown annually in spring and twice for hay in summer	3,14 ± 2,64

does penetrate the soil may be lost more slowly in protected than
in regularly burnt grassland.   Evaporation rates will be low
because of the dense canopy cover above the soil, while
transpiration rates are also likely to be low in protected
grassland because of the small amount of living tissue on plants
which remain undefoliated.   On veld which does not carry a dense
canopy into the spring, burning will reduce growth rate (Anon
1974) and therefore reduce transpiration rate.

     As a result of the interactions between burning, rainfall in-
tensity and the condition of the grassland, results of investigations of soil moisture renewal and depletion patterns with and
without burning are confusing.   Phillips (1919) reported that
soil moisture increases more with rain on burnt veld than on unburnt veld but Scott (1952a) and West (1965) have reported better
moisture penetration on unburnt than on burnt veld.   Researchers
have generally agreed, however, that soils dry out more rapidly
on burnt than on unburnt veld (Phillips 1919; Theron 1937; Cook
1939b; Irvine 1943), although Dillon (1979) was unable to show
any such trends at Ukulinga.

EFFECTS OF FIRE REGIME ON WATER PRODUCTION AND QUALITY

     Scott (1952a) reported that runoff from plots in a veld burn-
ing trial at Estcourt was highest from protected plots and least
from regularly mown plots.   Burnt plots were intermediate.   The
highest rates of soil loss in this trial were reported from annual August and triennial spring-burnt veld (le Roux 1968), although Scott (1971) did record high rates of soil loss in some
years from completely protected veld.   This he attributed to the
loss of soil loosened by rodents, which were often particularly
active in these plots.   Du Plessis and Mostert (1965) have reported high runoff rates from burnt and grazed plots in the
Orange Free State, but Haylett (1960) could find no effect of
fire on runoff from veld in the southern Transvaal.

Nanni (1960) has cited a number of reports of decline in streamflow following fire in the catchment, although other reports have suggested either little effect (Bosch 1979) or an increased streamflow following fire. From his own work in the Cathedral Peak catchment, Nanni (1970) concluded that fire in the catchments had no apparent effect on streamflow. However, he did show that exotic plantations reduced runoff by as much as 500 mm yr^{-1} through their greater use of water and in spite of the greater infiltration of rainwater into soil of wooded communities, and he suggested that indigenous woody vegetation may do likewise. Long-term protection, which leads to the replacement of grassland by woody vegetation may, therefore, be expected to reduce runoff. Nanni (1972) has, in fact, shown that the removal of riparian vegetation (mostly *Leucosidea sericea* and sclerophyllous shrubs such as *Cliffortia linearifolia, Philippia evansii* and *Myrsine africana*) does increase streamflow in the Cathedral Peak area.

CONCLUSIONS

In the management of the grassland biome, fire is deliberately excluded only from those sites in which successional development to scrub or forest is being encouraged, in arid sweet grassland where the canopy material remains acceptable to grazing animals even when mature, and in highly intensive grazing systems on mixed veld and sourveld where canopy accumulation can be strictly controlled. Such areas occupy only a small proportion of the grassland region, so that over most of the area fires are used extensively to control forage quality and to prevent successional changes from fire climax grassland to communities which, judged from the point of view of forage production, are less useful. In general, it is the fire climax communities which provide the most useful forage and which are, therefore, most effective in maintaining high levels of secondary production.

Chapter 7 Fire in Savanna

W. S. W. TROLLOPE

INTRODUCTION

In the savanna areas of Africa fire is recognized as having an important ecological role in the development and maintenance of productive and stable savanna communities (Phillips 1965; Lemon 1968; Austen 1971; Gillon 1971a; van Wyk 1971; Vesey-Fitzgerald 1971; West 1971). Nevertheless, except for the wildlife areas, the general attitude regarding its practical use tends to be negative; veld burning is applied as a last resort. This view has arisen through the deleterious effects burning has on veld when used injudiciously and has resulted in a reduced number of veld fires in the savanna areas of South Africa. This reduction in the frequency of fires dates from about 1946 when the Soil Conservation Act was proclaimed. Strict procedures governing the use of fire were laid down and the practice of controlled burning in arid savanna was virtually eliminated. Scott (1970) drew attention to this phenomenon when discussing the pros and cons of eliminating veld burning in South Africa and the question arises whether an important or even essential factor of the ecological stability of savanna ecosystems of South Africa is not being inadvertently eliminated. This point emphasizes the necessity of assessing the ecological effects of fire in savanna in order to establish the role fire plays in this ecosystem. Unfortunately this is a difficult task because a review of the literature shows that there is a distinct lack of quantitative information on the effect of fire in savanna, particularly the arid savanna biome which is the larger of the two savanna biomes as defined by Huntley (this volume, chapter 1; West 1965; Scott 1970, 1971; van Wyk 1971; Trollope 1974, 1978a).

CHARACTERISTICS OF FIRE REGIME AND FIRE BEHAVIOUR

TYPE OF FIRE

In the savanna areas both crown and surface fires occur but the most common are surface fires burning with or against the wind as head or back fires. Crown fires develop only under very dry conditions when the fuel moisture is low and the prevailing weather is characterized by high winds, high air temperatures and low relative humidities. Surface fires are generally more frequent than crown fires in savanna because the relatively nonflammable foliage of tropical and subtropical trees and shrubs will ignite only under extreme atmospheric conditions. This is in contrast to fynbos vegetation where the leaves are very flammable due to the presence of terpenes, and crown fires readily develop. A very interesting aspect of fire behaviour in savanna is that bush clumps are very resistant to fire even under extreme burning conditions. Fires generally skirt around the edges of the bush clumps, leaving the centre unburnt. Unpublished data indicates that this phenomenon is caused either by a lack of grass fuel or by relatively nonflammable grass species growing under the trees and shrubs of the bush clump. In the eastern Cape two common grass species occurring under bush clumps are *Panicum maximum* and *Kaerochloa curva*, both of which generally have higher moisture contents than the grasses growing between the bush clumps (Trollope 1980a). The practical significance of this phenomenon to the stock farmer is that once bush encroachment has progressed to the bush clump stage, then fire is a far less effective management tool than during the initial stages of encroachment.

NATURAL FIRE REGIME

Consideration is given here to the fire regime in savanna areas little disturbed by man and attributable to fires caused by factors other than man. A study of the literature shows that there is virtually no information available on the ancient fire regime that existed prior to the advent of man or before his presence had a significant effect on the savanna areas of South Africa. Nevertheless, it is logical to expect that the factors that played the greatest role in the season, frequency and intensity of natural fires in the savanna were fuel load, fuel moisture and the incidence of lightning. Savanna in South Africa is largely confined to the summer rainfall region with a dry season from ca May to October, at the end of which the herbaceous grass fuel layer is very dry. Komarek (1971a) stated that Africa has a unique fire climate that accentuates the probability and occurrence of lightning fires because at the end of the dry period, dry lightning storms frequently occur and ignite many fires. The importance of lightning as an ignition source is illustrated by Siegfried (1980) who reported that in the Etosha National Park, where a policy of fire exclusion is applied, at least 54% and probably 73% of all fires that occurred during the period 1970 to 1979 were caused by lightning. In the Kruger National Park Gertenbach and Potgieter (1979) found that lightning caused 45% of all unscheduled fires during the 1977/78 season. Conversely Macdonald et al (1980) concluded from fire records that lightning was an insignificant ignition source in the Hluhluwe-Corridor-Umfolozi Game Reserve Complex in Zululand, Natal, during the period 1955 to 1978. Controlled burning and arson were the most important ignition sources. However, this finding does not necessarily indicate that lightning was not previously an important ignition source but merely reflects the dominant ignition sources under the present system of land-use and management. It is probable that when human populations were low in the adjoining areas and there were no constructed fire breaks and fire fighting services, lightning induced fires were more prevalent and burnt larger areas. An indication of the effect of the absence of human interference is provided by the occurrence of fires caused by lightning in the Kalahari Gemsbok Park during 1977/78 when approximately 350 000 ha of the park were burnt (G A Robinson and P van Wyk, personal communications, 1982).

Concerning the season of burning that occurred in the natural fire regime, Komarek (1971a) quotes the Secretary of Forestry in South Africa (1967) as stating that most of the fires of any consequence that are initiated by lightning occur during the early summer months, October and November, before significant summer rains have begun. This evidence would suggest that burns under the natural fire regime occurred most frequently at the end of the dry season and just prior to the first spring rains. Obviously fires also occurred at other times of the year in response to unseasonal drought periods and other ignition sources like rock falls.

The frequency of burning in the natural fire regime would have been largely influenced by the rate of accumulation of sufficient grass fuel to support a fire. Rainfall is the most important factor affecting the productivity of the grass sward under veld conditions and, therefore, the accumulation of grass fuel. Thus fires were undoubtedly more frequent in moist savanna (>600 mm rainfall yr^{-1}) than in arid savanna not only because of the higher rainfall but also because of the unacceptability of the mature grass to herbivores in these moist areas. Present day research would suggest that the natural frequency of fire in moist savanna must have ranged between annual and biennial, depending upon the seasonal rainfall and the degree of utilization of the vegetation by wild ungulates. Evidence for this fire frequency is provided by Scott (1971) who found that in the Southern Tall Grassveld (720 mm rainfall yr^{-1}) of Natal, which Acocks (1975) describes as open savanna, complete protection of the grass sward for 3 yr caused it to become moribund and die out. Conversely, annual and biennial burning maintained a vigorous grass sward with a far greater basal cover. Furthermore, in the Kruger National Park, where fire is an important component of the veld management strategy, it has been concluded from burning experiments initiated in 1954 that the most desirable burning frequency under grazing conditions in moist savanna is annual or biennial, depending upon grazing and grass fuel conditions (Gertenbach 1979).

In the arid savanna the frequency of fire must have been far lower than in the moist savanna because the rainfall is both less and highly erratic and the grass sward remains acceptable to grazing animals even when mature, thus reducing the rate of accumulation of grass fuel. The frequency of fires would have been determined by the occurrence of exceptionally wet seasons. Studies by Tyson and Dyer (1975) showed that periods of above and below average rainfall occur at cyclic intervals of approximately 10 yr. Results presented by Gertenbach and Potgieter (1979) for the mopani shrubveld in the Kruger National Park showed that under grazing conditions annual and biennial burning significantly reduced the basal cover of the grass sward and resulted in an increase of pioneer grass species when applied during the dry periods of the rainfall cycle. Conversely, these treatment effects were reversed during wet periods of the rainfall cycle. Bearing these results in mind and considering the period 1910 to 1980, Gertenbach and Potgieter (1979) concluded that annual and biennial fires were the probable frequencies during wet periods, whereas fires probably occured once every 3 to 5 yr or less frequently during dry periods. Thus, in arid savanna, fire frequency apparently was lower than in moist savanna and depended largely on the rate of accumulation of grass fuel in response to the amount of rainfall and the stocking rate of grazing animals. The finding of Kennan (1971) lends support to this viewpoint. He stated that at the Tuli Experiment Station in southwestern Zimbabwe, a burning trial was abandoned because it was impossible to apply burning treatments in a regular sequence. The area has very low and erratic rainfall (450 mm yr^{-1}) which causes very marked fluctuations in the seasonal production of grass material and therefore wide fluctuations in fuel loads.

It seems reasonable to assume that the intensities of fire occurring during the natural fire regime of the past were far greater than those of present day fires. Acocks (1975) has presented widely accepted botanical evidence indicating that the grass component of the veld in South Africa has been drastically altered and reduced in all veld types, including savanna, since the advent of settled agricultural practices. The effect on the production of grass fuel of a drastic reversal in grassland succession to a pioneer stage is illustrated by data presented by Danckwerts (1980). He found that in the False Thornveld of the Eastern Province the phytomass of grass produced per unit area by pioneer veld dominated by species like *Aristida congesta* was only 13% of that produced by climax veld dominated by *Themeda triandra*. Since grass constitutes the major fuel component in savanna fires and is the most important determinant of fire intensity, the fires of the natural fire regime were probably far more intense than those of today. Also, wild fires often are more intense than controlled management burns as applied at present. Obviously intense wild fires do occur during present times but are the exception rather that the rule.

The intensity of fire in the natural fire regime was probably higher in moist savanna than in arid savanna because of greater fuel loads. However, fire behaviour data would suggest that moist savanna of the southern and eastern seaboard experienced cooler fires than the northern and western savanna of the interior because grass fuel moisture and relative humidity are generally higher along the coast.

In conclusion, the natural fire regime in savanna undoubtedly resulted in a fire mosaic of areas burnt by different types and intensities of fire occurring at various times and frequencies, all of which maintained a diversity of vegetation types which provided an ideal habitat for a wide range of animals.

CURRENT FIRE REGIME

In contrast to the "natural" situation dealt with in the previous section, here the circumstances are largely those of savannas managed and manipulated by man who also is the primary cause of fires. The current fire regime is greatly influenced by and is the product of the system of land-use being applied in an area, namely, commercial ranching, subsistence ranching or wild-life management.

In the commercial ranching areas the use of fire is controlled by legislation which has as its objective the conservation of the natural resources. This underlying objective has had the effect of significantly reducing the frequency of fires in the savanna areas used for commercial ranching. Generally in the moist savannas burning is conducted on a biennial to quadriennial basis, with annual burning occurring as wild-fires or through the injudicious use of fire in contravention of the governing legislation. In the arid savannas burning is permitted only under very special circumstances such as for controlling bush encroachment, but generally it is seldom recommended or permitted and therefore fires are very infrequent in this type of savanna.

The season of burning is strictly controlled and administered by legislation and is generally limited to the end of the dormant period immediately after the commencement of the first spring rains. This regulation has resulted in relatively low intensity fires because of the comparatively humid conditions prevailing at this time of the year. It has also caused fires to be applied late in the season because of ill defined spring rains. This in turn has resulted in the burning of relatively green grass, causing low intensity fires. There are no regulations governing the types of fires to be used but in practice the majority of controlled burns are surface head fires. Of course, wild fires do occur as either head or back surface fires depending upon circumstances. Crown fires occur only under extreme burning conditions.

In the subsistence ranching areas the fire regime is theoretically controlled by legislations similar to that in the commercial ranching areas. However, in practice this legislation is completely ineffectual and fires are applied indiscriminately. The fire regime is largely determined by the availability of grass fuel and the prevailing weather conditions. Generally in the moist savannas annual fires occur while in the arid savannas fires are very rare because of the denuded condition of the veld caused by excessive overstocking and overgrazing. Fires occur at any time of the year when the grass is dry enough to burn. The intensity of the fires is generally low because of insufficient grass fuel and all types of surface fires occur because of the uncontrolled and indiscriminate nature of the burning practices.

In the wild-life areas the fire regime is very strictly controlled by the responsible wild-life agency. In the moist savannas of the Kruger National Park, the frequency of burning varies from annual to biennial whereas in the arid savannas burning ranges from every 4 to 8 yr, depending upon rainfall conditions (Gertenbach 1979). In the extremely arid savannas, such as the Etosha National Park in South West Africa, controlled burning is not practised (Siegfried 1980) and the frequency of fires depends upon the occurrence of lightning strikes and the availability of adequate levels of grass fuel in response to above average rainfall conditions. The main types of fires that occur are surface fires either in the form of head fires or back fires. In the wild-life areas back fires burning against the wind are more common than in the commercial ranching areas because of the extensive areas that are burnt at any one time. Thus fires that may have been initiated as head fires can be converted to back fires by a sudden change in the wind direction or by burning down the slope of landscapes with an undulating topography. The intensity of the fires occurring in the wild-life areas is influenced by the amount of rainfall, the season of burning, and the prevailing atmospheric conditions at the time of the fire. Generally, fuel loads of grass are higher in the moist savannas than in the arid savannas, therefore resulting in more intense fires in the former.

The intensity of a fire is influenced by the season of burning and the related moisture content of the fuel. For example, in the Kruger National Park fires are applied to different areas before the spring rains (August/September), after the first spring rains (September/October), in midsummer (January/February) and during autumn (April) (Gertenbach 1979). Thus the intensity of the fires is greatest when burnt before the spring rains when the moisture content of the fuel is very low. Conversely, fire intensities are relatively low in the burns applied during mid-summer and autumn when the grass is relatively green and the moisture content of the fuel is high. However, the major portion of the Kruger National Park is burnt at the end of the dormant season both before and after the first spring rains, resulting in fires of relatively high intensity. The intensity of the fires in the wild-life areas is also influenced by the atmospheric conditions prevailing at the time of the burn. For example, in the Kruger National Park, the most intense fires occur before the first spring rains, followed by those burnt after the first spring rains, during autumn and during mid-summer respectively (W P D Gertenbach, personal communication, 1982). The most important atmospheric factor causing these variations in the fire intensity at these different times is the humidity of the atmosphere.

EFFECT OF FIRE REGIME ON VEGETATION STRUCTURE AND DYNAMICS

THE GRASS/BUSH BALANCE

Considerable attention has been given to the effect of fire on the balance of grass to trees and shrubs in savanna (Scott 1947, 1952b, 1955, 1970, 1971; West 1955, 1969; Donaldson 1969; Roux 1969). The general conclusion reached is that fire per se favours the development and maintenance of a predominantly grassland vegetation by destroying the juvenile trees and shrubs and preventing the development of more mature plants to a taller fire-resistant stage. However, once bush has become dominant and is suppressing grass, fire no longer has this effect because of insufficient grass fuel for intense fires.

Conversely van der Schijff (1957) quoted observations made in the Kruger National Park and at Mara Research Station in the northern Transvaal that the development of a dense vigorous grass cover and the withdrawal of fire resulted in the significant dying-off of *Dichrostachys cinerea* (sickle bush) and *Acacia* species. This author concludes that, in the drier areas of South Africa, it is possible to restore the grass/bush balance by resting it for an indefinite period and protecting it from fire. Pienaar (1959) supports these observations and reports that at the Towoomba and Soutpan Research Stations and in the Pietersburg district of the northern Transvaal, *D. cinerea*, *Acacia karroo* (sweet thorn), *A. nilotica* (scented thorn) and *A. tortilis* (umbrella thorn) are successfully being reduced in density by excluding fire and resting the veld. Both van der Schijff (1957) and Pienaar (1959) state that burning often merely destroys the aerial portions of trees and shrubs, causing them to coppice and produce numerous stems. However, Pienaar (1959) feels that when the increase in bush is still in the initial stages it may be possible to control it with fire.

Van Wyk (1971) refutes the observation that *D. cinerea* is fire-dependent and unsuccessfully competes with a dense grass cover. He concluded from quantitative data obtained in the Kruger National Park that *D. cinerea* increased in density with the exclusion of fire and showed no increase in numbers on burnt plots. However, Gertenbach (personal communication, 1979) is of the opinion that the anomaly concerning *D. cinerea* is due to the existence of subspecies of *Dichrostachys* which react differently to fire. The subspecies *africana* occurs in moist savanna and, as van Wyk (1971) maintains, is not encouraged by fire and does not succumb to increased grass competition. The subspecies *nyassana* occurs in arid savanna and, as van der Schijff (1957) and Pienaar (1959) claim, is stimulated to coppice and develop profusely after fire but is susceptible to increased grass competition.

The author has also observed the depressive effect of the exclusion of fire and increased grass competition on *D. cinerea* and *A. karroo* in the mixed bushveld and sourish mixed bushveld in the Thabazimbi district of the northwestern Transvaal. However, this phenomenon, of a localized nature in that area, is apparently associated with deep, heavy soils. It does not apply to other bush species in the area like *A. tortilis*, *A. erubescens* (blue thorn), *Grewia flava* (brandy bush) and *Ziziphus mucronata* (buffalo thorn).

Thus a rather contradictory situation exists in the literature concerning the effect of fire on the balance of grass and bush. From personal observations made during extensive travels through southern African savanna and research findings obtained at the University of Fort Hare in the eastern Cape, Trollope summarizes the effect of fire on the grass/bush balance as follows: Generally, the tree and shrub species of savanna are very resistant to fire due to dormant buds at the base of the stem from which coppicing occurs (Trollope 1974). In the higher rainfall regions (above 600 mm yr^{-1}) it is possible to maintain the balance with fire alone, because even though the bush species coppice, rainfall is sufficient and reliable enough for adequate grass material to accumulate under grazing conditions to support frequent fires which burn the coppice growth and control bush seedlings. In the drier rainfall regions (below 600 mm yr^{-1}) which constitute the major portion of South African savanna, rainfall is too low and erratic to support a sufficient number of fires under grazing conditions to prevent the regeneration of bush from coppice and seedling growth. These conclusions led Trollope (1974) to hypothesize that the ecological significance of fire in influencing the grass/bush balance in dry savanna is due to the fact that fire maintains bush at a height and in a state highly acceptable to browsing animals rather than due to the fire effect alone. Under the natural conditions of the past fierce fires destroyed the aerial growth of encroaching bush species, thus providing coppice growth at an acceptable height and in a highly acceptable state for browsing by wild ungulate species. Here the degree to which fire and browsing will influence the balance of grass and bush will be determined by the intensity of the fire, the acceptability of the different coppicing bush species and the intensity of browsing.

Research has been conducted at the University of Fort Hare to test the above hypothesis. In a *Themeda triandra*- dominated grassland moderately invaded by *A. karroo* and other bush species (1 625 ± 119 plants ha^{-1}) a single intense head fire resulted in an 80,8% topkill of trees and shrubs, of which 71,5% coppiced and only 9,3% were destroyed (Trollope 1974). Contiguous plots of the burnt area were subject to treatments comprising continuous browsing with goats (1 goat ha^{-1}), no browsing (control), and annual spring burning. After 5 yr the browsing treatment reduced the original bush density by 90% and the burning treatment reduced bush density by 32%. On the control plot the bush recovered completely. In subsequent years the bush density on the burnt plot has steadily increased despite the annual fires, albeit in the form of dwarf coppicing bushes, whereas the browsing on the third plot has prevented any re-establishment of the bush (Trollope 1980a). The author has noted similar evidence of the effect of fire and browsing on the recovery of bush after intense fires in the Mkuze Game Reserve in northern Natal and in the Thabazimbi district of the northwestern Transvaal.

SEASON OF BURNING

Very little published quantitative information is available on the effect of season of burning on the grass sward in savanna. The results from burning experiments in the Kruger National Park are confounded with grazing and van Wyk (1971) has drawn attention to the cumulative effect of grazing after fire, particularly in the annual spring burns and to a lesser extent in the biennial burns applied in April and August. These effects of grazing make it very difficult to identify the true effect of season of burning on the herbaceous grass layer.

Preliminary results obtained at the University of Fort Hare on the short-term effects of season of burning on the grass sward indicated that there was no difference in effect between fires in midwinter and fires immediately after the first spring rains. However, burns applied during early summer when the grass was actively growing had a disastrous effect on the productivity and basal cover of the grass sward. Further work investigating the effect of fire during a midsummer drought when the grass was dormant suggests that the physiological state of the grass plant, rather than the season of burning, is the most important factor determining the response of the grass to fire. Actively growing plants are apparently more susceptible to damage by fire than dormant plants (Trollope 1980a).

West (1965), reporting on the effect of season of burning on the grass sward in savanna of Zimbabwe, also stressed the importance of burning when the grass is dormant and advocated burning just prior to the spring rains if the objective is to control bush encroachment. This is in conflict with Scott (1971) who stated that burning in winter damages the grass and recommended

burning after the first spring rains to control bush encroachment. However, Scott (1971) quoted data from the Southern Tall
Grassveld of Natal, where the mean grass basal cover of plots
burnt in autumn, late winter and after the first spring rains for
a period exceeding 20 yr was 12,8; 13,0 and 14,4% respectively.
The absence of large differences in the mean grass basal cover
obtained with these different seasons of burning would suggest
that for all practical purposes there is very little difference
in the effect on the grass sward itself when burning before or
after the spring rains while the grass is dormant. This conclusion is supported by Tainton et al (1977) who also found that
there was no difference in the recovery of veld burned before or
after the first spring rains in the Tall Grassveld of Natal.

It is difficult to ascertain the effect of season of burning
on trees and shrubs in savanna because generally it is confounded
with fire intensity. Van Wyk (1971) stated that in the Kruger
National Park fires during late winter and early summer (end of
dry season) were very intense, whereas fires during summer (wet
season) were much less intense. West (1965) postulated that
trees and shrubs are probably more susceptible to fire at the end
of the dry season than at the beginning of the dry season for the
following reasons:- (1) the initial temperature of the plant
tissue is high and therefore closer to the lethal temperatures;
(2) most of the trees have already produced new leaves probably
resulting in the plant reserves being depleted; (3) less protection is provided by the bark because moisture content probably
increases, thereby increasing thermal conductivity of the bark,
with the resumption of active growth; and (4) as new leaves are
very susceptible to heat damage, the trees are more readily
defoliated and are forced to draw upon already depleted plant
reserves to produce new leaves.

Kennan (1971) supports this view, stating that at the Matopos
Research Station in Zimbabwe damage to trees was greatest when
burnt in spring after the trees had flushed. It was difficult
however to assess this effect because a complete kill of plants
was rarely obtained in order to be able to quantify the effect.

The effect of seasonal burning on the production of seed by
grass plants was recorded in an experiment at the University of
Fort Hare where a *T. triandra*- dominant sward produced significantly more *T. triandra* seed when burnt during a drought in
midsummer than when burnt immediately after the rains a month
later. Burning after the first spring rains virtually prevented
production of seed (Trollope 1980a).

In an experiment investigating the effect of burning or
mowing on the seeding of *Anthephora pubescens*, an important grass
species in savanna of the northern Cape Province, Nursey and
Kruger (1973) found that burning at the beginning of the growing
season produced 19% more seed than mowing at this time. They
also found that both treatments significantly depressed the
production of seed when applied later in the season at the early
piping stage.

The effect of fire on seed germination has not been studied
on a seasonal basis but from the point of view of a heat treatment per se West (1951) found that the germination of fresh
T. triandra seed was significantly increased by a heat treatment

involving pre-drying at temperatures of 30 to 40°C. Trollope (1980a) conducted an investigation in savanna of the eastern Cape which indicated that fire may stimulate the germination of *T. triandra*. In a survey conducted on burnt and unburnt veld dominated by *T. triandra*, 18 days after a wild-fire burnt an extensive area, the density of *T. triandra* seedlings was 190,5 m^{-2} in the burnt area and 0,2 m^{-2} in the unburnt area. Germination tests on seed collected from the soil surface in the burnt and unburnt areas showed that only the seed from the unburnt area germinated (2,7% germination). Mowing the unburnt veld to expose the soil surface failed to stimulate any germination of *T. triandra* seed. These results suggest that in the burnt area only seed that was embedded in the ground germinated. The soil would have insulated the seed, which still could have been stimulated by heat.

The effect of fire on the germination of seed of trees and shrubs was investigated by Story (1951). He quoted Sim (1907) as stating that the germination of seeds of *A. karroo* is greatly enhanced by a severe heat treatment. He also found experimentally that treating *A. karroo* seed with either boiling water or a ground fire stimulated germination significantly. He concluded that breaking the hard seed testas made it more permeable and thus stimulated germination. However, the author observed after numerous fires in savanna of the eastern Cape that seeds of *A. karroo* are not necessarily stimulated to germinate after a fire. Macdonald (1980) reported similar findings in the Hluhluwe Game Reserve in Zululand where single fires did not give rise to any significant establishment of seedlings of *A. karroo*, *A. davyi* (corky-bark acacia) and *Euclea divinorum* (magic guarri) during the first postfire season. Possibly the germination is only stimulated when conditions are very dry, fire intensities very high and the burn is followed by adequate moisture.

FREQUENCY OF BURNING

In considering the effect on vegetation of fire frequency, two complementary variables must be born in mind. These include the number of times that the treatment has been applied and the type of management that is used during the interval between fires. For example Kennan (1971) at Matopos Research Station in Zimbabwe found that initially, annual burning had the most deleterious effect on trees and shrubs but that as the grass sward deteriorated with the application of this treatment so it became progressively less damaging to the bush. Therefore the effect of annual burning varied according to the number of times that the treatment was applied.

The effect of the management that is applied during the interval between burns is very important and in most of the experiments in South Africa and Zimbabwe it would appear that this factor is confounded with the frequency of burning. For example van Wyk (1971) stated that in the Kruger National Park overgrazing of the grass sward is a very serious problem in many of the experimentally burnt plots and is correlated with the frequency of burning, the most apparent effect being manifested on the annual and to a lesser extent biennial burning treatments. He drew the general conclusion that factors such as overgrazing, drought and frost complicate the interpretation of the results to such an extent that cause and effect are indistinguishable.

Further evidence of the confounding effect of the type of management during the interval between burns is provided by Robinson et al (1979) who found that under conditions of no grazing in the eastern Cape annual burning resulted in a high rooted frequency of grasses but a low rooted frequency of forbs. Conversely, quadriennial burning caused a significant decrease in grasses and a significant increase in forbs. However, complete protection for 5 yr also resulted in a reduction in the rooted frequency of grasses and in an increase in the rooted frequency of forbs. Therefore it would appear that burning once every 4 yr is confounded with the effect of resting and that the grasses decreased due to their becoming moribund through a lack of defoliation and not because of being burnt once every 4 yr. Tainton and Mentis have also reported a similar observation (this volume, chapter 6).

Different fire intensities resulting from different fuel loads accumulating during the interval between fires are another confounding effect in burning frequency treatments applied under conditions of no grazing. Generally, the longer the interval the greater the fuel load and therefore the greater the fire intensity. Research at the University of Fort Hare clearly illustrates that the reaction of vegetation to burning is significantly correlated with fire intensity (Trollope 1978a).

On the basis of the above discussion it would appear that only limited conclusions can be drawn from the published research data on the effect of frequency of burning in savanna. Van Wyk (1971) presented long-term data (15 yr) on the effect of annual, biennial and triennial burning treatments on the grass component in the Kruger National Park but as already mentioned the effects are confounded with the grazing that occurs after the fire. At Matopos Research Station, Kennan (1971) found that after 14 yr under conditions of no grazing the effect of fire was greater in thornveld which occurs on heavier soils than in sandveld which has lighter soils. In the former, annual burning resulted in very poor basal cover with perennial grass species being replaced by annual grass species. Less frequent burning resulted in increased basal cover and dominance of perennial grass species. Apparently in the dry climate of Matopos the extended period of no defoliation between fires had no significant detrimental effect on the grassland.

Robinson et al (1979) found at the University of Fort Hare that frequent burning favoured the dominance of *Themeda triandra*. Similar results are being obtained in another experiment at the University of Fort Hare and the effect of annual spring burning for 7 yr on grass basal cover and botanical composition of the veld is presented in Table 1 (Trollope 1980a). The significant drop in the basal cover of the control treatment is caused by grazing in winter, a treatment which does not favour lateral tillering in grasses and a resultant good basal cover. The similarity between the results for 1976 and

1978 suggests that the number of annual burns is no longer having an effect on the grass but rather that the burning frequency is now the dominant factor.

Table 1   The effect of annual spring burning for 7 yr on basal cover and botanical composition of the grass sward in the false thornveld of the eastern Cape expressed as a percentage (Trollope 1980a).

| Grass species | Basal Cover (%) | | | | | |
| | 1973 | | 1976 | | 1978 | |
	Control[a]	Burn[b]	Control	Burn	Control	Burn
Themeda triandra	6,0	7,7	5,3	5,2	7,6	6,3
Digitaria eriantha	2,5	1,9	2,0	1,3	1,3	1,2
Sporobolus fimbriatus	1,1	0,8	1,1	0,7	0,5	0,5
Panicum stapfianum	3,4	2,7	0,6	0,2	0,6	0,1
Cymbopogon plurinodis	0,4	2,4	0,6	0,2	0,6	0,2
Eustachys mutica	0,5	0,3	0,6	–	0,3	0,1
Eragrostis chloromelas	0,7	0,2	0,2	0,1	0,3	–
Setaria neglecta	–	–	–	–	0,2	–
Eragrostis obtusa	0,2	0,3	–	–	–	–
Total	14,8	16,4	10,4	7,6	11,5	8,4

[a]Control: One initial spring burn (11th September, 1972) followed by grazing with cattle in winter for 6 yr.
[b]Burn: Annual burning after first spring rains for 7 yr.

At the Matopos Research Station in Zimbabwe, Kennan (1971) found that provided there was sufficient grass fuel to ensure an intense enough fire, all frequencies of burning resulted in top-kill in the smaller trees and shrubs, the majority of which coppiced again.   The only effect of frequency of burning was the degree to which the plants recovered during the interval between fires.   After a period of 15 yr no significant changes which could be attributed to the different burning frequencies had occurred in the densities of trees and shrubs.   Similar conclusions can be drawn from data presented by van Wyk (1971) from the Kruger National Park where after 15 yr the mean change in plant density was only 14,7 ± 4,8%, which is minor in biological terms.

The effect of annual spring burning on the density of various bush species at the University of Fort Hare is presented in Table 2 (Trollope 1980a).

The results in Table 2 indicate that initially annual burning caused a mortality of plants but since 1976 the density has increased significantly.An analysis of the 1977 data showed that 88% of the bushes were less than 0,5 m in height.   The data suggests that a significant proportion of the original trees and shrubs have survived by coppicing and that further increases are due to the successful establishment of new seedlings.   Observations in the field confirm these results (Trollope 1980a).

Table 2   The effect of annual spring burning for 6 yr on the
density of different bush species in the False Thornveld of the Eastern Cape expressed as number of plants
per hectare and percentage change (Trollope 1980a).

Year	Plant Density No. ha^{-1}			
	Control[a]	%Change	Burn[b]	%Change
1972	315		501	
1975	288	− 9	253	−50
1976	463	+ 47	340	−32
1977	1 298	+312	788	+57
1978	1 697	+439	863	+72

[a]Control: One initial spring burn (11/9/1972) followed by
grazing with cattle in winter for 6 yr.
[b]Burn: Annual burning after first spring rains for 7 yr.

TYPE AND INTENSITY OF FIRE

The effect of burning on vegetation depends to a large extent
on the type and intensity of the fire (Trollope 1978a). As mentioned earlier the most common types of fire in savanna are surface fires, burning either as head or back fires, with crown
fires occurring only under extreme fire conditions. Trollope
(1978a) reported on the effects of surface fires, occurring as
either head or back fires, on the grass sward in savanna of the
eastern Cape. Results showed that back fires were more intense
at ground level than head fires, and that this had a significant
depressive effect on the recovery of the grass, resulting in
lower yields.

Savanna trees and shrubs are very sensitive to various types
of fires because of differences in the vertical distribution of
the release of heat energy. Fire research studies in the eastern
Cape have shown that crown and surface head fires caused the
highest kill of stems and branches of A. karroo and other bush
species as compared with back fires. This is because heat energy
in these types of fires is released above the soil surface at
levels closer to the terminal buds of the aerial portions of the
trees and shrubs (Trollope 1980a).

Apparently no published data are available on the effect of
different fire intensities on the grass sward in savanna. Only
unpublished information is available on the effect of fire intensity on savanna trees and shrubs in the eastern Cape where research has shown that there was a highly significant correlation
(P = 0,01) between fire intensity and the topkill of stems and
branches of trees and shrubs (Trollope 1980a). This effect is
illustrated in Figure 1.

The results in Figure 1 show that topkill of bush increased
with greater fire intensities but that the trees and shrubs became less susceptible with an increase in their height. The
greater resistance of the taller trees and shrubs was caused by
the fire-tender terminal buds being borne at increasing levels

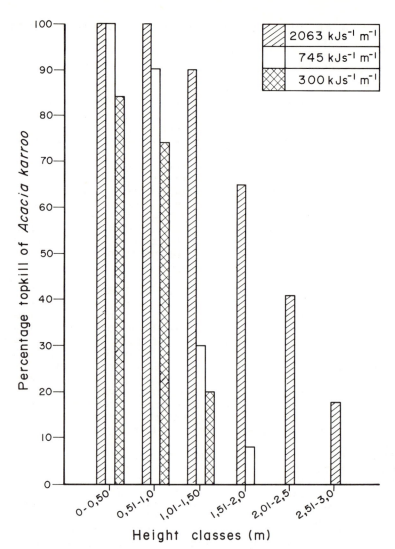

Figure 1.　Topkill of *Acacia karroo* (sweet thorn) in response to different fire intensities occurring during three surface head fires in the false thornveld of the eastern Cape.

above the main heat zone of the flames. These results are corroborated by Macdonald (1980) who found that in Zululand *A. karroo, A. davyi and Euclea divinorum* plants suffered a topkill only when the flame height exceeded plant height.

EFFECTS OF FIRE REGIME ON HERBAGE PRODUCTION AND QUALITY

HERBAGE PRODUCTION

There is limited quantitative information available on the effect of fire regime on the production of herbage in savanna. The short-term effects of the season of burning on the production of a *Themeda triandra*- dominated grass sward has been investigated in savanna of the eastern Cape. There was no significant difference in the production of herbage from areas that had been burnt in midwinter or immediately after the first spring rains. Burning in midsummer caused a 37% reduction in grass yield during the first growing season and the standing biomass of grass at the end of the second growing season was still 31% lower than in the areas burnt during spring and midwinter (Trollope 1980a). Fires in midsummer when the grass plants were actively growing caused a high mortality of elevated shoot apices and grass tillers. Subsequent investigations also showed that fire in midsummer, when the grass was dormant during a drought period, did not affect grass production adversely when compared with burning immediately after the first spring rains (Trollope 1980a). No quantitative data are available on the effect of season of burning on the production of browse by trees and shrubs in savanna.

As mentioned previously the true effect of the frequency of burning on vegetation has not been adequately investigated in savanna of South Africa and only limited quantitative data are available. Research in the eastern Cape has shown that annual burning over a 6 yr period reduced the yield of *Themeda triandra*-dominated grassland in the subsequent growing season by up to 41% compared to grazed grassland. The reduction in yield varied quite markedly from season to season, apparently in response to different amounts of rainfall and varying fire intensities; unfortunately it has not been possible to determine the individual effects of these confounding factors in this study (Trollope 1980a). No information is available on the effect of frequency of fire on the production of browse by savanna trees and shrubs.

Information on the effect of the type of fire on the production of herbage from the herbaceous grass layer is limited to surface fires with and against the wind. Trollope (1978a) found that back fires significantly ($P = 0,01$) reduced the yield of grass by approximately 10% during the first growing season when compared with head fires. The depression in yield was caused by a critical temperature of approximately 95°C being maintained for 20 seconds longer at ground level during the back fire which resulted in a greater mortality of shoot apices and tillers in the grass tufts.

The factor that is possibly responsible for much of the controversy surrounding the use of fire in South Africa is the type of grazing management that is applied after burning. Despite all the controversy, very little quantitative information is available on the effects of different grazing and burning regimes on the grass sward. What particularly interests veld managers is the period of time after fire that should elapse before resuming grazing, and the degree of stocking. Tainton et al (1977) provide some very pertinent results, albeit not from true savanna but from similar veld in the Tall Grassveld of Natal. Experimental results showed that the shorter the interval between harvesting (by mowing) and time of burn, the greater the reduction in total seasonal yield of the grass. This effect is particularly marked in the case of burns applied long before growth begins in spring. These results clearly illustrate the impact of different defoliation treatments after burning and emphasize the significant ecological role of the interaction between burning and grazing on the grass sward.

Similar information is required on the interaction of fire and browsing on the recovery of trees and shrubs after burning. Trollope (1974) has shown that continuous browsing with goats on coppice growth of bush 150 to 300 mm high after one intense fire resulted in maintenance of the coppice growth at that stage. Later results have shown that after 5 yr this treatment destroyed 90% of the palatable bush (Trollope 1980a). As mentioned earlier the profound effect of the interaction of browsing and burning on bush has also been observed with impala and other wild ungulates in the Mkuzi Game Reserve in northern Natal and in the Thabazimbi district of the northwestern Transvaal.

HERBAGE QUALITY

West (1965) stated that the fresh green shoots of new growth on burnt grassland are very high in protein and sought after by grazing animals. He reported that Plowes (1957) found that the average crude protein content of herbage after burning was 19% for 20 common grass species growing on three soil types at the Matopos Research Station in Zimbabwe. Tainton et al (1977) found in the tall grassveld of Natal that initially the protein content of new leaves of grass burnt shortly before (September) and after (October) the first spring rains was ca 2,6% higher than for grass mown at the same times. Conversely, there was no difference in the protein content of new regrowth in grasses that were burnt or mown in late winter (August).

Apparently no information is available on how burning affects the chemical content of browseable material of savanna trees and shrubs.

EFFECTS OF FIRE REGIME ON FAUNAL STRUCTURE AND DYNAMICS

Very limited information is available on the effect of the fire regime on animals in savanna, as most of the attention of biologists has been on the effect of fire on vegetation. This situation led Komarek (1971b) to propose at the fire ecology conference on "Fire in Africa", that more attention must be given to studying animal relationships in fire-induced habitats in order to determine the influence of different fire regimes on animal populations. Despite this appeal a deficiency of information in respect of the savanna of southern Africa still exists.

When considering the effect of fire on fauna it is necessary to distinguish between direct and indirect effects on animal populations. The indirect effects involve the influence of burning on the habitat, including the quantity and quality of the food supply and the microclimate of the habitat. These indirect effects can and often do constitute the major influence of fire on the fauna.

SEASON OF BURNING

An important effect of the season of occurrence of fire on large wild ungulate populations is the influence on the availability of acceptable and nutritious grass herbage. Since 1926 different burning regimes have been applied in the Kruger National Park involving autumn burning and burning after the first spring rains (Brynard 1971), neither of which were found to be completely suitable for the wild ungulate populations. Research results obtained from 1954 to 1975 have led to the development of the present burning policy where 80% of the Kruger National Park is burnt in rotation before the first spring rains, after the first spring rains and during midsummer. The present burning policy was introduced to meet the requirements of both fauna and flora. The most pressing faunal requirement was for a continuous supply of short, nutritious grass, particularly for the declining black wildebeest (Connochaetes gnou) and Burchell's zebra (Equus burchelli) populations (Gertenbach 1979). Burning at different times of the year provides short green grass on a year-long basis.

Brooks and Berry (1980) investigated the responses of 18 ungulate species to fire in the Hluhluwe and Umfolozi Game Reserves in Zululand. The study concentrated on the short-term responses to changes in the availability and quality of food in areas burnt in winter (May to July) and spring (August to September). The study indicated that, overall, the grazing ungulates preferred burnt veld. However, they generally preferred winter burns to spring burns because of the greater difference after the winter fire between the quality of the green flush and to that of the unburnt mature growth of the dormant grasses. The different responses amongst grazing species were associated with habitat preferences, size of home range, dependence on riverine communities in the dry season and tolerance to long grass on the burnt areas in late summer. The mixed feeders impala (Aepyceros melampus) and nyala (Tragelaphus angasi) were less attracted to burnt veld and did not prefer areas burnt during winter or spring. The browsing ungulates were generally either randomly associated with the different burnt areas or showed significant avoidance of them, eg giraffe (Giraffa camelopardalis) (Brooks and Berry 1980).

FREQUENCY OF BURNING

The frequency of burning also influences the availability of suitable grazing for ungulates and can affect the structure of the habitat. Since the proclamation of the Kruger National Park in 1926 different frequencies of burning have been applied with significantly different effects on the wild ungulate population. From 1926 to 1946 annual burning was the accepted policy in the Kruger National Park and was applied as far as was practically possible. Between 1946 and 1954 a policy of infrequent burning, not more than once every 5 yr, was adopted. This change in burning policy caused numerous animals to migrate in search of short, nutritious grass. This effect was particularly serious in the sourveld areas around Pretoriuskop, where the dominant grass, *Hyperthelia dissoluta*, became overgrown and unacceptable for grazing, causing a steady decline in animal numbers (Brynard 1971). Infrequent burning also led to bush encroachment in this area which further reduced the herbaceous grass layer and caused grazing ungulate species to move to more open habitats (Brynard 1971; Komarek 1971b; Gertenbach 1979). The policy of infrequent burning was altered in 1954 to a programme of triennial burning and further changed in 1975 to one of variable burning frequencies ranging from annual and biennial burning in the moist sourveld areas to once every 4 to 8 yr in the dry, sparsely grassed sweetveld areas. These changes in the burning policy of the Kruger National Park have been made partially to provide short, acceptable grazing for the ungulate population (Gertenbach 1979) and to inhibit bush encroachment.

Another important effect of the frequency of fire on faunal structure and dynamics is the extent to which fire may increase competition between animal species by allowing habitat-tolerant species into the preferred areas of more habitat-specific species. For example, various habitat-specific species such as blue duiker *(Cephalophus monticola)*, bushbuck *(Tragelaphus scriptus)* and common and mountain reedbuck *(Redunca arundinum* and *R. fulvorufula)* have declined or disappeared from the Hluhluwe and Umfolozi Game Reserves since the 1950s. Increased frequency of burning since the mid 1950s may have been a contributing factor. The frequent burning of long grass and forest margins is likely to have reduced the cover required for bushbuck and the other species and attracted competitors into these habitats (Brooks and Berry 1980).

TYPE AND INTENSITY OF FIRE

As with the other components of the fire regime the study of the effect of the type and intensity of fire on the structure and dynamics of the fauna in savanna has not received much attention in South Africa.

Brynard (1971) stated that one of the consequences of the infrequent burning policy applied in the Kruger National Park from 1946 to 1954 was the occurrence of intense fires in response to the accumulation of excessively high fuel loads of old moribund grass. During the spring of 1954 numerous wild-fires burnt out approximately 5 180 km^2, 25% of the Kruger National Park. Considerable numbers of wild animals were destroyed by these intense fires and on two occasions 40 animals comprising impala, lion *(Panthera leo)*, elephant, *(Loxodonta africana)*, kudu *(Tragelaphus strepsiceros)*, waterbuck *(Kobus ellipsiprymnus)*, steenbok

(*Raphicerus campestris*), roan antelope (*Hippotragus equinus*), grey duiker (*Sylvicapra grimmia*) and warthog (*Phacochoerus aethiopicus*) were found dead or maimed (Brynard 1971). No information is available on the types of fire that occurred during these accidental burns but it could be expected that they were primarily swift, intense surface head fires and crown fires with considerable flame heights, making escape through the flames by even highly agile animals difficult.

Because of these high intensity fires the policy of infrequent burning in 1954 was replaced by one of more frequent burning applied after the first spring rains so as to ensure cooler fires and less adverse effects on fauna (Brynard 1971). Even in the current burning policy, implemented since 1975, where some of the burns are applied before the first spring rains, the intensity of the fires is generally lower because of reduced fuel loads caused by more frequent burning.

Gandar (1982) showed in detail the effects of a low intensity fire on the animal population of the Nylsvley Nature Reserve in the northern Transvaal. Studies conducted on burnt and unburnt sites in the *Burkea* savanna showed that there were no significant differences in the bacterial biomass and microbial activity at the two sites. The beetle population was not affected by the fire until two months after the burn. This result suggested that the larvae and pupae, which live in the soil, survived the fire, but that later the population declined in response to a depletion of food or desiccation of the soil. Observations showed that the fire had minimal direct effects on the termite population because these insects could quickly take refuge in subterranean galleries below the soil surface. Even foraging termites in wood were not affected because apparently very few termites were present on the soil surface and in upper ground layers when the fire started in the early evening. Subsequent foraging by termites during the first month after the fire was significantly reduced because of decreased forage and shelter.

Surveys conducted on two tree species, *Dombeya rotundifolia* (wild pear) and *Ochna pulchra* (lekkerbreek), which were 2 to 4 m high, showed that the insect population of the trees was completely eliminated by the burn despite the fact that the intensity of the fire was low and temperatures were significantly less than 260°C in tree canopies (Gandar 1982).

Other studies showed that only 30% of the grasshopper population was killed during the fire. This was possibly because the majority of the grasshoppers were highly mobile adults, the patchy burn provided adequate escape routes and burning at night reduced predation by insectivorous birds like the forktailed drongo (*Dicrurus adsimilis*). The egg pods of grasshoppers and stick insects in the soil also survived the fire but many nymphs were killed. Conversely, there was a high concentration of grasshoppers on the unburnt portions of the fire mosaic but the average biomass of grasshoppers for the entire burn decreased by 58% after four months, apparently in response to the high mortality of nymphs and increased predation by birds like grey hornbill (*Tockus nasutus*) on the burnt patches (Gandar 1982).

The small mammal population was not directly affected by the fire per se but composition and size of the population varied according to the plant cover and food available after the fire (Gandar 1982).

Pre- and postfire censuses showed that the impala population increased by approximately 93% on the burnt areas. However, the impala only moved onto the burn in significant numbers 10 days after the fire, when the grass commenced rapid regrowth, and reached a peak population after 20 to 30 days. Animal numbers gradually decreased after 30 days but the density of impala was still relatively high three months after the fire. The impalas preferred burnt *Burkea* savanna to burnt *Acacia* savanna possibly because the forage grasses, like *Setaria perennis*, commenced growth sooner after the fire and there was a greater diversity of plant species in this savanna type (Gandar 1982).

ADAPTIVE RESPONSES OF ORGANISMS TO FIRE REGIMES

ADAPTIVE RESPONSES OF PLANTS

Gill (1974) is of the opinion that many so-called adaptations of plants to fire are instead life cycle characteristics which ensure species survival in the face of fire rather than being specific adaptations to fire per se. This viewpoint seems to apply to the responses of plants to fire in the savanna of South Africa. For example the germination of numerous *Acacia* spp is enhanced by a heat treatment of the hard seed coat as experienced during a fire but a similar effect is also obtained if the seed passes through the digestive tract of a ruminant. Similarly the coppicing habit of most savanna trees and shrubs makes them particularly adapted to fire but this regenerative trait makes these species equally adapted to mechanical damage caused by frost, elephants or bulldozers! Nevertheless, fire does have a specific and unique effect on the ecosystem that is different from other forms of defoliation. Therefore, it is likely that there are fire-specific adaptive responses amongst plants. Unfortunately these have not been well studied or reported in respect of plants of the savanna.

Further, plant species are adapted to the components of the fire regime comprising season of burn, intensity of fire, frequency of burn (Gill 1974) and the type of fire rather than to fire per se. Unfortunately a serious lack of quantitative information on adaptive responses of plants to the fire regime (Frost 1979) makes possible only a general descriptive account for savanna.

Season of burning

The adaptations that enable plants to survive different seasons of burning depend upon both the growth form and the physiological state of the plant at the time of fire. Grasses and other perennial herbaceous plants are better adapted to intense dry season fires than trees and shrubs because grasses have dormant buds at or below the soil surface that are largely protected from the fire (West 1971). Conversely trees and shrubs have buds located in the vulnerable aerial portions of the plant. Their susceptibility is more marked at the end of the dry season when trees and shrubs have initiated the spring flush of leaves while grasses are still dormant and fire resistant (West 1965). On the contrary fires burning during the moist growing season are more detrimental to the herbaceous grass layer than the woody stratum. At this time the shoot apices of the grass plants have been elevated to a vulnerable height above the soil surface and Daubenmire (1968), West (1965) and Tainton et al (1977) all mention the harmful effect of burning when the grass is actively growing.

Trees and shrubs are better adapted to burning at this time because the aerial growing points are generally well above the slow-spreading and low intensity fires that occur during the moist growing season.

Frequency of burning

Grasses are especially adapted to frequent burning because of the tillering habit of these types of plants. Species differences do occur and Robinson et al (1979) found in the eastern Cape that *Themeda triandra* is more resistant to frequent annual burning than *Cymbopogon plurinodis*.

Many savanna tree and shrub species are adapted to frequent burning by being able to coppice repeatedly from dormant buds located at the collar region of the junction between the stem and roots of the plant. Observations made in the eastern Cape show that *A. karroo* specimens have been able to survive eight annual fires by coppicing after each burn.

Type and intensity of fire

The type of fire greatly influences the vertical distribution of the heat energy released during combustion and this has a significant effect on the ability of plants to survive different types of fire. Grasses and herbaceous plants are more tolerant of crown fires and surface head fires because the majority of the heat energy release during these fires is well above ground level and away from the shoot apices of these species. Trees and shrubs are, on the contrary less adapted to these fires because the shoot apices of the stems and branches are more likely to be in the zone of maximum heat release.

Most savanna trees and shrubs are resistant to back fires because the release of heat energy occurs below the level of the terminal growing points of the stems and branches. Experience and research in the eastern Cape showed that *A. karroo* savanna is hardly affected by back fires whereas head fires burning under the same conditions cause a significant topkill of trees up to a height of 3 m (Trollope 1974). Grasses and herbaceous plants are predictably less adapted to back fires because the heat energy is released closer to the soil surface. Trollope (1978a) found that back fires significantly retarded the recovery of grass as compared to head fires.

Adaptive characteristics that enable plants to survive high
intensity fires are those which provide maximum protection to the
living plant tissue. West (1971) stated that trees exhibit different degrees of heat tolerance and this is correlated with the
thickness and composition of the bark. Woody species like *Acacia
sieberana* (paperbark acacia) and *Cussonia spicata* (cabbage tree)
have very thick, well-insulated bark and are highly resistant to
intense fires. Conversely, *Ehretia rigida* (wild lilac) and
Grewia occidentalis (four corner) have thin bark and the stems
and branches succumb to even low intensity fires.

The most important adaptive response that enables savanna
tree and shrub species to survive high intensity fires is the
ability of the majority of species to coppice from axillary buds
located at the collar region. When the above-ground portions of
the plant are killed during a fire, coppicing occurs in the
absence of apical repression and the numerous stems produced lead
to the recovery of the plant.

Cryptogeal germination by certain savanna tree and shrub
species enable seedlings to withstand intense fires. This type
of germination involves the production of an apparent radicle
from a seed lying on the soil surface and the subsequent development of new shoots from below ground level. This ensures that
the root crown develops below the soil surface and therefore protects the dormant buds from fire. This pyrophytic habit occurs
in *Combretum molle* (velvet bushwillow) and *C. collinum* (bushwillow), both found in South African savannas (Jackson 1974).

ADAPTIVE RESPONSES OF ANIMALS

As with plants, the majority of traits that enable animals to
survive a burning regime are not necessarily limited to with-
standing fire. Nevertheless specific fire-adaptive traits may
exist among animals in the savanna areas which have not yet been
recognized. For example Komarek (1971b) quotes Evans (1964) who
found that certain fire beetles of the genus *Melanophila* have
infrared sensory pits on their hind legs which enable them to
detect and locate forest fires over extensive distances. This
attraction to fires is apparently in response to reproductive
processes such as courtship and mating (Komarek 1971b) because
these insects mate only in the presence of smoke (E V Komarek,
personal communication, 1978).

Very little attention has been given to the adaptive responses of animals to fire in South Africa. Most sedentary species,
particularly invertebrates, survive fire either by selecting
protected sites such as termite mounds or bush clumps or by
sheltering in cracks in the soil, in the bark of trees or the
basal tufts of grasses. Larger mobile animals frequently avoid
fire by moving to unaffected areas (Frost 1979).

Observations made in eastern Cape savanna showed that rodents
survived fierce surface head fires by taking refuge in underground burrows. Hares, duikers and steenbok were able to successfully escape through the flames of back fires but it is sus-
pected that they would not have been able to withstand the intense flames of a raging head fire. Conversely tortoise are

apparently well adapted to fires because on two occasions specimens 10 cm and 15 cm in diameter survived surface head fires with intensities of 3 804 kJ s^{-1} m^{-1} and 1 068 kJ s^{-1} m^{-1} respectively. The first fire was an extremely intense burn and the tortoise was unaffected except for minor heat-frayed portions on the edge of the shell. Presumably the tortoise retracted their heads and legs into the shell during the fire.

The phenomenon of fire melanism reported by Hocking (1964) in grasshoppers on burnt areas in central Africa is an adaptive response enabling these insects to better survive the effects of fire. Melanism is the process whereby the cuticles of insects change in colour from light to dark shades. In South Africa Gandar (1982) has recorded the occurrence of melanism among grasshoppers after a fire in the Nylsvley Nature Reserve in the northern Transvaal. In this case the adaptive advantage is believed to be that the insects are less conspicuous and, therefore, less prone to predation by insectivorous birds.

EFFECTS OF FIRE REGIME ON THE EDAPHIC ENVIRONMENT

A perusal of the annotated bibliography of fire in South Africa by Schirge and Penderis (1978) indicates that there is very limited information available on the effect of fire on the edaphic environment in the savanna areas.

In attempting to assess the effect of fire on the edaphic environment it is necessary to distinguish between the direct effects of fire and the indirect effects resulting from the exposure of and the addition of partially burnt plant material to the soil surface.

It would appear that surface and crown fires have very little direct effect on the soil because soil temperatures change very little during a fire. West (1965) cited results from various centres in the world where the soil temperatures recorded during surface fires seldom exceeded 100°C immediately below the soil surface. Cook (1939b) found on the Transvaal highveld that even when the temperature at the base of a grass tuft rose to ca 600°C, there was very little increase in the soil temperature at a depth of only 5 mm. The reason for this is that soil conducts heat very poorly and has a high specific heat. Observations in the eastern Cape indicate that the soil temperature is even less affected when the soil is moist because temperatures cannot exceed 100°C until all the moisture is boiled off, which is most unlikely during a normal surface grass fire.

No quantitative data are available on soil temperatures after a fire in the savanna areas but Daubenmire (1968) states that burning increases postfire soil temperatures by removing the vegetal cover and litter on the soil surface. Gandar (1982) reported that the albedo on burnt and unburnt areas in the northern Transvaal was 7 and 13% respectively. This explained why postburn soil temperatures are higher than preburn temperatures.

West (1965) stated that burning can have an adverse effect on postfire soil moisture content due to reduced infiltration, increased runoff and increased evapotranspiration. This is supported by results from the Nylsvley Nature Reserve in the northern Transvaal where Gandar (1982) found that soil moisture content tended to be lower in a burnt than in an unburnt area.

Studies in the Kruger National Park by Webber (1979) showed that moisture content at the soil surface of both red apedal and duplex soils was significantly lower in areas burnt biennially in December and annually in August respectively, than in protected control areas. Other studies limited to the red apedal soils also showed that the moisture content in the B horizon of the burnt areas was 105% higher than in the areas protected from fire. These differences in moisture content between the surface and B horizon were ascribed to the fact that the burnt areas comprised open tree communities with an actively growing grass sward that depleted the moisture at the soil surface. On the other hand, the areas protected from fire were dominated by denser tree and shrub communities that drew on moisture supplies from subsurface levels via deeper root systems.

Webber (1979) found that the effect of burning on soil erosion in the Kruger National Park was very dependent on soil type. In duplex soils annual burning in August caused a 33% greater loss of soil from the orthic and perched grey horizons when compared with adjacent areas that were protected from fire. Conversely in deep, red apedal soils there were no significant differences in soil depth in areas burnt biennially in December compared to areas that were protected from burning. Duplex soils are highly erodible because when the aerial grass cover is burnt off in August the surface develops a dry, slightly hard surface crust. When this surface crust is broken by animal trampling or wind, a loose, friable surface is exposed which is extremely susceptible to water erosion during early summer rainstorms.

Webber (1979) also studied the effect of burning on the chemical properties of soils in the Kruger National Park but no firm conclusions can be drawn from his data. Nevertheless, burning may have a significant effect on the recycling of minerals in savanna ecosystems through combustion of plant material and deposition of soluble ash on the soil surface. Estimates of the organic constituents of grass material that were lost and that remained after head and back surface fires in the eastern Cape are presented in Table 3 (Trollope 1980a).

Table 3   The organic and inorganic constituents of grass fuel lost and remaining after different types of surface fires expressed as a percentage.

Constituents	Head fire	Back fire
	%	%
Organic matter lost	83,4	87,8
Organic matter remaining	5,6	1,2
Mineral ash	11,0	11,0

The results in Table 3 give the approximate proportion of organic matter that was lost and indicate the greater degree of combustion that occurred during back fires, which produced grey ash in contrast to the darker coloured ash from head fires. Daubenmire (1968) stated that nitrogen and sulphur are volatilized during a fire but in the case of nitrogen not all of this element is lost and partially combusted ash will contain 0,01 to 0,76% nitrogen on a dry mass basis. The amounts of these elements lost during a fire would have negligible effects, based on the figures presented in Table 3. Daubenmire (1968) further stated that the other macronutrients are not volatilized during a fire but are changed into simple salts that are water soluble and hence immediately available at the soil surface. Using the data presented in Table 3 and assuming a grass fuel load of 3 000 kg ha^{-1}, which is that recommended for controlling bush encroachment in the eastern Cape, the quantities of ash deposited on the soil surface after head and back fires are 498 kg ha^{-1} and 366 kg ha^{-1} respectively. Unfortunately only the nitrogen content of the ash was determined. The ash from the head and back fires comprised 0,565 and 0,137% nitrogen respectively (Trollope 1980a), which is equivalent to 2,8 kg ha^{-1} and 0,5 kg ha^{-1} of nitrogen. However, in the region of 30 kg ha^{-1} of nitrogen is likely to be lost to the atmosphere when such veld is burned. Estimates of the possible amounts of phosphate, potassium, calcium and magnesium remaining in the ash can also be made. With the mineral content of 11% presented in Table 3, the quantity of minerals deposited on the soil surface after head and back fires with a grass fuel load of 3 000 kg ha^{-1} is 330 kg ha^{-1}. Based on chemical analyses presented by Weinmann (1955) and Bishop (1980), the mineral content of mature grass fuel and the equivalent yield of the individual macro-elements can be estimated as follows:

$$
\begin{array}{llll}
\text{Phosphate} & = 0,2\% & = & 6 \text{ kg ha}^{-1} \\
\text{Potassium} & = 1,2\% & = & 36 \text{ kg ha}^{-1} \\
\text{Calcium} & = 0,4\% & = & 12 \text{ kg ha}^{-1} \\
\text{Magnesium} & = 0,2\% & = & 6 \text{ kg ha}^{-1}
\end{array}
$$

It is difficult to assess the biological significance of these quantities of minerals without knowing the responses of fauna and flora to varying amounts of the different elements. In agronomic terms the quantities of nitrogen appear to be insignificant but the amounts of the other elements suggest that more attention should be given to the effect of fire on mineral cycling in savanna.

EFFECT OF FIRE REGIME ON WATER YIELD AND QUALITY

The annotated bibliography of fire in South African ecosystems by Schirge and Penderis (1978) indicates that no research data have been published on the effect of fire regime on yield and quality of water in savanna. There clearly is a need for such research to be done. Wide fluctuations in streamflow, periodic floods and high silt loads are a feature of the savanna regions. Fire regime could well have a pronounced effect on the hydrological features and requires assessment.

Chapter 8 Fire in Forest

J. E. GRANGER

INTRODUCTION

This chapter deals only with the indigenous forests of South Africa. Bioclimatic studies such as those of Poynton (1971), Phillips (1973) and Schulze and McGee (1978) have described climatic zones suitable for the existence of indigenous forest, the areas of which are greatly restricted in South Africa by low rainfall and in parts, by excessive cold in winter. For the most part the forest zone occurs as a narrow belt around the eastern and southern seaboard of South Africa, extending inland as far as the Great Escarpment (Figure 1). Although the area includes parts of both the summer and winter rainfall areas, the climate for the most part is humid or subhumid. The severity of frost varies from none to severe for relatively short periods. Severe droughts do occur, albeit infrequently (Schulze and McGee 1978). If, however, a comparison is made between the present occurrence of forest and these bioclimatic zones, it appears that very little of this potential is actually realized (Huntley, this volume, chapter 1).

One possible explanation for the restriction of the area under forest may lie in the major fluctuations of climate which are known to have occurred since the Quaternary (Cooke 1964; Tyson 1978; van Zinderen Bakker 1978). The effects of such change may have been direct in that they produced conditions that were physiologically unsuitable for forest (Cooke 1964). In addition, they may have played an indirect role in creating conditions that favoured the extensive establishment of grassland and other similar readily combustible communities which in many places bordered on the forests. Consequently, the periodic fires that occurred in such communities caused by lightning strikes and rock falls may have been sufficiently frequent to restrict the distribution of forest.

However, no matter what the role of past climates in determining the distribution of forests, such changes can only be regarded as a partial explanation. The growing body of archaeological evidence leaves little doubt that it is man's use of fire and exploitation of the forest that is primarily responsible for the present limited occurrence of this vegetation type (Hall, this volume, chapter 3).

CHARACTERISTICS OF FIRE REGIMES AND FIRE BEHAVIOUR

ANTHROPOGENIC FIRES

While it can be accepted that the association between man and fire is very old, it is virtually impossible to affix a definite age to the relationship. In the forest biome as delineated by Huntley (this volume, chapter 1), a few Early Stone Age but a greater number of Middle Stone Age sites have been found at various localities throughout the area (Klein 1972a, 1979b; Deacon 1976, 1978, 1979; Inskeep 1978). Thus it is possible that anthropogenic fires have been a feature of this biome for the last 150 000 to 180 000 yr (Maggs 1977). If such is indeed the case, then any assessment of the long-term influences of fire on

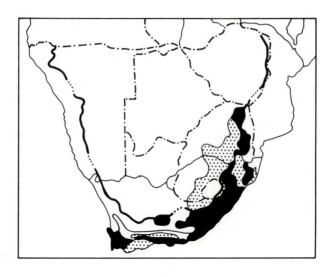

ZONE	CLIMATE TYPE	MOISTURE INDEX	THERMAL EFFICIENCY INDEX	FROST	APPROXIMATE MEAN MONTHLY MINIMUM TEMP. FOR COLDEST MONTHS
optimal ▮	subtropical warmer temperate (mesothermal)	>40-0	1140-570	occasional to light	5°C 0°C
intermediate ▦	cooler temperate (mesothermal)	-20 0	590-997	moderate to severe	0°C < -5°C

Figure 1   Distribution of areas where the climate is suitable for the existence of forest.   The thick line indicates the position of the Great Escarpment (based on Poynton 1971 and Schulze and McGee 1978).

forest must be made concomitantly with an assessment of the effects associated with major changes in climate.   Evidence for such changes within the biome during this period is summarized by Inskeep (1978).

Probably of even greater importance than the period during which fire has played an important role, however, is the frequency and seasonality of anthropogenic fires.   Hall (this volume, chapter 3) contends that nomadic Stone Age peoples used fire as a tool to manipulate the environment by maintaining grasslands in a state attractive to the large herds of animals which were hunted, and to possibly induce flushes of edible herbs.   Furthermore, he argues that because of seasonal changes in climate, vegetation, game movement and possibly the availability of suitable rock shelters, these people followed specific migration routes with some degree of regularity.   Such proposals suggest a number of implications.

First of all, anthropogenic fires would have occurred at specific times of the year in different geographical areas and at fairly regular intervals. In the case of the summer rainfall area in the Drakensberg and its foothills, burning in the uplands would have taken place in spring and in the lowlands in winter (Carter 1970). In the southern Cape, however, a different pattern, determined largely by the winter rainfall, would have existed. Here spring and early summer burning (October to December) would have been the rule. During this period conditions are climatically suitable for fire; regeneration of heath from seed is suppressed (Kruger 1977b) and some summer weather and a wet winter lie ahead during which a grass cover suitable for grazing can develop.

As regards the frequency of burning in Natal, Hall (this volume, chapter 3) suggests that anthropogenic fires in the lowlands were less frequent than in the uplands. Beyond this it is not possible to determine what the rotations may have been. To what extent such a model is applicable to the southern Cape is difficult to judge. Here an important factor may have been the dense stands of heath which spring up soon after burning and displace grass cover, particularly when burning has taken place in late summer or autumn. Thus, other than to burn early in the dry season and kill the plants before the seed set, there may have been a tendency to burn certain areas very frequently or to burn when conditions would be likely to result in a very hot fire.

A second characteristic of these Stone Age fires is that deliberate burning was apparently almost exclusively confined to grassland communities. Thus damage to the forests would have been confined to the margins and only in exceptionally dry years would there have existed the possibility of fire entering the body of the forest. Again, it is feasible that this situation differed from summer rainfall to winter rainfall regions. In the summer rainfall areas the fringing vegetation would mainly comprise grasses which in most fires would have been rapidly consumed at comparatively low temperatures and without producing very tall flames. In the southern Cape, however, where the fringing vegetation would in many instances be tall heath (Phillips 1963; Cameron 1980), hotter fires of longer duration capable of setting the canopy alight would have been possible. The importance of these facts would obviously be considerably modified by the time period between fires. If in some areas this was fairly short as Hall (this volume, chapter 3) implies, then the opportunity for adequate quantities of potentially destructive fuel to accumulate would have been reduced.

Whatever the damage wrought to the forests by Stone Age man it seems that because of his low population density (Carter 1978) and the fact that there were no pressures that would have made it necessary for him to change the balance of the communities making up his environment, his impact was probably minimal. The same cannot, however, be said of the Iron Age farmers and white settlers who subsequently appeared in this biome, the former during the 2nd century AD (Hall, this volume, chapter 3) and the latter in the mid-17th century. As pastoralists, the Iron Age peoples used fire extensively to maintain the grasslands in a suitable condition for grazing for as long as possible. In addition, they planted some crops and so made use of fire to clear patches of fertile forest soil for planting. They also exploited the timber within the forests for the construction of huts and stockades and for the production of charcoal required in "smelting" (Hall 1980). As the numbers of people and domestic stock increased man would have exerted an ever increasing effect on the forests, first in the lowlands and later in the higher regions of southern Africa (Hall, this volume, chapter 3).

With the arrival of the white settlers, many of whom were graziers who were quick to follow the example of their Iron Age neighbours (Holden 1855; Sim 1907; Clark 1959; McKenzie 1978), the scale and frequency of veld burning increased. Exploitation of the forests for timber also increased at an alarming rate, this being particularly so in the southern Cape. As the forests were opened up, the resulting spaces were colonized by communities in which heath and grass species predominated. Thus potentially hazardous fuel conditions developed within the body of the forest and as is well known, these areas were regularly burnt by graziers and hunters (Phillips 1931, 1963, 1965, 1974; Edwards 1967).

It therefore emerges that over the past 2 000 yr man has applied a particularly drastic pattern of exploitation and burning which has led to the eradication of much forest. The use of fire in this process has been both direct and indirect and in view of the latter, it is possible that the retreat of forest margins is closely correlated with the burning regimes practised in the adjoining grasslands.

NATURAL FIRES

The term "natural" is used here to describe fires started and influenced by factors other than man. Among the more important factors in this biome are lightning, rock falls and climate (Edwards, this volume, chapter 2).

Lightning

West (1965) has drawn attention to the numerous records that exist of fires caused by lightning, while Downing (1972, 1980) ascribed the present distribution of woody vegetation in the Umfolozi Game Reserve to the frequency of lightning-started fires. More recently, however, the studies by Berry and Macdonald (1979) and Macdonald et al (1980) on causal factors and by Hall (1980) on archaeological evidence tend to contradict this view. Likewise, in the Natal Midlands Moll (1976) and in the Natal Drakensberg Nanni (1956), Killick (1963), Mentis et al (1974) and Scotcher (1980) all report the occurrence of lightning-started fires but point out that they are very infrequent and therefore not a particularly significant ecological factor.

Similar conclusions were made by Moll et al (1980) for the southern and western Cape and by Phillips (1931, 1974) for the

Knysna forests.   Such views, however, contrast markedly with other information from the southern Cape provided by le Roux (1979a), Kruger and Bigalke (this volume, chapter 5) and Horne (1981), and from the Etosha Game Reserve, albeit in a different biome, by Siegfried (1980).   In Figure 2 the data of Horne (1981), Berry and Macdonald (1979) and Scotcher (1980) are compared.   In Figure 2A monthly totals of accidental fires and fires due to incendiarism are summed and expressed as a percentage of all fires.   This is done because in some instances the differentiation between incendiarism and an accident is vague and because both seem to reflect the seasonal changes in susceptibility of vegetation to fire.   A comparison of Figures 2A and B shows that the majority of fires in all areas are caused by man.   The fact that the incidence of such fires appears far greater in Zululand than elsewhere is probably due to the difficulties in regulating the use of fire in the countryside which surrounds the Hluhluwe complex, which for the most part is occupied by a large population of haphazardly settled black pastoralists.

Data presented in Figure 2B suggest that the southern Cape experiences a far higher incidence of lightning fires than elsewhere.   This possibility concurs with le Roux's (1979a) contention that the catchment areas of the southern Cape forest region experience more than double the number of lightning fires than the national average for Forestry Department land (Edwards, this volume, chapter 2).   An explanation for this trend is not immediately obvious but it may lie in the nature of the topography as suggested by Horne (1981) or in the presence of a more readily combustible fuel type.   The above data also reveal a very marked seasonal trend in the number of lightning fires occuring in the southern Cape, with fires being most common between late spring and early autumn (November to March).   In the summer rainfall areas, on the other hand, there does not appear to be a similar clearly defined seasonal pattern.   This fact does somewhat contradict observations made by Killick (1963), Mentis et al (1974), Moll (1976) and myself that such fires generally occur during spring and summer (September to February).   The explanation for this discrepancy may lie in the fact that lightning-started fires occurring during this period of the year are soon extinguished by the rain which accompanies the thunderstorms (Moll 1976; Horne 1981).   Furthermore, grasslands at this time are either actively growing or already green and consequently do not easily catch fire.   Thus many of the ground lightning strikes which occur over upland Natal (Edwards, this volume, chapter 2) may start fires which go undetected.   Such a possibility is also suggested by the large number of lightning-killed canopy trees seen, for example, in the Ngome Forest.

Rockfalls

Fires started by rockfalls are known to occur in the forest biome.   Such falls may occur as a result of extremes in soil moisture on steep slopes causing rocks to become dislodged, as a result of normal geological weathering of steep rock faces or in response to seismic disturbances.

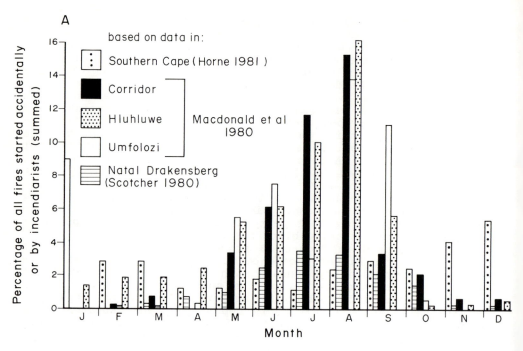

Figure 2A   Monthly percentage of accidental fires and fires started by incendiarists.

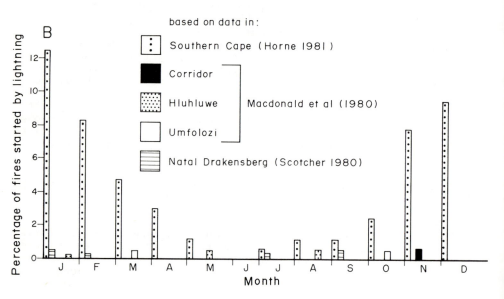

Figure 2B   Monthly percentage of fires started by lightning.

While such fires have been reported from areas situated throughout the biome (Wicht 1945; Nanni 1956; Phillips 1965, 1974; Moll et al 1980) they seem to be rare.

Climate

The importance of climate lies not only in producing atmospheric conditions conducive to fire but also in determining quantity and quality of fuel.

In the summer rainfall areas the greatest risk of accidental and incendiarist-started fires exists during the dry winter and early spring months (Macdonald et al 1980; Scotcher 1980). Spring fires may be especially hazardous due to high velocity, hot, dry bergwinds which occur at this time. Likewise in the southern Cape, le Roux (1979a), Horne (1981) and Kruger and Bigalke (this volume, chapter 5) have drawn attention to the importance of the seasonal distribution of rainfall and wind in determining the incidence of fire. While the driest conditions invariably prevail during the summer months (when a high percentage of accidental incendiarist fires occur), it is not unusual for Fohnlike bergwinds to occur during the wet winter months (Phillips 1931; le Roux 1979a), thereby producing conditions suitable for burning. Indeed, the relatively high proportion of manmade fires occurring between June and September in the Groot Swartberg area may very likely be correlated with such conditions (Horne 1981).

Drought also may be regarded as an important factor in this biome for although prolonged droughts are infrequent, when they do occur they offer the opportunity of an extended burning season in grasslands. Furthermore, such droughts may be broken by rain that is accompanied by thunderstorms and ground lightning and as a result, otherwise low or nonhazardous fuels may be ignited. Very prolonged droughts may increase the vulnerability of forest to fire by producing exceptionally high falls of leaves, twigs, branches and bark, thereby increasing the quantity of ground fuel. With associated conditions of low relative humidity and high air temperatures, such material is potentially destructive if ignited.

FIRE BEHAVIOUR

South African forests are, for the most part, evergreen. Thus, even in the drier facies of the southern Cape, fire in the body of the forest (except in islands of easily combustible vegetation) is rare. As has already been mentioned the majority of fire damage to forests occurs along the margins and therefore the type, quantity, quality and vertical and horizontal distribution of fuel at this interface is important.

Forest fires may be grouped under three categories, namely crown fires, ground fires and flank fires, all of which may be either hot or cool. The generally extensive but rare crown fires do little harm to the soil and to young trees even though high temperatures may be reached (Phillips 1931). On the other hand, ground fires, which are invariably associated with crown fires, generally result in very high temperatures, often with long dwell periods where individual trees take fire. Depending on the depth and moisture content of the litter layer such fires may even affect the root mass (Phillips 1931; Macdonald 1978a). However Beadle (1940) has stated that below the soil surface temperatures fall off very sharply.

Flank fires are generally characterized by their very rapid advance to the forest margin where they may flare up to considerable heights, resulting in severe scorching and even death of canopy trees. Because such fires often occur frequently in the same area and because the forest floor and litter are often damp, the quantity and quality of fuel generally tends to restrict penetration into the forest to a few metres. Where, however, drought and hot, dry, windy conditions prevail, extensive ground and crown fires may develop. The tendency for fires to often approach from the same direction may prove critical for many forest trees. Death may follow as a result of progressive leaf loss or because of repeated burns on one side of the trunk, which ultimately make it possible for a variety of organisms to attack the core of the tree.

The consequences of opening the body of the forest and thereby increasing the quantity of fuel have already been noted. Where the fuel contains volatile oils, which is often the case in heath species, very hot fires may be produced. The importance of the vertical distribution of such fuel has also been mentioned.

In contrast to the hot fire of the intensive fire regime (Hall, this volume, chapter 3) is the so-called "cool" burn developed by conservation managers to preserve indigenous forest. Such fires, usually referred to as fuel reduction burns, are applied to small areas when potentially hazardous fuel loads are green and/or damp from rain or dew and wind velocities are low. Under such conditions a slow-moving, easily controlled fire with low flames burns up to the forest margin, where it dies out.

In general then it may be concluded that fires started by lightning and rockfalls have probably had little influence on the present distribution of indigenous forests. To a slightly lesser degree, the same may be said of fires applied by Stone Age peoples. However, the Iron Age and white colonists are probably responsible for drastic changes in the forests as a result of the combined effects of exploitation, an increase in the frequency of burning, the deliberate application of very hot fires and an expansion of the fire season into periods beyond that which was likely to have been determined by lightning and rockfalls. Yet despite evidence of change, it is not possible to conclude that the present grassland areas of South Africa were once all forest, as suggested by Acocks (1975).

Evidence provided by Tainton and Mentis (this volume, chapter 6) on the abundance and distribution of grassland vertebrates in the highland sourveld of Natal shows that a forest-grassland mosaic has existed for a very long time. What cannot be disputed, however, is that the ratio of forest to grassland has altered considerably in the recent past.

ADAPTIVE RESPONSES OF ORGANISMS TO FIRE REGIME

FLORA

Microflora

Because fire occurs infrequently in forest it seems unlikely that forest microorganisms would be fire-tolerant. As pointed out by several authors (see Cass et al, this volume, chapter 14) lethal temperatures are likely only at the soil surface and a few mm below. Consequently, that portion of the population occurring at greater depths could be expected to replace those which had been destroyed. Since forest soils are likely to be favourable habitats for large numbers of such organisms, microorganisms are probably rapidly replaced. This concurs with data given by Meiklejohn (1955). Indeed, there is some evidence (Corbet 1934 cited by Meiklejohn 1955) that burning may even lead to an increase in the numbers of such organisms.

Macroflora

The ability of forest forbs and trees to survive fire varies considerably and is determined by features such as thickness and moisture content of the bark, root depth, ability to coppice, nature of the seed coat, allelopathy and age of the plant. The effectiveness of these features is, however, dependent on the maximum temperature achieved during the fire and the "dwell time" of abnormal temperatures. West (1965) states that the thermal death point for average mesophytic plants lies between 50 and 60°C. Cambium temperatures in this range for a period of 2 to 4 minutes is sufficient to cause death (Kayall 1963). Thus where a forest fire may smoulder at a particular spot for days or even weeks, it is unlikely that even the thickest bark would protect the tree (Phillips 1974).

Because of its poor diffusivity, bark is a good insulator against heat. Its thickness, which is likely to be of great importance, varies considerably with age and from one species to the next. For the Knysna forests Phillips (1931) lists 11 forest tree species that have a bark 19,05 mm or more in thickness, 9 with bark ca 12,70 mm thick, 20 with bark ca 8,47 mm thick and 2 with bark 3,18 mm thick.

Root depth may prove critical where very high temperatures persist for long periods at a particular spot. According to Phillips (1931) at least four tree species of the Knysna forests have the majority of their roots at depths of between 0,6 and 1,07 m where they would be expected to be well protected from surface fires.

Resprouting or coppice production from dormant epicormic buds on the stem or at the stem/root junction at or just below the soil surface, or from subterranean roots and lignotubers is a feature shown by a number of woody forest species. A number of forest trees including *Burchellia bubalina* (wild pomegranate), *Calodendrum capense* (Cape chestnut), *Celtis africana* (white stinkwood), *Cussonia spicata* (cabbage tree), *Euclea crispa* (blue guarri), *Halleria lucida* (tree-fuchia), *Ilex mitis* (African holly), *Myrica* spp (wax berries), *Ocotea bullata* (stinkwood), *Olinia emarginata* (mountain olinea), *Podocarpus latifolius* (real yellowwood), *Rhamnus prinoides* (dogwood), *Scolopia mundii* (red pear) and *Xymalos monospora* (lemon wood) all show some ability to coppice after fire, but this depends on the severity and frequency of fire. On the other hand other species survive burning by the same mechanisms but seem less prone to being killed by fire, whether regular or hot. In the Natal Drakensberg such species tend to predominate in forest precursor communities and along forest margins. In a study of four such species Smith (1978, 1979) found that *Buddleia salviifolia* (sagewood), *Leucosidea sericea* (ouhout) and *Widdringtonia nodiflora* (mountain cedar) all showed an ability to coppice. In the case of the first two species both epicormic and lignotuber sprouts were produced following both hot and cool fires, although *Buddleia salviifolia* produced more epicormic shoots after a cool burn than after a hot burn. On the other hand, regeneration of *W. nodiflora* occurred chiefly from buds located at the base of the stem or in the lignotuber. Smith's results also suggest that the onset of the ability to survive burning by such regeneration varies from one species to the next. The age of the plant and the frequency of burning are also important as both Smith's (1979) and Scriba's (1976) studies of *W. nodiflora* have shown.

The fourth species studied by Smith (1978, 1979), *Philippia evansii*, showed a different survival strategy. This ericaceous species sets seed between the end of winter and midspring when many wild-fires and hot, dry, high velocity bergwinds occur. Thus it appears that when the abundant fine seed is blown onto a recently burnt site it encounters conditions for germination more suitable than those prevailing in unburnt vegetation. On sites burnt during summer, seedling survival did not appear to be as high as on the earlier burnt sites. This difference in seedling survival may be due to the destruction during the hotter winter and spring fires of allelopathic compounds produced by *Pteridium aquilinum* (bracken fern), a plant common on sites where *P. evansii* appears (Everson 1979). Improved site conditions for germination of forest species following fire have also been noted for *B. salviifolia* and *H. lucida* (Sim 1907), *Virgilia oroboides* (keurboom) (Henkel 1912), *Gleichenia polypodioides* (climbing fern) (Phillips 1931), *Panicum* spp and *Isoglossa woodii* (buckweed) (Macdonald 1978b). Such conditions may also be exploited by undesirable exotics such as *Acacia* spp, *Asimina* spp, *Cestrum* spp, *Chromolaena odorata* (triffid weed), *Euphorbia* spp, *Lantana camara* (common lantana), *Melia azedarach* (syringa), *Psidium guajava* (guava) and *Solanum* spp (Macdonald 1978b).

Fire may result in the opening of seed capsules in certain forest species, including *W. nodiflora* (F R Smith, personal communication, 1980; Scriba 1976) and *Leucadendron coniferum* (dune conebush) (Taylor 1961), while increased temperatures during the fire or following it due to increased penetration of sunlight, appear to lead to increased germination of seed of the *V. oroboides* (Phillips 1974) and *Trema orientalis* (pigeonwood) (Pammenter 1979).

FAUNA

There is little to be found in the South African literature to suggest that forest animals have evolved specific adaptations to enable them to survive fire. Conversely, it appears that conditions following fire in and around forest may prove favourable to such animals (Phillips 1974). In the Natal Drakensberg, for example, *L. sericea* plants which have coppiced after burning may be preferentially browsed by grey duiker *(Sylvicapra grimmia)*, bushbuck *(Tragelaphus scriptus)* and Cape eland *(Taurotragus oryx)*. Burning may also open up these forests and allow patches of forest grasses to develop which may be grazed by bushbuck and eland. In coastal forest Macdonald (1978b) noted that fire killed trees, then became perches for birds such as hadeda ibis *(Bostrychia hagedash)* and nesting sites for goldenrumped tinker barbet *(Pogoniulus bilineatus)* and white-eared barbet *(Stactolaema leucotis)*. Both Macdonald (1978b) and Miller (1979) further pointed out that dead trees provide microhabitats for a wide array of insects such as species of lauxoniid flies, amphipoda, acarina, diplopoda and collembola.

Clancey (1964), examining the consequences of destroying large bodies of forest, pointed out that there are 14 species of birds characteristic of coast forest whose survival is threatened by the disappearance of this vegetation. He also stressed the importance of *Podocarpus* forest in Natal and western Zululand as a distributional corridor for species which occur down to sea level in the Cape, but which are averse to high temperatures and high relative humidity and so become montane in the eastern and northern regions of their continental range.

As regards herpetofauna, Broadley (1966) lists 13 species as being arboreal forest dwellers. While the more agile of these may survive the initial consequences of fire, they may suffer later through destruction of suitable habitats. He further lists 20 terrestrial forest species which may survive destruction of their habitat, as long as there remains some thick cover that provides cool, damp conditions at ground level and a layer of leaf mould in which to burrow. In a more recent publication Passmore and Carruthers (1979) list 16 species of frogs found in forest. Of these, representatives of the genus *Breviceps*, which burrow into the forest floor, and of the genus *Leptopelis* which are arboreal, are especially vulnerable to fire.

The sensitivity of forest-dwelling shrews to fire was noted by Meester (1978) in his study of the effects of fire in coast forest and he has tentatively suggested that the species *Thallomys paedulcus*, in preferring stable forest or bush habitat, is sensitive to fire while another species, *Praomys natalensis* (multimammate mice), is not.

In general, then, it appears that many forest plants possess mechanisms to survive fire while animals do not. This may be simply due to the fact that animals are able to flee. It is difficult to establish whether the survival mechanisms exhibited by many plants are a direct response to fire per se or are adaptations to some other environmental stress which have also proved valuable in coping with fire. The answer to such questions will provide considerable insight into the length of the period of the association between fire and forest.

EFFECT OF FIRE ON VEGETATION STRUCTURE AND DYNAMICS

Plainly, postfire changes in structure and dynamics in forest and forest margin communities are, to a great extent, determined by the adaptive responses of forest and forest margin plants to fire. The typical abrupt margin of many forests whose surrounds are subjected to regular fires substantiate this.

Trapnell (1959), reporting on the results of 23 yr of burning treatments in *Brachystegia-Julbernadia* woodland in Zambia, found that early burning (June and July) maintained a closed canopy woodland in which there was regeneration of canopy species. Late burning (in October), on the other hand, resulted in hot fires which thinned out the woody vegetation and encouraged the invasion of a grassy ground cover. This trend resulted in subsequent fires becoming progressively more destructive so that there was no regeneration of canopy species and an increase in the death rate of large canopy trees. This treatment was also characterized by a gradual increase in the number and variety of fire-tolerant woody species. Exclusion of fire led to a very dense stratified thicket and invasion by a variety of fire-intolerant, shade-loving evergreen species. A similar pattern of increasing density which first produces a dense scrub that may ultimately succeed to forest has been noted in the Natal Drakensberg (Killick 1963; Edwards 1967; Granger 1976b), in the Natal Midlands (Edwards 1967; Moll 1976), in the Knysna forests (Phillips 1931, 1974) and in the southwestern Cape (Taylor 1961).

The appearance of woody communities which are seral to forest may be rapid, as in Catchment IX in the Masongwane Valley in the Natal Drakensberg (Granger 1976a) and in coastal forest (Macdonald 1978a,b), with few intermediate woody stages, or they may be slow with several distinct woody stages as described by Phillips (1931) for the Knysna forests. Since many of the species comprising such precursor communities are fire-tolerant, these intermediate stages may be held in check for considerable periods by burning, an observation also noted by Edwards (1967) for valley bushveld, southern tall grassveld and sour sandveld in Natal.

This ability to produce coppice growth can lead to considerable modification in the overall structure of the community. Growth-inhibiting substances produced in the crowns of the trees tend to keep coppice buds in the dormant condition. Thus when burning results in total topkill, a plant with a shape quite different from the original may develop. In *L. sericea*, for example, previously burnt plants are often fan-shaped while in the *W. nodiflora* a rounded "dumpy" cylinder rather than a tall, slender plant may develop. Where only partial topkill occurs, intermediate situations may develop on recovery. Such patterns of coppice production often obliterate definite strata and increase the impenetrability of the community. Similar observations have been made by Phillips (1965).

Species richness differs from forest to woody precursor communities. Obviously, while a greater variety of tree species occurs in forest, the variety of shrubs and herbs may be far greater in the precursor communities, especially in the first few years after fire (Phillips 1974). The only known thorough study of such changes is that of Macdonald (1978a,b) in Natal coast forest where he found that richness of woody species in a burnt area of forest was almost as great as in the adjoining unburnt forest (32 woody species in the unburnt forest of which 25 were present in the burnt forest). A further 12 species not present in the unburnt forest were recorded in the burnt area. A number of these, eg *Eugenia capensis* (dune myrtle) and *Passerina rigida* (dune gonna), were typical of earlier stages of dune succession (Moll 1972). Other species such as *Calpurnia aurea* (wild laburnum) and *Trema orientalis* were characteristic of disturbed forest while species such as the *Halleria lucida* and *Maesa lanceolata* (maesa) were characteristic of forest margins (Moll 1967). Canopy species found only in unburnt forest were *Apodytes dimidiata* (white pear) and *Olea woodiana* (forest olive) while the shrubs *Acokanthera oblongifolia* (dune poison-bush), *Pavetta revoluta* (dune brides-bush) and *Psychotria capensis* (cream psychotria) occurred in the understorey. Of the species common to both burnt and unburnt forest *Canthium inerme* (turkey-berry) was 13 times more dense in the burnt than the unburnt area and *Brachylaena discolor* (wild silver oak), a species characteristic of early succession on dunes (Moll 1972), 11 times more dense in the burnt area. Conversely, in the unburnt forest, *Tricalysia sonderana* (dune tricalysia) and *Monanthotaxis caffra* (dwada-berry) were four times more dense than in the burnt area.

It would therefore seem that the changes in structure and species composition which follow fire in forest and forest pre-cursor communities are to a great extent governed by the adaptive responses of the various species to fire.

EFFECTS OF FIRE REGIME ON FAUNAL STRUCTURE AND DYNAMICS

VERTEBRATES

Archaeological evidence such as that of Klein (1972a, 1979b), Moffet and Deacon (1977), Schweitzer and Wilson (1978), Deacon (1976, 1978, 1979) and Deacon et al (1978) suggests that the distribution and numbers of forest-dwelling animals has been drastically altered through the disappearance of forest. Similar observations have been made more recently by Chapman and White (1970) and Phillips (1974). In addition to habitat destruction, fires such as the one which occurred in the Knysna area in 1869 show that a single massive conflagration may damage large animal populations beyond recovery (Phillips 1963; J D Scott, personal communication, 1980).

For smaller vertebrates, there is some indication that chang-es in vegetation following burning may favour different species in succession (Neal 1970). In the Cathedral Peak area of the Natal Drakensberg Rowe-Rowe (1977) recorded the presence of *Thamnomys dolichurus* and *Graphiurus murinus* only in *Podocarpus* forest and forest margin communities during the warm seasons of the year. In addition, two further species of rodent *(Rhabdomys pumilio* (four-striped field mouse) and *Dendromus mesomelas)* and one species of shrew *Myosorex varius* (forest shrew) were also found in forest, forest margins, woody communities dominated by

Leucosidea sericea, *B. salviifolia*, *W. nodiflora*, *Philippia evansii* and in *Themeda triandra* grassland. These *L. sericea*, *B. salviifolia*, *W. nodiflora* and *P. evansii*- dominated communities also provided a habitat for four additional species of rodent [(*Praomys natalensis*, *Otomys irroratus* (vlei rat), *Mus minutoides* (pygmy mouse) (Rowe-Rowe 1977), *Thamnomys dolichurus* (Pexton 1979)] and one shrew *Crocidura flavescens* (Rowe-Rowe 1977). Exclusion of fire from these communities led to a decrease in the variety of rodent and shrew species (Rowe-Rowe 1977; W L van Wyk, personal communication, 1980). In the cold, dry winter months, population densities of all species declined but only *T. dolichurus* and *G. murinus* seemed to disappear completely (Rowe-Rowe 1977). Tentative findings by Pexton (1979) suggest, however, that winter (July) burning in scrub communities dominated by *L. sericea*, *B. salviifolia* and *P. evansii* may lead to an increase in *R. pumilio* while the same burn may be responsible for an increase in *T. dolichurus* in the *L. sericea*-dominated areas only. Summer (December and January) burning on the other hand is thought to be the reason for the absence of the *R. pumilio* in *L. sericea*- dominated areas and the decrease in numbers of the same species in *B. salviifolia*- and *P. evansii*-dominated communities.

A further example of small mammals' response to fire-induced differences in woody vegetation are the studies of Meester (1978) and Meester et al (1979), who in Natal coast forest found that the rodent species *T. paedulcus* occurred far more frequently in unburnt than in burnt forest while *P. natalensis* was invariably found in recent burnt forest.

In recently burnt Natal coast forest Lawson (1979) has found some indications of the inability of certain bird species to use newly burnt areas. Of the 54 species recorded 14 were forest species that showed very little inclination to use the burnt area while 8 species appeared to prefer the burnt to the unburnt area. The remainder showed equal preference for both types of habitat.

INVERTEBRATES

While the number and diversity of vertebrates found in forest is small, the same cannot be said of the invertebrates. Because of its ameliorating effects on temperature and moisture, the forest provides habitats quite different from those found in the surrounding grassland, and on the forest floor this is especially so. Consequently many forest invertebrates are probably restricted to this habitat and therefore extremely vulnerable to fire. Some such as the slow-moving ground-dwelling *Onychophora* may not survive at all, while other more mobile groups such as the Lauxanid (Diptera) flies which occur throughout the profile of the forest may avoid the fire and even flourish in its aftermath (Lawrence 1953).

Comparing numbers of Lauxanid flies found in burnt and unburnt Natal coast forest, Miller (1979) found that the species *Homoneura* "S" and *Xangelina* were approximately three times more abundant in burnt than in unburnt forest, while species *Homoneura* "B" was never found in burnt forest. In the case of the species

Cestrotus *"T"* similar numbers were trapped in burnt and unburnt forest and in communities seral to forest. Overall, there appeared to be a preference for the burnt area where 108 individuals were trapped as compared with 76 in unburnt forest and 41 in seral vegetation. No explanation for these results is given but they may reflect the advantages of good mobility and ability to exploit new habitats.

The distribution of 15 species of Mutillidae (Hymenoptera) revealed some tendency for species to prefer either burnt or unburnt forest. Again this may reflect their high degree of mobility and ability to exploit new environments but it may also be a response to changes in numbers and distribution of other bees and wasps upon which they are parasitic (Skaife 1953).

A far more pronounced response to burning was found in the case of invertebrates confined to the litter layer. Groups such as the Diplopoda were able to exploit the increased quantities of grass and improved moisture conditions of burnt forest. Others like the Collembola, which are basically leaf litter inhabitants and therefore highly susceptible to moisture variations, were found only in low numbers in burnt forest where much of the litter had been destroyed.

EFFECT OF FIRE REGIME ON SOIL PHYSICAL AND CHEMICAL PROPERTIES

CHANGES IN THE LITTER LAYER, SOIL MOISTURE REGIMES AND RATE OF SOIL REMOVAL

Raising the temperature of leaves to 55°C for 3 minutes or to 60°C or more for a few seconds is usually fatal (Luke and Mac-Arthur 1978). Thus it is not uncommon to notice, soon after a fire in or near forest, severely wilted and dead leaves in the canopy located several metres above what was the mean flame height. Subsequent leaf fall is likely to intercept a greater portion of net rainfall at the soil surface and at the same time reduce evaporative losses (Malherbe et al 1968). The production of such unusually large quantities of litter may increase temporarily the fire hazard in forest but in a subtropical system like that of South Africa, characterized by intense fungal, bacterial and detritivore activity, decomposition will rapidly reduce susceptibility to fire (Borman and Likens 1979).

Ground fire in forest may result in total destruction of the litter layer (Phillips 1931, 1965; Macdonald 1978a). Consequently, there may be marked changes in soil surface temperature regimes even down to depths of 15 cm (Phillips 1931). The marked decrease in albedo and increase in temperature, net radiation and exposure to wind following such fires are likely to lead to increased evaporative losses. Such a pattern may, however, occur only near the surface since Phillips (1931) found this trend to be reversed at depths greater than 15 cm. Changes in microclimate together with the "puddling effect" of heavy rainfall may also lead to the soil becoming indurated (Phillips 1965; Malherbe et al 1968) and as a result, water absorption, infiltration rate and hydraulic conductivity may decrease (Cass et al, this volume, chapter 14). The persistence of such effects is difficult to judge but Macdonald (1978b) found that even 3 yr after burning the litter layer had not become as deep as that in adjacent unburnt forest. Destruction of the litter layer does not always appear to lead to increased soil loss although as Cass et al (this volume, chapter 14) point out, the subsequent reduction in organic matter may lead to instability of soil aggregates. An increased tendency to erode may also follow as a result of the deflocculation of clay minerals by ash (Phillips 1974).

NUTRIENT STATUS

The rapid growth rates characteristic of many plants that appear soon after fire may be due to improved conditions of light and temperature. However, the nutrients which are released by burning are also likely to enhance growth (Cass et al, this volume, chapter 14). Regrettably this aspect has been little researched in South African forests, thereby often making it necessary to infer effects from the results obtained in other situations.

While burning a grassland may reduce soil organic carbon through loss of windborn ash (West 1965; Daubenmire 1968), the production of charcoal in forest following fire may lead to an increase of this component (Daubenmire 1968). Particularly violent forest fires are likely to produce temperatures sufficiently high to volatilize nitrogen, sulphur and phosphorus (Cass et al, this volume, chapter 14). However, Nye and Greenland (1950 cited by Phillips 1965) found no significant changes in carbon and nitrogen contents following burning of the humus layer in a forest in Ghana, while Sly and Tinker (1962 cited by Phillips 1965) on the other hand, working in Nigerian forests, reported slight increases in organic carbon and nitrogen levels in the soil following the burning of felled slash. At Cathedral Peak in the Natal Drakensberg analyses of samples of topsoil collected along a transect running from biennially spring-burnt *Themeda triandra* grassland through *W. nodiflora*- dominated forest margin, unburnt for 15 yr, and into *Podocarpus*- dominated forest, have yielded average organic carbon values of 10% in forest, 6% in the woody margin and 4% in the grassland. Nitrogen levels followed the same trend: 1,3% in forest, 0,6% in the margin and 0,4% in grassland (Granger 1976b). However, changes in nitrogen content following burning is determined by factors other than fire per se. Ammonium ions for example may be strongly held on cation exchange sites or fixed on organic matter or clay. Thus the extent to which organic matter is destroyed following burning and the quantities of different clay minerals in the soil play an important role. Further, nitrates, being highly soluble, are easily leached out of the system, thereby making precipitation after fire an important determinant of subsequent soil nitrogen levels. The proportions of fire-sensitive aerobic nitrogen fixers and fire-tolerant anaerobic fixers may also enter the picture (Meiklejohn 1955).

Soil pH in forest is usually raised following burning (Phillips 1965) and Granger (1976b), in the same transect referred to previously, found a trend of increasing pH from grassland to forest. In the southern Cape, however, J C van Daalen (personal communication, 1980) found no significant differences in pH (H$_2$0 and KCl) across fire-induced forest edges where burning had last occurred 36 to 50 yr before.

Changes in cation exchange capacity (CEC) result largely from altered organic matter levels. Decreases in CEC levels that co-incided with destruction of organic matter were reported by Nye and Tinker (1962 cited by Phillips 1965) while Nye and Greenland (1960 cited by Phillips 1965) found that CEC, pH and availability of cations increased following recovery from burning in forest.

As regards other elements, Phillips (1965) stated that fire normally returns appreciable quantities of phosphate, potassium, calcium and magnesium to the soil. However, additions of these elements following fire may be evident only in the upper few mm of mineral soil (Cass et al, this volume, chapter 14). Results from analyses of topsoils collected by Granger (1976b) along a grassland/forest transect showed that sodium levels tended to be slightly higher in burnt grassland than in forest while potassium was higher in the woody margin than in either of the other two communities. However, calcium, magnesium and phosphate tended to be present in progressively increasing amounts in a transect from grassland to forest. Exchangeable aluminium levels were much lower in forest than in grassland, suggesting that calcium may be acting as an ameliorator (Granger 1976a). It therefore seems possible that burning in the forest might destroy this effect and consequently lead to phosphate becoming less readily available to forest plants, particularly at the seedling stage. Similar changes in nutrient levels following burning of felled forest are reported by Nye and Tinker (1962 cited by Phillips 1965) who postulated that burning may tend to conserve sodium and potassium and lower calcium and possibly magnesium levels.

EFFECT OF FIRE ON HERBAGE PRODUCTION AND QUALITY

Very little information on the effect of fire on herbage production and quality in forest communities is to be found. There is, however, some recent evidence on the response of forest margin shrub species in the Natal Drakensberg to fire. F Smith (personal communication, 1980) has noted that regeneration of the forest precurser *Leucosidea sericea* is most pronounced after winter-burning, a fact that he ascribes to total removal of crown dominance by hot winter fires. Tentative results from J J B Scotcher's (personal communication, 1980) studies tend to support Smith's findings. In addition, Scotcher has concluded some analyses of the mineral and biochemical composition of *L. sericea* foliage in order to determine quality of browse for eland. Thus far it appears that browsable foliage from unburnt *L. sericea* growing on basalt-derived soil is higher in crude protein, phosphate, calcium and magnesium and lower in crude fats, fibre content, potassium and sodium than *L. sericea* growing on soils derived from Clarens Formation Sandstone. Following burning in these two different sites however, crude protein levels were approximately three times greater in the browsable coppice harvested from basalt soils than from sandstone-derived soils. In addition, crude fat, calcium, magnesium and sodium levels were also higher in plants from the basalt soils while fibre content and phosphate and potassium levels were lower than those from the sandstone soils. Similar trends of improved nutrient quality in postburn coppice of woody savanna species is also reported by Brooks and Berry (1980).

EFFECT OF FIRE REGIME ON WATER PRODUCTION AND QUALITY

As the vegetation type on a site changes from grassland to forest it may be expected that there will be parallel increases in water loss by transpiration (Wicht 1949). Schulze (1975), using a water balance estimation technique in the Natal Drakensberg, confirmed this view as did other workers in the same area, in which gauged catchments previously covered by grassland were planted with *Pinus patula* (patula pine) (Nanni 1970).

Evidence for the possibility of causing at least a temporary reversal of this trend by burning and felling is provided by a number of workers. Rycroft (1947) and Banks (1964) both reported short-term significant increases in winter peak flows from gauged catchments at Jonkershoek following burning in autumn. This trend, however, persisted for only 1 yr after the burn. Removal by cutting of riparian *L. sericea*-dominated vegetation at Cathedral Peak led to reduced vapour losses and an increase of winter base flow by 1,1 m^3 per day for every 100 m of streambank cleared (Nanni 1972). A similar response to removal of riparian heath was obtained by Rycroft (1955) at Jonkershoek in the southern Cape although Banks (1961, 1962) expressed doubt that this treatment alone was responsible for the effect.

While changes such as the above may be the result of the removal of large volumes of transpiring leaves, destruction of these and small twigs will obviously lead to a drastic decrease in interception. Consequently, greater volumes of water are able to reach the soil surface and this may be reflected by increased streamflow. In situations where this additional input occurs as heavy rainfall, an increase in soil and nutrient loss may be expected (Borman and Likens 1979).

CONCLUSIONS

Forests are disappearing from the humid tropics of Africa, Asia and Latin America at a rate of 11 million ha per year. Much of the blame for this can be laid on itinerant farmers who slash and burn an area of forest, grow crops and move on. In addition, the collection of firewood and extraction of timber for commercial purposes also takes its toll (Anon 1979a). The consequences of such activities are often major changes in microclimate. Thus the delicately balanced conditions required by many forest plants and animals may be severely disturbed.

While the comparative rarity of forests provides good reason to apply special conservation measures to protect them, it is also recognized that many forests play an important role in stabilizing steep terrain. Thus their role in the character of run-off makes it important that they be given special consideration in catchment management plans.

Finally, because of the tendency for forest and grassland to occur as a mosaic, the distinctive character of the forest environment dictates that they be regarded as terrestrial islands in the grassland.   They may serve to ensure the survival of many grassland plant and animal species.

Thus in addition to sentiment, there are also sound scientific reasons why the remaining forests of South Africa should be preserved, and to do this fire needs to be excluded from the forests themselves, and carefully controlled in adjacent grasslands and forest margin communities.

Chapter 9 Fire Behaviour

W. S. W. TROLLOPE

INTRODUCTION

The effect of fire on natural ecosystems depends on the response of living organisms to the release of heat energy through the combustion of plant material. The expression **fire behaviour** describes the release of heat energy and is dependent on fire intensity, rate of spread of the fire front, flame characteristics and other related phenomena. The manner in which heat energy is released and the factors that influence this currently form the basis of any study of fire behaviour. Such a study necessitates a basic understanding of the phenomenon of combustion. Brown and Davis (1973) state that combustion is an oxidation process comprising a chain reaction in which the heat energy from fire originates from solar energy fixed by the process of photosynthesis. Combustion is similar to photosynthesis in reverse and is clearly illustrated in the following two general formulae:

Photosynthesis

$$CO_2 + H_2O + \text{solar energy} \rightleftarrows (C_6H_{10}O_5)_n + O_2 \qquad (1)$$

Combustion

$$(C_6H_{10}O_5)_n + O_2 + \text{kindling temperature} \rightleftarrows CO_2 + H_2O + \text{heat} \qquad (2)$$

The kindling temperature in the combustion formula has a catalytic role of initiating and maintaining the combustion process.

There are three phases in the combustion of plant fuels. The first is the **preheating** phase in which plant material ahead of the flames is raised to its ignition point and involves the driving off of moisture and the generation of flammable hydrocarbon gases. The ignition of these gases heralds the second phase which is characterized by **flaming combustion.** In the third phase the remaining charcoal is consumed by **glowing combustion,** leaving a small amount of residual ash. The amount of heat energy released during the flaming and glowing phases of combustion varies with different fuel types. Heavy fuels with low flames generally release more heat energy, albeit at a slower rate, via glowing combustion (Brown and Davis 1973) whereas light fuels such as grass material release most of their heat energy during flaming combustion. The three phases of combustion can overlap and occur simultaneously during a fire but are easily recognized as three characteristic zones in a fire. In the first zone the leaves and other fine fuels curl and are scorched by the preheating of the oncoming flames. Second is the flaming zone of burning gases followed by the third but less conspicuous zone of burning charcoal (Brown and Davis 1973).

Maintaining the chain reaction of combustion involves the transfer of heat energy to the adjacent potential plant fuel via the processes of conduction, convection, radiation and the movement of hot or burning plant material through spotting (Steward 1974). Besides spotting, the transfer of heat in a moving fire front is mainly due to convection and radiation. Convection currents are primarily responsible for the preheating of the higher shrub layers and tree crowns, while radiation from the flames accounts for most of the preheating of the fuel ahead of the fire front (Luke and McArthur 1978).

The effect of fire on plants and animals depends upon the amount and rate of and the height at which heat energy is released. In South Africa there is a serious lack of knowledge concerning fire behaviour and virtually no attempt has been made to quantify the dynamics of the release of heat energy during a fire and the subsequent response of plants and animals. The determination of such relationships will help explain many of the apparently inexplicable and sometimes contradictory effects of fire which are often cited in the literature.

In the USA and Australia three broad **types of fire** are recognized according to the layers in which the vegetation burns, namely ground, surface and crown fires (Brown and Davis 1973; Luke and McArthur 1978). A **ground fire** is a fire that burns below the surface of the ground in deep layers of organic material (Luke and McArthur 1978) and plant debris. A **surface fire** is one that burns in the surface vegetation, the most common form being a grass fire either in grassland or in understorey in wooded communities (Luke and McArthur 1978). A **crown fire** burns in the canopies of trees and shrubs and can be more or less independent of a surface fire. In practice all three types of fire may occur simultaneously or in all possible combinations (Brown and Davis 1973). In Africa, Phillips (1974) distinguished only between ground and crown fires. But his ground fires are synonymous with the ground and surface fires recognized in the USA and Australia. However, in South Africa ground fires are rare and generally confined to old mature fynbos communities and forests that burn under extremely dry conditions. Surface fires are most common and in tree and shrub vegetation can develop into crown fires when foliage ignites and carries the fire above the surface of the ground. Fynbos vegetation is very prone to crown fires whereas in savanna communities crown fires develop only when fuel moisture is low and atmospheric conditions include high winds, high air temperatures and low relative humidities.

Fires can be further subdivided into those burning with or against the wind. Trollope (1978a) referred to these as **head fires** and **back fires** respectively and according to Phillips (1974) they can have significantly different effects in open plant communities. Crown fires occur only as head fires but surface fires occur as either head or back fires. These two very common types of surface fire have different fire behaviour characteristics that are very pertinent to an understanding of the effect of fire and its use in the management of ecosystems for livestock, wildlife and water catchment purposes.

PARAMETERS OF FIRE BEHAVIOUR

The parameters which are relevant to a study of fire behaviour are those which influence fire intensity (heat energy released per unit time per unit area) and the vertical distribution of the heat which is released (flame profile). Both these factors are believed to be important in determining the response of plant communities to fire.

FIRE INTENSITY

Fire intensity is determined by the **amount** of available heat energy and the **rate of heat energy release.** The amount of energy released is in turn dependent on the **available heat energy** in the fuel, and this in turn on the **fuel load** and the **heat of combustion** or more particularly, the **heat yield** of a unit mass of that fuel. To understand these relationships, it is necessary to understand each of these parameters in turn, and to appreciate the role of each in determining the response of the vegetation.

Amount of available heat energy

As indicated above, the available heat energy at any site is dependent on the fuel load and the heat of combustion. The fuel load is defined as the mass of fuel available for combustion per unit area (Luke and McArthur 1978). It represents the total amount of heat energy available for release. It determines the heat load to which living cells are subjected and research has shown that fuel load is highly positively correlated (P=0,01) with topkill of stems and branches of savanna trees and shrubs during a surface head fire (Trollope 1980a).

The total amount of heat energy contained per unit mass of fuel, the **heat of combustion,** is expressed in kilojoules per kilogram (kJ kg^{-1}). In both the USA and Australia the average heat of combustion of fuels consumed in forest and bush fires is assumed to be 20 000 kJ kg^{-1} dry mass (Brown and Davis 1973; Luke and McArthur 1978). Some examples of the heat of combustion of different grass and shrub species in areas commonly burnt in South Africa are presented in Table 1.

These data indicate that heat of combustion of fuels in South Africa is not substantially dissimilar to that quoted for the USA and Australia.

During a fire not all heat of combustion is released. Unburnt material remains in the ash and is lost in smoke and heat energy is lost in driving off fuel moisture. Therefore available heat energy is always somewhat less than the heat of combustion of natural plant fuels. This available heat energy is referred to as **heat yield,** and is defined as the amount of heat energy available for release per unit mass of fuel. It is closely related to current moisture content of the fuel. The mean heat yield quoted for grass and forest fuels in Australia is 16 000 kJ kg^{-1} (Luke and McArthur 1978). In the USA Albini (1976) quotes the average heat yield for forest fuels as 18 640 kJ kg^{-1}. In South Africa Trollope (1980a), le Maitre (1981), Smith (1982) and Smith et al (1983) have determined the heat yield in different situations (Table 2 and Figure 1). The data of Trollope (1980a) are for fully cured, dormant winter grass where research has shown that with fuel moisture contents of less than 40%, maximum fuel combustion occurs. The heat yield for grass fuels burning

as back fires was slightly higher (5,3%) than that for head
fires. This result was supported by the production of grey ash
by back fires and the production of black ash by head fires,
indicating a higher carbon content and less complete combustion
of the grass fuel in the latter case. The data of Smith (1982)

Table 1   The heat of combustion of different fuel types commonly
occurring in burnt veld expressed as kilojoules per
kilogram (kJ kg^{-1}) on a dry mass basis (Trollope 1980a;
Smith 1982; Smith et al 1983).

Grass species	Description	Heat of combustion kJ kg^{-1}
Cymbopogon plurinodis	Vegetative leafy stage	17 643 ± 48,1
C. plurinodis	Mature leaf/culm stage	18 133 ± 46,0
Digitaria eriantha	Vegetative leafy stage	16 722 ± 140,2
D. eriantha	Mature leaf/culm stage	17 538 ± 96,3
Panicum maximum	Vegetative leafy stage	17 936 ± 144,4
P. maximum	Mature leaf/culm stage	17 677 ± 56,5
Sporobolus fimbriatus	Vegetative leafy stage	17 543 ± 157,0
S. fimbriatus	Mature leaf/culm stage	17 212 ± 46,0
Themeda triandra	Vegetative leafy stage	17 170 ± 16,7
T. triandra	Mature leaf/culm stage	17 727 ± 44,0
Semi arid grassland	Mean composite field sample	18 024 ± 149,0
Humid mountain grassland	one year old	20 506
Humid mountain grassland	two years old	18 497
Buddleia salviifolia shrubland	herbaceous plants and litter	18 023 ± 534,0
Leucosidea sericea shrubland	herbaceous plants and litter	17 188 ± 636,0
Philippia evansii heath	**fine fuels (< 6 mm dia):**	
	forbs and grasses – winter	16 368 ± 1 426
	forbs and grasses – summer	20 147 ± 1 341
	bracken fern	19 388 ± 356
	orthophyllous plants – summer and winter	19 519 ± 418
	sclerophyllous plants – summer and winter	23 726 ± 519
	heavy fuels (> 6mm dia):	
	winter and summer	19 621 ± 453
Widdringtonia nodiflora thicket	**fine fuels (< 6 mm dia):**	
	herbaceous plants and litter summer and winter	18 649 ± 322
	sclero- and orthophyllous woody plants, winter	20 698 ± 297
	heavy fuels (> 6 mm dia):	
	winter	20 647 ± 340

are for morning and afternoon burns and suggest that heat yield is influenced by the time of the day at which the vegetation is burnt. However, the effects are relatively small in spite of some large differences in the moisture content of the fuel at these different times.

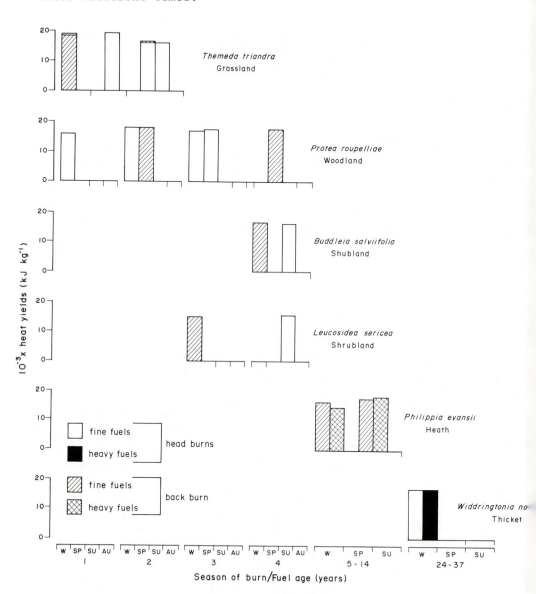

Figure 1   Heat yields (kJ kg⁻¹) for a number of communities subjected to head and back fires (Smith et al 1983).

Table 2   The heat yield (available fuel energy) measured in some
           South African communities (data for the two grasslands
           from Trollope 1980a and that for fynbos from Durand
           (cited by le Maitre 1981). The remaining data is from
           Smith 1982).

Type of fire	Heat yield kJ kg^{-1}	Fuel moisture %
grassland - head fire	16 890	32,4
grassland - back fire	17 781	36,0
fynbos	19 646	-
Buddleia salviifolia shrubland-		
summer head burn (11h22)	14 781	120,6
summer head burn (14h25)	17 347	94,6
winter back burn (08h49)	16 336	28,7
winter back burn (14h00)	17 061	5,3
Leucosidea sericea shrubland-		
summer head burn (12h26)	15 440	74,9
summer head burn (15h04)	15 309	60,5
winter back burn (09h01)	15 360	36,1
winter back burn (14h17)	14 967	51,2
Widdringtonia nodiflora thicket-		
winter head burn (09h15)	16 785	85,3
winter head burn (15h39)	16 895	68,6

The amount of heat energy (kJ m^{-2}) released during a veld
fire is the product of the fuel load (kg m^{-2}) and the heat yield
(kJ kg^{-1}). From this it is clear that the total potential amount
of heat energy released during a fire is greatly influenced by
the fuel load. The total amount of heat released can also be
estimated by examining the magnitude and duration of the rise in
temperature. The area underneath the temperature vs time curve
represents the total amount of heat energy released. Tunstal et
al (1976) have also found that the area underneath the temperature curve is positively correlated with the maxium temperature
reached during a fire, while Trollope (1980a) and Trollope and
Potgieter (1983) have shown a strong positive correlation between
the fire intensity and the maximum temperature reached. This
correlation was shown to be particularly strong within the grass
canopy and at a height of 1 m above the grass canopy. Temperatures generated at ground level were shown to be less well correlated with fire intensity. Maximum temperatures reached can also
serve as an estimate of the total amount of heat energy released
during a veld fire and therefore of the intensity of a fire.
     Fuel load characteristics vary widely in different South
African biomes in a number of respects. In particular, the mass
of material, its physical structure and its horizontal distribut-

ion in the profile, will vary widely according to the component species in the community. They are normally closely related to annual rainfall at any site since it is the availability of moisture which largely determines plant growth rate in most South African biomes. Hence fuel loads are normally lower in arid zones than in humid zones for any particular inter-fire interval. For inter-fire intervals of 2 yr in grasslands, for example, fuel loads may be expected to vary from 1 t ha^{-1} in arid zones to about 4 t ha^{-1} in humid zones. In humid mountain vegetation, Smith et al (1983) recorded fuel loads of over 13 t ha^{-1} in *Philippia evansii* shrubland and between 15 and 18 t ha^{-1} in *Widdringtonia nodiflora* thicket, while in fynbos vegetation of the Western Cape Province, le Maitre (1981) recorded fuel loads ranging between 10 and 18 t ha^{-1}. However, in grasslands, a large proportion of the fuel is available for combustion, whereas in savanna and thicket communities, only a relatively small fraction of the fuel may burn in any given fire. Hence, in *W. nodiflora* communities, Smith et al (1983) reported that fine fuels less than 6 mm in diameter comprised only about half the fuel load. In these communities, the reduction of the fuel load resulting from burning declined to as low as 41%. A similar situation exists in the fynbos, where le Maitre (1981) found that fine fuels (undergrowth and litter) constitute about 65% of the fuel load in the spring, although the contribution of this component may rise to as high as 90% in the autumn. Here fire has been shown to consume up to 95% of the undergrowth material and litter, but only between 10 and 19% of the heavier material produced by the tall shrubs. The overall consumption of fuel by a fire may therefore decline to as low as 60% in the spring, but is normally somewhat higher in the autumn.

Rate of heat energy release

Albini (1976) states that the rate of heat energy release during a fire is one of the most poorly understood measures of fire behaviour. It is normally estimated in practice from measurements of the rate of forward movement of the fire front (Brown and Davis 1973; Albini 1976; Luke and McArthur 1978; Cheney and Vines, undated). It is recommended that the term **rate of spread** be used to describe the rate of this forward movement of a fire front per unit of time.

Determination of fire intensity

The parameters, heat yield, fuel mass and rate of spread are used to estimate fire intensity according to the following equation:

$$I = H \, w \, r \tag{3}$$

where

I = fire intensity (kJ s^{-1} m^{-1})
H = heat yield of fuel (kJ kg^{-1})
w = mass of available fuel (kg m^{-2})
r = rate of spread of the fire front (m s^{-1}).

In the USA fire intensity is expressed as British thermal units per second per unit length of the fire front (BTU s^{-1} m^{-1}) (Byram 1959; Brown and Davis 1973; Albini 1976). In Australia it is preferred to express fire intensity in the units of power (heat flux) rather than those of energy. Hence the units kilowatts per metre (kW m^{-1}) are used instead of kilojoules per second per metre (kJ s^{-1} m^{-1}) (1 kilowatt = 1 kilojoule per second). However, units of energy are more appropriate than units of power in the context of fire behaviour and fire effects. Therefore it is strongly recommended that fire intensity be expressed in units that are in accordance with the concept originally conceived by Byram (1959), ie kJ s^{-1} m^{-1}.

Albini (1976) considers that Byram's fireline intensity has proved to be very useful in fire behaviour studies and quotes van Wagner (1973) who found that fire intensity was significantly correlated with the height of lethal scorching of coniferous tree crowns. Trollope (1980a) has also found highly significant correlations (P = 0,01) between fire intensity and the topkill of stems and branches of savanna trees and shrubs, while Smith (1982) established the same relationship for shrub species in the Natal Drakensberg. Smith (1982) showed a greater incidence of aerial resprouting in *Buddleia salviifolia*, *W. nodiflora* and *L. sericea* after low intensity summer burns than after high intensity winter burns. However, basal resprouting of these shrubs increased with an increase in the severity of fire damage, and was therefore greater for winter than for summer burns.

VERTICAL DISTRIBUTION OF HEAT ENERGY

A reliable indicator of the vertical distribution of heat energy during a fire is the height distribution of flames above ground level ie **flame height.** The vertical distribution of heat energy in a fire can also be measured by recording temperatures at different heights above the ground. Trollope (1978a) investigated the effect of surface fires occurring as either head or back fires on the grass sward in eastern Cape savanna. He found that at ground level temperatures were generally higher during a back fire than during a head fire. In a grassland sward, the critical temperature of approximately 95°C was maintained for 20 s longer in the back fires than in the head fires. In fynbos, Ashton et al (1980 cited by le Maitre 1981) produced temperature profiles at four heights within the canopy during an autumn burn. A maximum temperature of ca 400°C was reached at ground level ca 45 s after ignition, remained at this level for a further 45 s, and then declined slowly to 145°C after 180 s. At a height of 0,6 m within the canopy, the temperature rose sharply to a maximum of ca 770°C after 56 s, and then declined rapidly to 110°C after 180 s. At 1,2 m, the temperature also rose to ca 770°C and remained relatively high for 70 s, whereas at a height of 1,8 m the temperature rose only to 500°C before declining rapidly to ca 50°C after 180 s. Extremely high temperatures are therefore produced, particularly at intermediate levels within the canopy, where they remain greater than 95°C for periods in excess of 180 s.

BEHAVIOUR OF DIFFERENT TYPES OF FIRE WITH SPECIAL REFERENCE TO HEAD AND BACK FIRES

As mentioned earlier, ground, surface and crown fires have markedly different fire behaviour characteristics which in turn result in significantly different responses from fauna and flora. To date only preliminary information is available on the behaviour of surface fires in grassland and savanna of South Africa.

RATE OF HEAT ENERGY RELEASE

No published information is available in South Africa on the intensity of crown and ground fires although the data presented for *Widdringtonia nodiflora* and for the fynbos community in Table 3 represent a combined surface and crown fire.

Table 3   Fire intensities of head and back surface fires (data for the two grasslands are from Trollope 1978a and for the fynbos from le Maitre 1981. The remaining data is from Smith 1982).

Type of fire	Fire intensity $kJ\ s^{-1}\ m^{-1}$
grassland head fire	1 877 ± 215
grassland back fire	124 ± 8
Buddlia salviifolia shrubland	
summer head fire (11h22)	209
summer head fire (14h25)	88
winter back fire (08h49)	162
winter back fire (14h00)	191
Leucosidea sericea shrubland	
summer head fire (12h26)	149
summer head fire (15h04)	493
winter back fire (09h01)	137
winter back fire (14h17)	417
Widdringtonia nodiflora thicket	
winter head fire (09h15)	899
winter head fire (15h39)	1 617
fynbos community	
autumn back fire	8 644
spring back fire	3 614 - 6 749
summer head fire	6 558
autumn head fire	3 208 - 7 609

The behaviour of surface grass fires burning as head and back fires have been compared in the eastern Cape and the mean fire intensities of these types of fires are presented in Table 3 (Trollope 1980a), together with data from Smith (1982) working in the Natal Drakensberg and from le Maitre (1981) working in the fynbos.

The results in Table 3 show that, in grassland, the head fires were approximately 7 times more intense than the back fires but that in the shrub communities the differences between head and back fires were less pronounced. Furthermore the standard errors of the mean grassland fire intensities indicate that the head fires were more variable than the back fires and were therefore presumably more greatly influenced by environmental conditions prevailing at the time of fire. Because rate of spread is an important component of fire intensity it followed the same pattern of behaviour for head and back fires as did fire intensity (Trollope 1978a).

Considering maximum temperature as an index of fire intensity, Trollope (1978a) also found that head fires had a greater potential than back fires for developing higher maximum temperatures given the appropriate environmental conditions. The maximum temperature recorded with a chrome-alumel thermocouple during grassland head fires was 557°C and during the back fires 390°C. In the fynbos, however, head fires produced considerably higher temperatures than in grassland or mountain shrubland and thicket.

VERTICAL DISTRIBUTION OF HEAT ENERGY

There is no published data in South Africa on the vertical distribution of heat energy during ground and crown fires. However, Brown and Davis (1973) have stated that ground fires which consume the organic material beneath the surface litter are characterized by glowing rather than flaming combustion. Consequently the heat energy released during these fires is distributed at and below the soil surface.

Conversely crown fires consume the foliage of trees and shrubs above the surface of the ground and can release considerable heat energy at some distance above ground level. The author has observed flame heights of up to 10 m in crown fires in fynbos vegetation (1 m high) in the Amatole Mountains of the eastern Cape.

The vertical distribution of the release of heat energy during surface grass fires is positively related to the pattern of flame distribution during a fire (Trollope and Potgieter 1983). The flame heights recorded during head and back fires are presented in Table 4. These data clearly illustrate that grassland head fires had markedly higher flames than the back fires, but that the opposite was true of the shrub communities. The standard errors of the mean for the grassland fires also indicate that the flame heights were more variable for the head fires than for the back fires. These results suggest that there is a greater vertical distribution in the heat load in grassland head fires than in back fires. A frequency distribution of the maximum temperatures recorded with chrome-alumel thermocouples at ground level, at grass canopy height and 1 m above grass canopy during head and back fires supports this conclusion (Table 5). It is important to note, however, that Smith's (1982) data suggest that the opposite would be true in the shrub communities.

Table 4   Flame heights of head and back surface fires (data for the grassland fires are from Trollope 1978a. The remaining data are from Smith 1982).

Type of fire	Mean flame height m
grassland - head fire	2,8 ± 0,4
grassland - back fire	0,8 ± 0,1
Buddleia salviifolia shrubland	
summer head fire (11h22)	0,45
summer head fire (14h25)	0,46
winter back fire (08h49)	0,85
winter back fire (14h00)	0,90
Leucosidea sericea shrubland	
summer head fire (12h26)	0,38
summer head fire (15h04)	0,67
winter back fire (09h01)	0,70
winter back fire (14h17)	1,25
Widdringtonia nodiflora thicket	
winter head fire (09h15)	2,33
winter head fire (15h39)	1,50

The data in Table 5 also show that the majority of the head fires were cooler than the back fires at ground level. At grass canopy height the maximum temperatures in both head and back fires were higher than those at ground level, a result which is also supported by data produced in the fynbos by Ashton et al (1980 cited by le Maitre 1981). Generally, back fires in grass-land tended to be hotter than head fires at grass canopy height but nevertheless the highest temperature recorded at this level was during a head fire, indicating the greater potential of this type of fire to produce high fire intensities given the appropriate set of environmental conditions. Finally, at 1 m above the grass canopy height the results clearly indicate that the major-ity of head fires were hotter than the back fires.

These findings are largely supported by those of Potgieter (1974) who recorded the maximum temperatures reached at different heights above-ground during head and back fires in the Kruger National Park. The results are presented in Table 6.

Table 5   Frequency distribution of maximum temperatures recorded at ground level, grass canopy and 1 m above the grass canopy height in head (HF) and back (BF) surface fires expressed as percentages.

Temperature (°C)	Ground level		Grass canopy height		1 m above grass canopy	
	HF	BF	HF	BF	HF	BF
130	67	23	–	–	45	78
131–200	–	44	20	11	33	22
201–300	11	33	50	33	11	–
301–400	–	–	20	56	11	–
401–500	11	–	–	–	–	–
501–550	11	–	10	–	–	–

Table 6   The mean maximum temperatures (°C) recorded during head and back fires at different heights in *Acacia nigrescens - Sclerocarya caffra* woodland in the Kruger National Park (Potgieter 1974).

Height mm	Head fire °C	Back fire °C	[a]Significant difference
0	336	324	N S
50	306	259	* *
100	257	204	* *
150	227	174	* *
200	205	138	* *
250	178	109	* *
300	136	92	* *
350	117	77	* *

[a]N S   = nonsignificant difference
 * *   = difference significant at $P < 0,01$.
Least significant differences = 24,3°C ($P \leq 0,05$)
                             = 32,0°C ($P \leq 0,01$)

It can generally be concluded that back fires are more intense than head fires at ground level. Conversely head fires are more intense overall at levels corresponding to and above the canopy of the grass sward. These conclusions are in accord with those of Lindenmuth and Byram (1948, cited by Stinson and Wright 1969), who stated that head fires are consistently hotter 18 inches (0,46 m) above the soil surface while back fires are consistently hotter below this level. Hare (1961, cited by Stinson and Wright 1969), also concluded that head fires develop more heat than back fires because more fuel burns per unit time.

SPOTTING

Spotting is the initiation of a new fire ahead of a main fire by an airborne firebrand or ember (Luke and McArthur 1978). It depends upon the availability of firebrand material and the flammability of the fine fuel components where the firebrands land. Not all vegetation types are equally prone to spotting. For example, in Texas, mesquite communities are not prone to spotting because mesquite shrubs burn slowly and give off few firebrands, while the grass understorey burns rapidly and produces no firebrands. Conversely, shrubby chaparral in California contains highly flammable volatile oils which release their heat energy very rapidly on ignition and produce numerous firebrands of various sizes which can remain hot for an extended period of time. These firebrands have been known to cause spotting from 150 to 6 400 m ahead of the main fire front (Bunting and Wright 1974). Spotting distances of 30 km or more have been recorded in Australia where it is a particularly serious problem in eucalypt forests (Luke and McArthur 1978).

There are no quantitative data available on spotting in South Africa but experience indicates that it does occur during very intense surface and crown fires burning with the wind. Crown fires are generally more prone to spotting because of the greater availability of firebrand material in the form of fine branches, twigs and sections of bark in the crowns of trees and shrubs. The vegetation type most prone to spotting in South Africa is fynbos, which contains highly flammable volatile oils. During extreme fire conditions crown fires develop rapidly in fynbos and in the Amatole Mountains of the eastern Cape spotting has been observed up to distances of ca 0,5 km. Conversely, spotting seldom occurs during surface fires in grassland and savanna because the trees and shrubs are large, nonflammable and the grasses burn too rapidly to permit the transport of burning embers any significant distance. However, in savanna of northeastern Natal and the Transvaal spotting is conceivably more frequent than in the evergreen savanna of the southern and eastern regions because numerous tree and shrub species have large deciduous leaves. Where these leaves are highly flammable, as in *Colophospermum mopane* (mopane) where they contain highly combustible oils (W P D Gertenbach, personal communication, 1980), spotting may be moderately frequent. There is also a considerable amount of standing dead material in the form of branches and twigs to act as firebrands.

Factors that influence the degree of spotting are ease of transport of the firebrands and flammability of the fine fuels where they land. Increasing wind speeds and steeper slopes cause greater rates of spread and the development of updrafts and convection currents that transport the firebrands. Fuel moisture is the most important factor that influences the flammability of the fine fuels; others are air temperature, relative humidity and period since the last rain (Brown and Davis 1973; Bunting and Wright 1974; Luke and McArthur 1978).

FACTORS INFLUENCING FIRE BEHAVIOUR

There is a serious lack of quantitative data on the effect of various factors on behaviour of fire in South Africa. Conversely in the USA and Australia the study of fire behaviour is at an advanced level and very sophisticated mathematical models have been developed to predict the behaviour of fires. This is particularly so in the USA. However, Luke and McArthur (1978) in Australia believe that for practical field use the fire models that have been produced by Rothermel (1972) and others in the USA are difficult to apply and prefer instead simpler models based on general fuel characteristics such as particle size, distribution, quantity and moisture content together with slope, relative humidity, air temperature and wind speed.

A similar approach has been adopted in recently initiated fire behaviour studies in South Africa. For the sake of brevity the discussion will be largely limited to the effect of different variables on fire intensity. This is because research in the eastern Cape has shown that fire intensity is significantly correlated with rate of spread, flame height and maximum temperatures recorded at different heights above-ground during fires (Trollope 1980a).

FUEL

Fuel characteristics such as particle size, distribution, compaction, moisture content and quantity have very marked effects on fire intensity but have not been studied to any significant degree in South Africa.

Particle size

According to the ease with which different fuel sizes ignite and burn Luke and McArthur (1978) have classified plant fuels into two broad types, namely fine fuels and heavy fuels. Fine fuels comprise all plant material with a diameter up to 6 mm and burn very readily (in a grass fire almost complete combustion normally occurs). Conversely combustion in heavy fuels (such as are present in forest), is incomplete because of the great bulk of some of the dead material. Data from le Maitre (1981) and Smith (1982) clearly illustrate the greater combustion of fine compared with heavy fuels in mountain shrubland and fynbos in South Africa. Where insufficient fine fuels are available, great difficulty may in fact be experienced in achieving a successful burn, as Smith (1982) has shown.

Fuel distribution

Fire behaviour is greatly influenced by the vertical distribution of plant fuels and Brown and Davis (1973) recognized three broad groups, namely, ground, surface and aerial fuels.

Ground fuels include all combustible material below the loose surface litter and comprise decomposing plant material. These fuels support glowing combustion in the form of ground fires and are difficult to ignite but are persistent once ignited (Brown and Davis 1973). **Surface fuels** include standing grass swards, shrublet communities, seedlings, forbs and loose surface litter. These are fine fuels and can support intense surface fires in direct proportion to their quantity per unit area (Brown and Davis 1973). **Aerial fuels** include all combustible material, live or dead, located in the understorey and upper canopy of tree and shrub communities. The main components are mosses, lichens, epiphytes and branches and foliage of trees and shrubs (Brown and Davis 1973). This fuel type can support high intensity crown fires, as shown by the data presented in Table 3 for fynbos communities.

Fuel compaction

Fuel compaction refers to the placement of individual pieces of fuel in relation to one another. Combustion is optimized when the fuel is sufficiently loosely packed to enable adequate quantities of oxygen to reach the flame zone but dense enough for efficient heat transfer to occur. Fuel spacing is especially critical in heavy fuels but generally adequate ventilation occurs in the majority of fuel types (Luke and McArthur 1978). This is particularly true for fine grass fuels in South Africa where it has been shown that fuel compaction had no significant effect on the intensity of surface grass fires (Trollope 1980a). No other quantitative data are available in South Africa on the effect of fuel compaction on fire behaviour.

Fuel moisture

Fuel moisture, normally expressed on a dry mass basis, is a critical factor in determining the intensity of a fire because it affects ease of ignition, quantity of fuel consumed and combustion rate of different types of fuel. The most important influence of moisture on fire behaviour is the smothering effect of water vapour leaving the fuel and diluting the oxygen in the air immediately surrounding the fuel (Brown and Davis 1973).

Luke and McArthur (1978) distinguish between the moisture content of live and dead fuel. In the former it varies gradually in response to seasonal and climatic changes whereas in the latter it is hygroscopic and the moisture content is affected more rapidly by adsorption and desorption in response to changes in the relative humidity and atmospheric temperature.

Evidence for the important role which fuel moisture plays in modifying fire behaviour in South Africa is provided by results from the eastern Cape where fuel moisture contents ranging from 29 to 89% significantly affected the rate of spread and flame height of head fires (Trollope 1978a). Further results indicated that the threshold moisture content between living and cured plant material for grass fuels is ca 40% and that fuel moisture per se has a significant effect on fire intensity only when it is greater than this value (Trollope 1980a). The important effect of fuel moisture is also illustrated by research conducted in the Kruger National Park where the quantity of green grass and the preceding months' rainfall were the only factors that had a significant effect on the mean maximum temperatures recorded during fires applied at different frequencies and seasons of the year (Potgieter 1974).

Fuel load

Fire intensity is directly proportional to the amount of fuel available for combustion at any given rate of spread of the fire front (Brown and Davis 1973). Research in South Africa has shown that fuel load is a major contributor to fire intensity, generally accounting for between about 30 and 60% of the variation in intensity between grassland fires (Trollope 1980a; Trollope and Potgieter 1983).

ATMOSPHERIC AND PHYSIOGRAPHIC CONDITIONS

Air temperature

The direct effect of air temperature on fire behaviour is to influence the temperature of the fuel and therefore the quantity of heat energy required to raise it to its ignition point (Brown and Davis 1973). It also has indirect effects via its influence on the relative humidity of the atmosphere and moisture losses by evaporation (Luke and McArthur 1978). Research has shown that the intensity of surface grass fires may increase significantly with higher air temperatures (Trollope 1980a), but that this is not always so (Trollope and Potgieter 1983). In order to ensure that fires are relatively safe ($<$ 3 500 kJ s^{-1} m^{-1}), Trollope and Potgier (1983) have nonetheless suggested that air temperatures should not exceed 30°C where other characteristics are conducive to hot fires.

Relative humidity

Relative humidity of the atmosphere influences the moisture content of the fuel when it is fully cured and not unexpectedly, therefore, has a negative effect on fire intensity, particularly when the fuel moisture content is $<$ 40% (Trollope 1980a). Practical experience shows that the intensity of a fire is potentially high when the relative humidity is $\leq$ 30%.

Wind

The combustion rate of a fire is directly influenced by the rate of oxygen supply to the fire (Brown and Davis 1973), and so wind speed tends to be positively related to the rate at which energy is released by the fire. Wind also causes the angle of the flames to become more acute and with increased wind velocities the flames are forced into the unburnt material, resulting in more efficient preheating of the fuel and greater rates of spread in surface head fires (Luke and McArthur 1978). Beaufait (1965) found that wind speeds ranging from 0 to 3,6 m s^{-1} increased the rate of spread of surface head fires exponentially but had no effect on the rate of spread of back fires. Apparently its lack of effect on back fires is a widely observed phenomenon (A M Gill, personal communication, 1980). Beaufait (1965) suggested that even though the flames are blown away from the fuel immediately adjacent to the fire front during back fires, flame propagation results from preheating and ignition mechanisms occurring beneath the surface of the fuel.

Both Brown and Davis (1973) and Luke and McArthur (1978) state that increased wind speeds cause greater rates of spread and therefore more intense fires. However, flame height is negatively associated with wind speed because increased wind speeds cause the flames to assume a more acute angle and this partly explains why crown fires do not always occur during high winds.

Fire behaviour studies in South Africa have shown that wind speed has no statistically significant effect on intensity and flame height of surface grass fires under conditions of controlled burning where the wind speed normally does not exceed 5,6 m s^{-1}. In one study the mean wind speed for 90 controlled burns was 2,9 ± 1,7 m s^{-1} (Trollope 1980a). The conclusion is that at relatively low wind speeds, overall atmospheric wind conditions do not significantly affect the behaviour of surface head fires and that these fires are largely subject to the air movements generated by the convection column.

No quantitative information is available on the effect of wind speed on ground and crown fires in South Africa.

Slope

Slope significantly influences the forward rate of spread of fires burning up-slope by increasing the degree of preheating of unburnt fuel immediately in front of the flames. This is achieved, as with wind, by creating acutely angled flames with slopes exceeding 15 to 20°. Conversely, a down-slope decreases the rate of spread of surface fires (Luke and McArthur 1978) and at low wind speeds has the effect of converting a head fire into a back fire. Experience gained in the USA indicates that the increasing effect of slope on the rate of spread of head fires doubles from a moderate (0 to 22°) to a steep slope (22 to 35°) and doubles again from a steep to a very steep slope (35 to 45°) (Luke and McArthur 1978). Cheney (1981) has proposed the following general relationship between slope and rate of spread:

$$R = R_o e^{bx}$$

where
R = rate of spread (ms^{-1})
R_o = rate of spread on level ground (ms^{-1})
b = 0,0693
x = angle of slope (°)

No quantitative data on these effects are available for South Africa.

USE OF FIRE BEHAVIOUR DATA IN STRATEGIES FOR ECOSYSTEM MANAGEMENT

In South Africa fire behaviour knowledge has been intuitively used during application of controlled burns and in combatting wild-fires. A largely undocumented body of knowledge has been gained through experience in the field and generally pertains to safe application of controlled burns rather than to the achievement of predetermined effects on the ecosystem. While recognizing the fundamental importance of using fire with a minimum risk to life and property it is believed that with existing knowledge and future research it is both feasible and necessary to use fire behaviour data to achieve management objectives based on known reactions of ecosystems to different types and intensities of fire.

Using the results from South African work as a basis, the following preliminary conclusions regarding the use of fire in veld management can be drawn.

1   Controlled burns should be applied as head fires because they may cause least damage to the grass sward but can effect maximum damage to woody vegetation if necessary.

2   When burning to remove moribund, unacceptable grass material a low intensity fire is required to remove the material and cause least damage to the grass sward. This can be achieved by burning when the air temperature is <20°C and the relative humidity is >50%.
    These conditions frequently prevail during the period 15h30 to 11h00. The fuel load should be as low as possible but sufficiently continuous to carry the fire.

3   When burning to eradicate or prevent the encroachment of undesirable plants an intense fire is required. In the case of fynbos, karoo and encroaching herbaceous species, the plants are themselves normally highly flammable and the grass fuel load required to destroy these plants is therefore less than that needed to destroy tropical and subtropical trees and shrubs which have nonflammable foliage. Research and experience indicate that a fire sufficiently intense to destroy the aerial portions of bush to a height of ca 2 m will be obtained when the grass fuel load is > 3 000 kg ha^{-1}. Finally, in both the flammable and nonflammable communities the air temperature must be > 25°C and the relative humidity < 30% to ensure an intense fire. These atmospheric conditions frequently occur between 11h00 and 15h30.

4   In all cases the grass fuel must be fully cured and the wind speed should not exceed 5,6 m s^{-1} for safety reasons.

Chapter 10   Effects of Fire on Vegetation Structure and Dynamics

F. J. KRUGER

INTRODUCTION

In this chapter an attempt is made to summarize our understanding of the changes caused by fire in vegetation of different South African biomes. Concepts of succession are reviewed as a background to what follows. Then the responses in vegetation structure that have been documented in the region are summarized, as well as published information on the different vegetation structural variables that have been shown to respond to fire. Finally, information on fire effects is summarized for fynbos, forest, grassland and savanna. Information on the karoo biome is too scant to justify a review.

In some cases plausible and influential hypotheses have been offered to explain patterns of fire effects in different biomes and these are discussed below. Responses of vegetation to fire must by and large be analysed by examining the responses of individual constituent species in order to understand the mechanisms of fire's effects. The scant information for South African biomes is summarized here, largely within the framework of current succession theory.

SUCCESSION

Many of the effects of fire on vegetation must be interpreted in terms of ecological succession which may be defined as the more or less orderly process of change in ecosystems over time, cumulative and directional for the duration of a limited interval, and involving a progressive change in the structure and composition of the vegetation and fauna. Here, secondary succession, ie changes following disturbance of a previously vegetated site, are considered. The concept does not include seasonal change, and in this chapter also excludes fluctuation change due to year-to-year or longer-term changes in the controlling environmental factors, such as the dynamics described by Macdonald (1978c) which will be discussed below.

Concepts of succession and the climax were introduced to South Africa by Bews (1916) and Phillips (1931) and were latterly based largely on the system proposed by Clements (1916, 1936). This approach was applied more or less rigorously by many subsequent investigators (Killick 1963; Edwards 1961), and continues to strongly influence approaches to resource management (Tainton 1981b).

Expressed briefly, Clementsian theory reads as follows: given certain climatic conditions and absence of disturbance, vegetation that occupies a site will change progressively until it reaches an equilibrium characteristic of the prevailing climate, irrespective of the original condition of the site. This, the climatic climax, comprises species fully adapted to their environment and assembled so as to fully utilize the resources of the site. Succession encompasses a number of fundamental processes, which may be "...successive or interacting." In the initiation phase, the processes include nudation - the processes that cause the site to be exposed; migration - the arrival of propagules at the site; ecesis - germination, establishment and growth; and reaction - the effect of the established community on the site. Reaction modifies the site in favour of new immigrants. In the continuation phase the established community develops further through the processes of competition - absent or ineffective hitherto - as well as those operating in the initiation phase, until the community equilibrates during the stabilization phase as the climax formation. The climax is analogous to the organism, which has emergent properties and the capacity for regeneration. Succession is analogous to organismic development: "As an organism, the formation arises, grows, matures, and dies" (Clements 1916).

Clements recognized the influence of disturbing factors within the context of climatic control. The proclimax was identified as a class of stable, persistent communities that had not attained climax status, and included the following types: the subclimax, representing a community which is maintained by recurrent disturbance, especially by factors such as fire, ie a community of a kind typical of the successional stage preceding the climax; the disclimax which closely resembles the subclimax, but results from "...the modification and replacement of the true climax...or from a change in the direction of succession...", as would result from, for example, the displacement of native dominants by exotic plant invaders, or the effects of introduced herbivores; the preclimax, which includes communities of plants adapted to earlier climatic conditions, surviving as relicts following an amelioration of climate; and the postclimax, which includes those relicts that survived a deterioration of climate.

Clementsian theory has been shown to be insufficient to explain existing vegetation patterns or successional sequences or both in a large number of important cases (Drury and Nisbet 1973; Colinvaux 1973; Connell and Slatyer 1977; Miles 1979). The theory itself is criticised on the grounds that most of the theoretical features of succession and the climax (for example, trends to maximum biomass and species diversity) are simply the inevitable consequences of growth and other processes over time, rather than of internal properties of the community, and that many other characters are deductions based on the invalid organismic concept. Connell and Slatyer (1977) therefore propose an explicit hypothetical framework for the study of succession, in the form of models to explain succession by processes and mechanisms involved, rather than the "emergent" properties of the ecosystem. The three models advanced assume for each that any site exposed by disturbance is occupied by species with colonizing ability and therefore that "...early occupants modify the environment so that it is unsuitable for further recruitment of...early-succession species". Their first model, the "facilitation" model, is identical with Clementsian theory. Only certain pioneer species are able to establish and these early species react on the site to favour invasion by later-succession species and to disfavour recruitment of their own kind, and so on in relay, until the sequence terminates when the site is occupied by species that do not facilitate invasions. In the case of the other two models, any species "...that are able to survive there as adults can establish themselves". In the tolerance model, later successional species succeed whether or not they are preceded by early succession species, but species are assumed to differ demographically so that fast-growing species may dominate the site early, but slow-growing species tolerate shading and/or other effects of the closing stand to survive and grow. The composition of the dominants adjusts as shorter-lived species die and those among them that are not tolerant are excluded. Tolerant species grow from established plants and/or invade, and the stand is ultimately dominated by these species. In the inhibition model, the earlier colonists occupy the disturbed site fully and no further invasion is possible. Slow-growing later-successional species are suppressed and the stand develops through the normal processes of growth among these pioneers. No recruitment occurs during development. However, when the stand is fully developed, dominants begin to die. These may be replaced by species already present and the composition of the stand does not change. But the space released by mortality of dominants can allow entry of species of late-successional character and if such species are available succession may proceed once more. Also, plants of late-successional species that arrived originally at the disturbed site may survive in a suppressed state and grow to ultimate dominance when released by mortality among early-successional dominants. Thus "...later species cannot grow to maturity in the presence of earlier ones; they appear later because they live longer and so gradually accumulate as they replace earlier ones". Whereas early successional species are killed in competition with later-successional species in the first two models, in the inhibition model they are not and die through local disturbance or natural mortality factors.

Connell and Slatyer's (1977) proposals rely on the distinction between early- and late-successional species. The former are seen to be those that are highly vagile, quick-growing, short-lived and intolerant of competition for resources, while the latter are less vagile, slower-growing, long-lived, and tend to tolerate competition for resources. They are therefore respectively equivalent to r- and K-species in terms of evolutionary ecology.

Few South African studies provide tests for these models. Nevertheless, where data are available their validity will be discussed. In doing so, a distinction will be made between pyric succession – the changes in vegetation between one fire and the next – and secular changes, that occur over a long time in response to a change in fire regime.

VEGETATION RESPONSES TO FIRE REGIME

STRUCTURAL VARIABLES SENSITIVE TO FIRE REGIME

All vegetation variables are more or less sensitive to fire regime and the chapters in this volume contain many examples of how fire influences biomass, cover, height, species composition, and the relative proportion of woody to herbaceous species. But what have not yet emerged are general principles to explain such responses. For example, basal cover responds to fire frequency in grassland, savanna and fynbos, and the hypotheses to explain

the nature of this response in grasses are presented below. Of
interest is whether these hypotheses will survive experimental
trial, and whether the same hypotheses can be proposed for
fynbos. Some simple generalizations concerning the relationship
between grass and woody components in savannas are emerging but
can these generalizations be extended to all South African
biomes?

Community diversity changes with succession and fire regime.
Thus, species richness changes with pyric succession in fynbos
(Adamson 1935) and in other vegetation. In fynbos, species
richness apparently increases with fire frequency (Campbell and
van der Meulen 1980; van Wilgen 1981b), though successional and
fire frequency effects interact and have yet to be separated.
Relative changes in diversity seem to depend on the relative
dominance of overstorey plants (Campbell and van der Meulen 1980)
so that reductions in diversity are greater in tall dense shrublands than elsewhere. This apparently supports Specht and
Morgan's (1981) generalization for Australian vegetation. Though
high fire frequencies may eliminate some shrub species, the
number of woody species increases. In savanna, by contrast,
marked increases in numbers of tree and shrub species occur where
fire is deferred (Trapnell 1959; I A W Macdonald, personal
communication, 1979; though data in Gertenbach and Potgieter 1979
show no such response). For arid savanna at Matopos, Macdonald
reports double the number of woody species in plots protected for
27 yr, as compared with those regularly burnt although richness
on plots burnt at frequencies ranging from annually to once in 5
yr did not vary significantly by treatment. Data for the herbaceous stratum were not reported. For false thornveld savanna in
the eastern Cape Province, Robinson et al (1979) show a marked
increase in the numbers of species in the herb layer of protected
veld, relative to frequently burnt veld, mainly due to increases
in forb species. This appears to be the general trend, judging
by mention of such enrichment in many reports. There could
therefore be directly opposite trends in fynbos and savanna. The
patterns in grassland have apparently not been described, but
probably resemble those in savanna. Thus the flora of fynbos
contains numerous species adapted to frequent regeneration by
fire, whereas the same can be said only of graminoids and certain
other herbs in grassland and savanna. These biomes, by contrast,
contain many woody species not always evident in the community,
that have traits not adaptive in a regime of frequent fire.
Study of this contrast may allow a better understanding of the
phenomenon in general. The reasons for such a difference could
lie in fundamentally different successional processes in fynbos.

Dominance and equitability are also affected by fire. Thus,
in dense fynbos, mature stands are often dominated by one or a
few shrubs, whereas after fire biomass is usually distributed
more uniformly. Exceptions occur, as for example when conditions
favour a post-fire flush of legumes. Frequent fire also tends to
favour equitability rather than dominance concentration (van
Wilgen 1981b, 1982). Post-fire recovery in tropical coastal
forest was marked by dominance of *Trema orientalis* (pigeonwood),
which constituted 73% of total basal area (and hence approximately of biomass) as opposed to five species that constituted about

72% of total basal area in the adjacent, unburnt stand (Macdonald and Pammenter, 1979). In grassland, equitability responds little to fire but where fire is long deferred, dominance concentration may increase as one or a few shrubs invade (Granger 1976a). Such stands react like fynbos. Here again responses to fire appear to reflect fundamental differences in successional processes in the different biomes. May (1978) has noted how tropical plants tend to have evolved competitive ability, rather than the tendency for "weediness" shown by temperate plants (K- vs r-selection). Hence, few plants in the tropical coastal forest are good colonizers, and these few dominate the post-fire community, as opposed to the temperate fynbos, with many woody 'r-species'.

Pattern also responds to fire regime. Thus, Tainton et al (1978) show how irregular burns result in "...large widely spaced grass tufts...", relative to the sward produced under a regime of intensive defoliation through burning plus mowing. Trapnell (1959) describes a pattern of open, grassy "fire pockets" alternating with patches of thicket that developed under the early burning experimental regime in savanna woodland in northern Zambia, a phenomenon which could no doubt be replicated in South African equivalents. Local fuel concentrations such as prostrate tree-trunks and consequently severe local heating of the soil can initiate enduring patterns of grass distribution (Macdonald 1978c). Grassland and fynbos subject to regular burns show little pattern, and plants of different forms are closely intermingled. Frequent fire, in defoliating the cover regularly and opening space indiscriminately, appears to a large extent to mask factors governing patterning of species and individuals in the stand.

DYNAMICS OF VEGETATION IN RELATION TO FIRE

Through the process of pyric succession in the interval between fires in the normal regime the original pre-fire vegetation is replaced more or less perfectly. There is abundant evidence that, in fire environments, vegetation regains its original physiognomy given sufficient successional time. What kinds of change in vegetation follow a change in regime?

Certain concepts are important here. In a biome that is prone to fire one may assume that the biota evolved under the selective pressure of a given fire regime, which we may term the normal fire regime. In chapter 5 the kind of normal fire regime that may characterize fynbos has been described. However, in any given element of the landscape the vegetation formation presently found may owe its existence to a particular regime whose mean frequency and seasonality, for example, differ from those of the normal fire regime, though included in the normal probability distribution. This may be called the prevailing fire regime. Under the prevailing regime the vegetation is in dynamic equilibrium - it takes on a limited range of states or structures that intergrade continuously in the process of succession. If the prevailing regime is modified the vegetation will change as a new dynamic equilibrium is established. Such a change may or may not involve major changes in physiognomy and may be more or less reversible, depending on local patterns of invasion and extinction. For example, in fynbos the species composition of a stand will apparently remain essentially stable if fire recurs on average once every 8 to 30 yr. Frequencies of less than once in 8 yr will tend to eliminate seeding shrubs, and elimination is nearly complete when frequencies exceed once in 4 to 6 yr. A shrubland is then converted to a herbland in the extreme case. Once this condition has been induced, decreasing the frequency to less than 8 yr will not necessarily allow immediate return of a shrubland, because seeding shrubs have become locally extinct and seed dispersal from outside is poor (Bond 1980). For this reason, and because fire recurrence intervals that coincide with or slightly exceed the youth periods of seeding shrubs severely limit the individual reproductive potential, frequencies may need to fall well below once in 8 yr to allow recovery of shrubland. Conversely, where conditions are suitable, diminution of the shrub component due to senescence when frequencies are much less than once in 30 yr may be accompanied by immigration of rain forest precursors which, since they have sprouting ability, could tend to persist even if frequencies were increased to about once in 30 yr. Similar arguments could be advanced for montane grassland. Thus we see that changes in the prevailing regime may effect quantitative as well as conditionally persistent **qualitative** changes in the vegetation, and these may be reinforced by changes in the nature of fuels that accompany changes in plant dominants and in microclimate.

EFFECT OF FIRE INTENSITY

For the purposes of this review, fire intensity will be regarded as the net effect of those behavioural variables that determine the amount of energy delivered to an organism or organ of interest, and the rate of delivery. Fire intensity affects vegetation structure and dynamics through: (a) differential effects on survival of plants and propagules on the site, (b) variable stimulation of on-plant or soil-stored propagules, and (c) differential effects on the physical and biological factors that define the regeneration niche of any given species, and this includes the indirect effect of the relative amounts of vegetation removed. Thus fire intensity can have a profound effect on the initial composition of the community in pyric succession. Examples are the phenomenon of locally persistent vegetation patches induced by burning logs and branches reported by Macdonald (1978c), and the differential effects of head and back burns reported by Trollope (this volume, chapter 9). Persistent differences in fire intensity per se can apparently have a marked effect on savanna structure. Thus West (1965) explains the death and disappearance of savanna trees in Trapnell's burning trials, and their persistence under similar burning regimes in semi-arid savannas of Zimbabwe, as being due to the hotter fires in the former case, because of greater fuel load under more mesic conditions.

Although there are many references to observations of the relative effects of "hot" and "cool" fires on vegetation in the preceding chapters and the South African literature in general, there have been very few controlled studies on the effects of fire intensity, aside from Trollope's (1978a) pioneering work. Investigators have concentrated on testing fire season and rotation in their trials since these variables apparently have a stronger effect than intensity. Seasonal and frequency effects are now fairly well understood and extensive investigation of intensity effects would be justified, particularly since they are so commonly alluded to in the literature.

EFFECT OF SEASON OF BURN

The season in which fire occurs affects subsequent structure of vegetation because it interacts with plant phenology and post-fire weather to moderate plant survival and reproduction.

Plants survive fire best if burnt when dormant. In Natal tall grassveld, Tainton et al (1977) showed that varying the time of either mowing or burning between 1 August and 16 October had little effect on tiller survival and subsequent regrowth. Slightly later fires, when shoot growth was active, markedly reduced tiller survival and recovery growth rates. Sympatric grass species vary in their seasonality of growth and reproduction and thus variation in timing of fire around the season of growth initiation will differentially affect sward composition. Tainton and Booysen (1963, 1965a,b) have shown this for the sympatric tufted grasses *Tristachya leucothrix*, *Hyparrhenia hirta*, and *Themeda triandra*. Phenological differences often correlate with growth form as in the contrast between trees and herbs, or between the "pre-rain" or spring geophyte floras and autumnal aspect plants among the summer-growing hemicryptophytes of grasslands (Bayer 1955; Roux 1969; and see chapter 6), and these often underlie the structural changes that follow changes in season of fire. Unseasonal summer burns in the grasslands of the Drakensberg reduced sward productivity and basal cover, and reduced the frequency of *Themeda triandra* and other sensitive grass species relative to previously less common species such as *Rendlia altera* (Scotcher and Clarke 1981).

Survival rates of some species that regenerate vegetatively are not sensitive to the season of fire. For example, in fynbos, mortality in fire among *Protea nitida* and *Watsonia pyramidata* varies little seasonally (Haynes 1976; see also chapter 6). Such species may form a relatively stable component of the vegetation, compared with others.

Species that regenerate after fire from seed may also be phenologically sensitive to season of fire, depending on seasonality in availability and condition of seed, as suggested for *Protea repens* (sugar bush) by Jordaan (1949, 1965), or specific seasonal requirements for germination post-fire as in *P. magnifica* (bearded protea) (Deall and Brown 1981). Thus, where regeneration in dominant shrubs is influenced by fire season, marked changes in vegetation structure are possible if fire season deviates from the normal.

In herbaceous species that sprout, vegetative recruitment as well as sexual reproduction is affected by fire season. Thus the

Jonkershoek sample of *Watsonia pyramidata* burnt in autumn responded by a 27% growth due to vegetative reproduction and a 7 500%
growth due to seedling recruitment, while a similar sample burnt
in spring did not respond at all (Kruger 1978). Positive sexual
and vegetative reproductive responses to fire in the right season
are common in grasses (Daubenmire 1968; Vogl 1974; Tainton and
Mentis, this volume, chapter 6) and there are many South African
examples but the rule is not uniform. For example, *Anthephora
pubescens* markedly increases seed production after spring burns
(Donaldson et al 1972), as does *Eragrostis curvula*, but in
Themeda triandra flowering is inhibited (Tainton and Booysen
1963). The effect depends on the seasonality of tiller
elongation. Experiments by Nursey and Kruger (1973) show how
total seed yield from *Anthephora pubescens* populations are
markedly increased by burning in early spring, ie at the start of
seasonal growth, as compared with yields from stands burnt in
late spring (as inflorescence shoots began to elongate) and
unburnt controls. Seed also ripened much earlier in the latter
than the former case. Burns in certain seasons, eg late spring
and summer, or autumn on an annual cycle, can inhibit or prevent
flowering (chapter 6). Differences in reproductive responses
between sympatric species are often reported, and in such cases
variation in the season of fire within the "favourable" period
can lead to changes in vegetation composition (West 1951 for
Trachypogon spicatus vs *Monocymbium ceresiiforme*).

Fire interacts also with climatic seasonality to effect
structural changes. The effect of subsequent weather on seed
regeneration in fynbos is sometimes seen in seedling mortality
during drought after "late" (spring) burns, which in turn affects
the balance between seeding and sprouting species in the vegetation (see Specht et al 1958 for a detailed description of the
phenomenon for analogous Australian heathland). Contrasting
conditions - warm humid weather following spring burns - have
been seen to cause seedling mortality through damping off.
Interactions with weather are various and have many effects. For
example, late winter burning ameliorates ground frosts and
permits early resprouting of grass in Dohne Sourveld. In the
Drakensberg, as in the southern Cape (Granger 1976a; Bond 1980),
autumn burning can be followed by severe deflation during bergwinds, with apparent net loss of nutrients in ash. Leaching of
bases through rains on spring burns in the Bankenveld significantly reduced concentrations of available bases as compared with
soils of sites burnt in winter (White and Grossman 1972).
Climatic control on moisture content of soil and bark, and hence
of their thermal conductivity, can play a role in determining
plant mortality rates in fires at different seasons (West 1965).
Initial tissue temperatures vary similarly and also affect
survival (West 1965). These relations are vague, however, and
have yet to be established in terms of the structural response of
vegetation.

Fire regime is a third-order ecological variable, and is
determined principally by climate and vegetation (Gill 1974).
Hence, in any given biome fires tend to occur during the season
when vegetation is driest and thus very often dormant, and when
climatic variables favour fire. This seasonality has interacted

with other environmental factors as a selective force to determine the kinds of plant species and hence form of vegetation in the biome, and this vegetation is usually highly stable under such a "natural" seasonality. Thus, fire in the favourable season acts as a cue both for enhanced reproductive output among sprouters and enhanced recruitment by vegetative or sexual reproduction. In the *Protea magnifica,* seed released after fire requires exposure to moist-cool conditions to break dormancy, thus ensuring germination in the fynbos winter (Deall and Brown 1981). Hence, natural communities of species adapted to local environments stabilize under favourable fire seasonalities. Sympatric species differ in their responses to fire season as a result, for example, of asynchronous phenologies and differences in reproductive biology, and variability in the incidence of fire within the favourable fire season would contribute to the continued coexistence of species by allowing fluctuations around the mean composition.

Changes in fire season can lead to changes in composition but not physiognomy, as where the composition of the grass sward changes from one dominated by *Themeda triandra* to another with other grass dominants (Scotcher and Clarke 1981; Tainton and Mentis, this volume, chapter 6). If the regime changes beyond the adaptive capacity of the dominant plants the effect on structure may be marked. Thus, unseasonal fires can eliminate dominant fynbos Proteaceae, and change a tall shrubland to a low shrubby herbland in a single event (Jordaan 1965; W J Bond, personal communication, 1981). The apparent increase in forbs in summer-burnt Drakensberg grassland (Scotcher and Clarke 1981) suggests that changes as great as those in fynbos can be caused in these grasslands by changes in fire season.

The nature and magnitude of vegetation responses to fire season are too poorly understood to allow proper prediction of fire regime effects and prescription for management in South Africa, and considerable research is necessary. Available evidence shows that such research should begin with the reproductive strategies of plants, and how these relate to environmental seasonality. Attempts to find and apply a "natural" fire season without understanding plant responses are less than profitable (Scotcher and Clarke 1981).

EFFECTS OF FIRE FREQUENCY

The effects of fire frequency on vegetation are usually readily evident. The more frequent the fire, the greater is the herbaceous component, and the less frequent the fire, the more abundant the woody component. Nevertheless, this relationship is not sufficiently understood to allow proper management of vegetation. Thus there is considerable controversy about prescriptions for fire frequency in fynbos, even with agreement on management goals (Moll et al 1980).

Noble and Slatyer (1977, 1981) have established the logical framework for analysing vegetation response to fire frequency in their system describing plant vital attributes. South African examples are discussed here in this context.

Mode of plant persistence

Noble and Slatyer recognized two different categories of mechanism that allowed plants to persist through a disturbance on a site. The first of these relates to species that lack the ability to sprout after fire and must regenerate from seed and, implicitly, other propagules on the site. These include:

(a) species unable to persist in situ and regenerating from seed dispersed to the site from surrounding, undisturbed vegetation (vital attribute D); (b) species regenerating from a long-lived store of seed in the soil and where a balance of dormant seed remains in the pool after disturbance (vital attribute S); (c) species regenerating from soil stored seed where the entire seed store is exhausted at disturbance (vital attribute 9); and (d) species regenerating from seed stored in the canopy, this source being exhausted after any given disturbance (vital attribute C). The second set includes those species which regenerate vegetatively from plant parts surviving the disturbance. This includes (e) those species which resprout but which must pass through a juvenile stage before maturing (vital attribute V); (f) those which are virtually unaffected (vital attribute U); and (g) those which are virtually unaffected at the adult stage but are exterpated in the juvenile stage (vital attribute W). Also included are combinations Δ, ε and γ which correspond to D, S and G attributes but where the adult stages sprout and are immediately reproductively mature.

(a) **Sprouters** (vital attributes V, U and W). It is a truism that species which reproduce vegetatively withstand highest fire frequencies, but species response to variation in frequency is little understood. The sprouting trait is apparently usually linked to some requirement for periodic defoliation to maintain vigour, both in herbs (as in *Themeda triandra* and other sward-forming grasses - chapter 6) and woody plants (as in savanna, geoxylic suffrutices (Frost, this volume, chapter 13) and in sprouting *Protea* spp (Rourke 1980)). Because sympatric species vary in this respect, local, relatively small variations in fire frequency can strongly influence the relative importance of different sprouting species in the stand. Because of high relative growth rates and tillering in graminoids, very high fire frequencies favour herbaceous sprouters over woody species though these latter are extremely persistent. For example, Trollope (1973) reduced the relative biomass of "macchia" species from dominance to relative insignificance by short-rotation burning, but most or all species continued to survive. Trapnell (1959) quotes numerous cases of woody species and vines that were reduced from their previous prominence in woodland to relative obscurity in a wooded savanna by frequent burning but the woody species continued to survive and retained the capacity to recover when fire frequency was reduced once more. Thus, variations in fire frequency have largely quantitative effects on vegetation composition and structure but limited qualitative effects that result in local extinction or immigration of species. Because of the persistence of sprouting trees and shrubs even under high fire frequency, a reduction in frequency can result in rapid changes in vegetation structure as such woody species are allowed to increase in stature. Thus, variation in fire occurrence between high and intermediate frequencies will govern vegetation structure mainly through regulating the relative abundance of sprouters. When fires are infrequent, however, the vigour of sprouters can be reduced and qualitative changes in structure and composition follow as new species enter the community. Furthermore, because sprouters frequently respond to burning by flowering and since a number of them lose fecundity as shoots age (Frost, this volume, chapter 13), recruitment by sexual reproduction falls off as fire frequency decreases.

As noted by Rutherford (1981) and others (Frost, this volume, chapter 13), many shrubs and trees, especially in savannas, readily survive fires that pass through the herbaceous layer, because meristems or cambium or both are protected by bark or in some other way. Established populations of these species are apparently relatively insensitive to fire and therefore to changes in fire frequency, as witnessed by extensive savanna woodlands in areas which are frequently burnt.

(b) **Indispersal** (vital attributes D and Δ). Species which distribute seed widely are relatively insensitive to changes in fire frequency because seed is normally delivered to any given site in the habitat to replace adults killed by fire. Species that cannot mature on the site because of high fire frequencies are nevertheless present as seed or juveniles. Seed dispersal patterns in South African vegetation are hardly known, but evidence is now accumulating to indicate that different types may have distinct dispersal spectra. Thus at least some fynbos communities appear to comprise species adapted for local dispersal of seed within the community, with very few distributing seed over long distances (Levyns 1929b, 1935b; Wicht 1948b; Bond 1980; Bond and Slingsby 1983), whereas trees of forest and some in savanna are apparently predominantly adapted for long-range dispersal (Frost, this volume, chapter 13). The profound implications that dispersal patterns have are already partly implicit in attitudes to management of vegetation but dispersal in relation to fire regime has become a key research question as refinements to management begin to demand better understanding and evidence for interference in dispersal processes begins to emerge (Slingsby and Bond 1982, regarding the argentine ant).

(c) Soil seed banks (vital attribute S, G and Σ). If fires are not so frequent as to persistently eliminate parent plants before maturity, soil-stored seed can effectively buffer the plant species against variations in fire frequency. The range in frequencies that can be tolerated will depend on the dynamics of the particular seed bank, as described in chapter 13. Soil-stored seed is no doubt found in all South African biomes, but present evidence suggests that it is most important in fynbos (chapters 5 and 13), where mostly intolerant, rather short-lived shrubs are implicated. Here, fire frequency relates to vegetation structure in two ways: (i) where parent plants disappear through senescence, increasing intervals between fires would decrease the incidence of shrubs in the vegetation, and (ii) where members of the seed pool differ in duration of seed viability, eg large- and hard-seeded Fabaceae vs small-seeded Ericaceae, a shift toward lower fire frequency would favour long-lived members of the seed-pool. These suggested relationships are scarcely more than surmise and critical research is urgently needed.

(d) Canopy-stored seed (vital attribute C). This phenomenon is confined largely to vegetation of coastal and mountain fynbos. The effectiveness of canopy-stored seed is limited to the life-span of the parent. In intolerant species, lengthening the interval between fires beyond this life-span would result in local extinction but such low fire frequencies are seldom reported for fynbos. More important to management is the fact that variation in fire frequency will govern abundance of regeneration from such shrubs because reproductive potential of parents varies according to post-fire age.

Conditions for establishment

Distinction is made between tolerant species (T), where seedlings are able to establish in the stand at any time and to tolerate competition, intolerant species (I) that are able to establish only immediately after disturbance and are intolerant of competition in the established stand, and species that have some requirement for establishment such that they are unable to establish immediately after disturbance, but are able to do so when succession has ameliorated conditions (R).

Intolerant (I) species, in contrast to (R) species, will be favoured by high fire frequencies and ultimately eliminated by low frequencies. The dominant plant species of the different biomes often seem to fall into either one category or the other. Thus, forest species seem to require the special microclimate of older vegetation for establishment, whereas fynbos species require open sites.

Studies on germination and recruitment patterns in fynbos (Levyns 1929b; Kruger and Bigalke, this volume, chapter 5) indicate that intolerance is a feature at least of most shrub species. The little work done in forests indicates the opposite (Phillips 1931; Geldenhuys 1975) and the role of fire frequency in determining distribution of forest and fynbos is conventionally explained in these terms, though the notion has not been tested.

There seems to have been little work, aside from studies on individual species such as *Acacia karroo* (sweet thorn), on the establishment requirements for plants in grasslands and savannas. With respect to many woody species it appears that seedlings are intolerant, requiring the frequent exposure of establishment sites by burning (as in *Pterocarpus angolensis* (kiaat), and other cryptogeal species). On the other hand, the "late-successional" species that appear both in woodland (as in Trapnell's study) and grassland with protection or the lengthening of intervals between fires are apparently able only to establish under well-developed vegetation, though this could equally be due to a life-history character requiring infrequent and patchy disturbance of a kind with effects different from those of fire.

A knowledge of the spectrum of establishment requirements in the available flora could explain many of the patterns in grass-land and savanna woodland succession that accompany changes in fire frequency, as will be shown below.

Life stages

The third vital attribute incorporates life history stages critical in response to disturbance and its frequency. These include (i) the time taken for a species to reach reproductive maturity after a disturbance (m), (ii) the life span of the species in the undisturbed community (l) and (iii) the time taken for all propagules to be lost from the community ie for local extinction (e).

FIRE AND VEGETATION IN SOUTH AFRICAN BIOMES

FYNBOS

Pyric succession

The apparently typical pyric succession for fynbos has been described extensively in chapter 5. The general pattern fits Connell and Slatyer's (1977) inhibition model, in the special case where the regenerating stand is nearly identical in species composition to the parent stand. However, as noted elsewhere the composition of the parent and hence the regenerating stand may depend on the period elapsed since the previous fire, and of the regenerating stand by the season of the burn.

Levyns (1935b) described a striking pyric succession in coastal renosterveld near Riversdale. A stand dominated by *Elytropappus rhinocerotis* (renosterbos) was replaced as a dominant by *Falkia dichondroides* (a tropical member of the Convolvulaceae), tropical Acanthaceae, and a *Pelargonium* in the first year after fire, while the stand was dominated in the second, third, and fifth years respectively by *Selago corymbosa*, *Aspalathus spinosa*, and *Aspalathus microdon*. *E. rhinocerotis* was prominent by the fifth year and predicted to be dominant by the next and succeeding years. Marked and rapid senescence was noted among early-successional species. Nevertheless, this sequence was not a replacement series, every species in the sequence being present in the first year post-fire. Thus the autosuccessional inhibition model applied here too. As in renosterveld at Ida's Valley (Levyns 1929b), grasses played a relatively insignificant role in the succession. In fynbos of more fertile soils and in a more equable rainfall regime elsewhere (Martin 1966; Trollope 1973; Robinson et al 1979), grasses are often dominant in the early pyric succession. However, views of pyric succession in fynbos come mainly from nutrient-deficient sites with high rainfall and the patterns of succession as they vary with moisture regime and soil conditions need urgent study.

Secular vegetation replacement sequences

A single example of fynbos is used here to illustrate possible vegetation replacement sequences. This picture is then qualified by reference to examples from elsewhere. The species listed in Table 1 have been selected from a complete list for a tall proteoid shrubland on granite soils, receiving about 1 600 mm per yr under a winter rainfall regime. Species listed are dominant or typical of each stratum. Two species in the list were not recorded in the stand. *Aspalathus* spp would have been present as dormant seed, while *Kiggelaria africana* (wild peach) seed is regularly dispersed to this kind of site. Vital attributes have been given for each species according to Noble and Slatyer's (1981) scheme. Leaving aside questions of fire intensity and season, how would this vegetation, which has been maintained under a regime of fire once in about 20 yr (van Wilgen 1982), respond to changes in fire frequency?

Table 1   Vital attributes for representative species of a typical proteoid shrubland, Jonkershoek State Forest (from Kruger 1979). Vital attributes given according to Noble and Slatyer (1981). See text for explanation of symbols.

	Method of persistence	Conditions for establishment and maturation	Timing of life stage parameters, yr since fire			
			Maturity		Death (life span)	Local extinction
			Sprouts	Seedling		
Widdringtonia nodiflora	V	I	6	20	150	150
Protea neriifolia	C	I	–	8	50	50
Brunia nodiflora	V	I	3	20	70	70
Erica plukenetii	S	I	–	6	30	32
Erica hispidula	D	R	–	6	infinite	infinite
Restio triticeus	U	I	1	10	100	100
Watsonia pyramidata	U	I	1	10	150	150
Kiggelaria africana	D	R	–	20	infinite	infinite
Aspalathus spp	S	I	–	3	6	100

Widdringtonia nodiflora (mountain cedar) sprouts after fire but also carries seed in closed cones. Since these seeds are released mainly when tops are killed, seedlings are presumably intolerant. Sprouts produce new cones about 6 yr after fire. In vegetation protected against fire, *W. nodiflora* at Jonkershoek shows signs of shoot senescence (heart-rot, windfall) from about 40 yr on but individuals are presumably long-lived, and populations should last 150 yr. *Brunia nodiflora* is like *W. nodiflora* except that senescence is more marked from 40 yr, so the presumed life-span is 70 yr. *Protea neriifolia* (oleander-leaved protea), the tall (3 to 4 m) dominant shrub, is a seeder. Populations reach effective maturity (ie with sufficient ripe seed for self-replacement) by about 8 yr post-fire, carry seed in the canopy, and begin to senesce from about 30 yr, with an effective life-span of about 50 yr. No seedlings establish effectively in regenerating and mature vegetation. *Erica plukenetii* and *E. hispidula* share similar life-cycles but the former apparently relies on soil-stored, short-lived seed for regeneration. Seedlings are intolerant and the populations form a single cohort. In *E. hispidula*, germination and establishment is delayed until vegetation has recovered somewhat after burning, and occurs sporadically through the development of the stand. At least some germination is apparently from indispersed seed so that propagules are always available on site. *Restio triticeus* and *Watsonia pyramidata* have similar life-histories, sprouting and flowering readily after fire, but the latter has longer-lived ramets. *K. africana* is a forest precursor tree dispersed widely by birds but absent from frequently burnt and regenerating to mature vegetation. It apparently requires the conditions of a senescing stand for establishment.

If fire recurs within three years only sprouting plants and *Erica hispidula* and *Aspalathus* spp in the juvenile form survive. Because of limited life-spans and three years or more for sprouts to produce flowers, *W. nodiflora* and *B. nodiflora* will ultimately be eliminated from the site by such frequent fires, and the *Aspalathus* seed-pool will become exhausted and the species locally extinct within a century or so. Lengthening the fire-free interval to an average of 6 yr or slightly more allows for the survival and normal life-cycles of all species but for *P. neriifolia* and *K. africana*. If fires recur at between 8 and about 30 yr, the stand will comprise entire fynbos flora. *K. africana* may appear as juveniles as *P. neriifolia* senesces from about 30 yr but could not persist. Reduced frequencies result in an attenuation of the fynbos. *E. plukenetii* would not survive frequencies of less than once in about 30 yr, *P. neriifolia* once in 50 yr, and *B. nodiflora* once in 70 yr. As frequencies fall below once in about 50 yr, *K. africana* will have the opportunity to grow to maturity and form with *W. nodiflora*, *E. hispidula*, *R. triticeus*, *W. pyramidata* and *Aspalathus* spp (as a fugitive), a mixed forest precursor stand.

This analysis reflects the broad fire-induced patterns of vegetation at Jonkershoek and similar sites elsewhere (McKenzie et al 1977; van Wilgen 1982) except in certain important respects. First, when senescence in *P. neriifolia* at Jonkershoek opens the canopy, its seeds are able to germinate, and it establishes and matures once more, so that a cyclic population replacement is evident. This is not the rule, however. For example, Bond (1980) found no effective establishment of extant overstorey shrubs in open, senescent shrubland in the Swartberg, and surveys of senescent vegetation on Lebanon and Kogelberg State Forests (Kruger, 1980) produced similar results. These observations were from well-drained, infertile quartzitic soils, in contrast to the more fertile, finer-textured soils at Jonkershoek.

Secondly, establishment and growth of *K. africana* and similar forest precursors is variable. At Jonkershoek these precursors are abundant and have grown rapidly in long-unburnt vegetation near streams, but are sparse and variably stunted, 20 m or more away on the slopes, despite uniform overstorey vegetation. In surveys of senescent vegetation elsewhere, no forest precursors were found.

Thus, vegetation replacement sequences in fynbos, though poorly documented and understood, are clearly not uniform. Vital attributes and consequent replacement patterns seem to vary according to water balance as determined by climate and soil factors such as depth, texture, and local drainage patterns, to soil fertility status, and the available biotas. These patterns must be determined to allow an explanation of fynbos dynamics and its reaction to fire.

FOREST

Pyric succession

There is a notable dearth of descriptions of pyric successions in forest. In Knysna forest, the pattern of succession depends partly on the degree of disturbance, ranging from little change with light crown fires to an apparently complete replacement with intense ground fires (Phillips 1931). Because crown fires seldom occur in the forest except during extreme weather conditions, pyric succession following ground fires is the most frequent. Though most forest tree species sprout if defoliated or otherwise damaged (Phillips 1931; van der Merwe 1966b; C J Geldenhuys, personal communication, 1979) ground fires kill most trees except deep-rooted ones such as *Ocotea bullata* (stinkwood), *Curtisia dentata* (assegai tree), and *Cassine crocea* (red saffronwood) (Phillips 1931), but nearly all overstorey trees are often killed, as in the Woodville fire of 1963 (C J Geldenhuys, personal communication, 1979). Under these extreme circumstances, different pyric successions are evident. First, the site is rapidly occupied by perennial herbs such as *Pteridium aquilinum* (bracken fern), *Brachypodium flexum*, *Carex clavatum*, *Helichrysum petiolatum* and other congeners, *Senecio quinquelobus* and congeners, *Galopina circaeoides* and others, to form a dense tangled layer 1,4 to 1,8 m tall (as at Woodville) which apparently permanently occupies the site, or are sometimes replaced by the reptant fern *Gleichenia polypodioides* (climbing fern) (Phillips 1931), and here no further vegetation replacement is evident.

This is an extreme form of the inhibition model of Connell and Slatyer (1977). By analogy to the clearfelled site at the Forest Creek Concession Area (van Daalen 1981), herbaceous early-successional species can give way to Proteaceae, Ericaceae and other typical fynbos, with no further replacement.

Phillips (1931) describes the "usual" successional sequence as follows: (i) a stage of dense weed growth of Cyperaceae, *Helichrysum* spp, *Senecio* spp, *Rubus* spp and others, among which are coppice shoots of overstorey trees and seedlings of shrubs of the second stage; (ii) the second stage of "weak, woody shrubs", where *Psoralea* spp, *Podalyria* spp, *Erica* spp, species of the Bruniaceae, *Sparrmannia africana* (Cape stock-rose) and other short-lived species may form single-species or mixed stands, 3 m or more high within 18 months, in which seedlings of *Halleria* and *Burchellia* "...may be present at this time..."; (iii) if the site bore *Virgilia oroboides* (keurboom), then seedlings establish post-fire and grow through the first and second stages to dominate and form a stand 7 to 10 m tall, with seed as well as coppice regrowth of various overstorey forest species below the canopy; and (iv) replacement of the weak shrubs and/or *V. oroboides* by canopy species. Phillips implies that the canopy species enter the stand progressively and therefore that the facilitation model applies here, but the evidence is weak and the tolerance model could be equally valid.

These depictions of pyric successions must suffice as initial models for Afromontane forests. Is the pattern of pyric succession for tropical coastal forest similar? Macdonald and Pammenter (1979) give a precise picture of early regeneration after an apparently intense crown and ground fire in Zululand coast forest. This caused a major transformation in the forest. Vegetation analysed on the burnt site three years after fire was dominated by trees rather than herbs or soft shrubs, but tree basal area was reduced to about one-fifth of that of unburnt forest tree species composition had changed by 57%, and the regenerating forest was overwhelmingly dominated by a seeding tree, *Trema orientalis*, a pioneer r-strategist absent from the unburnt stand. Canopy species present in regenerating vegetation recovered mainly by sprouting. No data are given for herbaceous species, but the pattern of early regeneration is clearly different from that in many instances in Knysna forest. There is also no analysis of seedlings and young plants and it is therefore not possible to say which Connell and Slatyer model would fit the coast forest pyric succession.

Secular vegetation replacement sequences

It is uncertain to what extent the present distribution of forests reflects recent (100 to 2 000 yr BP) man-induced disturbance, including modified fire regimes, and therefore what the "natural" limits to forest distribution are under present circumstances. For example, Acocks (1975) maps potential Knysna forest to occupy some 3 800 km^2 and implies a reduction in its actual extent to about 650 km^2 owing to human influence, including anthropogenic fire. However, with respect to the Knysna

Forest region Phillips (1931) argued that"...macchia type appears to be climax in nature...(on)...upper mountain slopes, the whole of the summits of the range, portions of the foothills and certain limited lateritic portions of the plateaux ...". Macchia (fynbos) could constitute the climax on sites both too dry and too wet for forest.

Any consideration of fire regime and its effects on dynamics of forest vegetation must be placed in the framework of an explanation of the physical enviromental controls on forest distribution. In this respect, no critical work has yet been done in South Africa. General climatic maps are poor predictors of forest distribution (Schulze and McGee 1978). Within zones of putative forest climate, major forest boundaries are found that clearly are natural and coincide with soil factors (van Daalen 1981, for the Ysternek site). Both Schimper (1903) and Phillips (1931) have explicitly proposed that such physical limits are set not only by climate but also by physiographic and edaphic factors – soil depth, texture, internal and lateral drainage – that determine soil moisture-retaining capacity and hence local water balance (see also van Daalen 1981). Acocks (1975) has repeated references to such control while Tinley (1982) has emphasized how physiographic patterns and processes can effect a complex pattern of distribution of forest. If such an hypothesis is defensible then the rapid and nearly universal replacement of grassland by forest following fire exclusion and other protection in moist tropical coastal dune areas (Weisser 1978) with relatively uniform soils and local climates would be as readily explained as the patchy "relictual" pattern of forests in fynbos and montane grasslands in areas of strong relief and heterogeneous soils. Intriguing alternatives include the possibility that physiographic factors create suitable conditions for establishment by exposing a mineral seed-bed as well as by offering shelter in an otherwise hostile landscape, as in the case of the donga forests described by Acocks (1975).

Given that the question is confined to situations where the changes are possible, what replacement sequences will follow changes in fire regime, and how can these be predicted from a knowledge of the vital attributes of the species concerned? Within forests at least two species types are encountered among pioneers: local persistence through long-lived seed in *V. oroboides* (Phillips 1931), and probably extreme vagility in *T. orientalis*, both being intolerant species dependent in their life-cycles on periodic catastrophe. But as to other pioneers, no information is available. The limited work on late-successional species, mainly by Phillips (1931), suggests that these are highly tolerant species, able to survive at light levels as little as 1/500 those of full sunlight, but few data have become available on conditions required for seedling establishment. *Podocarpus falcatus* (Outeniqua yellowwood), however, indicates that the species is intolerant in its own presence but tolerant elsewhere. The studies on pyric succession above did not provide detailed information on establishment of a late-successional species. However, Phillips's (1931) accounts suggest that these species established either immediately post-fire, or soon after, and would classify as intolerant or tolerant, rather than as types that require an amelioration of the site before establishing.

How do forest species colonize grassland or fynbos? With regard to the latter, and regarding only sites that clearly have the potential to carry forest, two extreme positions are evident. Firstly, van Daalen (1981) has investigated forest-fynbos ecotones in the Knysna area and found several where the transition was not marked by any notable physiographic or edaphic boundary. These "artificial" boundaries, at least inferentially owing to fire, marked a sharp cutoff in the distribution of forest and fynbos taxa. No forest precursors were found in fynbos adjoining forest. Van Daalen concluded that the replacement of fynbos by forest was markedly inhibited, but did not choose among three explanations: constraints on forest establishment in fynbos owing to "leaky" nutrient cycling in the latter; persistence of a fire regime in fynbos that precludes forest species with life-histories maladaptive under that regime; and microclimatic conditions, specifically excessive seasonal moisture deficits, in fynbos that could not be tolerated by forest precursor seedlings and/or young plants.

Phillips (1931) reports forest precursors in fynbos adjoining forest and freely conceives of a replacement sequence where forest follows fynbos, with or without intervening the keurboom and other stages. He emphasized that extremely low light levels under dense fynbos (1/500 to 1/1 500 of full sunlight) could not be tolerated by forest precursors and only when cover declined could they establish. This view could also explain the sequence involving wild peach described above for Jonkershoek.

Thus, at this stage it is not possible to establish whether forest precursors are inhibited from colonizing fynbos because they are intolerant of the fynbos environment, or because they require some amelioration of the site, or because the life-history parameters are nevertheless maladaptive under a regime of even infrequent fire (less than once in 40 yr). The situation regarding forests and grasslands is similar. Whatever the case, the species' method of arrival of persistence on a site and the conditions required for establishment and maturation are presently the most urgent aspects requiring investigation in attempts to understand forest dynamics.

GRASSLAND AND SAVANNA

Pyric succession

In grassland and wooded savanna, pyric succession is essentially a process of vegetative recovery, rapid (requiring 12 months in humid tropical conditions, perhaps four years in semi-arid savannas) and seldom involving great changes in plant populations. This recovery process is usually trivial in relation to the overall dynamics of grassland and savanna ecosystems (Walker 1982). Nevertheless the immediate changes in palatability and accessibility of herbage, as documented in chapters 6 and 7, the pulse of plant reproductive activity, and pronounced changes in leaf area ratios and other foliage characteristics of woody plants (Rutherford 1981), effect the crucial role of pyric successions in faunal dynamics.

SECULAR VEGETATION REPLACEMENT SEQUENCES

For the present, grassland and savannas are conveniently subdivided in "climax" formations, where climatic or pedologic conditions determine the balance between herbaceous and woody strata, and subclimax formations, where fire maintains grassland or savanna instead of woodland or forest (chapters 2, 6 and 7). The matter of forest succession in "subclimax" grassland has been discussed briefly above, and this account focuses on the role of fire in climax grassland and savanna.

Climate, especially moisture regime, (Walter 1971; Walker and Noy-Meir 1982) but also frost (Acocks 1975), is usually accorded the major role in determining the structure of grasslands and savannas. "The structure of a savanna is ...primarily determined by competition between woody and grass plants for available soil water. Modifying factors are fire, herbivores and soil nutrients" (Walker and Noy-Meir 1982). Nevertheless, the evidence in this volume shows clearly that the effect of fire regime on dynamics and hence structure of grasslands and savanna determines the form of vegetation within the limits set by climate, substrate and biogeography, at least within those zones where climate and productivity allow fairly regular fire.

The grass sward

The key role of fire regime, with or without the role of other defoliation, in determining the nature of the grass sward has been shown by West (1965), Tainton and Mentis (this volume, chapter 6) and others. Deferral of fire results in accumulation of litter, senescence and mortality among plants in the grass layer and, presumably, ultimate extinction of the grass plants, and is accompanied by an overall decline in basal cover. Decline in the grass sward permits immigration and/or development of shrubs and trees. This occurs even with rainfall of 600 mm yr^{-1} and less, but the critical fire frequency tends to decrease with decreasing effective rainfall. Changes in composition of the grass sward include competitive displacement of aerial-tillering species such as *Themeda triandra* by others such as *Tristachya leucothrix* which tiller from underground stems. At least the initial phases of these changes are by inhibition of tillering due to the shading effect of litter (West 1965). The grass sward declines more quickly with more effective rainfall because the relationship between production and decomposition allows far more rapid accumulation of litter than in dry areas. This decline is reinforced by the higher intensities of fires when they do occur in stands where litter has accumulated (West 1965). Thus, responses of the grass sward to fire regime are not accommodated in the analytic system proposed by Noble and Slatyer (1981).

The sward in humid areas (rainfall exceeding about 1 000 mm yr^{-1}) retains its cover and vigour with annual burning, but in drier areas short rotations tend to reduce the density of the sward. Thus, at Potchefstroom (rainfall about 600 mm yr^{-1}), burning at a fire interval of three years or more is necessary to maintain the sward (Theron 1946). On the basis of experiment and observation West (1965) suggested that this was the result of increased soil moisture stress due to reduced rainfall infiltration caused by puddling of soils with frequent burning. This is apparently a factor only in semi-arid environments. In Zimbabwe, Kelly and Walker (1976) have shown how fire destroys litter and effectively reduces infiltration and hence soil moisture. By contrast, data presented by Tainton and Mentis (this volume, chapter 6) for a humid environment show how soil infiltration rates are reduced by burning and mowing treatments, but the reduced rates nevertheless still greatly exceed maximum rainfall intensities.

The woody stratum

In moist savannas, as noted previously, the development of woodland or forest following protection from fire apparently involves processes both of growth of already established savanna species, as well as immigration, establishment and growth of new "forest" species (Trapnell 1959). The picture for arid savannas is apparently similar. Thus, in all grassland and savanna experiments fire exclusion has resulted in increased species richness (including South African arid savannas - Gertenbach and Potgieter 1979), usually because of immigration of woody species. Thus, fire regime regulates the density of the woody stratum not only by governing the biomass accumulation of trees and shrubs but also through effects on survival, establishment and growth. As Walker (1982) has put it: "Owing to their long evolution with fire, most savanna (woody) plants are adapted to it, and the proportion of species which are easily killed is very low. They nevertheless exist, and there is a continuum from those which are highly susceptible to those which are extremely resistant. The relative abundances of the two extremes on any site is a fair reflection of the fire history of that site". Of 21 species of trees and shrubs investigated by Rutherford (1981) at Nylsvley, all sprouted after fire. There was a significant difference in overall mortality caused by head fires and back fires but differences were small (5% mortality in trees in the back fire vs 2% in the head fires and no real difference for shrubs). The unaffected reproductive capacity of most species was by the burn (U in the Noble-Slatyer system) though some may have required a year or two for shoots to mature (V). In one species, *Burkea africana* (red syringa), seedlings and juveniles survived poorly (W). Thus, the established woody stratum in savannas is resistant to high fire frequencies because of high survivorship and largely unaffected reproductive performance, but there is evidently a component of the flora that is sensitive to fire regime.

What determines relative performance of species? Seed of most woody plants in savannas is apparently well dispersed and available for germination and establishment at any site. Of the 21 species studied at Nylsvley (Rutherford 1981), at least 14 species had seed dispersed by animals, and hence highly vagile. Walker (1982) states that "most species are easily killed as seedlings, and their resistance increases with age, up to the point where they become senescent, and again susceptible." This generalization neglects the evidence for cryptogeal germination, an effective mechanism for seedling establishment in the face of frequent fire. It seems therefore that while the methods of persistence of savanna trees and shrubs are fairly well known, at least in general terms, knowledge of the requirements and mechanisms for establishment, and the life-histories of species types is required to allow a predictive understanding of this continuum of sensitivity to fire regime.

The grass-bush balance

Pasture scientists have paid close attentin to the effect of fire on grasses but have not often studied the responses of trees or shrubs, most being satisfied with experimental demonstration of gross developments in tree and shrub strata under different treatments. Attempts to explain the phenomenon of grassland replacement by shrubs or trees have had limited success. *Stoebe vulgaris* readily invades protected Bankenveld grassland, though it is readily excluded by regular spring burning, apparently because germination is precluded in the well-lit environment of burnt veld (Roux 1969). Thus, *S. vulgaris* appears to be a highly dispersed species with special requirements for establishment. Once established, it is not readily displaced by burning with or without grazing since it regenerates readily from adventitious buds on the stem bases, although further establishment is prevented by burning. Lecatsas (1962), however, has shown that season of burn has an effect on mortality, with about 50% mortality in summer (mid-November until the end of December) burns, as opposed to 5 to 7% mortality in October burns. He deduced from analysis of nitrogen content of resprout shoots and from laboratory trials that defoliation and resprouting during summer caused "...a general disturbance in nitrogen metabolism..." which enhanced mortality. By contrast, the invasion of grassland by karoo shrubs is ascribed to the open conditions of degraded grassland allowing germination and establishment of the invaders (Roberts 1981). This process, and its relation to fire regime, needs considerable further study. Thus Donaldson and Mostert (1958) obtained significant reduction in the density and basal cover of *Chrysocoma tenuifolia* (bitterbos) by means of spring burning, to the benefit of the grass stratum, in the western Orange Free State. Squires and Trollope (1979) have suggested that invasion of sweet grassveld of the eastern karoo by *C. tenuifolia* is facilitated by allelopathic inhibition of grass development, an effect which is drastically reduced by fire. Proper understanding of such processes could allow considerable refinement to the general recommendations offered by Roberts (1981) for veld reclamation under these circumstances. Studies of *Acacia karroo* as an invader of grassland have also been inconclusive as to the underlying mechanisms determining its success or failure (du Toit 1972b). However, Trollope (1974, 1979) presents experimental evidence to support the proposal that *A. karroo* is able to establish in grassland in areas of erratic rainfall during years when conditions are less favourable for grass, and that grasslands in such areas could be maintained only through the synergistic effects of fire and browsers in defoliating *A. karroo* and reducing its competitive advantage. Whatever the case, there is too little information to provide a general picture of the underlying mechanisms which determine interactions between fire and the woody components of grasslands and savannas.

Various hypotheses based on experiment and on general experience have been presented to explain the role of fire in the dynamic relations between the grass sward and shrub and tree strata (West 1965; Trollope 1980b). These may be reduced to the following: the competitive ability of species of the grass sward is apparently crucial and any factor which acts against this, including deferred burning, too frequent burning, and aseasonal burning, will favour development of woody components. Additionally, phenological differences between grass forms and tree and shrub forms permit differential effects of fire in different seasons. Since woody components usually begin growth in early spring before grasses are active, "late" dry season burns usually maintain grass at the expense of shrubs and trees (but the seasonal effect is confounded with fire intensity). Grass, on the other hand, is highly sensitive to burns in the growing season and can be thus weakened in favour of woody species. Frequency generally favours grass if high but not otherwise, for reasons outlined above and because of the relatively slower growth-rate of woody species. Intensity is an important variable, favouring grass if high but not if extreme as with high fuel loads when fire is deferred. Intensity is related to many variables but correlates strongly with grass biomass so that there is often strong positive feedback between grass growth and intensity. Finally, fire and herbivores often have a powerful synergistic effect.

A change in fire regime from say an annual rotation to a 5 yr rotation, induces changes which may stabilize quite rapidly in a new equilibrial vegetation structure. This may happen within six years in Natal Tall Grassveld, for example (Edwards 1961). This new equilibrium involves not only a new composition but also pyric succession processes which differ from the original (Scott 1971). In arid savannas, grass swards can be reduced quite rapidly below the minimum level required for relatively regular fires, and the vegetation quickly stabilizes in a new state where shrubs or trees dominate and can no longer be displaced by fire or even any form or combination of forms of herbivory (West 1965; Donaldson 1967). The change is apparently irreversible in nature. This process of bush encroachment is reinforced by the positive feedback between grass biomass and tree and shrub cover. The flammability characters of the grass fuels change also with change in growth form on base-saturated soils ("sweet" grasses, as opposed to "sour" grasses on leached soils). There may also be fundamental differences in fire behaviour and in its ecological effects.

CONCLUSION

Although imperfectly understood it is clear that fire regime exerts a discernible influence on vegetation of all South African biomes outside the succulent types, the communities of the arid west coast and forests, where its role is poorly perceived and in any event controversial. At least in mesic grasslands and savanna, fire regime is a crucial determinant of structure. In fynbos fire is a pervasive phenomenon playing perhaps a fundamentally different role in permitting high community diversity levels by accommodating plant life-cycles that cannot be completed in its absence - unlike those cases in other biomes where defoliation by, for example, herbivores can serve the same role - and possibly by recycling scarce nutrient resources.

Only in the case of mesic grasslands and savannas is it possible to formulate explicit statements linking fire regime to the response of dominant plant species and thus to the stand of vegetation. Even here, it is only the responses of grass forms that are reasonably well understood. It seems therefore that there are pressing needs for proper field trials in many types of vegetation, and for plant autecological studies of a range of representative species. Most important is the theoretical framework required to generalize from the few studies that resources will allow.

Chapter 11 The Effect of Fire on Forage Production and Quality

M. T. MENTIS and N. M. TAINTON

INTRODUCTION

Numerous estimates of primary production have been made in various parts of southern Africa. The topic was reviewed recently by Rutherford (1978), and additional studies were undertaken by du Plessis (1972), Porter (1975), Tainton et al (1978), van der Westhuizen et al (1978) and le Roux (1979b). Many analyses of the quality of plants, mostly grasses and bushes, and mostly in regard to those eaten by domestic and wild ungulates, have also been conducted (Henrici 1935, 1940; Botha 1938; du Toit et al 1940; Weinmann 1955; Mes 1958; Louw et al 1968a,b,c; Louw 1969; Joubert et al 1969; Roth and Osterberg 1971; du Plessis 1972; Hall-Martin and Basson 1975; Tainton et al 1977; Aucamp et al 1978; van der Westhuizen et al 1978; Mentis 1978; Downing 1979; Stindt and Joubert 1979; Tomlinson 1980; Mentis and Bigalke 1981a). There is, however, scant information specifically on the effect of fire on plant production and quality. Within this constraint of limited availability of information, this chapter aims to synthesize what direct and indirect evidence is available on the influence of fire on the quantity and quality of forage produced in South African ecosystems, with emphasis upon those which are characterized by a grass field layer.

Forage is here defined as plant material which may be consumed by secondary producers (herbivores). Not all plant material produced is or can be eaten by herbivores. Firstly, with the exception of some animals, such as baboons, mole-rats and grassland francolins which consume roots, corms and tubers, the underground plant material is not available to most herbivores. Secondly, a variable amount of the above-ground material either is not available to herbivores because it is out of reach, or is not acceptable because of particular physical structure, poor nutritive value, or because of the presence of spines, hairs or unpalatable or toxic compounds. In this synthesis fire is examined as a factor which may modify primary production, the acceptability and availability of the material produced, and hence forage production.

Gross primary yield is here used to represent the amount of plant material which accumulates over and above the respiratory needs of the plants and the flow to decomposers, but in the absence of large herbivores (ie the size of hares or larger) and fire. The gross accumulation rate describes the rate at which this yield accumulates. Net primary yield is defined here as the yield of plant material after losses to respiration and decomposers, and in the presence of whatever herbivores there are, and whatever fires occur. Net accumulation rate describes the rate at which yield accumulates in the presence of these defoliating agents.

EFFECT OF FIRE ON GROSS AND NET ACCUMULATION RATE AND YIELD

In terms of the above definitions, most if not all southern African systems have, at least in the short term, a positive gross accumulation rate. With the possible exception of forests and moribund communities, wherever large herbivores and fire are excluded, plant material accumulates. This rate of accumulation is variable. In the short term it is rapid in savanna, grassland and fynbos, slow in the karoo, and very slow if not approaching zero in mature forest (Rutherford 1978). In the long-term absence of significant defoliation (by large herbivores or fire or both), the gross accumulation rate declines, and must tend to zero since infinite growth in a finite system is impossible. With the accumulation of plant material, plants become moribund. The time scale for these events appears to depend on both gross primary yield and vegetation type (West 1965; Rutherford 1978). In humid grassland and humid savanna the moribund stage is reached in 2 or 3 yr. In arid grassland and arid savanna the time might be the same during a succession of wet years, but otherwise the process may take up to about 10 yr. In fynbos moderately high growth rates may apparently continue in undisturbed stands for several decades. In the karoo the growth rate within the community is low except in unusually wet years, so that yield normally remains low and a moribund condition may take many years to develop.

In contrast to the trends in accumulation of herbage in the absence of fire, grazing and browsing in southern Africa, it is commonly observed that the net accumulation rate over a period of 1 or 2 yr is generally low in unprotected sites. This is so simply because of the intensity of grazing, browsing and fire on most land. Recently, and probably to a significant extent in the evolutionary past (see chapters 5, 6 and 7), these defoliating agents have maintained the vegetation in a productive condition. However, in many cases present regimes of defoliation have been excessively intensive. Too frequent defoliation by animals and fire has both short- and long-term consequences for production.

SHORT-TERM EFFECTS OF FIRE

Where perennial grasses of the summer rainfall, humid grasslands have remained undefoliated for some time, individual plants become moribund or composed largely of inactive mature tillers. Defoliation at this stage will stimulate basal tillering (Drewes 1979) if there are basal tiller initials, so that growth rate will remain high. In Giant's Castle Game Reserve the above-ground net yield in grassland measured in winter was 261,4 g m^{-2} on an area burnt in spring 23 months previously, and 209,9 g m^{-2} on an area burnt in spring 11 months previously (Scotcher et al 1980b). In collecting these data no attempt was made to account for the amount of grazing since burning, or for the loss of plant material to decomposed litter. However, these two types of loss were probably small, so that accumulation in the second growing season was substantially less than in the first growing season following a spring burn. The implication is that in humid grassland the depressive effect of accumulated plant material on growth operates possibly in the first and certainly in the second growing season following defoliation. Thus in these kinds of situations fire rejuvenates the sward. However, if basal tiller initials are absent, fire simply kills the plants and depresses production. Where a sward of perennial grasses is defoliated, say grazed, frequently, then plant material may not accumulate sufficiently to inhibit basal tillering. If fire is applied at this stage it may destroy the apices of a large proportion of actively growing tillers, at least in swards dominated by *Themeda triandra*. Gross accumulation rate in the immediate postfire period is then depressed. This happens because the new tillers which develop after the fire, although continuing to grow relatively late into the summer, grow more slowly than the more mature but still active tillers would have grown had they not been burnt (Anon 1973/74; Drewes 1979).

The effect of fire on seeding by perennial grasses is variable. *T. triandra* produces flowers in the second growing season after burning (Tainton and Booysen 1965a). This happens because the tillers are biennial and the apices of tillers which flower in one season elevate late in the previous season, and thus are vulnerable to fire for an extended time which includes the normal burning period of spring. Other grasses, like *Eragrostis curvula*, have flowering in the immediate postburn period stimulated by burning (Field-Dodgson 1976). In this case tillering from the basal initials is stimulated by fire, and these tillers flower in the season of their initiation. Still other grasses, for example *Festuca costata*, do not flower unless they are burnt, and a spring burn is followed by more prolific flowering than burns at other times.

Vernal aspect forbs are stimulated to flower and produce leaf by early burning (ie winter to early spring) (Bayer 1955). The bared soil surface and consequently elevated soil temperatures are the stimulus. Where this early defoliation does not occur frequently, the failure to produce leaf is likely to depress production of underground storage organs which are characteristic of these forbs.

Regarding annual plants, fire may stimulate germination and growth, and therefore increase the gross accumulation rate in the short term. This happens where the burning removes a canopy which has been sufficiently dense to restrict the growth of the annuals through smothering by the canopy of perennial plants. This effect is particularly prevalent in fynbos where annuals are common only during the immediate postfire period and before the tall growing shrubs form a dense canopy (chapter 5).

Periodic fire every 4 to 30 yr rejuvenates the woody components of fynbos (chapter 5) and probably those of savanna as well. In fynbos, frequent fire may eliminate bushes which are not able to flower in the interval between burns. However, in the extended absence of fire, the bushes senesce, their foliage is reduced to tufts at the tips of branches, and mortality rises. To an extent the opening of the canopy as bushes die is followed by seed regeneration, but fire at this stage will either induce vigorous coppicing (as for example in the forest margins shrubs *Leucosidea sericea* (ouhout) and *Buddleia salviifolia* (sagewood)) or stimulate seed regeneration as in *Philippia evansii* (Smith 1982). Therefore, as with herbs, periodic fire stimulates continued growth of bush species in fynbos and in savanna, but generally the optimal frequency of fire is longer for woody plants than for herbs.

LONG-TERM EFFECTS OF FIRE

Since the frequency of fire affects the botanical composition of communities, and since plant species differ in their productive capacity, fire frequency may be expected to affect overall gross accumulation rate and yield. There have, however, been few attempts to document its long-term effect.

In the Moist Tall Grassveld of Natal, a range of frequencies of defoliation were applied for 18 yr. Defoliation included mowing or burning or both in several combinations ranging from 3 defoliations per yr to no defoliations whatsoever. At the start of the 19th or test year, all plots except those which had been protected (undefoliated) were mown in winter. With the experimental defoliation treatments suspended, the gross primary yield was measured for the growing season of the test year on all except the protected plots. Over the range from triannual to triennial defoliation, there was generally an increase in gross yield as the frequency of defoliation decreased (Anon 1973/74). This trend is the result of the effect of defoliation frequency on cover and botanical composition, rather than of the immediately preceding defoliation treatment. However, although there are no measurements, it is apparent that gross yield on the protected plots after 18 yr is low. From these data it might be concluded that in humid grassland a fire frequency between once in 2 yr and once in 18 yr maximizes gross accumulation rate in the first growing season after a winter defoliation. Nevertheless, frequent defoliation, compared to infrequent defoliation, over a number of years will produce a higher mean gross yield per year. This is because of the smothering effect arising under a regime of infrequent defoliation, as discussed previously.

In Giant's Castle Game Reserve the above-ground net primary yield of grassland not burnt for 9 yr was 1 656,7 g m^{-2} (Scotcher et al 1980b). This is almost eight times the net yield (209,9 g m^{-2}) measured in grassland 11 months after a spring burn. The implication is that, in humid grassland, the long-term absence of fire leads (at least before woody plants invade) to little decline in gross accumulation rate. This contrasts with the short-term effect of the absence of fire (see above), and there are perhaps two reasons for the difference. Firstly, the change in floristic composition induced by excluding defoliation is often towards a dominance of robust, relatively unacceptable, highly lignified plants such as evergreen *Festuca costata* in the montane region and *Cymbopogon* spp in other grassland. The unmeasured loss of material to herbivores is therefore likely to be less in unburnt *Festuca* or *Cymbopogon* veld than in frequently burnt *Themeda* veld. Secondly, dead material from these robust grasses is likely to decompose more slowly than that from *T. triandra* and its associates.

In the absence of data, it is only possible to speculate on these long-term effects in savanna, fynbos, arid grassland, karoo and forest. Possibly, the fire frequency which maximizes gross accumulation rate in the year following defoliation decreases from humid grassland and humid savanna to fynbos, arid grassland, arid savanna and karoo.

EFFECT OF FIRE ON FORAGE ACCEPTABILITY

"Acceptability" is used here to include all those factors which contribute to the attraction of an item as forage to an animal. Acceptability is thus a function of nutrient and energy content, digestibility, the effect of digestibility on intake, the presence of chemicals such as tannins, alkaloids and resins, plant surface factors like spines and hairs, the particular mixture of forage items, the type of animal and the physiological status of the animal. There is little direct information on the effect of fire on these factors.

Mes (1958) observed the spring regrowth in selected highveld grasses on burnt grassland as compared to unburnt grassland to have a higher nitrogen and ash content. The difference was, however, short-lived, and did not persist beyond the end of October. In the Moist Tall Grassveld of Natal the nitrogen content of spring-produced grass on burnt plots was substantially higher than that of new growth on veld mown at the same time (Tainton et al 1977). This difference persisted through to late summer, apparently because the growth on the burnt plots was almost exclusively from newly developed tillers and composed largely of leaf growth whereas on mown veld much of the recovery growth was generated from old tillers, carried over from the previous season, and including a proportion of stem material.

Measurements of the quality of herbage in relation to fire in grassland in the Natal Drakensberg have been made by Mentis (1978) and Scotcher et al (1980b). Grass regrowth after fire was high in crude protein, potassium and phosphorus, and low in crude fibre. The percentage of crude protein, potassium and phosphorus decreased and of crude fibre increased with time after burning. In the absence of fire the percentage of crude protein in grass was higher in summer than in winter, but the summer values were less than in recently burnt grassland. The calcium, magnesium and ether extract contents of grasses remained fairly constant. On areas burnt in autumn (March) the veld was of higher nutritive value to large herbivores in winter than on areas burnt in spring or summer. Forbs at all times had higher concentrations of crude protein than did grasses, and these concentrations, as in the grasses, were higher soon after rather than long after burning. The concentrations of potassium and phosphorus were also higher in the immediate postburn regrowth of forbs than in unburnt plants. The ether extract content of forbs as a whole was fairly constant. However, in some individual species (eg *Senecio bupleuroides*) the percentage of ether extract increased steadily to about 8% of the dry matter 11 months after burning. The genus *Senecio* is well known for its generally high alkaloid content. In the Weende proximate analysis, the ether extract fraction includes, in addition to fats and resins, whatever alkaloids the sample contains. The increase in the ether extract of *S. bupleuroides* with time since burning may therefore be an example of a chemically based adaptive response restricting defoliation by animals. Presumably, the immediate demands on the plant after burning are to recreate an effective photosynthetic area in competition with other plants. Once such leaf area has been developed the diversion of chemical resources to products which have a protective role may increase. The role of fire in making plants with these mechanisms vulnerable to defoliation shortly after burning has not been explored in South Africa, despite many fynbos and karoo plants characteristically having a high ether extract content (Louw et al 1967).

The direct effects of fire on the digestibility, spininess, hairiness and content of tannins, alkaloids and resins of woody plants are largely unexplored. It might nevertheless be expected that immediate postfire regrowth is unlignified and therefore digestible, not rigidly spiny, and low in those chemicals which generally render plants poorly acceptable to herbivores. The effect is that the postfire regrowth of many plant species is highly acceptable to herbivores and even vulnerable to overutilization. While the factors of availability and acceptability are often difficult to separate, this concept of burning to produce acceptable regrowth has been widely practised. Traditionally the grazier in Africa has burnt for this reason for millenia. Trollope (1974) in savanna has used fire to promote the browsing of the bush regrowth by goats. Continuous stocking with goats then may eliminate the bush, while controlled rotational browsing may permit sustained production from the acceptable bush material.

Large wild herbivores have been shown to select strongly for recently burnt grassland (chapter 6), as have *Spodoptera exempta* (army worm), which severely defoliated young regrowing grass on part of a summer burn, but did not infest nearby, more mature grass in the Natal Drakensberg (Scotcher and Clarke 1980). However, the many chemical interactions between plants and insects are complex (Dethier 1970). Individuals tend to aggregate on plants which provide a balanced diet. Some plants have chemicals which attract, and others chemicals which repel insects. Thus, wherever fire modifies the chemistry of plants, it may be expected to affect the plants' acceptability to and use by phytophagous insects.

The major foods of grassland francolins are the corms and tubers of grassland geophytes (chapter 6). Infrequent fire and the consequent failure of the geophytes to produce leaf annually, and probable depletion (by respiration) of the underground parts, are likely to lead to poor forage quality of low acceptability to the birds. Presumably the same applies in the case of other consumers of corms and tubers.

The effects of fire on the acceptability of forage so far considered are essentially of a short-term nature. Long-term effects include the role of fire frequency in determining the botanical composition. Not only do plant species differ in their gross productive capacity, but they also differ in nutritive value and internal and external physical properties. The species composition of a community, which is in part determined by the fire regime, thus influences the general acceptability of the plant material to herbivores. Obviously an important function here is the type of herbivore, its individual dietary requirements and preferences and its foraging strategy. Depending on these characteristics, the animal will or will not be favoured by the short- and long-term effects of fire on the acceptability of the forage. Especially among the small herbivores, such as

insects, rodents and birds, these effects of fire on acceptability are confounded by the role fire plays in modifying the
physiognomy of the plant community, and the quantity and accessibility of forage.

Nevertheless, the more or less characteristic postfire succession among herbivores (eg Mentis and Rowe-Rowe 1979) may be
expected to be determined in part by the changes in forage
acceptability resulting from fire regime. In regard to large
herbivores, the long-term effects of fire on acceptability are
relatively clear-cut. In fynbos and in the karoo mountains, fire
stimulates many highly acceptable herbaceous species at the
expense of less acceptable fynbos shrubs. In the savanna, periodic fire helps to maintain open grass-bush communities in which
many of the grasses produce highly acceptable forage. In the
arid grasslands and marginal karoo areas fire may help to counter
invasion by often unacceptable pioneer karoo shrubs. In the
humid grasslands, periodic fire prevents succession proceeding
from communities in which generally acceptable species such as
Themeda triandra, *Heteropogon contortus* and *Diheteropogon
amplectens* dominate, to communities in which more or less
unacceptable grasses such as *Tristachya leucothrix*, *Alloteropsis
semialata* and *Cymbopogon* spp dominate or, in the extreme, to
forest which provides little acceptable forage for large herbivores. These generalizations apply to ungulates, both domestic
and wild, as a group (Mentis 1977, 1980). However, individual
ungulate species vary in their preference for specific botanical
compositions induced by different defoliating regimes, including
fire (Mentis 1979b). Nevertheless, especially in humid grassland, humid savanna and fynbos, frequent fire maximizes plant
acceptability to the majority of large herbivores.

EFFECT OF FIRE ON FORAGE AVAILABILITY

Availability is used here in the sense of accessibility of
forage to herbivores. In grassland the main effect of fire on
forage availability is to make fresh regrowth readily accessible
and to remove the diluting effect of herbage from previous seasons. In this respect, availability and acceptability are difficult to distinguish. For large herbivores, such as cattle and
horses, which are incapable of extreme plant part selection in
feeding, the effect is largely on quality and therefore forage
acceptability (Mentis 1980). For intermediate-sized herbivores,
such as sheep, blesbok *(Damaliscus dorcas phillipsi)* and
impala *(Aepyceros melampus)*, which have small mouths and can
select plant parts to a fine degree, the effect essentially
concerns accessibility. In unburnt grasslands with an accumulation of a season or more of plant material, fresh growth is present but difficult for these intermediate-sized herbivores to
isolate. For small herbivores such as rodents and insects the
effect is perhaps minimal. However, periodic burning to remove
the top hamper would appear to greatly facilitate the accessibility of forage to grassland francolins (Mentis and Bigalke 1979).
Apparently these birds use the aerial parts of the feed plants as
a guide for where to dig for the corms and tubers. An accumulation of top hamper would probably hinder recognition of the aerial

parts, and in any case suppresses above-ground production. All these principles may be expected to apply throughout southern Africa wherever a vigorous herb layer occurs.

Forage-producing bushes may grow out of reach of mammalian herbivores. In this case the effect of a hot fire (ie a fire applied when the ambient temperature is above 20°C, the relative humidity is less than 30%, and the fuel load is in excess of 3 t ha^{-1}) may be used to kill the aerial portions of the bushes and induce either basal coppicing or regeneration from seed (chapter 7). Therefore, appropriately applied fire has an important effect in increasing the availability of browse material to mammalian herbivores.

DISCUSSION

We have seen that frequent defoliation maximizes the mean gross accumulation rate in southern African vegetation. In this statement the meaning of "frequent" is relative to the circumstances under consideration. The optimum frequency is higher for humid grassland and humid savanna than for arid grassland, arid savanna, fynbos and karoo. Recalling that relatively frequent fire modifies, usually in a way favourable to herbivores, the properties of forage acceptability and availability, frequent fire is generally in the interests of forage production. Obviously this does not apply when considering animals which are adapted to those situations which develop in the long-term absence of fire (eg in forest and mature fynbos). However, it is remarkable, particularly in grassland and savanna, that a regime of relatively frequent fire generally leads to the annual production of forage in the greatest quantity and of the highest availability and acceptability, and consequently with the capacity for supporting the largest biomass of herbivores. Grassland and savanna in particular may have been subjected to frequent burning, grazing and browsing in their evolutionary development. Possible adaptive responses are a resistance to these forms of defoliation or a recuperative capacity to facilitate recovery after defoliation. Such resistance and recuperative capacity are characteristic of grassland and savanna (chapters 6 and 7) and of fynbos (chapter 5). Possession of the recuperative capacity, rather than resistance to defoliation, implies that plants have a high capacity for gross production, because burnt plants without such capacity would be at a disadvantage in competition for the resources of light, water and nutrients. It is perhaps this competition which has provided the mechanism in the fire climax communities for selection in favour of grasses with a recuperative ability rather than a resistance to defoliation. In short, plants of the fire climax, especially grasses of the humid grassland and humid savanna, are not only productive plants which can tolerate periodic severe defoliation, but require it if they are to persist, and if high gross primary production and high forage production for the coevolved herbivores are to be maintained.

In regard to sustained high forage production, Holling (1973, 1974) has argued that economic ecological systems should be managed to maintain their resilience (ie a capacity to remain attracted to the former equilibrium despite stresses which may cause large changes in the state variables). This is proposed as a hedge against the imperfection of knowledge and against the unpredictability of future stresses. On these grounds it is proposed that management strategies, rather than be fail-safe, should be safe in failure. The essence of the latter type of strategy is to expose the system to stress so as to maintain its resilience. However, caution is required so that the stress is kept within bounds and the attempted maintenance of resilience does not amount to degradation or forcing the system into an undesirable domain of attraction. Indeed, many systems in southern Africa have already been overstressed by ill-conceived grazing, browsing and burning frequencies and intensities. An example is that portion of the humid grassland which is prone to invasion by *Aristida junciformis* (Edwards et al 1979). While veld so invaded is extremely resilient (at least in the short term) and has a high gross productive capacity, since acceptability of the herbage is poor, forage production is negligible. The *Themeda triandra*- dominated counterpart is less resilient and has a lower gross productive capacity, but the herbage is relatively acceptable so that forage production is high. The resilience and stability of the *T. triandra*- dominated sward are maximized by periodic severe defoliation (eg by spring burning) every second year or so. Summer defoliation prevents elevation of tiller initials so that the growth points of the plants remain relatively inaccessible to and protected from defoliating agents (Tainton and Booysen 1965a). As already discussed, the periodic severe defoliation also stimulates vegetative reproduction so that a high basal cover and a high forage productive capacity are maintained. The system may move from the *T. triandra* -dominated state to the *A. junciformis*- dominated state if the former is not defoliated. However, the change results mostly from grazing and burning regimes which weaken the plants of *T. triandra* and its associates and place them at a disadvantage in competition with *A. junciformis*. Thus, the stresses or perturbations which are required to maintain the dominance of *T. triandra*, are, in extreme forms, the very factors which degrade the system, not only for domestic livestock, but also for wild hoofed animals (Mentis and Duke 1976), and probably for all fauna.

In grassland and savanna, plant species richness is maximal under light or moderate defoliation regimes, and minimal under extreme defoliation (Walker 1974; Mentis and Collinson 1979; Robinson et al 1979). A high species richness is in the long-term interests of the resilience of a system.

Although little studied, it appears that many systems in southern Africa degraded by overuse are, in the short term, more resilient than their undergrazed counterparts (Walker 1980). However, as desirable as resilience is, the operator is cautioned against blindly stressing a system (eg burning) simply for the sake of resilience, while disregarding the factors which determine forage production and species richness. In principle, stresses such as burning, intended to maintain the resilience of the system in its desired domain of attraction, must only probe the boundaries of the domain and not penetrate them. In practice, this requires specific knowledge of how stresses (eg fire type, frequency and intensity) affect the components of the system, and in what specific ways resilience and long-term forage production may benefit.

Chapter 12 Effects of Fire Regime on Faunal Composition and Dynamics

R. C. BIGALKE and K. WILLAN

INTRODUCTION

In view of the apparent largescale occurrence of fire over evolutionary time in much of South Africa, the fauna is, not unexpectedly, often well adapted to it. Such adaptation has apparently taken a number of forms, and ranges from escape mechanisms which are typical of some species, to a range of survival mechanisms practised by others. Such differences in the strategies which permit the different species to survive in a fire-prone environment inevitably give rise to a wide range of short and long-term responses to fire. The populations of some species, and in particular those which escape fire, may be largely unaffected directly by a fire event, but their survival in the long term may be dependent on the habitat which is induced by fire. In contrast, the populations of some species may be reduced considerably by a fire event, but they may possess the capacity to recover rapidly in the post-fire environment. Yet other species occupy only those sites from which fire has been excluded for some time, and such species are therefore confined largely to fire refuges. However, even within the three examples of broad behavioural classes mentioned, large differences in the behaviour of individual species may exist. Detailed examination of different species is therefore essential if the different response mechanisms are to be identified. To date, however, only a relatively small number of species have received more than superficial attention, but sufficient data are available to provide a number of examples of the responses of different elements of the fauna to fire. These will be presented in this chapter in an attempt to provide some appreciation of the relationship between fire and the composition and dynamics of fauna in South Africa.

IMMEDIATE DIRECT EFFECTS OF FIRE

Fire can lead to faunal changes by killing animals or by causing them to disperse.

MORTALITY

Since even the most modest temperatures recorded in veld fires (Trollope, this volume, chapter 9) are well above lethal levels for most living organisms, death from heat, or asphyxiation, may be expected to be quite common. Records of fire-induced mortality are nonetheless rare.

Responses of soil fauna have been little studied. By analogy with work elsewhere (Ahlgren 1974) it is likely that much of the soil mesofauna - mites, collembolans and other very small arthropods - as well as spiders will be killed. However Lamotte (1975) states that fire does not greatly affect the fauna of the soil surface in tropical African savannas. Termites foraging in wood, but not those in the soil, are thought to have been killed in a broadleaved savanna fire at Nylsvley (Gandar 1982). Some arboreal insects of the order Hemiptera, Coleoptera and Lepidoptera survived in canopies of *Dombeya rotundifolia* (wild pear) trees 3 to 4 m high but all were totally destroyed on *Ochna pulchra* (lekkerbreek) trees of about 2 m in height (Gandar 1982). The same fire resulted in a 30% decrease in grasshopper (Orthoptera, Acrididae) biomass, although how much was due to mortality and how much to flight was not established. Gillon (1971b) sampled grasshoppers immediately after a fire in tropical savanna on the Ivory Coast and recorded minimum figures of only 4,5% burned, 7,7% alive and 87,8% which had fled.

Gillon (1971b) also reports that a spectacular variety of birds congregated about the fire, feeding on insects as they flew away from the flames. The effects could not be quantified. Insectivorous birds commonly gather at fires (Komarek 1969; Gandar 1982) and predation may be a significant additional cause of insect mortality.

Mortality may be high in flightless arthropods. Populations of the tick *Ixodes rubricundus* are reported to be significantly reduced by fire in mountains of the Karoo (Roux and Smart 1980). Among grasshopper nymphs death rates ranging from 4,5% in an African savanna (Gillon 1971b) to 100% in rangeland in the USA (Hunter 1905) have been reported.

There are few records of fire-induced mortality among vertebrates. During a grassland fire at Midmar Dam Nature Reserve "a few" small mammals were killed or injured (C N V Lloyds, personal communication to K Willan, 1977). Wild-fires in savanna in the Kruger National Park have killed or maimed about 40 mammals on each of two occasions. Species involved were elephant *(Loxodonta africana)*, lion *(Panthera leo)*, impala *(Aepyceros melampus)*, kudu *(Tragelaphus strepsiceros)*, waterbuck *(Kobus ellipsiprymnus)*, steenbok *(Raphicerus campestris)*, roan antelope *(Hippotragus equinus)*, grey duiker *(Sylvicapra grimmia)* and warthog *(Phacochoerus aethiopicus)* (Brynard 1971).

DISPERSAL

Dispersal of animals fleeing fire may be an important cause of faunal change. In tropical African savannas, fire tends to lead to the disappearance of strongly flying insect groups, indicating either dispersal or mortality (Lamotte 1975). More specifically, the species composition of pentatomids (Hemiptera) in an Ivory Coast study area was altered through dispersal of strongly flying heliophilous forms and death of sciaphilous species, which fly only weakly.

Emigration was considered to be mainly responsible for a decline of 55 to 90% in small mammal density following a fire in *Terminalia-Dichrostachys* savanna (Kern 1978). Most impala left the burnt area and moved to other parts of the reserve in broadleaved savanna at Nylsvley (Gandar 1982).

EFFECT OF TYPE AND INTENSITY OF FIRE

The fire in broadleaved savanna at Nylsvley reported on by Gandar (1982) was of low intensity. Temperatures were significantly less than 250°C in the canopies of trees. This may explain why arboreal insects were totally destroyed on *O. pulchra* trees while some survived on taller individuals of *D. rotundifolia*. Direct effects on termites and beetle larvae in the soil were negligible. The fire which was applied at Nylsvley burnt with an uneven front and left unburnt patches amounting to 21% of the area in which grasshoppers were studied. Mobile insects could escape through breaks in the fire front and shelter in unburnt patches. Grasshopper density in these patches was over three times prefire levels.

In contrast, conflagrations in the Kruger National Park, mentioned above, which caused the death of a variety of large mammals followed 8 yr of protection against fire (Brynard 1971). Dangerously high fuel loads of old grass had accumulated and about 25% of the Park's area was burnt out. Trollope (this volume, chapter 9) believes the fires to have been fast moving, intense surface head fires with considerable flame heights through which even agile animals would have had difficulty escaping.

EFFECT OF SEASON

Effect of burns at different seasons could vary considerably. For example, coming at a time when seasonally restricted activities were in progress, such as territory establishment, mating or breeding, fire would have a greater effect on populations than fires occurring at other times. There is little published information on this aspect. Gandar (1982) notes that the Nylsvley fire took place in September when most grasshoppers were adult and so able to dodge the flames effectively. The implication is that mortality would have been greater had there been more immature grasshoppers about. A fire mosaic of burns applied at different times of year maintains a richer and more varied insect population in tropical savanna on the Ivory Coast than areas burnt in only one season (Gillon 1971a).

EFFECT OF FREQUENCY

Type and intensity of fire are related to frequency and to the rate at which fuel accumulates, which in turn depends on vegetation type and climate. There is little information available on the influence of different fire frequencies on direct fire effects.

One consideration leading to the introduction of more frequent burning in the Kruger National Park was the desire to reduce fire intensity to avoid conflagrations capable of killing large mammals (Brynard 1971). In the Hluhluwe-Umfolozi complex, much of which is burnt regularly on a cycle of 1 or 2 yr, no ungulates were reported killed by fire from 1975 to 1977 (Brooks and Berry

1980). We have already noted the importance of refuges left by a patchy low intensity fire for grasshopper survival at Nylsvley and of a fire mosaic of burns applied at different times of the year on insect populations in tropical savanna on the Ivory Coast (Gillon, 1971a).

INDIRECT EFFECTS OF FIRE

Fire alters the physical environment and the nature and quantity of food and cover available to animals, while levels of competition and predation may also change. These factors greatly affect faunal composition and dynamics in the short term, much more so than the direct effects of a burn. The immediate consequences of a fire wanes as postfire succession proceeds and the environment returns to its condition before the burn. The time scale of short-term changes is influenced by the rate of plant succession and mean fire frequency, which may vary from less than a year in grassland to as long as 40 yr in fynbos and longer in forest. Where fire modifies or drastically alters vegetation structure and composition, long-term faunal changes may occur.

EFFECTS OF SHORT-TERM CHANGES IN FOOD RESOURCES

Reduction of food supply

Fire may reduce or eliminate food supplies. For a month after the Nylsvley fire foraging activity of termites was lower than usual, perhaps partly due to high surface temperatures on exposed soil and to desiccation of the soil, and partly due to food scarcity (Gandar 1982). Gandar (1982) also suggests a reduction in the supply of roots on which the larvae feed or of the quantity of carbohydrates contained in the roots (because of their diversion to newly stimulated top growth) as factors accounting for a decline in the number of adult beetles emerging from the soil two months after a fire. Egg pods of grasshoppers and stick insects (Phasmidae) in the soil survived the fire but young nymphs emerging on burnt areas a month later generally did not survive.

The food preferences of the majority of South African small mammals in which responses to fire have been studied are poorly understood, but there is sufficient information to allocate them to one of three broad categories, omnivorous, herbivorous or insectivorous (Table 1). Comprehensive feeding studies have been undertaken only on *Otomys irroratus* (vlei rat) and *Rhabdomys pumilio* (four-striped field mouse) (Curtis and Perrin 1979; Perrin 1980). In addition, digestive tract morphology, and hence adaptation to diet, of a number of species listed in Table 1 has been investigated, and the feeding categories to which they were allocated (Perrin and Curtis 1980) are included in this table.

Fire may totally eliminate the food supply of the specialist herbivore *O. irroratus* and other *Otomys* spp (Table 1), and their disappearance from burns may relate to food shortage. However, cover availability appears more important in the timing of recolonization (see below).

Table 1   Postfire successional status and feeding categories of some South African small mammals.   Succession: S = specialist; P = pioneer (for additional description see text).   Diet: O = omnivore; H = herbivore; I = insectivore; O/H = omnivore with tendency to herbivory; G/I = granivore/insectivore, consuming large amounts of insects and seeds.   Numbers 1-19 are references.

Species	Successional status	Diet	Digestive tract morphology
Rodents:			
Acomys subspinosus	S(18)	O (1,7)	
Aethomys chrysophilus	S (9)	O (7)	O/H (14)
Aethomys namaquensis	S (16)	O (1)	O/H (14)
Dendromus melanotis	S (13,16,18)	O (7,19)	
Dendromus mesomelas	S (16)	O (7,19)	
Desmodillus auricularis	P (8)	O (11)	G/I (14)
Gerbillurus paeba	P (8)	O (11)	
Lemniscomys griselda	S (9)	O (1,7)	O/H (14)
Malacothrix typica	P (8)	O (1)	
Mus minutoides	P (12)		
	S (13,18)	O (7,10)	O (14)
Praomys natalensis	P (2,3,4,11,12)	O (7,17)	O (14)
	S (9)		
Praomys verreauxi	S (16)	O (1)	
Otomys irroratus	S (12,13,16)	H (5,15,17)	H (14)
Otomys spp.	S (16,18)	H (1,16)	
Rhabdomys pumilio	S (8,12,13,16,18)	O (6,15,17)	O (14)
Saccostomus campestris	S (9)	O (1,7)	G/I (14)
Steatomys pratensis	S (9)	O (7)	G/I (14)
Tatera leucogaster	P (9)	O (7)	O (14)
Thallomys paedulcus	S (12)	O (7)	O (14)
Insectivores:			
Crocidura cyanea	S (16)	I (1)	
Crocidura flavescens	S (13,16,18)	I (1)	
Crocidura hirta	S (9)	I (1)	
Myosorex varius	P (12,13)		
	S (16,18)	I (1)	

1. Roberts (1951); 2. Hanney (1965); 3. Neal (1970); 4. Delaney (1972); 5. Davis (1973); 6. Brooks (1974); 7. Kingdon (1974); 8. Christian (1977a); 9. Kern (1978); 10. Willan and Meester (1978); 11. Christian (1979); 12. Meester et al (1979); 13. Mentis and Rowe-Rowe (1979); 14. Perrin and Curtis (1980); 15. Perrin (1980); 16. Willan and Bigalke (1982); 17. Willan (1982); 18. Bigalke and Pepler (1979); 19. K C Willan (personal observation, 1979).

The remaining 17 rodent species under consideration here are omnivores but six of these are pioneer species in at least some areas, remaining on burns, while 11 are eliminated (Table 1). Similarly, while three of the four insectivores disappear, *Myosorex varius* (forest shrew) may be present immediately after fire (Table 1). There are no published accounts of the specific dietary requirements of the majority of these species (ie except *R. pumilio* - Curtis and Perrin 1979; Perrin 1980), but of the six pioneer rodents (Table 1), four were dealt with by Perrin and Curtis (1980), who considered three to be true omnivores (eating seeds, green plant and invertebrate food) while the fourth was a granivore insectivore (eating mainly seeds and insects). Pioneer omnivores may change from primarily granivorous diets to herbivory, in accordance with prevailing supply (eg *Tatera leucogaster* (bushveld gerbil) (Kern 1978). This species apparently crops the flush of green shoots appearing after fire. In spite of this, increased movement on burns relative to unburnt controls (Christian 1977a; Kern 1978) suggests that food supply is probably reduced by fire. *Praomys natalensis* (multimammate mouse), a primarily granivorous omnivore (Kingdon 1974) which pioneers a variety of disturbed habitats (de Wit 1972; Meester et al 1979), may immigrate onto burns (Hanney 1965; Neal 1970). This species was unable to maintain weight on laboratory diets comprising only green plant *Pennisetum clandestinum* or only invertebrate *(Tenebrio* larvae or *Macrotermes* nymphs) food (Willan 1982). *R. pumilio* lost weight on *P. clandestinum*, but gained weight on invertebrate food (Willan 1982).

From the above it appears that species with the broadest food niches, at least among rodents, appear most likely to remain on burns immediately following fire (Table 1). However, elimination of a number of omnivores, albeit in at least some cases with narrower food niches than the true omnivore category (Perrin and Curtis 1980; Table 1), suggests that cover availability or some other factor or factors may be limiting in some cases.

Large herbivores move off burns, for example impala at Nylsvley (Gandar 1982) and common reedbuck *(Redunca arundinum)* in the Kruger National Park (Jungius 1971), but recolonization may be rapid (see below).

Increase in quantity and quality of food

For herbivores, regenerating vegetation soon provides a readily available source of palatable nutritious food and burns are often rapidly recolonized. Within a week two species of grasshopper appeared on the burn at Nylsvley, one of them a mixed feeder which took not only grass, forbs and litter but also ash. Three more species were found after three weeks (Gandar 1982).

Rodent species trapped more frequently after a burn than before at Nylsvley included *T. leucogaster* (but the percentage in the total catch did not change) and *Saccostomus campestris* (pouched mouse). They were thought to be feeding mainly on surviving tree seeds (Gandar 1979). However, *T. leucogaster* takes green shoots as well; together with *Steatomys pratensis* (rat mouse) it was found to immigrate onto triennially burnt plots in the months following a fire in the Kruger National Park (Kern 1978).

In burnt fynbos especially nutritious food resources such as seed released from plants, corms, cormlets and other structures among geophytes, and sprouts, are used by a wide variety of transients including birds such as francolins *(Francolinus* spp), canaries *(Serinus* spp) and doves *(Streptopelia* spp) (Kruger 1972). Levyns (1929b) and Kruger and Bigalke (this volume, chapter 5) found increased rodent mole activity on burnt plots, presumably in response to greater availability of underground storage organs of geophytes.

New green growth appearing after fire attracts a wide variety of herbivores, from tortoises to lagomorphs and large ungulates, in all major vegetation types. Levyns (1929b) observed "...buck, a hare and several tortoises..." foraging on recently burnt fynbos plots. Mountain reedbuck *(Redunca fulvorufula)*, grey rhebuck *(Pelea capreolus)* and oribi *(Ourebia ourebi)* select strongly for the green flush of grass shortly following a fire in the Natal Drakensberg (Oliver et al 1978). Mentis (1978) showed densities of grey rhebuck and oribi on a fine-scale mosaic of spring burnt and unburnt grassland with a network of firebreaks prepared annually in winter.

In savanna of the Hluhluwe-Umfolozi complex eight species of grazing ungulates were significantly attracted to winter and spring burns. Species responses were affected by their home range behaviour. Burchell's zebra *(Equus burchelli)* and buffalo *(Syncerus caffer)* with the largest home ranges, and black wildebeest *(Connochaetes gnou)* and white rhinoceros *(Ceratotherium simum)* in which home ranges are medium-sized, moved rapidly onto burns. Waterbuck and warthog, which have small home ranges, and which are closely associated with riverine habitats in winter, did not move onto burns quickly (Brooks and Berry 1980). In this case, as with impala at Nylsvley (Gandar 1982), a decline in the availability of young highly nutritive plant parts as the grass grew and matured caused animals to move off. Peak impala numbers were observed 21 to 30 days after the fire at Nylsvley. Thereafter numbers started decreasing gradually although density was still relatively high after 90 days. Brooks and Berry (1980) found differences between species in the stage of grass growth at which they abandoned the burns, related to their requirements for highly nutritive forage.

Feeding behaviour of springbok *(Antidorcas marsupialis)* and blesbok *(Damaliscus dorcas phillipsi)* on burns reflects their requirements for increased food quality (Novellie 1978). On unburnt grassland mean feeding station interval (time spent at each feeding station) was high on coarse mature swards high in crude fibre and low in crude protein levels. Feeding station intervals declined with seasonal reduction in fibre and increase in protein. On burns feeding station intervals were always low. The reasons proposed for this were the high nutritional value of resprouting grass, absence of obscuring mature plant parts and lower overall abundance of forage.

Predators may also benefit from conditions following a burn. At Nylsvley Gandar (1982) found a concentration of grey hornbill *(Tockus nasutus)*, which feed on grasshoppers, around the burn for a few weeks after the fire. The birds were exploiting insects exposed after fire.

EFFECTS OF SHORT-TERM CHANGES IN VEGETATIVE COVER

Food supplies alone are not the only variable influencing animal populations after a fire. Changes in the amount and nature of vegetative cover may be at least as important, if not more so, although it is sometimes difficult to determine the relative importance of these two factors.

Reduction of plant cover and exposure of the soil surface may affect microclimate: thus high surface temperatures on exposed soils may have curtailed the time of day during which termites could forage near the surface on the Nylsvley burn (Gandar 1982).

Increased insolation following removal of vegetation was partly responsible for drying of the soil, which may have been a factor in reducing emergence of adult beetles two months after a fire at Nylsvley (Gandar 1982).

Lack of cover, together with food shortage and increased vulnerability to predation, are likely to be largely responsible for postburn declines or disappearances of small mammals (Delany 1972). Cook (1959) and Neal (1970) found these changes in small mammal populations to be related mainly to the effect of fire on cover. It follows that species which survive on burns (or rapidly recolonize them) are able to tolerate reduced cover levels. Four of the species listed in Table 1 as postfire pioneers, include habitats with little cover in their normal ranges. *Gerbillurus paeba* (South African pygmy gerbil), *Desmodillus auricularis* and *Malacothrix typica* are found, among other places, in sparsely vegetated areas of the Namib desert (Coetzee 1969), and *T. leucogaster* in areas of less than 70% cover or litter in *Terminalia-Dichrostachys* savanna in the Kruger National Park (Kern 1978). Similarly, while *P. natalensis* occur at a variety of cover densities (de Wit 1972; Willan 1982), in some situations it may forage in the open (Kingdon 1974) in areas such as bare ploughed fields (Mendelsohn 1981). Hence, these four species appear pre-adapted to survive on burns. *Mus minutoides* and *Myosorex varius* are possibly sufficiently small (respectively ca 8 g and 12 g) to avoid predators by making use of cover and refuges which are inadequate for larger species.

While the above provides possible reasons for the continued presence of pioneer species on burns, it fails to explain the elimination of the majority of specialist species (Table 1). There is some evidence, however, that specialists may be eliminated by insufficient cover rather than by shortage of other resources (Kern 1978). The specialist herbivores *(Otomys* spp) have no food available to them immediately following fire, but the fact that they do not reappear for at least several months, during which considerable vegetative regeneration has usually occurred (Meester et al 1979; Mentis and Rowe-Rowe 1979), strongly implies a cover restriction in this case. Bond et al (1980) found a correlation between numbers of *Otomys* spp and the presence of dense, shrubby vegetation. While not entirely restricted to high cover situations, the *O. irroratus* appears to favour dense vegetation (Shortridge 1934; Roberts 1951; Davis 1973; Willan 1982). *R. pumilio* appears less cover-restricted than *O. irroratus* (Willan 1982), but even in the desert grassland habitat studied by Christian (1977a), where *R. pumilio* would be expected to have evolved greater tolerance to low cover availability than in higher rainfall areas (D P Christian, personal communication to K Willan, 1978), it had not reappeared on a burn within 12 weeks.

R. pumilio and *O. irroratus*, together with the majority of *Otomys* spp, are unique among the species listed in Table 1 in that they normally nest on the surface, often under grass tussocks (Davis 1973; Brooks 1974) or other suitably dense vegetation; hence, removal of cover by fire would prevent normal nesting, and in itself would be sufficient to promote emigration from burns. In addition, *R. pumilio*, *Lemniscomys griselda*, *O. irroratus* and *Otomys* spp are at least partially diurnal, with *R. pumilio* almost entirely so (Brooks 1974; Christian 1977b). *L. griselda* (Kingdon 1974) and *O. irroratus* (Davis 1973) are predominantly crepuscular. Thus, all three species are exposed to diurnal raptors, which hunt by sight and are presumably more efficient at low than at high cover densities. However, in compensation for increased predation by diurnal raptors, it is possible that predation by owls on crepuscular and nocturnal small mammals is reduced. Christian (1977a) noted the absence of barn owl *(Tyto alba)* and spotted eagle owl *(Bubo africanus)*, from a burn but found that they hunted on a nearby unburnt control.

In the Natal Drakensberg, greywing francolin *(Francolinus africanus)* and redwing francolin *(F. levaillantii)* are very rare or absent in cleanly burnt grassland (Mentis 1973; Mentis and Bigalke 1979), presumably in response mainly to cover destruction. Among fynbos birds, Cape sugar bird *(Promerops cafer)*, for example, depends on well-developed stands of Proteaceae about 8 yr old and older for food and nest-sites. Fire deprives it of a habitable environment (Burger et al 1976; Mostert et al 1980).

As an example of a large mammal responding to cover changes, the case of common reedbuck in the Kruger National Park may be quoted. Jungius (1971) found common reedbuck to vacate areas in which the tall grassland they inhabited was totally destroyed by fire. Old territories were abandoned and males competed for new sites in localities where food and cover was still available, such as gallery bush along river courses or remnant grass patches. Social reorganization included the formation of new associations between territorial males, females and juveniles.

LONG-TERM CHANGES

Fire may drastically alter vegetation structure and so create long lasting or even permanent faunal changes. Perhaps the most dramatic example is the destruction of forest with its dependent fauna. The extent to which forest cover has been eliminated is discussed by Granger (this volume, chapter 8). Fire-maintained climax grassland supports a grassland fauna.

In savanna and woodland, fire can alter the density of woody species and the grass-bush balance. For example Trapnell (1959) reports that 23 yr of early burning in June and July maintained closed canopy *Brachystegia-Julbernardia* woodland. Late burning in October thinned out the woody vegetation and led to increased grass cover. Bush encroachment, which resulted from frequent early dry season burning (and grazing) in the Kruger National Park, was accompanied by a decline in grazing ungulate populations and an increase in browsers (Brynard 1964).

INFLUENCE OF FIRE REGIME

Type and intensity

While one might expect the most intense fires to create the least favourable postburn environments for animals, evidence supporting this is limited. The low-intensity patchy burn at Nylsvley merely scorched leaf litter. Beneath it *Odontotermes* spp and *Thysanura* spp were found foraging shortly after the fire. The litter also served to protect tree seeds on which *Saccostomus capensis* and *T. leucogaster* were able to feed. Unburnt patches of grass provided food and cover for grasshoppers (Gandar 1982). In contrast, a fire as intense as that in the Cedarberg in January 1975, which killed most resprouting herbs (Kruger and Bigalke, this volume, chapter 5), might be expected to have destroyed most animal food and cover.

Season

Season of burn has a particularly striking effect on food in sour grassveld, where nutritive values are at their lowest in the coldest, driest months. From August to October, mortality amongst small antelopes reaches a peak in montane grassland of the Natal Drakensberg (Mentis 1978; Oliver et al 1978). There is evidence that the higher crude protein and phosphorus content of this grassland burnt in autumn reduces antelope mortality and that a change from predominantly autumn to spring burning has led to a decline of antelope numbers in Giant's Castle Game Reserve (Scotcher et al 1979).

Eight species of grazing ungulates were equally attracted to winter and spring burns in the Hluhluwe-Umfolozi complex. Mixed feeders (nyala and impala) showed a preference for spring burns. This may be because both species switch from browse to graze at the beginning of the rains and thus become less dependent on riverine habitats (which were not burnt) at that time (Brooks and Berry 1980).

Frequency

Fire frequency influences the quality of pasture for herbi-vores to varying degrees in different vegetation types and clima-tic zones. For example, when a policy of burning not more than once every 5 yr was introduced in the Kruger National Park, it led to the accumulation of moribund grass and emigration of grazing ungulates. Subsequently burning frequencies ranging from annual or biennial in moist sourveld areas to once every 4 to 8 yr in dry sweetveld were instituted to maintain acceptably short palatable grazing (Brynard 1971; Gertenbach 1979).

Food and cover are probably both involved in the response of mammal and bird populations to fire frequency in Drakensberg montane grassland. Mentis and Rowe-Rowe (1979) found the greatest abundance and species richness of francolin, small mammals and antelope up to 3 yr after fire. Thereafter numbers of both species and individuals were low (but another peak was found in fire-protected areas). Protection of grassland from defoliation for 2 or more yr renders it unattractive to guinea-fowl for nesting (Mentis 1972b).

Fynbos fires frequent enough to prevent regeneration of fynbos to the shrubland stage, required for example by the sugar bird (see above), would effectively exclude this species.

In summary, fire frequency determines how often vegetation is returned to the beginning of the postfire successional process, when food supplies for various species are either diminished or improved and when low cover availability encourages some species and excludes others. Changes in community composition reflect this and are probably most strongly influenced by frequency.

FIRE EFFECTS ON POPULATION STRUCTURE AND SOCIAL ORGANIZATION

Immediately following fire, vulnerability of grasshopper nymphs to predation on exposed areas, together with food short-age, combined to increase mortality so that the grasshopper population after the Nylsvley fire consisted mainly of large old individuals (Gandar 1982). One might expect food shortages to reduce reproductive success in many species, and competition on burns or in refuges to increase juvenile mortality, but these speculations require confirmation.

Social organization may be disrupted in various ways. Home range sizes of *Gerbillurus paeba* and *Desmodillus auricularis* (Christian 1977a) and *T. leucogaster* (Kern 1978) increased after fire. Animals emigrating from burns must be expected to affect social organization in the unburnt habitats they invade. Thus many common reedbuck abandoned their old territories and males competed for new sites in remaining refuges. The period of social reorganization saw the formation of new associations between territorial males, females and juveniles (Jungius 1971). Impala formed large aggregations on the Nylsvley burn (Gandar 1982).

It may be significant that of the three South African small mammal species whose social systems have been studied, one, *P. natalensis*, is highly sociable and nonterritorial (Cilliers 1972; de Wit 1972) and may remain after fire. *O. irroratus* and *R. pumilio* include territoriality in their complex social organizations (Brooks 1974; Marais 1974) and are eliminated from burns. Sociability may perhaps rank with a broad feeding niche and tolerance of low cover as a preadaptation to burns.

POSTFIRE SUCCESSION

Mortality, dispersal and responses to changes in food, cover and predation result in altered postfire communities. Available information on the nature and tempo of successional changes is reviewed here.

INITIAL PHASE

Early postfire communities studied to date are characterized by reduced species richness, population density and biomass. In the Namib desert grassland five rodent species were present on a control plot but only three on a burn (Christian 1979). Two small mammal species were trapped shortly after a fire in montane grassland, compared with seven 18 to 24 months later; postburn population density was low (Mentis and Rowe-Rowe 1979). Meester et al (1979) trapped only one rodent species three months after a fire in grassland near Cathedral Peak. In *Terminalia-Dichrostachys* savanna a single species of rodent was trapped two weeks after a fire and a second was present at two months. Peak small mammal biomass on annual burns was only about half that on unburnt controls (Kern 1978). Grasshopper biomass in a mosaic of burnt and unburnt patches of *Burkea* savanna immediately after a fire was 70% of that of unburnt savanna. It declined to 44% after six weeks and was 42% after four months (Gandar 1982). In transitional Coastal Renosterbosveld at Stellenbosch one species of small mammal was present in the first year after a burn, compared with four in the second and six to seven in subsequent years. Trap success was 3,6% in 1 to 2 yr old veld but 50,4% at age 3 to 4 yr (Bigalke and Pepler 1979).

Primary consumer species present in the early stages after a fire tend to be unspecialized feeders tolerant of sparse vegetation cover. From the first week after the Nylsvley fire two grasshopper species reinvaded, *Acrotylus diana*, a cryptically coloured species favouring open habitats, and *Acorypha pallidicornis*, a mixed feeder eating grass, forbs, litter and - on the burn - ash. There was evidence that these and other grasshoppers fed less selectively on burnt areas (Gandar 1982).

It has already been pointed out that rodents found on fresh burns tend to be those with broad food niches. Most also include habitats with little cover within their normal ranges, for example *G. paeba*, *Desmodillus auricularis*, *Malacothrix typica*, *T. leucogaster* and *P. natalensis*. Small mammal pioneers which do not fall into this category - *Mus minutoides* and *Myosorex varius* - may be sufficiently small to avoid predation by making use of cover or refuges inadequate for larger species.

That predation is important is suggested by the fact that most small mammals using fresh burns are nocturnal or crepuscular. Furthermore, diurnal grasshoppers were exposed to opportunistic predation by hornbills congregating at the Nylsvley burn (Gandar 1982).

TEMPORARY AGGREGATIONS

In apparent contradiction of the trend towards species-poor, low density communities following a fire, species exploiting abundant ephemeral resources may become common for a while. About three weeks after the Nylsvley fire the grasshopper fauna was augmented by the appearance of three more species. Another two followed a few weeks later (Gandar 1982).

Large herbivores often aggregate in spectacular fashion. At Nylsvley impala began to appear in increasing numbers 11 to 20 days after the fire and reached a peak at 21 to 30 days. They shifted their preference from *Acacia* communities - which were not burnt - to normally nutrient-poor *Burkea* which were usually avoided (Gandar 1982). Eleven species of ungulates were attracted to burns in the Hluhluwe-Umfolozi complex, eight of them to a marked degree (Brooks and Berry 1980). If limited areas are burnt high population densities may be attained and management must ensure that burns are large enough to avoid overgrazing (Edwards, this volume, chapter 16).

Aggregations of large grazers are a temporary phase in postfire succession. Impala numbers at Nylsvley decreased gradually from 30 days after the fire, although they were still relatively high after 90 days (Gandar 1982). In Zululand, species left when the burn no longer provided shorter, more palatable grazing than surrounding veld. The order of their going corresponded to their tolerance of long grass, warthog being the first to leave, zebra and buffalo the last (Brooks and Berry 1980).

Transients may also exploit seed released from plants, corms and sprouts, as do birds such as francolins, canaries and doves in fynbos. In this vegetation rodent moles also increase in abundance presumably in response to increased abundance or availability of geophytes after fire (Levyns 1929b; Kruger and Bigalke, this volume, chapter 5). Predators too may congregate temporarily. As noted above, Gandar (1982) found grey hornbills to be unusually abundant for several weeks after the Nylsvley fire, preying on grasshoppers which were readily available.

SUCCESSION OVER THE LONGER TERM

Successional changes are best documented for small mammals. They accompany and are apparently mainly the result of postfire changes in vegetation structure. Figure 1 summarizes data relating to species richness from seven different studies (Toes 1972; Lewis 1975; Christian 1977a; Kern 1978; Bigalke and Pepler 1979; Mentis and Rowe-Rowe 1979; Willan and Bigalke 1982). The data of Toes, Lewis and Willan and Bigalke are combined since they sampled similar habitats using similar techniques.

Three trends are indicated in Figure 1.

1   Species richness increased with time (but see point 3 below).

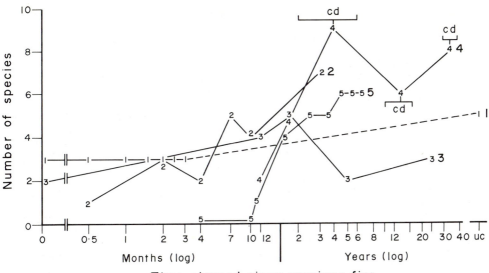

Figure 1   Number of small mammal species in relation to time
elapsed since previous fire. 1: desert grassland
(Christian 1977a); 2: *Terminalia-Dichrostachys*
savanna (Kern 1978); 3: humid montane grassland
(Mentis and Rowe-Rowe 1979); 4: Southwestern Cape
montane fynbos (Toes 1972; Lewis 1975; Willan and
Bigalke 1982); 5: Southwestern Cape fynbos "island"
(Bigalke and Pepler 1979) uc: unburnt control of
unspecified age, cd: combined data for the period
indicated.

2   Rates of changes are variable. Initially fewest species were
present in fynbos (data sets 4, 5) and most in desert
grassland (data set 1), where the three trapped immediately
after the fire are adapted to low-cover environments (see
above). Change was most rapid in *Terminalia-Dichrostachys*
savanna in the Kruger National Park where five species were
present seven months after burning (data set 2) but species
richness was greatest in montane fynbos at 2 to 6 yr (data
set 4).

3   In the two studies including relatively old postburn
vegetation (humid montane grassland, data set 3; montane
fynbos, data set 4) two peaks of species richness are
evident. In grassland the second is attained earlier than in
fynbos, a fact explicable by the slower rate of vegetation
change in fynbos (Kruger and Bigalke, this volume, chapter
5). Mentis and Rowe-Rowe (1979) have suggested that this
bimodality is the result of small mammal and antelope species
being adapted either to frequently burnt or fire inaccessible
grassland habitats but not to those of intermediate age.   A

simpler explanation is that some are preadapted to exploit postburn environments and decline in the absence of fire; others are restricted to stable vegetation seldom disrupted by burning.

Changes in species composition are also related to plant succession. In *Terminalia-Dichrostachys* savanna burnt triennially *T. leucogaster* was dominant while cover was less than 70% and there was little litter. By the end of the cycle, when very dense cover and litter had developed, the shrew *Crocidura hirta* was the dominant small mammal (Kern 1978). Similar patterns of change are reported from montane grassland (Mentis and Rowe-Rowe 1979) and fynbos (Willan and Bigalke 1982). Re-emergence of a shrub canopy in fynbos provides habitat suitable for sugar birds (Mostert et al 1980) and presumably also for other birds. Cody (1975) found species richness to be directly related to structural diversity of fynbos vegetation.

Abundance of small mammals as indicated by trap success has also been found to exhibit a bimodal distribution in montane grassland (Mentis and Rowe-Rowe 1979) and montane fynbos (Willan and Bigalke 1982), with the grassland peak occurring earlier than that in fynbos. In Kern's (1978) Kruger National Park study unburnt controls maintained a high stable density and biomass (and species composition) while in annually burnt plots the seasonal peak biomass was only half that of control plots.

In summary, available evidence suggests the following sequence of successional stages after a burn:

1   Survival of or rapid recolonization by a few species with broad feeding niches and which are tolerant of open habitats; densities and biomass are low.

2   A more or less strongly developed phase of temporary aggregation by opportunistic species exploiting ephemeral food resources. High biomass may be attained.

3   Gradual increase in species richness and population density as structural diversity of vegetation increases, with loss of some pioneers and appearance of species whose niche requirements are now met.

4   In the continued absence of fire, at least in montane grassland and fynbos, further species may be lost and density and biomass may decline, to increase again in the long term if and when an essentially different type of community has developed.

It is worth noting that successional changes may be influenced by fire behaviour and especially by the patchiness of a burn, which is linked to frequency, and by season. The effect of area of burn may be significant but has not been studied.

CONCLUSIONS

Much less is known about faunal responses to fire than is known about the response of flora. Available data come from a few widely scattered localities and relate mainly to some insects, birds and mammals, so that it is difficult to make satisfactory generalizations.

Fire appears not to kill many animals directly but more often results in significant dispersal. Type and intensity of a burn and the extent to which it leaves unburnt refuges are important variables affecting survival, especially of species of limited mobility. Scale is also likely to have a marked effect but has not been investigated. The inhospitable postburn environment has little cover and at first offers little food to primary consumers. Predators may however find abundant prey during and after a fire and may be an important contributory factor to the decline in animal density typical of fresh burns.

As the vegetation regenerates, temporary aggregations of primary consumers, especially large mobile forms, may exploit the accessible and palatable resources of high quality food which becomes available. At a time of year when unburnt vegetation is of particularly low nutritive value, as for example in the cold dry season in montane grassland, burns may significantly affect survival of antelope, and possibly of other species as well, by making green pasture available.

Change in vegetation structure, most marked in fynbos, appears to be the main feature influencing changes in species composition and population density in the course of postfire succession. From sparse populations of few species adapted to open habitats and using a wide spectrum of foods, communities grow in density and complexity. In high rainfall grassland and fynbos, where the phenomenon has been studied, species richness and population densities decline in the continued absence of fire, the time scale depending on rate of vegetation regeneration. Fire at appropriate frequencies thus maintains high species richness and density. Late seral species may however be eliminated by too frequent burning and a spectrum of habitats of different postburn ages is probably required to maintain maximum faunal diversity. The scale of such a mosaic is likely to be important especially to species of limited mobility requiring a diversity of vegetation forms within home ranges. Critical studies of faunal responses to burns at different intervals and seasons and on varying scales are needed.

Little is known of the effects of fire regime on population dynamics. Enhanced reproductive success and survival may be expected initially for recolonizing species with access to high quality food and little competition. Dispersal may be significantly affected. Topics such as levels of inter and intraspecific competition and predator-prey interactions on burns have not been studied. On many fronts there is a need for more research, particularly in order to provide a scientific basis for use of fire for faunal conservation and management.

Chapter 13 The Responses and Survival of Organisms in Fire-Prone Environments

P. G. H. FROST

INTRODUCTION

Fire is a widespread, naturally occurring phenomenon of great antiquity, influencing the structure, composition and dynamics of many ecosystems. Within southern Africa, grassland, savanna and fynbos ecosystems in particular are subjected to recurrent fires and fire is considered to have been of major importance in the evolution and maintenance of their biotas (Phillips 1930; West 1971; Kruger 1977b).

The focus of this review is on the effects of fire on plants and animals and the means by which they avoid, minimise, recover from, or exploit these effects. Fire may act directly on an individual, either through causing its death or by damaging or destroying tissue, thereby affecting growth and reproduction, or it may also act indirectly, through changing the environment within which an individual functions, thereby creating different challenges and opportunities. Fire may be mutagenic (Howe 1976) though for this to be significant it must be coupled with an appropriate ecological opportunity and some selective advantage.

In attempting to identify those features which confer advantage in a fire-prone environment it is necessary to interpose a caveat about presuming too readily that these features are adaptations to the circumstances of fire and its effects. Although potential advantages may be identified, this does not necessarily mean that these features were shaped by natural selection to serve that particular function (Williams 1966). They may not have originated through natural selection at all, or they may have been shaped by natural selection to serve completely different functions, in which case the additional advantage may be nothing more than the fortuitous consequence of the original function. This does not mean that such traits and responses are unimportant with respect to fire. Some may constrain the ability of an organism to accommodate changes in fire regime; others may serve as preadaptations, predisposing the bearer to further selection. All are important in contributing to the patterns of community structure and ecosystem functioning.

In the sections that follow, an attempt will, where possible, be made to differentiate between those traits and responses which seem to be adaptations to fire regime rather than to other ecological circumstances. None the less, present levels of understanding of these features is such that these interpretations should be treated as hypotheses for future research, rather than as documented instances of adaptation, or otherwise, to fire.

RESPONSES OF PLANTS TO FIRE

Plants can persist in a fire-prone environment through avoidance in space, escape in time, tolerance (including both resistance and recovery) and regeneration from seed (Wicht 1945; Naveh 1975; Gill 1977, 1981). Plants can also exploit the opportunities created in the post-fire environment, such as the greater chance for seedling establishment resulting from the lower level of competition from established plants and the opportunity to escape predation.

AVOIDANCE IN SPACE

In most environments exposed to regular fires there are areas
of vegetation which seldom, if ever, are burnt. These sites are
occupied largely by fire-sensitive or semi-tolerant plant
species, many of which, in the absence of fire, will invade the
community at large. In fynbos, species escape fires either by
being restricted to rocky areas *(Erica depressa:* Jackson 1976;
Maytenus oleoides (mountain maytenus), *Olea africana* (wild
olive), *Heeria argentea* (rockwood): personal observation, 1979),
or by being confined to perennially damp sites *(Crassula
pellucida, Disa uniflora* (red disa), *D. longicornu* (drip disa)
and *Cunonia capensis* (rooiels): Jackson 1976). Likewise, in
savannas, fire-sensitive species are confined to rocky outcrops
(eg *Rhus squammosa)* or termitaria *(Diospyros mespiliformis*
(jakkalsbessie), *Schotia brachypetala* (huilboerboon) and others:
W P D Gertenbach, personal communication, 1979).

In the False Thornveld of the Eastern Cape where *Themeda
triandra* grassland is being encroached by *Acacia karroo* (sweet
thorn) and other woody species (Trollope 1974), many of the
fire-sensitive bush precursors *(Ehretia rigida* (puzzle bush),
Scutia myrtina (cat-thorn), *Diospyros lycioides* (bluebush),
O. africana, Canthium inerme (turkey-berry) and others) occur
together in bush clumps. There they are protected from fires,
which normally skirt these clumps because of the lack of adequate
fuel (W S W Trollope, personal communication, 1979). This
clumped distribution may simply reflect higher survival of seeds
and seedlings in sheltered sites, or it may result from active
selection for, and dispersal to, such sites. The majority of the
species in these bush clumps produce small fleshy fruits adapted
for dispersal by birds. The main frugivorous bird species in the
area (blackeyed bulbul *(Pycnonotus barbatus),* speckled mousebird
(Colius striatus), redfronted tinker barbet *(Pogoniulus pusillus)*
and Cape white-eye *(Zosterops pallidus))* all occur predominantly
in the bush clumps (personal observation, 1979). Dispersal by
these species would provide the necessary mechanism for ensuring
directional dispersal of the seeds of fire-sensitive plants to
sheltered sites. This phenomenon of fire-sensitive plant species
being largely bird dispersed, and occurring in bush clumps where
they are protected from fire, appears to be common in many
savannas (personal observation, 1979).

Regular dry season fires tend to suppress woody vegetation,
particularly young plants. Rutherford (1981) has shown that
mortality among tree species, particularly *Burkea africana* (red
syringa) and *Ochna pulchra* (lekkerbreek), in a deciduous broadleafed savanna burnt during the late dry season is greatest among
seedlings and small saplings. Since this mortality must limit
the overall reproductive success of individuals, natural selection might be expected to favour particularly those traits which
enable seedlings and saplings to survive fires during the early
vulnerable years.

The survival of seedlings of a number of woody plant species
adapted to a fire-prone environment is promoted by cryptogeal
germination (Jackson 1974). This involves germination of the
seed on the soil surface followed by burial of the plumule as it

is drawn below the surface by an apparent radicle which is in fact part of the cotyledons. Cryptogeal germination has been recorded in a number of trees occurring in southern Africa: *Combretum apiculatum* (red bushwillow), *C. collinum* (bushwillow), *C. molle* (velvet bushwillow), *C. psidioides* (silver bushwillow), *C. zeyheri* (large-fruited bushwillow), *Elephantorrhiza burkei* (sumach bean) and *Piliostigma thonningii* (camel's foot) (Jackson 1974).

In *P. thonningii* the hypocotyl grows down into the soil and the cotyledons come to lie very close to the soil surface. A cup of tissue, formed by the petioles, protects the developing plumule while the radicle swells to several times the diameter of the hypocotyl and shoot. Damage to the shoot results in new shoots being produced from the swollen root crown (Jackson 1974).

In geophytes, where the corm or bulb of the adult plant is situated underground, but where the seed germinates on the soil surface, the stem base of the seedling is drawn well below the soil surface by contractile roots. For example, the young corms of *Watsonia pyramidata* are pulled down more than 2,5 cm in the first year after germination (Kruger 1977b). This ensures that the meristems generally are not damaged by fire or predators, and are insensitive to extremes of climate.

An alternative to cryptogeal germination as a means of distancing a seedling from fire is seed burial and hypogeal germination. Seed burial is particularly prevalent among grasses (Naveh 1975), especially the Andropogonae, where the seeds of most species have conspicuous hygroscopic awns, hardened tips and a fringe of basal hairs. Hygroscopic awns are well developed in *Themeda triandra*, *Heteropogon contortus*, *Hyparrhenia hirta*, *Hyperthelia dissoluta*, *Tristachya leucothrix*, *Sorghum versicolor* and others.

Seed burial is achieved by a twisting action of an awn which propels the seed into the soil. The awn is made up of diagonally placed fibres which are attached at an acute angle to the outer wall. On drying, the fibres contract and exert an asymmetrical force on the outer wall, causing it to twist. In some species (*T. triandra*, *H. dissoluta*) there is a longitudinal groove which appears to allow the awn to twist more tightly. Propulsion of the seed into the soil is aided by the distal end of the awn which does not contract and so acts as a propeller. Damage to the seed during its passage through the soil is prevented by the hardened tip, while the hairs at the seed tip probably serve to anchor the seed in the soil and so prevent the seed from withdrawing during the expansion and untwisting of the awn when it is wetted.

ESCAPE IN TIME

The susceptibility of plants to fire is partly a function of their phenological state at the time. Plants which are growing or reproducing will experience a greater loss of active tissue and, because of depleted reserves, a reduced capacity for regrowth, than will plants which are dormant. Generally, dormancy is a response to unfavourable environmental conditions, particularly drought and cold. It involves physiological quiescence, often coupled with die-back of all or some of the aboveground parts. Regrowth, when conditions are again suitable, is from reserves which are usually accumulated in underground storage organs. When dormancy coincides with the main fire season (usually during the driest time of the year) recovery is likely to be more assured. Escape in time therefore involves the scheduling of plant phenophases so that the least susceptible phase in the annual cycle coincides with the main fire season.

Many plants in fire-prone environments exhibit seasonal dormancy, coupled with some protection of the meristems. Perennial grasses, particularly those in the summer rainfall areas of South Africa, become dormant during the winter and most of the aerial parts of the plant die back to ground level. The dead leaf-bases insulate the basal meristems from environmental extremes, including fire. For some species, such as *Themeda triandra*, *Heteropogon contortus* and *Trachypogon spicatus*, the regular removal of this dead material appears necessary for these species to maintain their dominance, since they cannot produce tillers from heavily-shaded basal nodes (C Everson, personal communication, 1980). Late winter fires appear to be the main defoliant.

In the fynbos, grasses may remain almost dormant throughout most of the inter-fire interval, flourishing only in the first year or two after fire (eg *Merxmullera rufa*: F Kruger, personal communication, 1980). This may be related to shading by emergent shrubs, and to a less predictable inter-fire interval and fire season than is typical of the summer rainfall zone. Such a dormancy pattern enables the plant to persist in the community despite its early successional status, to survive the inevitable fires and subsequently to exploit the post-fire period without having to re-invade the community each time.

Dormancy, and the protection given to basal meristems by dead leaf-bases, enable grasses to survive intense dry season fires without any apparently detrimental effects. In contrast, grasses burnt after new growth has commenced are often severely damaged, even though the fires may be relatively 'cool', since a large proportion of the new season's tillers are destroyed (Tainton et al 1977).

Other monocots, especially species in the Iridaceae, Liliaceae, Amaryllidaceae, Orchidaceae and Hypoxidaceae, are geophytic, surviving the dormant period as underground bulbs or corms. There, the plants are efficiently insulated from the heat of the fire by the soil. In most cases, geophytes are seasonally dormant, but in some, such as the orchids *Satyrium rostratum*, *Orthopenthea bivalvata*, *Disa obtusa* and *D. racemosa* (Hall 1959; Schelpe 1976; F Kruger, personal communication, 1980), the plants may remain dormant throughout most of the inter-fire interval.

Seasonal dormancy also occurs in woody plants. In many species the perennating buds are located on well developed underground stems, lignotubers or rootstocks. In most of these plants the aerial shoots die back each year; in some, at longer intervals (Burtt-Davy 1922; White 1976). These geoxylic shrubs are most common in savannas. White (1976) lists 102 species for the Zambezian phytogeographic region, of which *Lannea edulis* (wild grape), *Parinari capensis* (sand apple), *Dichapetalum cymosum* (poison leaf), *Elephantorrhiza elephantina* (elandsboontjie) and *Pygmaeothamnus zeyheri* (goorappel) are common in South African savannas.

Finally, some plants may persist in a fire-prone environment through escape in time as seeds. Annual plants in particular would seem to have an advantage, especially where annual or biennial fires create open sites which can be colonized. Almost no data are available on the ecology of annual plants in relation to regular burning. However, the diversity of annuals in certain fire-prone environments is high, comprising 26% of the herbaceous layer flora in a South African *Burkea* savanna (Theron et al 1983) and 17 to 24% in various fire-maintained west African savannas (Cesar 1971).

Where intervals between fires increase, the advantage gained by annuals will be reduced (in the absence of any other factor causing significant disturbance favouring their establishment). This may account for the relative paucity of annuals in the fynbos where fire intervals range from 6 to 30 yr (Martin 1966; Kruger 1977b). In this case, some plants may survive by invading the post-fire community where they reproduce and disperse to new disturbed sites before becoming shaded out and before the next fire occurs at the original site. Martin (1966) mentions *Senecio pterophorus* (perdegifbos), *Indigofera stricta* and *I. hilaris* invading a post-fire community in the eastern Cape fynbos. The contrast between these 'fugitive' species and 'obligate reseeders' (discussed below) is that the former are not usually present in the prefire community while the latter are. Both, though, regenerate solely from seed.

FIRE TOLERANCE

Fire tolerance involves two attributes: **resistance** to fire, resulting from the protection of meristems and vascular tissues by thick, relatively non-flammable bark or by persistent leaf bases; and **recovery,** involving the capacity of the plant to resprout from dormant buds and thereby replace damaged or lost tissues.

Resistance

The damage experienced by a plant depends largely on the degree of protection of vital tissues from heat damage. Many authors have commented on the apparent protective function of thick bark in relation to fire (Phillips 1931; Wicht 1945; West 1971; Rourke 1972; Kruger 1977b) (Figure 1). Others have commented on the lack of resistance of some species to fire as a result of having thin bark (eg *Widdringtonia cedarbergensis* (Clanwilliam cedar): Luckhoff 1971), but there have been very few quantitative studies.

The extent to which a plant is damaged by fire depends also on the relationship between plant height and flame height, large trees generally being less susceptible to damage than small ones. In one study, 95% of all *A. karroo* trees experiencing

Figure 1   *Strychnos cocculoides* (corky-bark monkey orange): an
            example of thick corky bark protecting the stem
            vascular tissue against fire damage.

complete canopy destruction were under 2,5 m high (Trollope 1974)
(Figure 2).   Macdonald (1982) has shown that damage to above-
ground parts in *Acacia davyi* (corky-bark acacia) varies with fire
intensity; the extent of canopy damage in the taller plants being
greater in a more intense fire (Figure 2).   While these are
largely fortuitous consequences of large size, they suggest that
there might be some selective advantage in rapid growth and the
attainment of a sufficient size to enable the plant to survive
most fires.   However, no data are available to test this.
     Shape may also influence the degree of resistance of a plant
to fire.   Kruger and Bigalke (this volume, chapter 5) have
suggested that the dense canopy foliage and inverted conical
crowns of *Protea laurifolia* (laurel protea). *Leucospermum conocarpodendron* (tree   pincushions)   and *Leucadendron   argenteum*
(silver tree) facilitate the protection of apical buds by
deflecting hot air drafts rising from the fire below.   Although a
canopy shape which redirects convective heat upwards away from
the canopy would be advantageous to trees living in an environment where relatively intense ground fires regularly occur, it is
more likely that the shape of these plants is a consequence of
past fires killing buds in the lower canopy (Rourke 1972).
     Low growing plants must be particularly well protected
against heat damage since they probably experience greater and

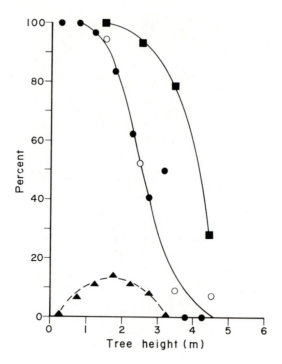

Figure 2   Percentage top-kill (———) and percentage mortality
(----) in *Acacia karroo* (sweet thorn) in relation to
tree height.   Circles represent data collected after
relatively 'cool' fires and squares, data collected
after a 'hot' fire (data from Trollope (1974) and
Macdonald (1982)

more prolonged elevation of temperatures during fires than do
taller plants.   Data from savanna fires indicate that, depending
on the grass canopy height, temperatures are greatest within
0,5 m to 1 m of the ground (Trollope 1974, and this volume,
chapter 7; Harrison 1978).   Within this zone, temperatures are
generally lower at ground level than at the top of the grass
canopy (Trollope, this volume, chapter 7).
     Grasses are among the most fire-resistant components of a
plant community, due primarily to their structure and patterns of
growth (Booysen et al 1963; Tainton and Booysen 1963, 1965a,
1965b; Tainton 1982).   Some grasses (eg *Alloteropsis semialata*,
Tristachya leucothrix, *Harpochloa falx*: C Everson, personal
communication, 1980) produce tillers from subterranean nodes on
rhizomes or from stolons.   The tiller initials, in the axils of
already formed leaves, lie close to or under the soil surface and
thus can survive all but the most severe defoliation.   In other
grasses, especially tufted perennials (eg *Themeda triandra*,
Heteropogon contortus), the tiller initials are slightly more
elevated but are protected by persistent leaf bases in a basal
tuft.   The close packing of these leaf bases ensures that fire

seldom penetrates the tuft. This protection is particularly effective when the plant is dormant, but once the tillers begin to grow they become progressively more susceptible to defoliation (Tainton 1982), though some protection is still provided by the leaves which develop from the base of the tiller and sheath the younger leaves and stem apex. In addition, in most species the tiller remains compact and close to the soil surface during the vegetative phase and only elongates once it becomes reproductive (Booysen et al 1963). These features ensure that tillers are well protected against both climatic extremes and defoliation by herbivores and fire.

Persistent leaf bases are also present in other herbs. In the Liliaceae, Iridaceae and Amaryllidaceae the leaf bases are often swollen and serve as storage organs, as well as protecting the meristems. These bulbs usually are situated underground, though they may protrude in some of the larger species (eg *Boophane disticha* (poison bulb), *Scilla natalensis* (slangkop)). In the Cyperaceae and Restionaceae the stem initials are situated basally where they are protected by older stems, and in some cases even arise from subterranean rhizomes. In the Cycadaceae, Velloziaceae and aloes (Liliaceae) the persistent leaf bases envelop the fibrous, sometimes woody stems and protect the leaf initials which are crowded together at the stem apex (Figure 3). Although these plants often stand out from the herb layer, the thickness of the leaf bases and their close packing provides adequate protection against even intense fires (eg *Encephalartos ghellinkii* (Drakensberg cycad) in the Drakensberg grasslands).

Recovery

Plants are often severely damaged by fire. Reductions in canopy volume and leaf biomass in the order of 40 to 100% are common, particularly among smaller individuals (Figure 2) (Trollope 1974; Rutherford 1981). Nevertheless, the proportion of individuals killed by fire is often relatively low (Table 1), and many plants display an impressive capacity for recovery from fire damage.

Recovery involves resprouting from dormant buds located in the branches, stem, root collar or in the roots themselves (Figures 4 and 5). Dormancy in these buds is maintained by correlative inhibition which is linked to apical dominance. When this dominance is broken by the destruction of the apical meristems, the dormant buds regain their meristematic activity and begin to differentiate and produce new shoots.

The extent of resprouting is apparently related to the degree to which apical meristems are damaged. In *A. karroo* the proportion of plants coppicing is greatest among plants which experience complete top kill irrespective of size and stem diameter (Trollope 1974). In *O. pulchra* the extent of basal regeneration increases exponentially as a function of the relative reduction in canopy volume, the increase being greater in a faster, apparently more intense burn, than in a slower, cooler burn, suggesting that fewer apical buds were destroyed by the slower burn (Rutherford 1981).

282

Figure 3   *Xerophyta retinervis* (Velloziaceae) showing fire blackened persistent leaf bases protecting stem vascular tissue. New leaves are produced from the stem apices.

Figure 4   *Olinia radiata* (Natal olinia), a forest species resprouting after an intense forest fire.

Table 1   Percentage mortality due to fire in some southern
          African plants (excluding species which experience 100%
          mortality and which regenerate solely from seed).

Species	Age Class	Mortality (%)	Remarks on circumstances of fire	Reference
CUPRESSACEAE				
Widdringtonia nodiflora	adult	41,0	ca 51-yr old stand	Scriba
	adult	67,4		(1976)
	45-mo old seedlings	15,0	experimental burn	Smith (1982)
W. cedarbergensis	all	97,3	30-40 yr old stand	
	all	39,7	17-19 yr old stand	Andrag
	all	33,3	16-17 yr old stand	(1977)
GRAMINEAE				
Andropogon schirensis	adult	21,0		
Aristida meridionalis	adult	14,3		
Rhynchelytrum spp	adult	12,3		Rutherford
Aristida stipitata	adult	5,9		(1975)
Digitaria pole-evansii	adult	0,6		
PROTEACEAE				
Protea roupelliae	seedlings	5,0	cool July burn	
	seedlings	71,0	hot July burn	P Frost
	seedlings	90,0	cool Sept burn	(pers.
	seedlings	68,0	hot Sept burn	obs. 1979)
MIMOSOIDEAE				
Acacia davyi	all	0,9		Macdonald
Acacia karroo	all	1,7		(1982)
Acacia karroo	all	9,9		Trollope 1974
Dichrostachys cinerea	all	0		B J Coetzee (pers. comm. 1980)
CAESALPINIOIDEAE				
Burkea africana	all	6,5		Rutherford (1975)
PAPILIONOIDEAE				
Lonchocarpus nelsii	all	4,3		Rutherford (1975)
ROSACEAE				
Leucosidea sericea	13-mo old seedlings	70,0	experimental burn	Smith (1982)

ANACARDIACEAE				
Rhus lucida	all	0		Trollope (1974)
TILIACEAE				
Grewia flavescens	all	0		Rutherford (1981)
Cliffortia linearifolia	all	33,0		Trollope and Booysen (1971)
OCHNACEAE				
Ochna pulchra	all	2,1		Rutherford (1975)
	all	5,0	slow burn	Rutherford
	all	1,0	fast burn	(1981)
COMBRETACEAE				
Combretum psidioides	all	1,1		Rutherford (1975)
Terminalia sericea	all	2,9		
LOGANIACEAE				
Buddleia salviifolia	13-mo old seedlings	35,0	experimental burn	Smith (1982)
EBENACEAE				
Euclea divinorum	all	0		Macdonald (1982)
ERICACEAE				
Erica brownleeae	all	97,3		Trollope and Booysen (1971)

The tendency to resprout depends not only on the extent to which apical buds have been damaged but also on the extent to which dormant buds have survived undamaged. This depends on the degree to which these buds are protected by thick bark and also by their position on the plant. In fire-adapted species, the aerial perennating buds from which post-fire coppice shoots originate are situated closer to the soil surface than in non-adapted species (van der Merwe 1966b). For example, in two fynbos plant communities experiencing regular fires, the proportion of vegetatively regenerating species is inversely related to the height of the perennating buds (Table 2).

Within one genus, *Leucospermum* (Proteaceae), 13 of the 47 species are capable of regenerating vegetatively after fire (Rourke 1972). These resprouting species can be grouped into two categories depending on whether new shoots arise from dormant buds located in the stem (6 species) or in the root stock (7 species). Only 30 to 50% of the individuals in a population which relies on regeneration from dormant buds in the stems survive fire, in contrast to 90 to 100% survival of individuals in populations which rely on regeneration from a subterranean rootstock or lignotuber (Rourke 1972).

Figure 5   *Lonchocarpus capassa* (apple-leaf) resprouting from the
root crown after an early winter fire.

Table 2   Percentage of species which regenerate vegetatively
after fire in two fynbos communities, classified
according to Raunkiaer life-forms.

	[a]Swartboskloof		[b]Jakkalsrivier	
	% species regenerating vegetatively	Total number of species in each class	% species regenerating vegetatively	Total number of species in each class
Phanerophyte	55,6	151	28,1	153
Chamaephyte	54,7	139	39,8	82
Hemicryptophyte	98,6	71	92,1	139
Geophyte	100	67	100	111
Therophyte	0	16	0	7
Unclassified	25,0	4	40,0	15

[a]data from van der Merwe (1966b)
[b]data from Kruger (1977b)

The close correlation between the capacity to resprout and the presence of a woody subterranean stem, rootstock or ligno-tuber from which numerous coppice shoots develop after burning, is well known and is considered to be a characteristic feature of vegetation in fire-prone environments (Burtt-Davy 1922; Martin 1966; West 1971; Rourke 1972; McMaster 1976; Carlquist 1977). Such plants occur in fynbos (*Leucadendron salignum* (geelbos), *Leucospermum hypophyllum* (slangbossie), *L. tomentosum*, *L. prostratum*, *Erica cerinthoides* (red hairy heath), *Staavia radiata* (altydbossie), *Grubbia tomentosa* (koolhout), *Metalasia muricata* (white bristle bush), *Acalypha peduncularis* and others), grasslands (*Protea dracomontana*, *P. simplex*, *Leucospermum cuneiforme*, *L. gerrardii*, *L. saxosum*, *L. innovans*, *Buchenroidera lotononoides*) and particularly in savannas (*Neorautanenia amboensis* (gemsbokboontjie), *Lannea edulis*, *Dichapetalum cymosum* and many others).

White (1976) has reviewed the occurrence of geoxylic suffrut-ices in African savanna floras. There are at least 109 species in 31 families, 102 of which occur in the Zambezian region and only 7 occurring in the Sudanian region. This disproportionate distribution has led White (1976) to conclude that the geoxylic growth form is primarily an adaptation to oligotrophic, season-ally waterlogged sandy soils in areas of low relief (which occur extensively in the Zambezian but not in the Sudanian region), rather than being adapted to fire or to frost (Burtt-Davy 1922; West 1971). (It must be pointed out that White has only consid-ered those species which have closely related species growing as trees. There are other geoxylic suffrutices but no data are available on their distribution through Africa. These species need to be considered before the apparent paucity of this growth form in the Sudanian region can be properly assessed).

White (1976) further suggests that geoxylic suffrutices are normally eliminated when forest or woodland are destroyed by annual fires and regress to secondary grasslands. This is contradicted by data from Zambia where suffrutices are most numerous in *chipya*, fire-maintained perennial grasslands with scattered small trees, and are less numerous in *miombo* and *mateshi* which are less regularly burnt (Lawton 1978). Fire is also important in maintaining the vigour of these plants. In the absence of fire the shoots produce progressively fewer flowers, eventually become moribund and die. This suggests that fire has been more important in the evolution of the suffrutex habit than White (1976) indicates.

Enlarged rootstocks and lignotubers develop early during the life of a plant. Pronounced swelling of the stem base has been noted in year old seedlings of a number of proteas (*Protea arborea* (waboom), *P. roupelliae* (silver protea), *P. gaguedi* (African protea), *P. welwitschii* (honey-scented protea)), species which regenerate vegetatively after fire (Figure 6). On the other hand, non-sprouting proteas (eg *Protea subvestita* (lipped protea), *P. repens* (sugarbush), *P. neriifolia* (oleander-leaved protea)) appear to lack this feature (personal observation, 1980). Similarly, the seedlings of the multistemmed *Leucospermum* spp (*L. saxosum* and allies) develop shoots in the axils of the lowermost leaves, including the cotyledons, at 8 months of age.

This is accompanied by a thickening of the stem base. These features do not occur in seedlings of non-sprouting, single-stemmed *Leucospermum* spp (Rourke 1972). Seedlings which have enlarged stem bases have the capacity to resprout after defoliation, the others do not.

Little information is available on the relative distribution of dormant buds in the branches, stem, root crown and roots. Considerable variation may be expected, perhaps related to the varying susceptibilities of different species to damage by fire. Species which are invariably burnt back to ground level during a fire *(Grewia flavescens* (donkey berry): Rutherford 1981) might be expected to have a majority of dormant buds concentrated in the root crown. Other species which have more resistant aerial parts might be expected to have dormant buds located well up the stem and branches. Plants which succeed in resprouting well towards the apices of the branches will be at an advantage over those that must resprout again from ground level, although both will have the advantage of continuing to occupy the same site as before the fire.

Figure 6   *Protea roupelliae* (silver protea) seedlings showing swollen root crowns. This swelling of the root crown occurs at an early age. It does not occur in non-resprouting species.

The number of basal shoots which regenerate after fire is often greater than the number killed by the fire. In *O. pulchra* almost twice as many new shoots were produced as were killed during the fire. In *Burkea africana* the ratio was 1,3 : 1 (Rutherford 1981). However, the capacity to produce new shoots may decline with age. Trollope (1974) demonstrated that mortality of *A. karroo* trees, following complete top kill, increased with increasing stem diameter and age. This probably reflects a progressive decline in the viability of the dormant buds in the root collar region (Trollope 1974).

Repeated burning, particularly successive burns at short intervals, also adversely affects the survival of resprouting species. For example, Trollope (1973) has shown that burning two years after an initial burn, followed by a further burn one year later, destroys *Cliffortia linearifolia*, a resprouting species which is dominant in lowland fynbos communities in parts of the eastern Cape. This mortality may be a result of the depletion of nutrient and energy reserves, with fires occurring too frequently to permit the plant to replenish them, leading to lowered vitality and a reduced ability to produce coppice shoots. The plants may also lack sufficient numbers of dormant buds from which new shoots can grow.

The capacity of plants to resprout from dormant buds after defoliation has not necessarily evolved solely in response to fire. Herbivory, pathogen attack, drought or frost damage can all cause defoliation and it is more likely that resprouting represents a general adaptive trait to defoliation, of whatever kind, than a particular response to any given one.

REGENERATION FROM SEED

Species which do not survive fires must either regenerate from seed or become extinct at that site. In some species the capacity to resprout is entirely absent and these species are obligate reseeders. They make up a significant proportion of the plant community in some fire-prone vegetation types. In the mountain fynbos communities at Swartboskloof and Jakkalsrivier, obligate reseeders comprise 34% and 37% respectively of the 448 and 508 plant species recorded in the two communities (van der Merwe 1966; Kruger 1977b). Mitchell (1922) lists 42 species occurring after a fire in fynbos on Signal Hill, Cape Town, of which 18 species regenerated solely from seed, 17 species resprouted and seven species both resprouted and produced significant numbers of seedlings.

Generally, resprouters predominate among the trees, larger woody shrubs, hemicryptophytes and geophytes, while obligate reseeders are predominantly the smaller shrubs and some herbs (Kruger 1977b). In the study of post-fire recovery of the vegetation on Signal Hill, the reseeding species belong to the families Compositae and Leguminosae, while the resprouters comprised mainly species in the families Anacardiaceae and Ebenaceae (Mitchell 1922). Obligate reseeders in fynbos often dominate the vegetation succession for many years (eg *Erica demissa* and *E. chamissonis:* Martin 1966; *Elytropappus rhinocerotis* (renosterbos): Levyns 1927, 1929a; *Cliffortia paucistaminea* and *Erica brownleeae:* Trollope and Booysen 1971; Trollope 1973), though they eventually become moribund in the absence of fire, and are replaced ultimately by larger woody shrubs and trees (Kruger 1977b).

Obligate reseeders appear to be rather uncommon among savanna and grassland plants. However, in forest and forest precursor communities there are many species which are fire-sensitive and which regenerate solely from seed (eg *Podocarpus latifolius* (yellowwood), *Apodytes dimidiata* (white pear), *Ekebergia capensis* (Cape ash), *Canthium obovatum* (quar), *Zanthoxylum capensis* (small knobwood), *Virgilia oroboides* (keurboom), *Trema orientalis* (pigeonwood), *Philippia evansii)*.

In a Natal coastal forest 74% of the tree species regenerated solely from seed after fire, though not all regeneration was confined to the immediate postfire period (Macdonald and Pammenter 1979). As in fynbos, some of these obligate seed regenerating species (eg *V. oroboides:* Phillips 1931; *T. orientalis:* Macdonald and Pammenter 1979; personal observation, 1980) dominate the community for a number of years after fire.

Seedlings become established after fire from seeds which have dispersed to the burnt area from adjacent unburnt stands of vegetation (eg *Erica chamissonis, E. demissa:* Martin 1966) or, more commonly, from the germination of on-site seed stores which have survived the fire (eg *Elytroppapus rhinocerotis, Borbonia cordata* (Cape gorse), *Psoralea hirta, P. uncinata* and others: Mitchell 1922; Levyns 1927, 1929a; *Protea repens, P. neriifolia:* Jordaan 1949; various *Leucadendron* spp: Williams 1972). Since the mortality rate among seedlings is often very high (Cook 1979) the maintenance of as large a seed store as possible seems likely to increase the probability of some of an individual's offspring becoming established in the post-fire community. The size of a seed store depends on the relative rates of seed production by the parent plant and the losses due to premature germination, predation, disease and senescence. In some plants there appears to be a regular input of many short-lived seeds (eg *Anthospermum aethiopicum, Relhania genistaefolia:* Levyns 1935b) while in others the maintenance of a large seed store depends on the gradual accumulation in the soil of fewer, longer-lived seeds. Although the viability of seeds in these species declines with age (eg *E. rhinocerotis:* Levyns 1929b, 1935b) (Figure 7), some seeds may remain viable in the soil for 15 yr or longer (eg *Orothamnus zeyheri, Mimetes stokoei:* Rourke 1976).

The longevity of seeds can be extended through seed dormancy. In some species, such as *E. rhinocerotis,* this involves innate dormancy, the seeds requiring a period after seed fall before they are able to germinate (Figure 7). In others, the dormancy appears to be enforced, the seeds ripening only after suitable environmental conditions occur in the seedbed. This appears to be promoted by a water resistant seed coat. Such hardseededness is found in the Gramineae, Restionaceae, Proteaceae, Leguminosae, Anacardiaceae, Malvaceae, Compositae and other families (Gill 1977). It is characterized by a lack of imbibition, which appears to increase as the seed moisture content decreases. Hardseededness may also be important in promoting longevity by deterring potential predators and rendering fungal attack ineffective.

One of the potential disadvantages of a hard seed coat is the necessity for extensive abrasion, cracking or chemically induced softening before imbibition and germination can occur. Too little damage will inhibit germination; too much will kill the embryo. Therefore the resistance of the testa is probably a compromise between the need for protection against predators, pathogens and fire, and the need for rapid germination when conditions are suitable. It is not known to what extent fire is important or necessary to initiate imbibition but exposure to high temperatures, temperature fluctuations, charring and cracking of the testa may all be involved (Gill 1977).

There have been few studies of fire-stimulated germination in southern African plants. Levyns (1929b) has investigated heat-stimulated germination in *E. rhinocerotis*. She showed that the percentage of fresh seeds germinating after exposure at 100°C for one hour increased from 2,5% to 11%. Exposure for longer periods, or to higher temperatures (250°C), adversely affected seed germination, while exposure to lower temperatures (50 to 60°C) for an hour or longer had no affect. Heating to 100°C followed by storage for one or more years did not affect subsequent germination success, though heat-treated seeds germinated about five days before the controls.

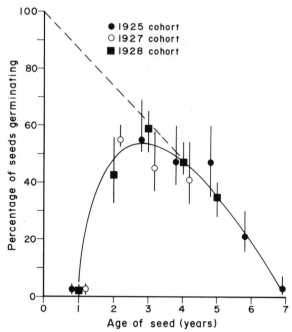

Figure 7   Percentage germination of the seed of *Elytropappus rhinocerotis* (renosterbos) in relation to seed age. Low germination in the first year represents inherent dormancy of the seed (data from Levyns 1935b).

Allelochemicals in the soil may inhibit germination and the extensive post-fire germination of seeds may simply be the consequence of the destruction of these chemicals by fire. For example, extracts from *Chrysocoma tenuifolia* (bitterbos) inhibit seed germination and suppress the early growth of seedlings, effects which are drastically reduced by fire (Squires and Trollope 1979). In *Orothamnus zeyheri*, the accumulation of litter (and perhaps associated allelochemicals) inhibits germination, which takes place only after fire (Boucher and McCann 1975).

An alternative to seed storage in the soil is seed retention on the plant. Here the seeds are protected from heat damage by being sheltered inside cones (eg *Widdringtonia* spp: Scriba 1976; Andrag 1977; *Leucadendron* spp: Williams 1972), within persistent fibrous bracts (eg *Protea* spp: Jordaan 1949; Lombard 1971) or in capsules (eg *Erica sessiliflora* (green heath): A J Rebelo, personal communication, 1982). Seed retention may be partial or complete, the seeds usually dehiscing after the death of the branch or stem on which they are borne (Figure 8). This usually occurs after fire but can occur at other times. In *Widdringtonia cedarbergensis* the seeds remain encapsulated for 1,5 to 2,5 yr (Andrag 1977); in *W. nodiflora* (mountain cedar), for a similar or even longer period (personal observation, 1979); in *P. repens*, *P. neriifolia* (oleander-leaved protea) and *P. subvestita* for 2 to 4 yr (Jordaan 1949; personal observation, 1979), and in *Leucadendron* spp, for up to 8 yr (Williams 1972). In *Leucadendron platyspermum* (kraaltolbos), the seed may even begin to germinate in the cone before it is released (F Kruger, personal communication, 1980).

The number of viable seeds retained on the plant will vary as a function of the age of the plant, the number of viable seeds produced each year, the duration for which they are retained and the loss of seeds to predators or to disease. About 900 to 1 300 seeds are present on 10 to 12 yr old *P. repens*, though only 9% are viable (Lombard 1971). There is a need for equivalent data from other seed-retaining species.

The capacity of an obligate reseeding species to survive in an environment subject to recurring fires depends on the frequency of fire in relation to the duration of the primary juvenile period (the period between germination and first seed production). The more frequently fires occur, the shorter this primary juvenile period must be if the species is to persist at a site in the absence of immigration. In *Anthospermum aethiopicum* flowering occurs less than 24 months after fire (Martin 1966); in *Erica mauretanica*, within 30 months after fire (Mitchell 1922) and in *P. repens*, *Leucadendron floridum* and *L. macowanii* between 3 to 5 yr (van der Merwe 1966; Taylor 1977). Kruger and Bigalke (this volume, chapter 5) give data on the juvenile periods of other seed regenerating species, ranging from 4 to 7 yr. Generally, the longer lived a species is, the longer is the juvenile period (Figure 9).

The time of year may also affect the capacity of a plant to regenerate from seed. Levyns (1929b) indicates that seeds of *E. rhinocerotis* germinate better after fires in the period December to March (summer) than after fires occurring during June to August (winter). Similarly, in *P. repens*, fires during the period January to March are favourable for germination, fires during the period April to June are much less favourable while fires occurring between July and December kill seeds (Jordaan 1949, 1965).

This interaction between the season of burning and germination success has practical implications for the management of favoured plant species. For example, the seeds of *W. cedarbergensis* cedar ripen from December to February, at the beginning of the natural fire season (December to April: Andrag 1977). Current management policies dictate that controlled fuel reduction fires should be applied during the wet winter months (June to August) so as to reduce the risk of dry season wildfires (Andrag 1977). This unnatural fire regime may be an important reason for the poor germination and seedling survival noted by Luckhoff (1971). The same considerations may apply in the case of *W. nodiflora*.

Figure 8   Fire-stimulated opening of the seed cones of *Widdringtonia nodiflora* (mountain cedar). The cones on nearby unburnt plants were not open.

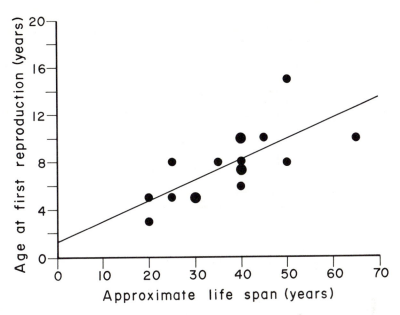

Figure 9   Relationship (y = 1,24 + 0,17x, (r^2 = 0,787; $p \leq 0,001$;
n = 17)) between age of first reproduction and average
longevity in some obligate seed-regenerating species
of fynbos plants.   Large circles represent two
values at the same coordinate (data from Moll et al
1980; E J Moll, personal communication, 1980).

POST-FIRE FLOWERING

Fire induces changes in the structure and functioning of the
post-fire environment, including changes in vegetation cover,
rainfall infiltration and albedo.   These in turn lead to changes
in microclimate, soil nutrient and soil moisture status.   In
addition, the death of established plants creates opportunities
for seedling establishment, while changes in animal populations
probably result, initially at least, in fewer seed and seedling
predators.   All these changes provide opportunities for enhanced
reproduction which many plants exploit.   This is manifested in
the marked post-fire flowering of the herbaceous flora in many
plant communities around the world (Australia: Gill 1977, 1981;
California: Muller et al 1968; Israel: Naveh 1974b; South Africa:
Hall 1959; Martin 1966; Kruger 1977b, 1980).   In South Africa,
and in the fynbos in particular, many species have been reported
to exhibit marked post-fire flowering (Figure 10, Table 3).
    Most of the species involved are geophytes.   Their ability to
survive fires, and the presence of underground energy and
nutrient reserves, predispose them to flowering soon after fire.
In some cases the response is remarkably rapid.   *Cyrtanthus
breviflorus* flowers within a week of fire (Gordon-Gray and Wright
1969) while *C. contractus* (fire lily) flowers within 14 days
(Martin 1966).   This rapid response presumably enables these
species to exploit pollinators and set seed before other plants
have begun to recover from the fire.

294

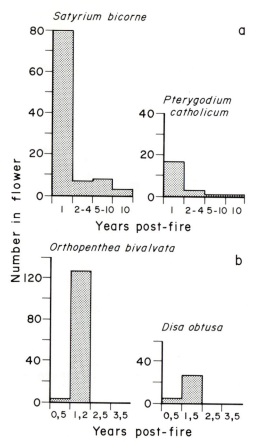

Figure 10   Postfire flowering in various orchid species:
A. numbers of plants flowering in different aged
postfire stands of mountain fynbos; B. numbers of
plants flowering on firebreaks of different postfire
ages (data from Hall 1959).

Some species flower only after fire (*C. contractus*: Martin
1966; *Haemanthus canaliculatus*: Levyns 1966a; *Moraea ramosissima*
(geeltulp):   F   J   Kruger,   personal   communication,   1980;
Orthopenthea bivalvata, *Disa obtusa*: Hall 1959; *Disa racemosa*,
Satyrium rostratum: Schelpe   1976;   F   J   Kruger,   personal
communication, 1980; *Aloe chortoliroides*: Reynolds 1974).   These
plants are therefore dependent on fire for flowering and some may
even remain dormant in the period between fires, for up to 25 yr
in the case of *Satyrium rostratum* (Schelpe 1976).   This postfire
flowering may reflect a dependence by the plant on a set of
seedbed conditions that exist only after fire, or it may enable a
plant to avoid specific flower, seed or seedling predators whose
populations would be limited by a lack of resources in the years
between fires (Gill 1977).

Table 3   Species which have been reported to show a marked
           post-fire flowering response.

Species	Response[a]	Locality	Reference
GRAMINEAE			
Eragrostis capensis	1	Eastern Cape	Martin 1966
Poa binata	2		Martin 1966
Themeda triandra	3		Martin 1966
Stiburus alopecuroides	2		Frost 1979
RESTIONACEAE			
Restio triticeus	3	Eastern Cape	Martin 1966
LILIACEAE			
Agapanthus africanus	2	Southwestern Cape	Levyns 1966b
Asparagus compactus	2		Kidd 1973
Asparagus capensis	2		Mitchell 1922
Tulbaghia alliacea	2		Levyns 1966b
Kniphofia uvaria	2		Levyns 1966b
Trachyandra revoluta	2	Western Cape	Mason 1972
Aloe chortoliroides	1	eastern Transvaal	Reynolds 1974
Aloe dominella	2	Natal	Reynolds 1974
Aloe integra	4	eastern Transvaal	Reynolds 1974
Aloe woolliana	4	eastern Transvaal	Reynolds 1974
AMARYLLIDACEAE			
Cyrtanthus augustifolius	1	Southwestern Cape	Kruger 1980
Cyrtanthus ventricosus	1		Levyns 1966b
Cyrtanthus contractus	1	Eastern Cape	Martin 1966
Cyrtanthus breviflorus	1	Natal	Gordon-Gray & Wright 1969
Haemanthus rotundifolius	2	Southwestern Cape	Levyns 1966b
Haemanthus coccineus	2		Levyns 1966b
Haemanthus canaliculatus	1		Levyns 1966a
Amaryllis belladona	2		Levyns 1966b
Boophane guttata	2		Levyns 1966b
Brunsvigia orientalis	2/4		Taylor 1972
IRIDACEAE			
Bobartia indica	2	Eastern Cape	Martin 1966
Bobartia burchelli	1		Martin 1966
Gladiolus brevifolius	4	Southwestern Cape	Mitchell 1922
Moraea trita	1	Natal	J D Macdonald (pers. comm. 1982)
Moraea ramosissima	1	Southwestern Cape	Kruger 1980
Aristea macrocarpa	4		Jackson 1976
Aristea spiralis	4		Jackson 1976
Watsonia pyramidata	2		Kruger 1977b
Watsonia tabularis	2		Levyns 1966b
Watsonia humilis	2		Levyns 1966b
Tritonia scillaris	2		Kidd 1973

ORCHIDACEAE

Satyrium rostratum	1	southwestern Cape	Schelpe 1976
Satyrium coriifolium	2		Jackson 1976
Satyrium bicorne	2		Hall 1959
Disa obtusa	1/3		Hall 1959
Disa cornuta	3		Hall 1959
Disa salteria	2		Kidd 1973
Disa ophrydea	1		Hall 1959
Pterygodium catholicum	2		Hall 1959
Monadenia micrantha	2		Hall 1959
Orthopenthea bivalvata	1/3		Hall 1959
Orthopenthea atricapilla	3		Hall 1959
Ceratandra atrata	3		Hall 1959
Eulophia tabularis	3		Hall 1959
Penthea patens	3		Hall 1959
Disperis capensis	2		Jackson 1976
Schizodium obliquum	2		Jackson 1976

RANUNCULACEAE

Anemone capensis	2	southwestern Cape	Kidd 1973
Anemone caffra	1	eastern Cape	Martin 1966

CRUCIFERAE

Heliophila meyeri	2	southwestern Cape	Jackson 1976

EUPHORBIACEAE

Clutia heterophylla	1	eastern Cape	Martin 1966
Graderia scabra	1		Martin 1966

ANACARDIACEAE

Rhus rosmarinifolia	2	southwestern Cape	Kidd 1973

MALVACEAE

Hibiscus aethiopicus	2	southwestern Cape	Mitchell 1922

APIACEAE

Thunbergiella filiformis	2	southwestern Cape	Kidd 1973

LABIATAE

Ajuga ophrydis	2	eastern Cape	Martin 1966

COMPOSITAE

Gerbera asplenifolia	1	eastern Cape	Martin 1966
		southwestern Cape	Levyns 1966b
Gerbera viridifolia	1	eastern Cape	Martin 1966
Gerbera crocea	2	southwestern Cape	Jackson 1976
Alciope tabularis	2		Jackson 1976
Haplocarpha lanata	2		Levyns 1966b
Berkheya ilicifolia	2		Levyns 1966b
Corymbium africanum	2		Kidd 1973
Senecio subcanescens	2		Levyns 1966b
Senecio othonnaeflorus	2	eastern Cape	Martin 1966

---

[a]The responses of the plants have been classified as follows:
1 - flowering only after fire (very rarely at other times);
2 - flowering after fire, less so at other times;
3 - little or no flowering in the first year after fire but prolific flowering in the second and sometimes third year;
4 - early flowering induced by fire.

Not all geophytes are stimulated to flower more profusely after fire than in its absence. The flowering of many geophytes appears to be governed by climate so that these species flower at the normal time (usually spring) irrespective of when they were burnt. Heat treatment of the dormant corms of various irises failed to stimulate early flowering or an increase in flower production (Bean 1962). However, the extent of postfire flowering in certain geophytes depends partly on the season of burning. In *Watsonia pyramidata*, plants burnt in autumn (March to May) flower profusely the following spring; plants burnt in spring (September to November) are not so stimulated (Kruger 1977 and personal communication, 1980). Competition from well-established grasses and restionaceous herbs may be responsible for the depressed flowering of *W. pyramidata* (F J Kruger, personal communication, 1980), though the mechanisms (such as shading or allelopathy) have not been identified.

The stimulus for flowering in fire-adapted geophytes is not fully understood. Changes in daily temperature fluctuations in the soil following fire probably trigger flowering in *C. contractus* (Martin 1966), though other effects such as increased soil temperatures and better light penetration after a fire, changes in the physical and chemical characteristics of the soil and reduced competition from other plants may also be important (Bean 1962; Martin 1966).

Among non-geophytes, fire generally depresses reproduction. Fire damages the stem apices of actively growing grasses, thereby reducing flowering and seed production. Although the death of the stem apex breaks apical dominance and leads to the development of lateral tillers, few of these tillers are able to mature and fruit in the same season (Booysen et al 1963). However, in some grasses (eg *Stiburus alopecuroides*: personal observation, 1979) flowering in the first season after fire is greatly increased over flowering in adjacent unburnt swards. Fire also appears to depress flowering among woody plants, though this may be followed by prolific flowering 2 to 3 yr later (Rutherford 1975). Some plants (eg *Acacia davyi*, *A. caffra* (common hook-thorn): I A W Macdonald, personal communication, 1980), while experiencing depressed fruiting as a result of canopy destruction, have the capacity to fruit from ground-level coppice shoots in the first post-fire season.

RESPONSES OF ANIMALS TO FIRE

Animals in general have a major advantage over plants in that they are mobile and thereby can avoid the direct effects of fire. Mobile insects, such as grasshoppers, phasmids and mantids can flee ahead of a flame front moving at about 1,4 m s^{-1} (Gillon 1971b). Most vertebrates can move even faster than this. This mobility enables animals to escape to peripheral habitats which are unaffected by fire. These include vegetation islands such as termite mounds or bush clumps which seldom burn completely, or patches of unburnt vegetation. Gandar (1982) found a marked increase in the numbers and biomass of grasshoppers on unburnt patches of savanna immediately after an early spring fire. The numbers of grasshoppers per unit area of unburnt ground (which comprised 23% of the area) was 280% higher than the prefire density in the same area. Correspondingly, the number of grasshoppers per unit area of burnt ground declined by 94% (Figure 11). Similar observations have been made in west Africa (Gillon and Pernes 1968).

Less mobile invertebrates which cannot flee the fire must take shelter in situ. For ground dwelling invertebrates, sheltered sites might include cracks in the ground, rodent burrows, termite mounds, rocks or any other site where some relief from high temperatures can be obtained. These fire-sensitive species should have well developed sensory capabilities to detect and respond to an approaching fire. For example, ticks drop to the ground and seek shelter at the slightest sensation of smoke, apparently reacting to volatile substances which are released only at high temperatures (T Bosman, personal communication, 1979). Such responses enable many slow moving invertebrates such as arachnids, blattids, tetrigids, lygeids and myriapods, as well as substantial numbers of mantids, grillids and carabids to survive fires (Gillon and Pernes 1968). Subsequently though, most of the survivors disappear, presumably because of the unsuitability of the immediate post-fire environment.

Arboreal insects do not appear to survive fires well. Gandar (1982) reports almost complete destruction of the arboreal insect fauna on *Ochna pulchra* and *Dombeya rotundifolia* (wild pear) during a savanna fire. Eggs and pupae may survive in sheltered sites (such as beneath bark or in hollows) and some adults may be able to fly to unburnt sites, but the exposed environment in trees, and the heat and smoke from the fire below, makes survival difficult.

Insect populations recover after fire through immigration or through the development of larvae which, as eggs deposited in the soil, survive the fire in situ. For example, after a savanna fire, grasshopper numbers gradually increased on the burnt areas while the numbers on adjacent unburnt areas decreased (Figure 11), suggesting immigration to burnt areas as the vegetation recovered (Gandar 1982). At the same time, there was no significant difference between the numbers of Scarabaeidae and Curculionidae emerging within two months of the fire on burnt and unburnt plots, indicating that the eggs, larvae and pupae living in the soil were unaffected by fire (Gandar 1982). In the fynbos, scarab beetle larvae are often found in *Amitermes hastatus* termite mounds (F Kruger, personal communication, 1980). Similarly, the larvae of a number of lycaenid butterflies (eg *Lepidochrysops trimeni*, *L. methymna*, *L. variabilis*) shelter inside the nests of the ants *Anoplolepis custodiens* and *Camponotus maculatus* with which they have symbiotic relationships (Clark and Dickson 1971). In these cases, escape from fire may merely be a consequence of associations which have evolved in response to other selection pressures, though it is noteworthy that the food plants of these species (principally *Selago* spp, including *S. serrata*, and possibly *Aspalathus sarcantha*) are more common after fire (Clark and Dickson 1971; Jackson 1976).

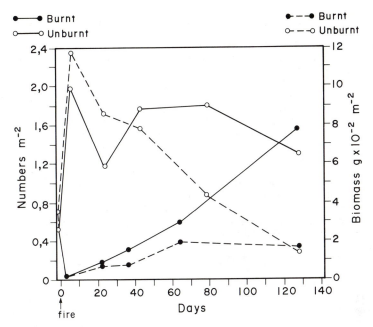

Figure 11   The numbers and biomass of grasshoppers in burnt and unburnt patches of *Burkea* - *Ochna* savanna before and after fire (data from Gandar 1982).

Most vertebrates are capable of avoiding fire directly and it is only the slower moving forms, such as tortoises, which are especially vulnerable. How tortoises, which are common in both fynbos and savanna, survive fires is not known, though habitat selection may be important. Reptiles and amphibians avoid fire, either through their habitat preferences (eg moist sites: anurans) or by escaping underground in holes, beneath rocks, up trees or into water. The breeding seasons and site selection of oviparous species such as snakes, lizards and geckos, in relation to fire-avoidance, deserves study.

Most small mammals also shelter from fire in burrows or holes. Whereas survival during fire is often high, marked changes in the composition and abundance of small mammal faunas occurs (Kern 1978; Mentis and Rowe-Rowe 1979; J P Watson, personal communication, 1980). Species preferring open habitats, such as *Tatera leucogaster* (bushveld gerbil), *Steatomys pratensis* (rat mouse) and *Saccostomus campestris* (pouched mouse), predominate after fire while species which prefer dense cover, such as *Lemniscomys griselda* and *Crocidura hirta*, emigrate.

Larger mammals avoid fire simply by fleeing ahead of, round the side or back through the advancing flame front. However, the young of those ungulate species which lie out for a period after birth, and which respond to disturbance by lying still rather than by fleeing, are especially vulnerable to fire, though parturition usually takes place in late spring or summer in savannas and grasslands and therefore after the peak of the

annual fire season (Tainton and Mentis, this volume, chapter 6).
Likewise, groundnesting birds such as pipits, larks and gamebirds
generally nest after the main fire season (Winterbottom 1972).

Many of the responses by animals to fire involve exploitation
of the fire or the post-fire environment. Insectivorous birds in
particular are attracted to fire where they catch fleeing insects
(Komarek 1969; Thiollay 1971; Gillon 1971b; Winterbottom 1972;
Hamner 1978). Abdim's (whitebellied) stork (*C. abdimii*) white
stork (*Ciconia ciconia*), black kite (*Milvus migrans*), especially
Dickinson's kestrel (*Falco dickinsoni*), lilacbreasted roller
(*Coracias caudata*), purple roller (*C. naevia*), hornbills (*Tockus*
spp), forktailed drongo (*Dicrurus adsimilis*), black swift (*Apus
barbatus*), Alpine swift (*A. melba*) and starlings (*Lamprotornis*
spp) are some of the more frequently recorded species. Some
species, such as the hornbills and cattle egret (*Bubulcus ibis*),
patrol the periphery of the fire, catching insects fleeing to unburnt ground. Other species, like ground hornbill (*Bucorvus
leadbeateri*), walk over burnt ground eating small animals killed
by the fire.

Birds also exploit burnt areas for some time after fire.
Gandar (1982) noted a concentration of grey hornbill (*T.
nasutus*), feeding on grasshoppers on burnt ground for a couple of
weeks after a fire. Bald ibis (*Geronticus calvus*) consistently
prefer burnt areas during late winter in Natal where they feed on
dead and exposed animals (Manry 1982). Concentrations of forktailed drongos, lilac-breasted rollers), and yellowbilled hornbill (*Tockus flavirostris*), have been observed catching insects
on burnt savanna some days after fire. Redwing francolin
(*Francolinus levaillantii*) and greywing francolin (*F. africanus*)
regularly exploit burnt grassland where this occurs close to
suitable cover. They feed on the corms and bulbs of geophytes,
locating these by searching for the aerial portions of the plants
which are more conspicuous than in unburnt grassland (Mentis and
Bigalke 1979). The concentration of food, or its increased
availability after fire, may enable some birds to start breeding
earlier than those in areas which have not been burnt, though
there is apparently no published data on this.

A number of birds appear to breed preferentially on burnt
ground. These include lesser blackwinged plover (*Vanellus
lugubris*) and blackwinged plover (*V. melanopterus*) (Figure 12),
bronzewinged courser (*Rhinoptilus chalcopterus*), Temminck's
courser (*Cursorius temminckii*), redwing (collared) pratincole
(*Glareola pratincola*), pennantwinged nightjar (*Macrodipteryx
vexillaria*) (Figure 13), and dusky lark (*Pinarocorys nigricans*)
(Pitman 1932; Dean 1974 and personal communication, 1981,
G L Maclean, personal communication, 1979). The regional movements of these birds appear to be related to the seasonal occurrence of burnt veld and the species show a number of adaptations
to nesting on blackened ground. In *Vanellus* spp, *Rhinoptilus*
spp, *Cursorius* spp and *Glareola* spp these include dark coloured
eggs and heavily pigmented downy chicks (Maclean and Kemp 1973)
(Figure 14). In the dusky lark the nest is placed in a depression over which there is some cover (Figure 15), since the normal
vegetation cover, in which other larks nest, is absent. The
advantage of nesting on burnt ground may be related to better

Figure 12   Blackwinged plover *(Vanellus melanopterus)*, a species
adapted to exploiting recently burnt veld (photograph
G L Maclean).

predator detection, fewer predators and, for insectivorous birds
nesting in a mosaic of burnt and unburnt patches, more concentrated food.
    Other animals also use burnt areas at different stages. Some
exploit the opportunity to locate food which was less conspicuous
before the fire (eg honey badger *(Mellivora capensis)*, excavating
rodent burrows: personal observation, 1979).   Other species may
use the opportunity to obtain minerals from plant material which
may not have been easily obtained before the fire.   Both
elephant *(Loxodonta   africana)* and   Burchell's   zebra *(Equus
burchelli)* regularly   eat burnt twigs of *Colophospermum mopane*
(A J Hall-Martin and S C J Joubert, personal communications,
1979).   These twigs are high in calcium, sodium, potassium,
phosphorus and other minerals.   Although elephant do eat the
terminal branches of unburnt mopane (W Gertenbach, personal
communication, 1979), the branches are flexible and not easy to
break. Resinous oils, which are volatilized during the fire, may
also inhibit intake of unburnt material.
    The best example of the use of the post-fire environment is
the tendency for ungulates to concentrate onto burnt areas as
grasses and other plants begin to flush.   Gandar (1982) quotes
unpublished data which show that impala *(Aepyceros melampus)*
densities increased to eight times the prefire average in burnt
Burkea-Ochna woodland.   Numbers reached a maximum 20 to 30 days
after the fire, at the time when the grasses were growing fast-
est.   The higher protein content of grasses flushing after fire
(Tainton et al 1977) is probably one of the major attractions for
herbivores.

Figure 13   Female   pennantwinged   nightjar *(Macrodipteryx
             vexillaria)* incubating   eggs   on   burnt   ground
             (photograph W R J Dean).

Figure 14   Nest, eggs and chicks of blackwinged plover *(Vanellus
             melanopterus)* on recently burnt veld.   Note the
             broad, dark blotches on the eggs.   This species
             breeds in late winter (just after the peak of the
             fire season), 1 to 2 months earlier than other
             dry-land plover species (photograph G L Maclean).

Figure 15   Nest and eggs of dusky lark *(Pinarocorys nigricans)*,
             another species adapted to nesting on burnt ground.
             Note the sheltered nest (photograph W R J Dean).

There is a succession of ungulate species moving onto burnt
areas during the post-fire recovery period (S C J Joubert, personal communication, 1979; Brooks and Berry 1980).   Zebra are
invariably the first species to move onto a burnt area, followed
by blue wildebeest *(Connochaetes taurinus)* and, in Natal,
white rhinoceros *(Ceratotherium simum)*.   Buffalo *(Syncerus
caffer)*, also move onto newly burnt areas in Natal (Brooks and
Berry 1980), but in the Kruger National Park they are one of the
last species to utilize burnt areas (S C J Joubert, personal
communication 1979).   Impala also respond rapidly, but being
sedentary, they are not attracted from any great distance.   Other
grazers, such as sable antelope *(Hippotragus niger)*, roan
antelope *(H. equinus)* and tsessebe *(Damaliscus lunatus)* in the
Kruger National Park, usually move onto burnt areas only when the
grass is 8 to 10 cm high.   Browsers such as kudu *(Tragelaphus
strepsiceros)* begin to exploit burnt areas once forbs start to
emerge and the woody plants begin to resprout.
Attraction to burns tends to be influenced by the season of
the burn and the habitat preferences of the species during that
season.   Thus, in Natal, nyala *(Tragelaphus angasi)* and impala
both prefer spring burns, due largely to their dependence on
wooded habitats during winter and a reluctance to move out of
them to open, burnt areas.   Grazers, with the exception of
waterbuck *(Kobus ellipsiprymnus)*, which use riverine habitats in

winter, prefer winter burns to spring burns (Brooks and Berry 1980). However, grass height apparently is a major determinant of the degree of attraction, the grass generally being shorter following winter than spring burns. Although the opportunity to exploit emerging grasses and forbs is probably the main reason why animals congregate on burnt areas, other advantages may include better opportunity for predator detection, and a warmer microclimate, especially at night.

Certain insects may also exploit the postfire environment. Evans (1971) lists 31 species in eight families worldwide which are attracted to fire and which lay their eggs in freshly burnt wood. Only one, *Chrysops silacea* (tabanid fly), is recorded from Africa. This probably reflects our lack of knowledge since various unidentified cerambycids have been noted as being attracted to camp fires (personal observation, 1979). A number of the species listed by Evans are highly adapted to fire, having sense organs sensitive to peak infrared wavelengths of fire, and wax glands which protect the insect against extensive water loss (Evans 1971).

Insects which remain on burnt areas are often conspicuous against the dark background of burnt earth. Burtt (1951) demonstrated experimentally that *Phorenula werneriana* (grasshopper) could change colour to match its background, including becoming dark when on burnt ground. Hocking (1964) showed that, in the Sudan, geophilous grasshopper species were usually dark-coloured while the phytophilous species tended to be predominantly pale. He lists 10 species which showed some degree of fire-melanism. Various acridids, mantids and lepidopterans have been reported to show fire-melanism in a west African savanna (Gillon and Pernes 1968) though no details have been published. Gandar (1982) has recorded fire-melanism in *Pnorisa squalus* and *Parga xanthoptera*, two grasshoppers occurring in deciduous broadleafed savannas. In *P. xanthoptera*, which is normally straw-coloured, the cuticle darkens after the final moult, suggesting the capacity to change colour according to circumstances. Lem (1930) also mentions melanistic grasshoppers from the fynbos but did not note if this was associated with a preference for burnt areas. Fire-melanism may provide camouflage against potential predators as well as enhancing radiant heat absorption, thereby extending the activity range of the individual.

DISCUSSION

Fire represents only one of the set of selection pressures facing plants and animals. In order to distinguish fire-adapted traits from those which might have evolved under other selective regimes having qualitatively similar effects, the significance of each trait needs to be assessed within the overall context of a species' life history (Gill 1977). In this respect, few of the studies reported on here are supported by sufficient life-history information to enable an assessment to be made of the various costs and benefits associated with each trait. There is a pressing need for such information, particularly on mortality and fecundity schedules and on the role of fire in affecting these, either directly, by influencing survival probabilities and features such as fire-stimulated reproduction, or indirectly, through fire's effects on the environment and on an organism's competitors and predators.

Although individual organisms are exposed to and are affected by particular fires, it is the fire regime that is important in evolutionary time. The components of fire regime include the types of fire that normally prevail (ie ground fires, crown fires etc), the frequency or average return-time of fire, fire intensity and seasonality (Gill 1977, 1981). Within the South African context, very little is known about the types of fires and their effects, so that this feature is subsequently ignored. Fire seasonality is usually represented in terms of calendar periods or seasonal climatic cycles. In the context of its effects on the survival and success of an organism, it is perhaps best viewed in relation to whether or not the organism in question is active at a particular time of year.

At the simplest level of abstraction, fire regimes can be represented as particular combinations of fire frequency, intensity and seasonality (Figure 16). Each of these combinations is likely to impose rather different selection pressures on the organisms concerned, though on our present information it is not easy to rank all these different combinations in terms of their potential severity to different organisms. Obviously, not all the combinations are equally likely to occur in nature either (Figure 16). However, the scheme does provide a preliminary framework within which to assess the types of responses that can evolve.

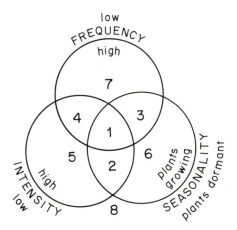

Figure 16   Venn diagram illustrating possible combinations of fire frequency, intensity and seasonality giving rise to different fire regimes. Regimes numbered in approximate order of severity to the organisms concerned. Not all combinations are equally likely to occur in nature. Within South African biomes, combination 2 probably applies to forest, 2 and 5 to fynbos, 7 (or possibly 4) to moist savannas and grasslands, and 8 to arid grass and shrublands.

The responses of plants to fire must also be seen within the context of community dynamics, in particular plant succession, and the role of fire in those processes. Plant successional theories have been reviewed critically by Drury and Nisbet (1973), Connell and Slatyer (1977) and others, all of whom have emphasized that classical succession theory fails to account for many patterns of vegetation change. Post-fire succession is one of these.

Post-fire successional sequences are determined largely by the species composition at the site immediately after disturbance and by the manner in which these species survive the fire (Noble and Slatyer 1977). Some species are present as propagules which have either reached the site from elsewhere or which were present at the site prior to disturbance and which survived as seed. Other species are represented by already established individuals which have either survived the fire intact or regenerated vegetatively from undamaged parts. Because individuals which survive and regenerate vegetatively can outgrow and outcompete seedlings, the opportunities for seedling establishment are determined largely by the extent of damage to, and the rate of recovery by, vegetatively resprouting species.

Since only those species which are present in the immediate post-fire community, either as seeds or as established plants, normally feature in the post-fire succession, selection should favour those plant attributes which enable individuals or their offspring to remain in the community from one disturbance-succession cycle to the next. The types of attributes which will be favoured will depend on the frequency and intensity of fire and its effects on individual survival and subsequent reproductive success.

There is a general inverse relationship, within similar climatic zones, between fire frequency and fire intensity so that the greater the interval between fires, the more intense those fires will be. Plant survival, in turn, is determined largely by fire intensity, modified to varying degrees by the various plant attributes. Consequently, plant survival tends to be high under a regime of frequent fires. Mostly it is juvenile trees and shrubs which are killed so that plants showing avoidance, escape and resistance tend to be favoured (West 1971). Avoidance is favoured where there is considerable spatial heterogeneity in the environment which creates some fire-safe sites. Escape in time is possible where fires show strong and predictable seasonality, while resistance is exhibited by those plants which are regularly exposed to fires of non-lethal intensity.

With increasing intervals between fires, fuel loads tend to accumulate, leading to more intense burns (see data for fynbos in Kruger and Bigalke, this volume, chapter 5). Destruction of all or part of the aboveground biomass, but not the root crowns or stem bases, favours resprouting. Rapid post-fire recovery and the ability of resprouters to outgrow seedlings suggests that resprouting should be favoured over reseeding in most circumstances (Keeley and Zedler 1978).

The advantages of the obligate reseeding strategy are less obvious. Keeley and Zedler (1978) have suggested that there are two main advantages. Firstly, since seedlings do not compete very successfully with established plants, they must exploit clearings within the community. Clearings occur after fire. The size of these depends on the intensity of fire, the extent to which established plants are burnt out and on the average size of the plants. Similarly, larger individuals progressively dominate the community with increasing time since the last fire (data for fynbos: Kruger 1977b), so that the size of post-fire openings can be expected to increase with longer intervals between fires. Keeley and Zedler (1978) suggest that, since the probability of fire-induced mortality increases among sprouters as the period since the last fire lengthens, plants should allocate proportionately more energy to seed production than to growth and maintenance as they become older. This would compromise the capacity of these species to resprout, further enhancing the advantages of reseeding when the interval between fires is very long. The large number of obligate reseeding species in fynbos and forests (which experience intense fires, usually at long intervals) strongly suggests that infrequent fires have been important in the evolution of obligate reseeding.

The second advantage of obligate reseeding is that individuals reproduce sexually, thereby maximizing the genetic heterogeneity of their offspring. The period following a fire, during which seedlings of many individuals and species are establishing themselves, is likely to be a time of intense selection among the various genotypes. However, the post-fire environment is not necessarily similar from one fire cycle to the next, and selection pressures can be expected to vary. Consequently, in the fire-free period, it would be advantageous for individuals to maximize the variety of phenotypes in which their genes are represented, thereby enhancing the possibility that their genes will be selectively favoured during the next post-fire selection of seedlings (Keeley and Zedler 1978).

These various responses of plants to fire involve different patterns of resource allocation in respect of energy and nutrients for maintenance, growth and reproduction. In terms of evolutionary fitness, the resources available for reproduction are crucial. Resources allocated to maintenance and growth are important only in terms of the ultimate contribution that these processes make to the reproductive success of the individual.

The apparent advantage of fire-tolerant and resprouting species over obligate reseeding species, as already mentioned, places a premium on survival and on the diversion of available resources from immediate reproduction to features which enhance tolerance to, and the ability to recover from, fire. However, the increased allocation of resources to maintenance and growth must involve at least a temporary decrease in the resources available for reproduction, at least until such time as the plant has recovered fully from fire.

Generally, if opportunities for seedling establishment in the interval between disturbances are few, selection should favour the deferment of germination and establishment until conditions are suitable. Fire creates such opportunities. Some of these will be taken up by seeds already present at the site and others by seeds which enter the site soon afterwards.

Obligate reseeding necessarily implies efficient reproduction since the selective advantage lies with those plants which produce the largest number of seeds giving rise to reproducing offspring. Efficient pollination is a prerequisite for successful reproduction and the pollination systems should reflect the different patterns of resource allocation in reseeders and resprouters. Carpenter and Recher (1979) predicted that reseeders would allocate more energy to flower, nectar and seed production than should resprouters; reseeders should be more attractive than resprouters to pollinators; and reseeders should be partly self-compatible to ensure that some seed is set on occasions when pollinator activity is low or directed elsewhere. In contrast, resprouters should be self-incompatible since they already reproduce vegetatively, which tends to result in decreased genetic variability and the possibility of reduced fitness of any seedlings that manage to establish themselves after fire in a variable post-fire environment.

These predictions have been confirmed in at least two contrasting *Banksia* spp (Proteaceae) in Australia (Carpenter and Recher 1979) and two *Arctostaphylos* spp (Ericaceae) in California (Fulton and Carpenter 1979). There have been no similar studies in southern Africa though comparisons between *Erica cerinthoides* and *E. glumaeflora* (resprouters: Martin 1966) and *E. chamissonis* and *E. demissa* (obligate reseeders: Martin 1966) would be instructive.

Maximum seed production is also essential among those plants which only or primarily flower after fire. Since they appear at irregular intervals they must be able to attract suitable pollinators, irrespective of the presence of competing nectar sources. Many of them (*Watsonia* spp, *Cyrtanthus* spp, *Haemanthus* spp) are bird-pollinated with well developed pollinator attracting mechanisms (conspicuously coloured flowers, high quality nectar rewards).

Since many opportunities for seedling establishment exist in the post-fire environment there is an advantage to obligate reseeders in producing large numbers of small seeds which can be dispersed widely by wind or water to open, well insolated sites (eg many species of *Erica*: Martin 1966). Alternatively, some obligate reseeders (eg some *Leucadendron* spp: Williams 1972) produce seeds which have no obvious dispersal mechanisms and which fall in the vicinity of the parent plant, either before or immediately after the fire, thereby ensuring that the resulting seedlings become established on the same site that the parent plant had occupied successfully prior to the fire.

In contrast, animal-mediated seed dispersal seems to be much less favoured in the initial post-fire succession since seeds which are dispersed by animals are often large and tend to be clumped on dispersal, usually in middens or around the base of regular perches. This mode of dispersal appears to be more important for those species which enter the community later in the succession and which usually require large, well provisioned seeds in order to compete successfully for space in the post-fire community. Ant-dispersed seeds though are an exception. About

20% of the flowering plants (over 1 300 species) in the fynbos flora have seeds bearing elaiosomes and are presumed to be dispersed by ants (Slingsby and Bond 1982). Within the Proteaceae alone, 53% (175 species) are adapted for ant-dispersal, including all the species in the genera *Diastella*, *Leucospermum*, *Mimetes*, *Orothamnus*, *Paranomus*, *Serruria*, *Sorocephalus* and *Spatalla* (Slingsby and Bond 1982). Although these seeds are seldom carried far from the parent plant (up to 17 m, Slingsby and Bond 1982), ant-dispersal is advantageous in that the seeds are taken below the soil surface, where they are protected from fire and possibly from other sources of mortality such as fungal attack, so leading to a build-up of seed reserves in the soil (Slingsby and Bond 1982).

Most of the above discussion has focused on the responses of plants to different fire regimes, and the consequences of these responses in terms of the allocation of resources to survival, growth and reproduction. What patterns exist in animals?

Whereas the direct effects of fire on plants and animals are similar, animals are generally mobile and can often avoid these effects. Thus, in situ survival strategies do not seem to be well developed. More importantly, those animals, particularly herbivores, that survive a fire in situ are faced with a temporary disruption of their resource base and a loss of shelter. For many species, this situation makes the evolution of in situ survival mechanisms less advantageous, unless they are accompanied by additional means of overcoming the relatively harsh post-fire environment. Emigration and diapause are two obvious mechanisms though they have not been adequately researched locally in the context of fire. Diapause can be expected to be favoured in situations where the degree of displacement of community structure and ecosystem processes is minimal and in which there is a fairly rapid recovery to pre-fire levels. This probably occurs in areas subjected to regular, predictable fires of low intensity, such as in savannas. However, where fire causes massive changes in community structure and ecosystem functioning and where these recover only very slowly to pre-fire levels, as in forests and fynbos, emigration and subsequent immigration to the site would seem to be more advantageous. There is some evidence for this in rodents (Kern 1978; Mentis and Rowe-Rowe 1979) but little information on other animal groups. Clearly, there is scope for more research in this area.

In conclusion, although the details are generally lacking, there is much to suggest that fire has been important in the evolution of a wide variety of plant and animal attributes in South African ecosystems. Much more attention needs to be placed on the evaluation of apparently fire-adapted traits in relation to other components of an organism's life-history, and the circumstances in which these responses are advantageous. As Noble and Slatyer (1977) have indicated, these responses play an important role in determining community structure and the processes of successional change in this. If we are to move beyond merely describing community patterns, more consideration will have to be given to the processes involved. In this context, understanding plant and animal attributes and the circumstances in which they are advantageous is of fundamental importance.

Chapter 14 The Effect of Fire on Soil and Microclimate

A. CASS, M. J. SAVAGE and F. M. WALLIS

INTRODUCTION

The effect of fire regime on soil properties and microclimate has not been studied in sufficient detail and breadth to allow complete understanding of fire ecology in South Africa. For this reason, what information is available is incomplete and very often conflicting. The complexity of most ecosystems is the fundamental cause of this difficulty in understanding the inter-action between fire regime and the physical environment. Factors such as climate, vegetation, soil type and human activity create widely divergent conditions that have a profound influence on the long-term response of soil and microclimate to fire.

The extent to which fire influences soil properties, micro-biological populations and microclimate depends on the intensity of the fire, the nature of the vegetation, the increase in soil temperature occasioned by the fire and the frequency of fire occurrence. The role of fire in causing erosion and surface runoff and in changing soil moisture dynamics has been a subject of much concern in studies of the effects of burning. Since fire often changes the vegetation suddenly and drastically, it will also affect the hydrological response of the ecosystem. However, such changes vary greatly with the conditions of the soil, vegetation, topography and climate.

The main agency by which fire influences soil chemistry is the ash resulting from combustion of organic matter present on the soil surface. The residual ash affects various soil chemical properties, including pH and the concentration of soluble elements. Soluble constituents in the ash are carried into the soil and become part of the soil solution. Some may be lost by surface runoff or by wind erosion.

Because vegetation changes may be dramatic and often permanent, microclimatic responses to fire and fire regime may be equally dramatic. These changes in microclimatic properties in turn influence soil properties, vegetation growth and microbial populations. Moore (1960) concluded from his investigations that the major effects of fire in Nigeria resulted from vegetation changes induced by fire (fire regime) rather than from the direct effects of fire itself.

SOIL PHYSICAL AND CHEMICAL PROPERTIES

CLAY MINERALOGICAL COMPOSITION

There is little evidence to show that fire and fire regime are responsible for clay mineralogical transformations in soil. However, it is not impossible to conceive of some changes in clay mineral properties if the increase in soil temperatures is sufficiently high. For example, if soil temperatures exceed 550°C during burning, kaolinite may be altered and Fitzpatrick (1980) presents some evidence for this. However, clay mineral properties such as cation exchange capacity (CEC) are not altered by burning of grasslands where soil temperatures seldom exceed 250°C (Coutts 1945; Cass 1978) during a fire.

Iron oxides, however, appear to be influenced by fire regime. Fitzpatrick (1980) has presented evidence to show that burning of brushwood in wattle and pine plantations could induce transformation of geothite to maghaemite, but this depended on a number of conditions which presumably affect the soil temperature during burning. In grassland fire-research sites, Fitzpatrick could not demonstrate such transformations.

ORGANIC MATTER AND LITTER LAYER

The higher the temperature induced by the burn and the greater the frequency of fire, the greater is the change in organic matter that can be expected (West 1965). Surface temperatures of 690°C have been found to destroy all the surface litter and 99% of the soil organic carbon (Raison 1979). Soil temperatures during burning are, however, generally less than 200°C and high enough to destroy only humic acids (West 1965). Some reports of an increase in organic matter following burning exist (Greene 1935; Moore 1960; Wells 1971; Owensby and Wyrill 1973) but Daubenmire (1968) attributes such increases to an accumulation of charcoal in soil rather than organic matter as such. Generally, fire tends to decrease the organic matter content of soils (West 1965; Daubenmire 1968) but many researchers, including Hervey (1949) and Reynolds and Bohning (1956), were unable to detect any such change. Burning of grassland and commercial wattle plantations in Natal has not been shown to produce any change in soil organic matter content (Beard and Darby 1951; Beard 1961; Edwards 1961; Cass 1978). However, White and Grossman (1972) have demonstrated a significant decrease in the amount of organic matter in very sandy soil (8% clay) exposed to regular veld burning in the Transvaal.

BULK DENSITY AND POROSITY

The majority of studies indicate that fires are not hot enough to produce direct effects upon the structure of soils (Isaac and Hopkins 1937; Sampson 1944; Trimble and Tripp 1949) although Heyward (1937) has found that excluding fire from pine forest for periods as brief as 10 yr has resulted in a more porous, penetrable soil. Secondary effects may however operate, and soil porosity may be reduced because fire destroys insects and other macroorganisms which channel in the soil (Phillips 1931; Wells et al 1979).

In evaluating long-term burning experiments on grassland in Natal, Edwards (1961) and Cass and Collins (1983) found that soils from burnt and unburnt treatments manifested no difference in bulk density nor pore size distribution. However, Cass and Collins (1983) report that the soil surface appeared to be less porous in burnt plots, forming a weak crust less than 5 mm thick.

Jansen (1959b) and Edwards (1961) have also suggested that crusts develop on burnt sites in grassland and Phillips (1931) reports increased soil compaction from burning of fynbos. Generally, experience in other countries supports the conclusion that burning often results in surface structural deterioration (Wells et al 1979).

AGGREGATE STABILITY

Although there is considerable evidence to show that burning is often associated with increased soil erosion, the relationship between fire regime and aggregate stability is less clear. Some evidence that indicates little direct effect of burning on aggregate stability has appeared (Edwards 1961; Cass and Collins 1983), but this may depend primarily on the effect of the particular fire regime on soil organic matter content. Where fire intensity is high, destruction of organic matter may weaken aggregates and promote particle detachment during rainfall, but often fire temperatures and burning frequency may not be high enough to affect soil organic matter at least in grassland and savanna soils in southern Africa where organic matter content is often low and relatively unimportant in determining aggregate stability.

The other major component of erosion, such as transportability, may, however, be considerably enhanced by burning because of the destruction of plant cover and the surface litter layers. Wells et al (1979) have reviewed the effect of fire on soil erosion and cite evidence to show that fire normally accelerates erosion on steep slopes, on soils with low infiltration rates, on veld which recovers slowly after burning and on soils which have not formed surface crusts. Minimal vegetation destruction (less than 60% of surface cover) or rapid revegetation of burnt sites reduced erosion considerably, regardless of the type of invader species. Considerable comment on the effect of fire regime on soil loss in southern Africa is available (Phillips 1931; Thompson 1936; Cook 1939b; Guilloteau 1957; Jansen 1959b; I'Ons 1960; Edwards 1961; West 1965), and there is general agreement on the adverse effects of burning in relation to erosion. However, no evidence for the reduction of aggregate stability as a result of burning has emerged. Rather the reason for increased soil erosion is enhanced soil transportability where appropriate topographical, climatic and vegetative characteristics lead to increased surface runoff of water after burning.

Vegetation cover and the litter layer play an important role in protecting surface soil from raindrop impact (Pase and Lindenmuth 1971). Although aggregate stability is weakened only by very intense fires, the exposure of soil surfaces to direct impact by rain may result in particle detachment if aggregate strength is naturally low (Arend 1941; Sampson 1944; Beaton 1959; Wells et al 1979). Given appropriate environmental conditions, this will result in erosion; but if the topography and the climate are such that the transport of particles is limited, it may alter the surface structure of soil (Dyrness and Youngberg 1957). Formation of a surface crust may reduce erosion, but generally, crusts will form only on sites where transportability is low.

Both wind and water are important agents of soil transport during the erosion process, although wind may be particularly important in the erosion of ash after burning and may be responsible for an appreciable loss of nutrients from burnt sites (Beard 1961). On very steep slopes in mountain areas, burnt sites may become susceptible to landslip erosion as a result of the destruction of vegetation and removal of the stabilizing effect of plant roots (Wells et al 1979).

SOIL STRENGTH

Reports on the effects of fire on soil strength have been inconsistent (Wells et al 1979). Some workers have demonstrated increased strength while others show a reduced strength and the development of a more friable surface soil. Again this differential response appears to be occasioned by differences in fire regime, climate, vegetation and soil type. In Natal, Cass and Collins (1983) were unable to show an increase in the tensile strength (modulus of rupture) of surface soil as a result of 30 yr of burning, but a thin surface crust present on the surface of burnt sites imparted a greater penetrometer strength to the soil than was evident on unburnt sites.

INFILTRATION

Entry of water into soil is primarily dependent upon surface structure and on those soil properties which determine hydraulic conductivity. Surface structure is, however, sensitive to changes in the litter layer, vegetation cover and faunal activity. Generally, fire has been reported to have a destructive effect on litter, vegetation and soil fauna and to reduce water adsorption and infiltration rate and soil water hydraulic conductivity (Arend 1941; Austin and Baisinger 1955; Beaton 1959; Jansen 1959b; Edwards 1961; Anderson 1965; McMurphy and Anderson 1965; Buckhouse and Gifford 1976; Wells et al 1979; Cass and Collins 1983). The magnitude of such alteration may be dramatic. Cass and Collins (1983) showed that ponded infiltration rate of soil under grassland burnt each year for 30 yr in the early spring decreased from a value of 30 to 1,3 m day^{-1}. This decrease can be attributed to the formation of a thin crust of soil at the surface, where bulk density was higher and porosity lower than that of grassland not subjected to fire. It should be noted, however, that not all investigators have reported such responses to fire, and Veihmeyer and Johnson (1944) and Linnartz et al (1966) could not find any effect of fire on water entry characteristics into soils.

The development of water repellency in sandy soils under a fire regime is an important contributing factor to reduced infiltration of water (Wells et al 1979). Repellency may be a surface effect or it may occur at depth. It arises as a result of the distillation of organic aliphatic hydrocarbons by fire and subsequent deposition onto soil particles, causing nonwettable surfaces to develop. Fire-induced water repellency is known to occur in sandy soils in many areas of South Africa but its general importance in controlling the hydrology of burnt areas is not known at present.

NUTRIENT STATUS

Fire has variable effects on nutrient availability in soils. In some cases nutrient mobilization occurs; in others fire induces deficiencies and in yet others no discernable affects have been observed. Although changes in availability have often been demonstrated, the underlying causes have seldom been identified. Results from numerous studies show that plants generally respond to nutrient elements released by burning, but in addition, plants will also respond to soil sterilization induced by burning. In the case of nitrogen, fire causes increased mineralization (Sharrow and Wright 1977) which generally has a beneficial effect on plant growth.

Burning materials high in a particular mineral element increases the concentration of that element in the soil. Conversely, burning the same amount of material low in that element may not measurably change the abundance of the element in the soil (Raison 1979). An excess of basic cations such as potassium, calcium and magnesium over anions such as phosphate and sulphate in the ash neutralizes soil acidity. After the burn, these elements, initially present as oxides, may be converted to carbonates which are acid soluble only (Viro 1974; Fitzpatrick 1980). The change in soil properties induced by ash depends on the properties of the ash, the amount of ash and the nature of the soil (Raison 1979; Wells et al 1979). Therefore, the release of relatively large amounts of basic elements by fire will not significantly change the soil if it is already rich in these elements. These general considerations are applicable to mineral elements, but fire effects on volatile elements, especially nitrogen, are less predictable.

In the case of phosphorus, potassium, calcium and magnesium, burning usually produces trends towards higher concentrations of these elements in the upper few mm of mineral soil (Lunt 1950; Bean 1962; Daubenmire 1968; Viro 1974; Raison 1979). Nevertheless Wells et al (1979) and Raison (1979) cite many cases where the levels of soil phosphorus, calcium, magnesium and potassium in response to fire either remain unchanged or decrease. These conflicting changes appear to result from widely varying vegetation characteristics, fuel loads, fire intensity, climate and soil type. For example, in sandy soils where cation exchange capacity is often a function of organic matter content rather than clay mineralogy, burning may impair retention of cations if it destroys organic matter. Accordingly, in South Africa, White and Grossmann (1972), working with such soil, demonstrated that burning produced a loss of cations from the soil that was correlated with the amount of rainfall in the month following burning.

The pH of the surface soil layers may be increased if basic cations are released by burning. Soil pH change is usually temporary and depends upon the amount of ash released, original soil pH, chemical composition of the ash, soil texture and mean annual rainfall (Grier 1975; Wells et al 1979). The magnitude of pH change has been shown to vary from 0,5 pH units to zero in acid soils, but by as much as 2,5 pH units where large amounts of timber slash are burnt (Tarrant 1956). In Finnish forests where the litter layer is very fertile, Viro (1974) reported an increase of 0,2 to 0,4 pH units in soils. The effect lasted for 50 yr after the fire. However, the pH of surface soil immediately after burning was 2,5 to 4 pH units higher than unburnt sites. Fitzpatrick (1980) showed that surface soil pH values were 3,5 to 5 pH units higher on burnt sites than on unburnt sites in wattle and pine plantations in Natal but Phillips (1931) reported a decrease in surface soil pH after burning fynbos. In grassland soils where only small amounts of organic material are generally available for combustion, soil pH changes are minimal (Beard and Darby 1951; Reynolds and Bohning 1956; Cass 1978). Wells et al (1979) reported that Tarrant (1951), when heating soils to 315°C for 90 minutesm observed pH changes attributable to heating rather than the neutralizing effect of the oxides released from burning. This temperature effect may be as important as the chemical effect in changing soil pH.

Volatile elements such as nitrogen, sulphur, phosphorus and chlorine may be lost when soil temperatures exceed the temperature of volatilization. Nitrogen and sulphur are most important because they have a low volatilization temperature. For example, Kenworthy (1963) reports significant volatilization losses of nitrogen at fire temperatures in excess of 400°C. Surface erosion of plant residues, which may increase during the post-fire period, removes those nutrients closely associated with organic matter (N, P and S) while soil erosion will remove the entire spectrum of nutrients. Leaching losses of cations depend upon the presence of mobile anions (NO_3, $SO_4^=$ and organic acids) in solution, and fire may be implicated in increasing the solubility of minerals contained in the fuel. Such losses of mobile anions are of particular importance when they are essential nutrients such as nitrate and sulphate (Wells et al 1979).

Changes in soil resulting from shifts in microbial or higher plant populations contribute to the complexity of soil response to fire. For example, biological nitrogen fixation following fire may in some cases balance the nitrogen loss caused by fire. Wells et al (1979) state that there is evidence for both loss and gain of nitrogen following burning.

Nutrient losses from burnt sites are important only if they cannot be resupplied to the ecosystem to meet the requirements for optimum growth. For ecosystems in warm-temperate climates on soils derived from basic igneous parent materials or from sediments derived from these basic materials, nutrient elements are generally sufficient for plant growth. However, nitrogen and possibly sulphur may limit growth. In soils derived from acid igneous rocks and from highly weathered sediments, phosphorus, potassium and trace elements are usually limiting. In the former case nutrient removal should not limit productivity of ecosystems (Start 1977) but in the latter case, loss of nutrients by burning has been shown to cause deficiencies (Schutte 1960; Jorgensen et al 1975; Wells et al 1979).

MICROCLIMATE

SOIL TEMPERATURE

The importance of soil temperature is summarized by Geiger (1957); in high mountains with their generally low temperatures, plants can thrive only in the zone close to ground level where the soil acts as a heat reservoir and provides the necessary microclimate. The amount by which soil temperature exceeds air temperature increases with altitude and with it the dependence of vegetation for growth on the microclimate in the ground level zone. Phillips (1919) found in his grass-burning experiments that the temperature of bare soil during both day and night is considerably greater than that of soil covered with vegetation. Soil blanketed by vegetation does not exhibit the extremes of temperature found on bare soil.

Soil temperatures during burning

Norton and McGarity (1965) determined the effects of burning native pastures on soil temperature. Temperature changes greater than 10°C occurred only in the top 15 mm of the soil. There was no clear relationship between the amount of material burnt and the temperature increase. The extent of the increase appeared to be influenced largely by the amount of soil moisture present. They concluded that the effects of increases in soil temperature on organic matter, microorganisms, or seeds during the burning of native pasture would be confined to a comparatively shallow top layer of soil. They stated also that "the (soil) temperatures measured in the burns carrying normal cover suggest that fires of this type would be unlikely to have a direct influence on chemical breakdown by microbial activity". Scotter (1970) was able to predict the effect of "short-lived" grass fires on soil temperatures in various situations. He also reported a surprisingly small increase in soil temperature during grassland fires. A possible explanation for this is that only about 5% of the heat energy released during a fire may be partitioned to the soil (Packham 1969).

An important side effect of burning and the resultant increase in soil temperature is that of its possible influence on seed germination. In a laboratory study of simulated fires, Cushwa et al (1968) found that moist heat greatly increased germination rate and total germination. Germination increased markedly up to a 2 minute duration of heating at 80°C, but did not increase further with longer periods of heating. In a field study, Tothill (1960) found that burning favoured germination of buried speargrass seed when ambient temperatures were too low for this to occur in unburnt grassland.

Soil temperature after burning

Lemon (1967) found that occasional burning seemed to encourage vigorous growth and increased species richness in herbaceous vegetation. He maintained that this response was best explained by the increase in soil temperature immediately following burning.

Savage (1979a) measured soil temperatures at a depth of 50 mm on burnt and unburnt grassland at Ukulinga in Natal. Burning took place on 18 April 1979. Figure 1 shows the diurnal soil temperature variations for 1, 2 and 3 May for both sites and Table 1 shows the daily average soil temperature for both sites. It would appear that the soil temperature at this depth was greater during both day and night for the burnt site.

Table 1   Daily average soil temperature (°C) for burned (18/4/79) and control (unburned) sites, measured at a depth of 50 mm at Ukulinga Research Station, Pietermaritzburg, Natal.

Date	Burnt site	Control site
1/5/79	13,5	11,4
2/5/79	13,7	11,5
3/5/79	13,7	11,5

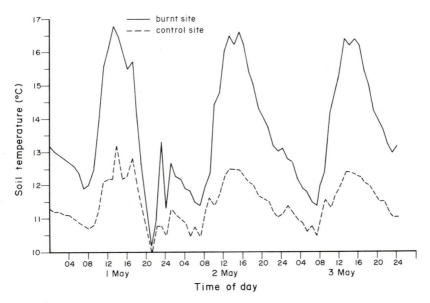

Figure 1   Soil temperature for 1, 2 and 3 May 1979 for the site burnt on 18 April and the control site (unburnt) at a depth of 50 mm.

Rice and Parenti (1978) concluded from their work that, whatever the mechanism of action, their data supported the suggestion that greater herbage production from the burnt grassland is primarily an effect of increased soil temperatures which stimulate earlier growth in the spring. With regard to the mechanism of action, Menhenett and Wareing (1975) found that in the case of tomato plants, soil temperatures of about 7°C markedly reduced root and shoot growth and the quantity of xylem exudate compared to temperatures of 22°C. They showed that for soil temperatures of 7°C, alterations in the hormone content of the sap may contribute to the observed reduction in shoot growth.

ENERGY BALANCE

The available energy input at any surface is determined by the seasonal distribution of solar (short-wave) radiation and, provided that water and nutrients are not limiting, this sets the ultimate limit to forage production (Cooper 1970). The total incoming solar radiant flux density R_T (W m^{-2}) incident at the earth's surface is converted into heat energy. Savage (1979b) discusses the terms and units used here. Part of the incoming energy flux density is re-emitted from the soil surface as long-wave radiation L_u (W m^{-2}). Some of this (L_d) is in turn scattered or reflected back to the earth's surface, so that the net loss in long-wave radiant flux density is:

$$L_{net} = L_u - L_d \qquad (1)$$

Part of R_t is reflected (rR_T). That part of R_T which is not reflected or back-radiated is termed the net radiant flux density R_{net} (W m^{-2}):

$$R_{net} = (1-r)\, R_T - L_{net} \qquad (2)$$

where r is the reflectivity or the reflection coefficient of the surface. This equation then describes the surface radiant energy balance. It should be noted that plants are not able to utilize all of R_{net} for photosynthesis but only that with wavelengths between about 380 and 710 nm. Table 2 shows R_{net} values for the burnt and control sites at Ukulinga following an autumn burn (burning date was 18 April 1979), as measured by Savage (1979a).

Table 2 Maximum and minimum R_{net} values (W m^{-2}) for the burnt (18/4/79) and control sites at Ukulinga Research Station, Pietermaritzburg, Natal.

Date	Burnt plot		Control plot	
	Max	Min	Max	Min
3/5/79	251	−27	198	−20
9/5/79	278	−52	254	−48
10/5/79	300	−49	279	−41

Harrison (1978) measured the mean reflectivity (r) of burnt and unburnt pastures for one month after a spring burn. He found that 13 days after the burn, r of the burnt site was nearly 7% compared with nearly 13% for the unburnt site. The reflectivity of the burnt site increased to 8% 16 days after the fire. On the 24th day it was measured as 10% and on the 45th day as 12%. The reflectivity of the unburnt site varied between 13 and 14% over the 45 day period. Gandar (1982) points out that two rain days occurred between the date of the fire and the first reflectivity measurements so that the reflectivity value of 7% for the burned site might have been lower immediately after the fire. Savage and Vermeulen (1983) measured reflectivity on the same site immediately before and after burning in spring. Reflectivity declined from 15% in unburnt grassland to 3% after the fire.

In an energy balance equation, R_{net} can be written as:

$$R_{net} = F_s + F_h + L_v F_w + F_p \qquad (3)$$

In this equation F_s is the soil heat flux density (W m^{-2}), F_h the sensible heat flux density (W m^{-2}), L_v the specific latent heat of vaporization (J kg^{-1}), F_w the flux density of water vapour from the surface (kg m^{-2} s^{-1}), and F_p is the energy flux density (W m^{-2}) represented by photosynthetically fixed assimilates. Of interest here is the manner in which the extra energy flux density associated with the daytime increase in R_{net} after burning, is partitioned between the soil (F_s), the atmosphere (F_h), in evaporating water ($L_v F_w$), for photosynthesis (F_p) or a combination of these (Savage 1980). Gandar (1982), commenting on the work of Harrison (1978), concluded that the burnt site was transferring more heat energy to the atmosphere by sensible heat than the unburnt site and that a small part of the energy may have gone to increase $L_v F_w$ as the soil on burnt sites dried. Savage and Vermeulen (1983) measured an increase in soil heat density of 50% between 08h00 and 16h00 after a spring fire. Sensible, latent and photosynthetic heat densities increased.

WIND SPEED

Old (1969) measured wind speed profiles above grassland that had recently been burnt and that burnt 4 yr previously. The wind speed at ground level on the unburned site was recorded as zero, and that on the recently burned site as 1,0 m s^{-1}. Greater wind speeds were recorded on the recently burned site to a height of 2 m above the soil surface. Above this height no differences could be detected.

Gates and Papian (1971) calculated the effect of wind speed on the transpiration rate per unit area of grassland (g m^{-2} s^{-1}) for various radiant energy flux densities absorbed by the leaf. At high radiant flux densities, the transpiration rate (g h^{-1}) decreased rapidly with an increase in wind speed from 0 to 1 m s^{-1}. At low radiant flux densities, there is almost no change in transpiration with change in wind speed, a result which was later contradicted by Grace (1977). The probable consequence of the results of Gates and Papian (1971) for burning is that the transpiration rate per unit area will be greatly affected by wind speed since the radiant flux density absorbed by the crop will be increased as wind speed increases but, again, there is no direct evidence to support this.

SOIL MOISTURE DYNAMICS AND EVAPOTRANSPIRATION

Where much of the plant foliage is destroyed, interception of rainfall and evapotranspiration will be reduced, resulting in increased soil water available for storage (Phillips 1919; Daubenmire 1968; Wells et al 1979). Where litter layers are consumed and mineral soil exposed, infiltration and soil water storage capacity may be immediately reduced. Accelerated oxidation of soil organic matter from greater radiation and changes in surface structure may decrease infiltration rate and water storage, leading to loss of water by surface runoff. For this reason, although the quantity of water present at the soil surface may be increased by burning, simultaneous increase in runoff will reduce the quantity of water entering soil (Edwards 1961). On balance therefore, the soil water status in burnt areas appears less favourable for plant growth than in unburnt areas, and is subject to wider fluctuations (Daubenmire 1968). In arid areas this may have severe consequences for plant regeneration (West 1965).

A diminution of the actual moisture content of the upper layer of soil following fire has often been observed (Beadle 1940; Sampson 1944), but such reduction in moisture content is only temporary. In general, intense fires decreased soil moisture while moderate fires had little or no effect.

The majority of investigators agree that moisture retention capability of soil is seldom affected by burning (Beadle 1940; Beard and Darby 1951; Cass and Collins 1983). It is only the destruction of the litter layer that appears to reduce water storage capacity.

The main influence of fire regime on soil water dynamics appears to result from the changes brought about to the vegetation by burning. Fisher (1978) has observed that in some tropical regions senescent pastures are burnt during the first part of the dry season in order to stimulate growth of green material at a time when the herbage is stressed for water. Although the plants experience severe water stress before burning, they frequently show new green growth immediately following a burn. Fisher (1978) compared the volumetric leaf water potential at 13h00, of two tropical pasture species which had been unburnt and of burnt plants 12 days after a fire. For unburnt plants the volumetric water potential was -1800 to -1400 kPa and for burnt plants -1100 to -900 kPa. The stomata of the unburnt plants were closed and no growth occurred, whereas the stomata of the burnt plants were open and the plants were actively growing. He concluded that complete defoliation by burning allowed the plants to make use of a limited store of soil water at a higher water potential. He explained the sequence of changes in leaf water potential and growth in the burnt plants as follows:

1   The fire removed the droughted but presumably still transpiring tissue and thus transpiration virtually stopped, at least
for a few days.

2   The remaining tissue rehydrated to a level where growth of
new leaves took place, with the water presumably coming from
the 100 to 900 mm depth where the soil water potential was
greater than the leaf water potential.

3   The subsequent increase in leaf area, and hence transpiration, together with a further decrease in soil water, led to
increasing lag of water uptake behind transpiration.

4   Tissue water therefore became increasingly depleted, which
caused a progressive decrease in leaf water potential in the
new leaves.

Much remains to be done to elucidate the relationship between
fire and plant and soil water status. Results to date show that
during years with below average rainfall, burning has no beneficial effect on grass production (Sharrow and Wright 1977; Wright
1978).

MICROBIOLOGICAL DYNAMICS

Information regarding the effect of fire on soil microbial
populations is fragmentary, especially with respect to grasslands
where relatively few papers have been published (Orput and Curtis
1957; Clark and Paul 1970; Wicklow 1973; Ahlgren 1974; Tiwari and
Rai 1977). In the African and South African context even less is
known. The only papers that the authors are aware of are those
by Phillips (1930), Cohen (1949), and Meiklejohn (1955).
Since temperature, available food, water content, aeration
and pH influence the soil microbial population (Alexander 1961;
Wells et al 1979), soil fertility will also be influenced by
disturbances affecting any of these factors.
The reported effects of burning on soil microbial populations
are understandably variable since the site conditions, fire
intensity and sampling methods are determining factors. Ahlgren
and Ahlgren (1965) and Renbuss et al (1973) state that hot fires
temporarily sterilize the soil. Corbet (1934), working in humid
tropical areas, reported that microbial populations rose
immediately after fire and declined to preburn numbers within 9
months. These authors were considering forest systems rather
than grasslands. On grassland local results have suggested that
even the most intense fires cause only a slight temporary drop in
numbers of microorganisms, and less intense fires caused a slight
increase in the total microbial population (Wallis and Price
1979).
Meiklejohn (1955) found that burning bushland in Kenya
resulted in a long-range reduction of numbers of bacteria,
actinomycetes and fungi. Ahlgren (1974) reports Froelich et al
as stating that although total numbers of bacteria, actinomycetes
and fungi were unaffected by fire, significant changes occurred

in the numbers of specific fungal genera and species. Jorgensen and Hodges (1970) were unable to show conclusively that a programme of annual or periodic burning altered the composition of the soil microbial population to the extent that metabolic processes in the soil were adversely affected.

Under local conditions the fungi, bacteria and actinomycetes responded differently to the different fire regimes applied. Duration of heating, maximum temperatures and soil water content appear to be the most important factors influencing these populations (Wallis and Price 1979).

Nitrogen is the main nutrient lost during burning and as South African soils are generally limiting in nitrogen this aspect is likely to be of particular importance in microbial responses to fire. The nitrifying bacteria are very important in the cycling of nitrogen and are particularly sensitive to heating (Wells et al 1979). This has important implications concerning plant nutrition. Research in this direction is strongly urged. Detailed studies of the nitrogen balance, particularly ammonium and nitrate nitrogen, have been published (Christensen 1973; Lewis 1974; Christensen and Muller 1975; Dunn et al 1979), but most pertain to forest or chaparral systems and no such data exist for South Africa.

As nitrogen is lost by burning some replacement mechanism must be present, since without this, site quality would decline in areas subjected to repeated fires. Jorgensen and Wells (1971) found that increased amounts of nitrogen are fixed by nonsymbiotic microorganisms following burning. An investigation of the effects of fire on the activities of microorganisms, particularly in the nitrogen cycle under South African conditions, is thus warranted.

CONCLUSIONS

The effects of fire regime on soil physical properties are not well understood, but the bulk of the evidence available suggests that the physical condition of the soil surface exposed to regular fires will generally exhibit retrogressive change. Quantitative data in support of this statement are generally lacking for southern African conditions but most researchers agree that secondary effects such as reduced infiltration rate, increased surface runoff and accelerated wind and water erosion are characteristic of most soils which have been subjected to regular burning.

Microclimatic responses to fire, although not well documented in the South African literature, can be predicted in broad direction if not in magnitude. There is, however, insufficient information for detailed understanding of the response of particular ecosystems to fire, especially at the level where modelling of the entire soil and atmospheric system is attempted. Hydrological responses within the entire soil-plant-atmosphere continuum are especially difficult to predict at present.

The effect of fire on nutrient cycling is perhaps one of the most important facets of fire ecology. Generally it is still not possible to predict whether burning has a beneficial or adverse effect on the overall nutrient status of particular ecosystems. Since fire has the potential for large-scale transformations of plant nutrients, regular burning could, under appropriate circumstances, result in substantial losses of essential elements from particular ecosystems, and particularly for such systems as sandy grasslands during periods of heavy rainfall. Surprisingly, this aspect does not appear to have received the research attention that is warranted by the widespread use of fire as a management device.

Generally, soil and microclimatic research in relation to fire ecology has been uncoordinated and fragmentary in the past. Comprehensive information on the general response of soil properties and microclimate in particular ecosystems to the short and long-term effects of fire is entirely lacking for southern African conditions.

Chapter 15 The Effect of Fire on Water Yield

J. M. BOSCH, R. E. SCHULZE, and F. J. KRUGER

INTRODUCTION

South Africa's climates are dominantly semi-arid and the country faces water scarcity. Available surface water amounts to about $52\ 000 \times 10^6\ m^3\ yr^{-1}$, of which about $21\ 000 \times 10^6\ m^3$ can be effectively used. By present population estimates this available surface water equates to 7 000 litres per person per day. By contrast, in Canada, the USA and Egypt the available surface water per person per day equals 430 000 l, 23 000 l and 9 000 l respectively (Hobbs 1980). By the end of the century the estimated surface water demand in South Africa has been projected to be $29\ 000 \times 10^6\ m^3\ yr^{-1}$, ie $8\ 000 \times 10^6\ m^3$ more than can be supplied.

The supply is distributed unevenly over the country because of large differences in and variability of rainfall. The annual rainfall for the western half of the country averages less than 300 mm, and for the entire country varies from less than 50 mm in places on the west coast to more than 2 000 mm in mountainous areas of the east and south.

Riverflow is even more variable than rainfall because of the added complexity of differential water losses to the atmosphere over the country. For example, in areas of 125 mm yr^{-1} or less precipitation only 0,45% of the rain is manifest as runoff, whereas streamflow constitutes as much as 80% of the rainfall in humid areas (Commission of Enquiry 1970). The relative contributions of different regions to the total water yield of the country are illustrated in Figure 1. The areas of high water yield are concentrated mainly in the northeastern and eastern parts of the country and in the southwestern part of the Cape. The greater proportion of this region is covered by veld, principally grassland and fynbos; hence sound catchment management of these areas is most important.

Mean annual streamflow in South Africa has been shown by Midgley and Pitman (1969) to increase as a power function of mean annual rainfall (Figure 2), emphasizing the significance of the limited high rainfall areas to water production in South Africa. Consequently the well-watered one twelfth of the country classified as mountain catchments yields one half of the total water supply of South Africa (Wicht 1971).

The fact that water yield can be influenced strongly by manipulation of vegetation has been demonstrated in catchment experiments in many parts of the world (Hibbert 1967), the results indicating that increases or decreases in water yield at any particular site are, in general, directly related to changes in plant biomass (Wicht 1971). Burning, one of the most important management tools and one which has such a dramatic effect on plant biomass, would, therefore, be expected to influence water yield.

The extent to which veld burning can be used to modify water yields from catchments is examined by reviewing results of South African experiments in the context of hydrological principles. In discussing effects of burning, concentration has mainly been on the streamflow response because it can be measured directly and is a factor of immediate economic importance.

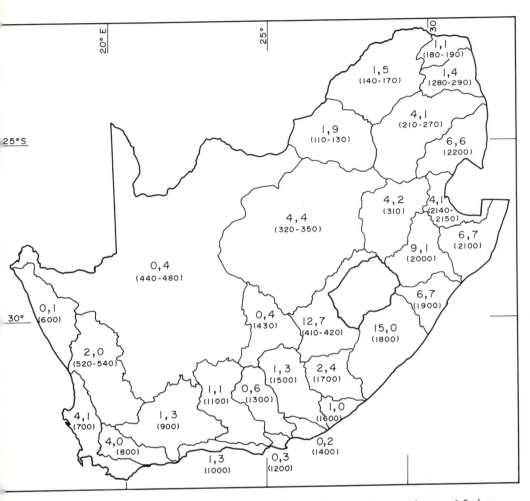

Figure 1   Runoff from hydrological regions of southern Africa,
           expressed as a percentage of the total runoff for the
           region.   Figures   in   parentheses   denote   drainage
           regions (after Commission of Enquiry 1970).

The influence of burning may also be expressed by changes in
the energy cycle, made manifest through evapotranspiration (E_t).
Schulze (1975), for example, developed a simulation model for
predicting changes in evapotranspiration, following changes in
vegetal conditions. Simulated changes in the evapotranspiration
output at a point in the catchment are, however, not necessarily
reflected by equal changes in measured streamflow, especially
when conditions antecedent to the burn are dry and the change in
vegetation structure is temporary, as where natural veld is burnt
in spring. The reason for this is that short-term changes in E_t
are expressed largely as short-term changes in soil storage, as
will be discussed below. However, the influence of fire on soil

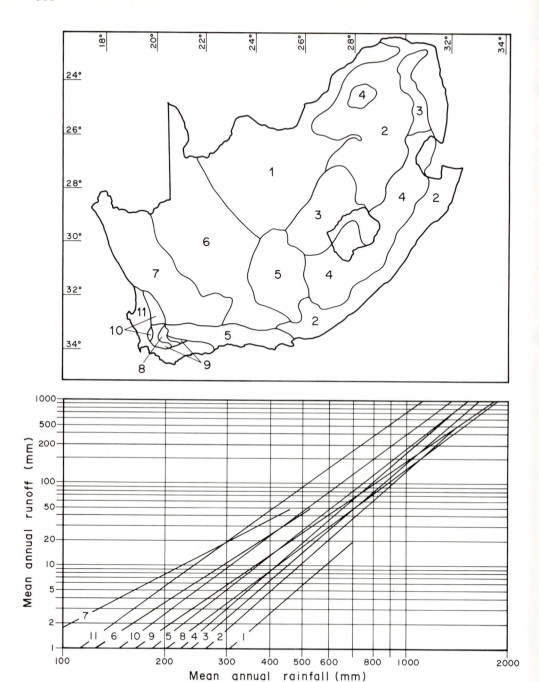

Figure 2   Rainfall-runoff relationships for different regions of
southern Africa (after Midgley and Pitman 1969).

moisture changes or plant-water relations will not be reviewed here. These aspects are dealt with in detail in other chapters.

THE RAINFALL-RUNOFF PROCESS

The effect of fire on water yield is discussed within the conceptual framework of the hydrological cycle and the energy balance.

THE HYDROLOGICAL CYCLE

The hydrological cycle as a system is depicted in Figure 3, which shows how precipitation is dissipated among various pathways by different processes. The water balance may be expressed as follows:

$$P = (T + I + E_{s+w}) + Q + S \qquad (1)$$

where

P = gross precipitation
T = transpiration
I = interception
E_{s+w} = evaporation from the soil and water surface
Q = streamflow and
S = change in soil moisture storage

When vegetation is affected by fire, changes in the major storages and processes of the hydrological cycle occur. Similarly, vegetation also interacts continuously with energy exchange processes. Thus the extent to which streamflow is altered by a fire is dependent on the relative rates prevailing in the hydrological and energy exchange processes at the time of the burn as well as on the vegetation recovery rate and pattern. For example, burning dormant grass, which is not transpiring, would have little effect on the transpiration losses; also, burning would have little effect on the interception component if there were no rain before the canopy had recovered.

EVAPOTRANSPIRATION (E_t)

Evapotranspiration includes transpiration and evaporation from the soil and other intercepting surfaces and accounts in most areas of South Africa for the largest loss component in the water balance equation. Evapotranspiration is regulated by interactions between vegetation and the water balance and energy exchange processes. These interactions are discussed below.

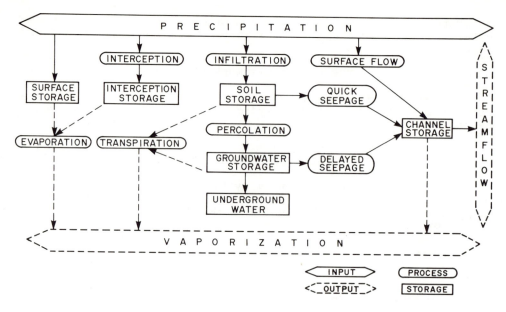

Figure 3   A systems representation of the hydrological cycle at catchment level (after Wicht 1971).

Water availability

Water availability, ie the amount of water available for direct evaporation and accessible to plants for transpiration, is determined by rainfall characteristics, soil properties, topographical features and plant rooting depth.   Provided water is available, the net radiant energy received by an ecosystem is dissipated largely as the latent energy required in evapotranspiration.

In South Africa's latitudes net radiation is seldom a limiting factor in the evapotranspiration process, whereas water availability is.   This is especially true during the seasonal droughts of the prevailing climates.   Thus, for example, changes in vegetation in the dry season will often have little effect on the water balance.

Because net radiation is not a limiting factor, actual evapotranspiration thus generally increases with increasing rainfall, as is readily confirmed by catchment water balance data (Bosch and Hewlett 1981). Hibbert (1971) has shown that changes in water yield (E_t savings) after clearing in shrubland in central Arizona may vary from as little as 50 mm yr^{-1} under conditions of limited water supply to as much as 300 mm yr^{-1} in the same catchment during high rainfall years.

Therefore, because of the effects of water availability, the immediate response of E_t to fire would be affected by season of burn, and burning of dormant grassland, for example, would be expected to have little immediate effect on E_t and thus on streamflow. Streamflow would, on the other hand, be expected to show a marked response to denudation of actively growing grassland during summer when there is normally an abundance of water available for transpiration. Evapotranspiration in sclerophyllous vegetation in areas with dry summers is likewise expected to be least affected by fires during summer when transpiration is minimal; some species of fynbos, for example, cease transpiring for certain periods in summer when under stress (P C Miller, personal communication, 1981).

Vegetation dynamics

Reductions in E_t due to burning of fire-adapted vegetation are comparatively short-lived. Where vegetation exerts a measurable influence on streamflow, ie in humid zones where runoff: rainfall ratios are low, discernible responses in streamflow to burning will depend on the timing of fire in relation to the season of maximum evapotranspiration, and on the vegetation regrowth rates. Burning during the dormant season may have little immediate effect, as noted above. Grassland may recover 50% of preburn cover and biomass within three to six months (Tainton and Mentis, this volume, chapter 6), while fynbos recovers 80% of its preburn canopy cover in less than 3 yr (Kruger and Bigalke, this volume, chapter 5). Thus, even when reduction of biomass by fire results in a response in streamflow, this response will be transient and difficult to observe, especially where preburn biomass is relatively small, as in grassland and in many fynbos types. As a corollary, one may expect increasing magnitudes of streamflow response to burning in dense, tall communities with slow relative recovery rates. Streamflow from fynbos catchments should, for example, respond more strongly than from grassland catchments.

In grassland most fires occur late in the dormant season and immediately prior to spring growth. Recovery of vegetation under such conditions is usually fast. The seasonal changes in vegetation biomass and structure are therefore relatively small and the major changes following fire are relatively short-lived and confined to the first one to six months after the fire.

Latent heat exchange

Radiation energy is dissipated in the heat energy balance and this process may be expressed as follows:

$$(1-r)\ S_t - L_{net} = R_n = B + H + L_v E \qquad (2)$$

where

R_n = net radiation energy flux
r = reflectivity coefficient (albedo)
S_t = total incoming solar radiation load

$$B \quad = \text{conductive heat flux}$$
$$H \quad = \text{convective heat flux}$$
$$L_vE \quad = \text{latent heat flux}$$
$$L_{net} \quad = \text{net long-wave flux}$$

Fire removes the vegetal cover and consequently affects evapotranspiration by partial reduction of transpiration and canopy interception of precipitation, ie an important part of the latent heat flux (L_vE). Burning thus favours reductions in E_t and should increase water yield by denudation of an area. It also tends to increase soil evaporation, since potential increases in soil evaporation result from the increased heat load at the soil surface, which is no longer shaded by vegetation.

The above generalizations are compounded by the effect of burning on the reflectivity of vegetation. For example, fire may increase the net radiant energy flux by darkening the soil surface and thus decreasing the reflectivity coefficient. This is most likely to be the case in grassland where tufts remain black for several weeks after a fire before changing to dark green when new growth starts. Reflectivity relationships for selected vegetation types are given in Figure 4. The diagram suggests possible changes of r from 22% for mature flat to gently sloping *Themeda* grassveld under cloudless conditions to 5% immediately after a burn (Schulze 1975).

Increases in net radiation by the above factors after a burn may result in increased soil evaporation rates. Accruals to the soil moisture store through elimination of interception and transpiration by burning could thus be balanced by increased evaporation losses, provided sufficient soil moisture is available in the top 200 to 300 mm of soil. Progressive surface drying lengthens the diffusion pathway in the soil and would eventually, particularly during daytime, restrict evaporation from the soil. Thus, increased net radiation received at the soil surface may be lost only partly by increased latent heat flux in evaporation, and balanced by increased net long-wave radiative cooling.

Interception loss

Precipitation intercepted by a canopy cover is readily available for direct return to the atmosphere by evaporation, and this interception loss is often an important part of evapotranspiration. For example, Zinke (1967) summarized the results of a number of experiments that showed that interception losses for coniferous forests vary mainly between 14 and 60% of gross annual precipitation and for shrubs between 4 and 6%. Hamilton and Rowe (1949) estimated interception losses from California chaparral as 5 to 14% of gross annual precipitation. Corbett (1968) gives estimates of gross interception losses ranging from 5 to 8% in grass and from 10 to 14% in chaparral. Losses in certain prairie grasslands were found to vary between 18 and 84% (Clark 1940).

In South Africa, gross interception loss has been recorded in an old stand of *Pinus radiata* (Monterey pine) in the western Cape, where it was found to average 30% of rainfall (Versfeld

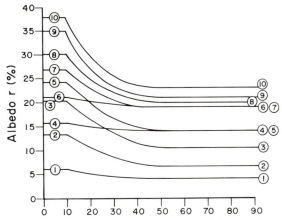

Angle and incidence between slope and solar beam, A

① Burnt Grassveld : ≤ 10 days after burning
   $r = 0,001287 A^2 - 0,13081 A + 7,3382$

② Burnt Grassveld: 11-15 days after burning
   $r = 0,002540 A^2 - 0,31280 A + 16,1335$

③ Burnt Grassveld: 16-20 days after burning
   $r = 0,00523 A^2 - 0,5479 A + 25,3112$

④ Forest (*Leucosidea, Pinus, Podocarpus*): Cloudy conditions
   $r = 0,00129 A^2 - 0,1139 A + 16,53317$

⑤ Forest (*Leucosidea, Pinus, Podocarpus*): Cloudless conditions
   $r = 0,00498 A^2 - 0,5524 A + 29,1794$

⑥ Grassland (*Themeda* : all stages): Cloudy conditions
   $r = 0,00093 A^2 - 0,1071 A + 21,998$

⑦ Grassveld (*Themeda* : senescent stage) and
   burnt Grassveld 21-25 days after burning:
   Cloudless conditions
   $r = 0,00492 A^2 - 0,4932 A + 30,9882$

⑧ Grassveld (*Themeda* : mature stage) : Cloudless conditions
   $r = 0,00491 A^2 - 0,5358 A + 34,2540$

⑨ Grassveld *Themeda* : new growth stage : Cloudless conditions
   $r = 0,00782 A^2 - 0,8012 A + 40,7594$

⑩ Brackenveld (winter): Cloudless conditions
   $r = 0,01154 A^2 - 1,0414 A + 46,6566$

Figure 4   Typical relationships of the reflectivity coefficient to selected vegetation types, growth phases, time after burning, sky conditions and relative solar altitude (Schulze 1975).

1978), and in an old stand of *P. patula* (patula pine) in the summer rainfall area, which was found to intercept 20% of the rain (Scott-Shaw 1976). Schulze (1980), using data extracted from de Villiers (1975), tabulated values for potential interception losses as follows: indigenous forest + 3,2 mm day^{-1}, bush-veld and savanna between 1,6 and 4,4 mm day^{-1}, fynbos between 0,8 and 2,0 mm day^{-1} and grassland between ca 1,2 mm and 2,6 mm day^{-1}.

Most studies show that the interception component of evapo-transpiration does represent a net loss of water to the atmosphere (Thorud 1967; Stewart 1977). Gross interception losses therefore depend on vegetation parameters governing the size of interception stores. Corbett (1968) calculated storage capacities of canopies of various grasses as varying between 0,5 and 5 mm, depending on average height and percent cover of the canopy. Leyton et al (1967) give storage capacities of 2,5, 1,3 and 1,5 mm for heather, bracken and Norway spruce, respectively. Zinke's (1967) summary showed that the storage capacities of vegetation vary from 0,25 to 9,14 mm, but concluded that no large errors would be made if a storage capacity of 1,3 mm for most grass-lands, shrublands and forests were accepted. However, gross losses also depend on local rainfall characteristics such as number, duration and intensity of storms (Jackson 1975; Schulze et al 1978).

Thus, while fire will reduce interception losses, the magnit-ude of the effect depends on a complexity of factors, and partic-ularly on the relative reduction in vegetation biomass and on post-fire recovery rates. Consider, for example, the hypothetic-al case depicted in Figure 5. If a grassland in the summer rainfall region is burnt during winter in three successive years and each of the winters is followed by summers favourable to high interception losses, the actual savings in losses may be high (Figure 5a). Conditions favourable for high interception would be high rainfall, frequent low intensity storms and little wind. On the other hand, if a grassland is burnt biennially in winter and each of the postfire years were low rainfall years with few but relative larger storms, savings in interception losses may be extremely small (Figure 5b). It has already been pointed out that grasslands in humid zones restore most of their intercepting surface rapidly.

It can also be shown that interception losses in fynbos, which restores most of its intercepting surface within 3 yr, is largely insensitive to season of burn. This is mainly because burning frequency in fynbos is normally much lower than in grass-lands and the immediate post-burn effect is spread over several years. Figure 5c shows a hypothetical initial saving in inter-ception loss due to burning in the beginning of the dry season (Burn "A" in Figure 5c). A burn in the middle of the wet season (Burn "B") would, however, result in little more, if any, savings in interception loss. The magnitude of saving would in this case be related more strongly to the postfire rainfall pattern.

The above arguments consider potential interception losses only. It will be realized from the previous discussions that the actual E_t losses depend on many factors other than interception. It must therefore be emphasized that a reduction in interception loss does not imply consequent equivalent reductions in evapo-transpiration or increases in water yield.

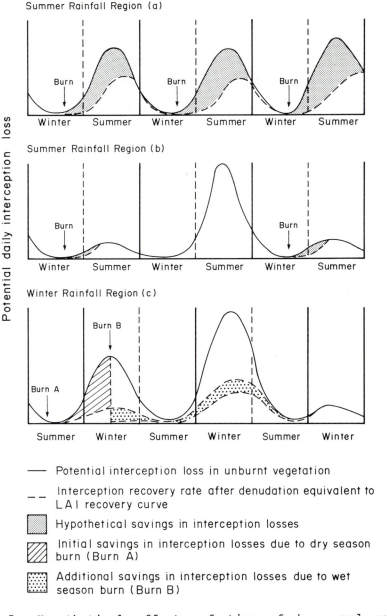

Potential daily interception loss

Summer Rainfall Region (a)

Burn

Winter | Summer | Winter | Summer | Winter | Summer

Summer Rainfall Region (b)

Burn

Winter | Summer | Winter | Summer | Winter | Summer

Winter Rainfall Region (c)

Burn B

Burn A

Summer | Winter | Summer | Winter | Summer | Winter

——— Potential interception loss in unburnt vegetation

— — Interception recovery rate after denudation equivalent to LAI recovery curve

▓ Hypothetical savings in interception losses

▨ Initial savings in interception losses due to dry season burn (Burn A)

▦ Additional savings in interception losses due to wet season burn (Burn B)

Figure 5   Hypothetical effects of time of burn and rainfall regime on interception losses in a high summer rainfall region (a), a low summer rainfall region (b) and in a winter rainfall region (c).

Transpiration and soil water evaporation

The extent to which E_t is reduced by reduced transpiration (through burning) depends on changes in the microclimate and the order of change in evaporation from the soil due to changes in microclimate. It also depends on prefire relations between the evaporation and transpiration processes, season of burn, recovery rate of the vegetation and availability of water. Constructive discussion is limited by the few available data on concomitant changes in evaporation and transpiration with changes in vegetation. The complexity of all the interacting factors that may or may not cause compensating effects has already been demonstrated.

INFILTRATION

Infiltration is the process by which water is absorbed into the soil profile, primarily through the surface, but also through crevices and other entry points (Hillel 1971). The rate at which rain infiltrates into the soil is a function of surface factors such as initial wetness, texture and structure, as well as of the hydraulic conductivity, uniformity and other physical character-istics of the entire soil profile.

Intense or frequent fires destroy the litter and organic layers of the soil and this tends to decrease the rate of infilt-ration through the surface (Arend 1941). Experimental results vary considerably, but most indicate that grassland and shrubland fires are not intense enough to change soil physical properties (Wells et al 1979). Under certain conditions fires cause tempor-ary repellancy in soils. Resistance to wetting and increased overland flow may be caused by residual ash dust. Heating of the surface layers in some soils may also result in the condensation of volatilized organic matter in underlying layers, promoting water repellancy. These phenomena have been observed in the USA (DeBano 1966) and in parts of South Africa (W Bond, personal communication, 1979), but no research has been undertaken in South Africa to investigate their effects on streamflow compon-ents or on erosion and sedimentation processes.

The emphasis that is commonly placed on the infiltration process with respect to burning stems from the precept that rainfall intensities frequently exceed the surface infiltration rates of soils, and that excess rainfall runs downslope to collect in streams. The amount of overland flow generated in this way may have regional significance in, for example, more arid areas characterized by crusted, eutrophic soils, on homogen-eous soil types with very low hydraulic conductivity, in pastures or cultivated farm land, or on soils with repellancy properties. Early observations by Fernow (1902), Zon (1927) and Hursh (1944) suggested that infiltrability was seldom exceeded by rainfall in humid areas and that surface infiltrability was not the major controlling factor of the stormflow volume from small first-order catchments. More recent work on small experimental catchments in the moist, forested northeastern USA (Hewlett 1961) has led to the variable source area concept as an alternative to concepts that incorporate overland flow as the major process producing

floods (Horton 1945). The variable source area concept, explained in detail by Hewlett and Troendle (1975), considers the major
controlling factor to be the porous soil mantle typical of high
rainfall regions with dense vegetation cover, and maintains that
overland flow in such catchments with undisturbed soils is generally limited to saturated zones around perennial channels. These
zones expand and shrink as the catchment gets wetter and dries
out, thus varying in size. Part of the expansion occurs as an
extension of the channel system. Detailed work on infiltration
and the way in which it is affected by fire should be preceded by
investigation of the importance and role of infiltration as
determinant of the pattern of streamflow.

The argument that the rate of infiltration in catchments of
the humid areas in South Africa is seldom exceeded by rainfall is
supported by a recent analysis of plot experiments at Jonkershoek
in the western Cape (Versfeld 1981). Overland flow never exceeded 0,05% of the rainfall in three fynbos catchments. Slashing
and burning of the fynbos had no effect on overland flow. In one
case, treatment was followed immediately by a 125 mm storm,
despite which no increase in overland flow was observed.

The variable source area concept has found application in
explaining many hydrological phenomena of moist areas (Freeze
1972; Hewlett and Troendle 1975; Harr 1977; Troendle 1979), but
little work has been done in explaining treatment effects in
these terms. Although most vegetation manipulation (including
burning) takes place in relatively humid areas, where the role of
infiltration in the generation of streamflow is expected to be
minimal, there are large areas of vegetation in semi-arid regions
of South Africa where water yield is critical. Hence there is a
real need to study differences in flow mechanisms occurring in
moist and arid areas.

SUBSURFACE FLOW

The subsurface flow component sometimes dominates the water
discharge process; this would, for example, be the case under
dry, rainless conditions. Assessing the short-lived effect of a
fire under these conditions would require detailed studies of
soil moisture status and movement along a catchment slope and
within the entire soil profile. Experiments performed in small
catchments (Patric et al 1965) showed that vegetation under
relatively dry conditions may create large potentials (suctions
in upper layers of the soil) which will draw water from moister
areas outside the rooting zone. If actively transpiring vegetation is burnt under these conditions, the root "tension" forces
are released, but water may move horizontally or vertically in
order to balance local changes in water potentials before moving
laterally to the stream channel. It is thus possible that more
water is retained in the catchment after elimination of transpiration by burning. Also, roots of rapidly recovering vegetation
could absorb and transpire the water before it ever reaches a
stream.

The soil water phase is the least understood and most complex
phase in the water cycle and merits detailed investigation, since

a large portion of rain that falls on South African catchments in humid areas is routed through the soil before reaching the streams.

HYDROLOGICAL RESPONSE

The observed response of streamflow to rainfall may be used as an indicator of differences among catchments with regard to mechanisms governing streamflow patterns. Statistics of storm-flow in relation to rainstorm depth provide such indices. These statistics, and the effect of treatment on them, may be interpreted without making assumptions about the relative roles of over-land flow and subsurface soil moisture movement in generating stormflow.

The hydrological response factor is used to describe the essential relationship between rainfall and streamflow in a given catchment. It provides a simple method of predicting the flood potential of an area (Woodruff and Hewlett 1970) and is similarly suited to testing the overall effect of treatment on stormflow volume.

The hydrological response (R) is defined as

$$R = \frac{Q_V}{P_V}$$

(3)

where Q_V represents the volume of stormflow and P_V the rain-fall volume.

Results of preliminary studies for certain areas in South Africa indicate very low response factors for stormflow volumes, at least for catchments in humid areas. Even for grassland catchments which are burnt regularly, response factors are in the order of 0,02. These response factors are not sensitive to large changes in vegetation biomass. Afforested catchments in many cases have response factors of 0,01 to 0,03 and these factors do not differ significantly from those in the natural (grassland) condition (Bosch 1980). It is only in very steep catchments that the stormflow volumes become relatively large (eg Langrivier, Table 1).

Mean annual hydrological response factors for stormflow volumes for some South African catchments in different regions are given in Table 1 together with values taken from Woodruff and Hewlett (1970) for the eastern USA. Almost all median values vary between 0,01 and 0,06 and indicate that these catchments exercise good control over the rain they receive.

The data presented in Table 1 also indicate that mountain catchments in humid areas of South Africa have similar stormflow responses to the selected USA catchments, implying that South African catchments have similar storage and infiltration charact-eristics. Catchment response, overland flow and the role of infiltration in arid and semi-arid areas of South Africa, however, still need to be studied in detail.

Table 1   Mean annual hydrological response factors for stormflow
           volumes in some South African catchments compared to
           catchments from the eastern United States of America.

Catchment description	Mean annual precip- itation (mm)	Mean annual stream- flow (mm)	Annual response factor of stormflow volumes		
			Mean	SD	Median
Cathedral Peak, Natal Catchment II (mature *Pinus patula* plantation)	1600	600	0,016	0,006	0,014
Catchment IV (grassland)	1400	700	0,025	0,009	0,025
Jonkershoek, western Cape Bosboukloof (mature *P. radiata* plantation)	1400	430	0,026	0,009	0,025
Langrivier (fynbos, steep topography)	2300	1500	0,306	0,056	0,299
Zachariashoek, western Cape (fynbos)	1100	410	0,074	0,049	0,060
Mokobulaan, eastern Tvl. Catchment A (mature *Eucalyptus saligna*)	1200	130	0,008	0,006	0,010
Catchment B (mature *P. patula*)	1200	220	0,020	0,013	0,035
Catchment C (grassland)	1200	170	0,024	0,011	0,020
Witklip, eastern Tvl. (mature *P. roxburgii*)	1400	350	0,040	0,010	0,040
Westfalia, northern Tvl. Catchment I (Indigenous forest)	1800	1000	0,103	0,108	0,064
90 eastern USA catchments[a]	–	–	0,078	0,056	–

[a]From Woodruff and Hewlett 1970.

EXPERIMENTAL RESULTS

CATCHMENT EXPERIMENTS

There is at present no hydrological model incorporating all the complex interactions of hydrological processes so as to accurately predict changes following burning, especially when the effect of fire is a short-term one. The integrated effects of fire on certain streamflow components can, however, be measured and these measurements compared with those for unburnt conditions in order to quantify the change. If the number of experiments under different conditions is large enough, statistical inferences and reasonable generalizations would be possible. This approach has been used worldwide in paired or multiple catchment experiments, as an alternative to the energy balance approach. Although small changes in flow may not be detected in a catchment experiment, Hewlett et al (1969) have shown that the method has been used satisfactorily to detect changes in the magnitude of flow of the order of 5 to 10%, whereas the energy balance approach is unlikely to detect changes smaller than 20%.

Results obtained from catchment experiments in South Africa, although limited, indicate that the magnitude of changes in vegetation type and composition need to be pronounced to have detectable influences on water yield. For example, fire has been excluded as far as possible from Catchment IX, a grassland site at Cathedral Peak in the Natal Drakensberg, since 1952. (It burnt out accidentally during 1956 and 1964, but the grassland communities have nevertheless, according to Granger (1976a), been replaced to a large extent by shrub and fern communities). No changes in streamflow have been detected when compared with biennially burnt adjacent catchments which have remained in grassland (Bosch 1979). One may therefore conclude that effects of fire on total water yield from grassland catchments in this zone are negligible. At Jonkershoek in the western Cape the ageing of fynbos in Lambrechtsbos A and Lambrechtsbos B for 26 yr and 18 yr respectively resulted in nonsignificant changes in annual streamflow (van Wyk 1977). Langrivier, another catchment at Jonkershoek, has been protected from fire since 1942. Van der Zel and Kruger (1975) concluded that this treatment resulted in a decrease in streamflow of 1% for each year of protection. Subsequent analysis of the experiment by van Wyk (1977), using additional records, has shown that this rate of decrease was not maintained after 24 yr and that the trend found by van der Zel and Kruger (1975) was in fact weaker than they had originally concluded. Van Wyk (1977) also points out that Langrivier represents a rather small area of high rainfall (it receives 2 000 mm yr^{-1} of which about 1 500 mm runs off) and also receives rain from "southeasters" during summer, with a large proportion of water thus being available for evapotranspiration. Reductions in streamflow from Langrivier were quantified by van Wyk (1977) as 23 mm yr^{-1} for the first 8 yr, 76 mm yr^{-1} for 9 to 12 yr, 211 mm yr^{-1} for 17 to 24 yr and 187 mm yr^{-1} for 25 to 32 yr of protection from fire. Experiments on afforestation at Jonkershoek (van Wyk 1977), Cathedral Peak (Bosch 1979) and Mokobulaan (van Lill et al 1980) have shown that the effects of converting veld to forest are detectable only after 3 to 8 yr. A recent review of all available catchment experiments worldwide (Bosch and Hewlett 1981) shows that in general, clearfelling of less than 20% of an area has little effect on annual water yield.

Wild-fire and other treatments analogous to burning in certain shrublands in the USA have been found to have significant but rather inconsistent effects on water yield. Brush control and conversion to grass of small catchments in Arizona chaparral, dominated by *Quercus turbinella* (shrub live oak) and *Cercocarpus betuloides* (western mountain-mahogany) resulted in yield increases varying between 50 and 150 mm annually, depending on the rainfall in a given year and its seasonal distribution (Hibbert 1971). In pinyon-juniper which is more of an open dwarf conifer vegetation type than a shrubland, clearing has had little or no effect on water yield. Small increases of 11 mm yr^{-1} were reported only from controlling juniper by herbicides at Beaver Creek, Arizona (Clary et al 1974). Results of the effects of clearings of forests in other countries are numerous (Bosch and Hewlett 1981) and they vary from yield increases of 20 to 600 mm.

Burning of 6 yr old sclerophyllous vegetation at Zacharias-hoek in the western Cape resulted in statistically nonsignificant increases in streamflow lasting for only 10 months after a burn (van Wyk 1977). A wild-fire in a 7 yr old *P. patula* stand at Cathedral Peak, Natal, resulted in nonsignificant changes in annual water yield (Bosch 1980). Rycroft (1947) found relatively large increases in peak discharge in the three months following an April burn in fynbos of Abdolskloof, Jonkershoek. There were also inconclusive indications that stormflow volume and total streamflow increased from this 12 ha catchment. These increases were, however, not related to annual yield. Banks (1964) found that even these short term effects had disappeared by the second rainy season after the fire.

The few effects of fire in grassland seem to be temporary. Nanni (1960) found no immediate effect on streamflow after spring burning of *Themeda triandra* grassland at Cathedral Peak. These findings were substantiated by Bosch (1980) who found that non-parametric tests showed no changes in monthly streamflow after several repeated spring burns in the same area. Stormflow volume from a catchment burnt biennially at Cathedral Peak has been analysed as a preliminary examination to changes in stormflow after burning (Bosch 1980). Monthly stormflow volumes from Catchment X during unburnt years were related in a linear regression to those from the adjacent Catchment IX, where vegetation was protected from fire and was relatively stable. The regression was repeated for years in which Catchment X was burnt, to test for differences. The results for October, November, December and March are presented diagrammatically in Figure 6 (a to d). Significant differences in stormflow between burning and nonburning were experienced in October (P 0,01) and November (P 0,05). The mean increase in stormflow from the burnt catchment constituted 18% of the total stormflow during October, which is only 1,3% of the total water yield for October and thus becomes negligible when compared to annual water yield. Changes in stormflow in grassland catchments therefore seem to be limited to short periods immediately after a burn. Increased sediment yield

344

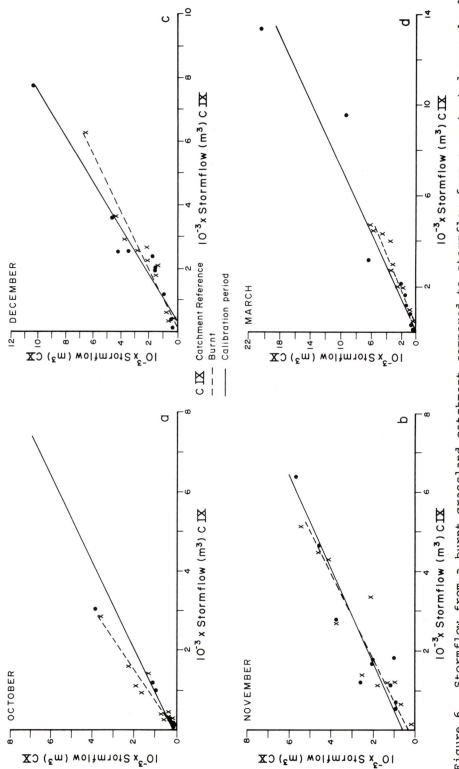

Figure 6   Stormflow from a burnt grassland catchment compared to stormflow from a protected grassland.

and erosion following fires may be of greater concern than possible changes in water yield, particularly in the western Cape.

PLOT STUDIES

A number of plot studies have been performed to evaluate relative changes in runoff and erosion due to a variety of treatments. Plot studies provide indications of responses in overland flow and erosion to treatment but do not supply information on total water and sediment yield from catchments. Such studies, if standardized, may supply valuable comparative data on certain factors such as soil erodibility, soil moisture changes in surface layers and its relation to vegetation parameters. However, the degree to which changes in soil moisture or surface runoff in a plot would relate to total yield from a catchment and other streamflow components is difficult to gauge.

Haylett (1960) reported that winter burning of veld in the Pretoria area combined with moderate grazing did not "materially" increase runoff and soil erosion in relation to unburnt veld. Erosion was significant on plots where soil was cleared, and slope had a significant influence on erosion in cases where the soil was relatively well covered by vegetation. This point illustrates that the flow energy of water is of lesser importance than raindrop energy in detaching and transporting soil particles. A study by du Plessis and Mostert (1965) showed increased runoff and soil loss from plots in *T. triandra* grassveld at Glen in the Orange Free State following moderate grazing during the growing season and annual spring burning. The poor correlation between rainfall and runoff (r = 0,0117), however, casts some doubt on results from this particular plot. Burning of plots in Tall Grassveld in Natal, combined with grazing, resulted in higher runoff and erosion relative to burnt but ungrazed veld (Scott 1952a).

Results from elsewhere on the conversion of vegetation types, ie treatments analogous to burning, in vegetation types similar to those found in South Africa, are limited. Based on soil moisture changes in plots in California, Rowe and Reimann (1961) indicated that water yield may be increased by converting shrubland to grassland. They concluded that "the amount of increase that can be obtained depends on such conditions as depth and storage capacity of the soil, amount and distribution of annual rainfall, and kinds of vegetation occupying the site before and after conversion". The conversion of mountain brush to grass in Utah has been suggested as the cause of evapotranspiration reductions of 130 to 150 mm annually (Johnston et al 1969). These suggestions stem from plot studies in which the mountain brush is composed largely of deciduous species, of which *Quercus gambelii* (Gambel oak) in shrub form dominated.

MANAGEMENT IMPLICATIONS

Until sophisticated models capable of predicting accurately water yield response to fire become available, managers will have to be guided by limited results from experiments under conditions and in vegetation types vaguely resembling their specific situations.

Results from a very limited number of experiments in South Africa imply that fire in grassland has no detectable effect on water yield. When considering the fire management options in grasslands, prospects for water yield augmentation by means of burning are therefore unappealing: choices of burning rotations are normally between 2 and 3 yr. Protection of grasslands for more than 8 yr on significantly large areas is seldom considered. If burning of a grassland site which has remained unburnt for ca 10 yr and of a 7 yr old pine forest had no significant effects on streamflow, the likelihood is very small for increasing streamflow by, for example, changing from a 3 to a 2 yr rotation.

Results on burning in brushland in South Africa and the USA are inconsistent, but suggest some potential for water yield increases. Management options in fynbos are more versatile: protection of fynbos for periods of 20 yr and more is, for reasons of ecology and fire hazard, no longer practised; rotations of 4 yr can also be discounted on grounds of erosion hazard. The main options would be between "short" rotation (ca 5 to 7 yr) and "long" rotation (ca 12 to 15 yr) burning. With one exception all studies on burning and protection in fynbos have suggested that increases in water yield following a burn are short-lived or very small. Evapotranspiration is presumably restored very rapidly and within the first 2 to 3 yr. Realistic estimates of the potential for water yield increase, if any, should thus distribute increases per unit area for the first three postfire years over the rest of the rotation span.

The water yield changes as determined by experimental catchments usually represent on-site changes in water yield under conditions of strict control and uniform treatment. It would be wrong to simply extrapolate experimental results to larger areas and to calculate potentials of increase in water yield on the assumption that experimental conditions resemble those of large management units. It can generally be assumed that treatment of larger areas would have a less pronounced effect on streamflow than that which has been demonstrated in small experimental catchments. Although there is no evidence for this assumption, studies of catchment experiment results from all over the world show generally lower response to treatment in larger catchments (Bosch and Hewlett 1981), probably because treatments on larger areas cannot be controlled to the same degree as in small experimental catchments, and treatments are not as uniformly applied. The same may be assumed for burning of veld. Although the burn may be uniform, there is usually a great diversity in plant communities and topographic features which may cause variable effects on water yield response to burning. A further factor which needs to be taken into account in converting plot data to water yield estimates is that part of the increased streamflow may be lost by channel evaporation and usage by riparian vegetation, depending on the distance to the point of storage or utilization. Hibbert (1979), for example, has estimated the downstream increases in streamflow after type conversions in Arizona chaparral to be only two-thirds of the on-site increase. The already relatively insignificant effect of burning on streamflow will therefore have an even smaller effect on the quantity of water available for storage and use.

Unconditional burning of grassland for maximum water yield may result in severe deterioration of the vegetation and eventually the soil mantle. These could in the long term destroy exactly those factors that are responsible for good infiltration, good water yield regulation, low sedimentation and relatively high biomass production, all conditions which have been shown to exist in some of South Africa's more important catchment areas.

In short, the balance between needs, cost and resource capabilities should be considered very carefully. Management should perhaps aim at conserving those qualities that are responsible for the existing, seemingly efficient water yield potential of our mountain catchment areas, rather than attempting to increase water yield per se.

CONCLUSION

Although there can be no doubt that drastic changes in plant biomass have marked effects on water yield from catchments, experimental results are insufficient to warrant conclusive statements on the effects of short-lived, relatively small biomass changes caused by burning of grassland and fynbos on water yield. Vegetation changes result in multiple interactions and balancing effects between energy exchange and water balance processes. Discussions of these processes show that, as a general rule, fire can be expected to have a relatively large effect on water yield when a vegetation type with high leaf area index or biomass is burnt during a period of vigorous growth and when sufficient amounts of water are available. Burning of dormant, low-structure vegetation during cool, rainless periods could, on the other hand, have very little immediate effect on water yield. The extent to which water yield would be affected over a longer period (> 1 yr) depends mainly on the rate of recovery of the particular vegetation and climatic conditions during the period of recovery.

Accruals to the soil moisture after burning are favoured by factors such as reductions in interception and transpiration losses. These gains in soil moisture may, however, be lost to the atmosphere due to increased soil evaporation following the more direct exposure of the soil and lower reflectivity coefficients of the evaporating surface after a fire. Additions to soil moisture during dry periods may also be retained in the soil, moving vertically and horizontally in an effort to balance moisture potentials created by the vegetation before fires and thus may not reach the stream channel.

Catchment experiments seem to support the above arguments. Burning of grassland in the Natal Drakensberg showed no immediate effect on baseflow and neither has the more than 20 years' successional development in one of the grassland catchments there resulted in a detectable decline in total flow from the catchment. Burning of 6 yr old fynbos in the western Cape resulted in negligible streamflow increases for a few months after the burn. Experiments on the protection of fynbos have, with the exception of one catchment, shown no reductions in streamflow. Results of experiments in burning conducted elsewhere and the conversion of vegetation types analogous to fynbos have shown variable results.

The potential of fire as a tool to augment streamflow in mountain catchments is hampered by several constraints, such as decline in water quality and increased erosion, and by plant ecological and multiple use considerations. Conclusions as to the potential for yield increases by means of fire should be drawn only after careful consideration of these factors.

Chapter 16 The Use of Fire as a Management Tool

P. J. EDWARDS

INTRODUCTION

Fire is widely accepted as being a valuable tool in the management of natural vegetation. It is a resource modifier (Cutler 1979) and can be used to change the composition of vegetation and its cover or to maintain plant communities in a certain stage of succession. So too in South Africa, where fire has, it would seem, played a role in determining the nature of vegetation for many hundreds of years (chapters 3 and 4). Not unexpectedly, therefore, it has continued to be used by farmers and others in the management of this vegetation. Here its use must be dictated by the desired objectives, the known reaction of the plant communities to burning, the management systems into which it is to be incorporated and by the local legislation pertaining to the use of fire. Previous chapters have dealt with the reaction of plant communities to fire and this chapter will deal with three specific aspects viz the objectives of burning, the incorporation of fire into some management systems and fire legislation.

OBJECTIVES OF BURNING

Before developing a plan of fire management for various systems of land-use the objectives of burning natural vegetation must be established. These objectives, with some comment on the success likely to be achieved under each, are considered in this section. The use of fire to achieve the objectives in various management systems will be discussed later in this chapter.

1   Fire can be used to remove surplus vegetation and facilitate access by man and animals. However, care should be taken that this advantage is not gained at the expense of plant composition, productivity and soil and water conservation.

2   Controlled burning will reduce the fuel load and thus the intensity and frequency of accidental fires. It can also be applied to make fire breaks which protect vulnerable areas. Such measures, if repeated too frequently on the same site, may have their own characteristic detrimental effects.

3   Fire can be used to maintain or achieve a plant composition which is optimal for a specific management objective. The changes which take place have been described previously (chapters 5, 6, 7 and 8).

4   Fire may be used to facilitate the introduction of exotic species into the vegetation (eg the introduction of improved forage species).

5   Burning can improve the acceptability and nutritional value of existing species for grazing and browsing animals. It may be applied at specific seasons for this purpose. However, burning in certain seasons of the year, particularly when followed by close cropping, can reduce the production of the vegetation and increase soil loss and water runoff (chapter 15).

6 Scott (1947) has suggested that burning will aid in the control of livestock parasites which spend certain phases of their life cycle on the vegetation. Some parasites such as ticks may be burnt in fires. However, evidence suggests that many avoid the effects of fire (T Bosman, personal communication, 1979) and that less drastic measures, eg dipping and dosing, are more effective. Fire has recently been used in the Kruger National Park to control anthrax (W P D Gertenbach, personal communication, 1980).

7 Burning may be used to maintain or develop the plant cover needed to conserve soil or water in a particular catchment. It affects both canopy and basal cover of vegetation and thus the infiltration and runoff of precipitation (chapters 6 and 15). These in turn influence the rate of soil movement (Edwards 1961). The response of these factors to fire on a specific site should be known before burning for this purpose.

8 Fire may be used to stimulate an out-of-season flush of growth as for example, by burning veld in late summer or autumn in the summer rainfall areas.

9 Fire may be used in Game Parks and other recreation areas to create habitats suited to certain game species and to induce game to graze otherwise non-preferred areas.

The objectives and consequences of the burn should be evaluated before including fire in a management system. It must also be remembered that the effects of fire are modified by climate, soil and in particular by use of the vegetation before and after the burn.

THE USE OF FIRE TO ACHIEVE MANAGEMENT OBJECTIVES

The relative areas of the various biomes in South Africa are fynbos 5%, karoo 32%, grassland 24%, savanna 34% and forest 5% (chapter 2). It is believed that the fynbos, grassland and savanna (63%) have been subject to frequent firing and the karoo and forest biomes (37%) to only sporadic fires over a long period of time (chapter 3). These frequency patterns among the biomes still exist today. The grassland and savanna biomes, which account for 92% of the frequently burnt areas, are used primarily by domestic herbivores but also for game farming and other activities. Thus the use of fire as a management tool has its greatest area of application in those systems concerned with domestic herbivores. In fynbos (5% of the area) fire also plays a significant role in achieving the management objectives of water and nature conservation and wild flower production. On the other hand, in the karoo, fire has management significance only following a succession of wet years and in the forest biome, its significance is solely related to the damage it does, or to its use in fire protection measures.

Burning is only one of many factors which influence vegetation composition and productivity. Its interaction with other management factors such as grazing and browsing must be considered and understood if optimum results are to be achieved by its incorporation into any system.

Proposals which follow for the use of fire in a number of systems of land use illustrate how various management objectives influence the choice of burning practice.

SYSTEMS WITH DOMESTIC GRAZERS AND BROWSERS

Optimum use of fire in grazing and browsing systems depends on the seasonal palatability of the veld, the stocking rate and consequently the intensity of utilization, the ratio of grazers to browsers, the plant species composition and vigour and the climatic conditions at each site.

Planning a burning programme on a farm starts with the planning of a grazing management and resting system. It is developed and modified, depending on the rate of plant growth and the stocking rates used over the whole season, until a final decision is made in winter.

Summer grazing practices which use all the available veld grass lead to veld deterioration. Experience in grassland indicates that 20 to 30% of the season's growth should remain unused at the end of summer on a well-managed farm. In good management systems which involve rotational grazing and resting, most of this ungrazed veld will be confined to specific areas of the farm, such as rested camps or camps due for a rest during the following season. Normally between a quarter and a third of the farm should be rested each year (Scott 1947). The mature unused material which remains on the veld (in August, in the summer rainfall area), if excessive, will lead to low animal intake in the short term and deterioration of the grazing value, particularly in sourveld, in the long term (sourveld and sweetveld differ primarily because the former is unpalatable when mature while mature material on sweetveld will normally be grazed). A burn will remove this material and improve the availability to grazing the new nutritious growth which normally follows burning. Rested areas and additional camps which it has not been possible to graze sufficiently during summer are candidates for burning if they are not used that winter. Similar considerations apply in the winter rainfall area where fire is used to remove obstructive unpalatable material and to stimulate palatable new growth (chapter 5). In both situations the old material can also be grazed off with the aid of supplementary licks (usually nitrogen) or mown, which achieves the same objective as burning and with fewer disadvantages (Scott 1947), and if veld is mown in the growing season, valuable hay can be provided. However, not all areas are mowable and because of relatively low yields the overhead costs and energy inputs of haymaking from veld tend to be excessive. Licks and sprays on winter veld may stimulate grazers' appetites and thus induce consumption of otherwise unpalatable material. However, as more acceptable plant species tend to be grazed more heavily than the unpalatable ones, the former may be detrimentally overgrazed.

These considerations apply to a lesser extent in mixed veld and sweetveld, because such veld is more subject to droughts and high summer temperatures and because the mature material is palatable, the need for burns to remove surplus material seldom arises. When burns are required in sweetveld for this or any other purpose, they should be followed by a rest of up to six months' duration.

When the camps scheduled for burning have been identified they should be burnt on a reasonably calm day, preferably with the wind (backburns result in higher temperatures at soil level than headburns and this may be more damaging to the grass cover). Suggested times for burning various vegetation types are discussed in the previous chapters. In practice, recommended burning times may be designed as much with an eye to postburning management, as to the direct effect of fire on the vegetation at different times. Veld can be badly damaged by grazing shortly after a burn. New growth is produced from plant reserves and if the area is grazed before an adequate leaf area has developed, subsequent regrowth is produced from an already depleted reserve source. This process continues with each subsequent grazing and the plant suffers the adverse effects of overuse. Also, the danger of overuse during the postburn period is very much dependent on the general fodder supply at this time, and so it may often be unwise to burn when fodder is likely to be in short supply for extended periods.

In veld types where browse is an important source of fodder (karoo and savanna) the effects of fire on browse species is important, in addition to its effect on the herbaceous layer. However, in the karoo vegetation types, because of the short stature of the browse plants and because of the general lack of fuel, fire seldom plays a useful role in management. Trollope (1978b) has, however, suggested that fire may play a role in eliminating some encroaching karroid species. In dry savanna, on the other hand, where browse can contribute considerably to livestock feed, much of the usable herbage may be above the browse line of domestic animals. At this stage these taller plants compete with the usable herbage for nutrients and water, but have only limited value for their pods and shade and it may be desirable to reduce their canopy height. In such areas herbaceous fuel may build up in high rainfall years and fire can be used advantageously to reduce the canopy level of browse plants. Such a fire must be preceded by a rest to obtain an adequate fuel load and must be followed by a long rest (six months at least depending on rainfall) to allow recovery of the herbaceous layer (Trollope 1980c). Browsing should then be allowed at an intensity which will maintain the browse plants in a productive condition and prevent them from again growing out of reach of the browsing animals.

In special circumstances, for example where undesirable species have invaded the ecosystems as a result of mismanagement, fire may be useful in the reclamation process. Examples of this are where fynbos (macchia) invades sourveld and where *Acacia* spp invade mixed veld or moist savanna. Fire aids in eliminating woody fynbos species from sourveld and *Acacia* spp may be eliminated from mixed veld and sweetveld with a low-cost combination of fire and goats (Trollope 1980c). An adequate fuel load is required to provide a hot, dry burn which, where the intention is to eliminate *Acacia* spp, is followed by continuous but controlled browsing by goats.

Thus, burning in a grazing system with domestic grazers and browsers is aimed at maintaining the optimum plant species composition, production and nutritional level so as to match the requirements of the herbivores. The ratio of grazers to browsers should be determined by the feed available, which can be manipulated to some extent by burning.

SYSTEMS WITH WILD GRAZERS AND BROWSERS

Included in this section are those systems in which the herbivore population is dominated by large to moderately large grazers and browsers which are able to exert a profound effect on the condition of the veld. The main objectives in managing such systems are to provide opportunities for hunting and game sighting and to manage for the production of meat and trophies.

Management systems used with grazers and browsers differ from those used for their domestic counterparts in two main respects. Firstly, it is seldom practical to erect internal fences which partition the veld into relatively homogeneous units for the control of area-selective grazing by wild animals. Secondly, a far wider spectrum of grazing and browsing habits are potentially available with game than with domestic herbivores.

The lack of internal fencing in the game situation results in either over-use of the whole area (from overstocking) or area selection of the vegetation at lower stocking rates. Because of large differences in palatability of different components of the vegetation in South Africa, it is impossible to obtain uniform use at any stocking rate short of a degree of use so high, that it results in basal cover decline and soil erosion. It may be theoretically possible to obtain uniform use with the variety of grazing and browsing habits of different species of South African game. Correct proportions of grazers (bulk roughage eaters and selective feeders) and browsers of different strata in relation to available herbage may even out the degree of grazing or browsing of different species in some seasons. However, seasonal variations in the production of various plant species, variations in the game population, the restricted supply of game of some species and veterinary consideration with respect to the use of other species, render such an exercise practically impossible. Restricted control of herd composition together with optimum placement of licks and water-points will aid in achieving even use. Nevertheless the system of continuous grazing of game in one paddock will inevitably result in uneven use, leading to a patchwork effect. If this is not corrected, the heavily used patches will increase in size, the vigour of the plants will decline and soil may begin to erode. Burning thus becomes almost essential in the wild herbivore system, even in sweetveld. Here fire is used to remove unpalatable, ungrazed herbage and to attract game to the palatable, nutritious flush after the burn.

This may relieve previously heavily used areas, although some game are very habitat specific and cannot be moved in this way. Allied to the use of fire to produce nutritious forage is its use in late summer and autumn to encourage an unseasonal flush of new growth for winter grazing. The well-being of essentially grazing species of game may largely depend on such practice in sourveld areas. However, the system is considered to be generally unacceptable because of the resulting soil exposure and potential for soil loss.

Burning to control plant invaders, to reduce the height of browse plants and to alter species composition also apply to areas allocated to wild game. The various vegetation communities must be burnt as dictated by their requirements (chapters 5 to 8). The same general principles of burning that apply to veld occupied by domestic herbivores also apply to that occupied by wild herbivores (such as burning in a season when vegetative recovery is rapid, and the need for an adequate fuel load and low humidity when controlling woody vegetation). However, because grazing and browsing after the burn cannot be controlled, it is necessary to burn large areas at any one time. The wild animals which are attracted to the burn are thus spread over a large area and do relatively little damage to the sprouting vegetation. Block burns of a quarter to half the area available are recommended, depending on the expected frequency of burning. On very large units more than one block should be burnt annually to cater for the species with small "home ranges" which it is intended to attract to the burn.

A combination of domestic bulk roughage eaters, such as mature steers, which should rotate within fenced camps, and wild herbivores to whom fences are no impediment and which roam over whole areas, would reduce the need for burning in game systems in the sweetveld.

Thus, while the objectives of burning a system for wild herbivores are similar to those for their domestic counterparts, since wild game movement cannot be controlled, fire must be used on a larger scale than is normally necessary for domestic herbivores.

SYSTEMS TO CREATE HABITATS FOR OTHER WILD ANIMALS

In this section the term "other wild animals" includes those animals which, though they have little direct impact on veld condition, depend on it for their survival. Although relatively little information is available on use of fire in the management of vegetation for such animals, Mentis and Rowe-Rowe (1979) have postulated a bimodal distribution in the species diversity and abundance of animals with respect to time elapsed since the last fire. Thus certain groups such as greywing francolin (*Francolinus africanus*) and redwing francolin (*F. levaillantii*) and small mammals occupy grasslands which are burnt frequently, while rednecked francolin (*F. afer*) occupy scrub which develops in the absence of fire. Similarly, it is probable that carnivores would seek protection in unburnt areas close to burnt areas which would provide food for grazing game. These classes of game are normally present on the same area as wild grazers and browsers. Burning frequencies in this situation would be adapted to the requirements of the class of game it is desired to encourage. If variety of animals is the main requirement then relatively frequently burnt areas should form a mosaic with unburnt areas, with the restriction that no burning practice should result in unacceptable amounts of soil erosion. A study of the preferred habitats of the desired species is a prerequisite to the design of any burning programme in such areas.

WILDERNESS AND RECREATION AREAS

In the first two systems discussed the objective of management was the maintenance of optimum amounts of usable herbage for herbivores. In this and the previous system, however, the objective tends to be the creation of vegetation diversity. While a uniform stand of grassland may be optimum for beef cattle, "game viewers" would soon tire of this scene.

In nature parks a wide variety of vegetation forms are needed to support a wide variety of animals, while in recreation and wilderness areas less game is found and the emphasis is on plant diversity and topographic variation. Because protection from fire or the application of fire at various times of the year or at different frequencies results in large variations in vegetation, fire is a powerful tool in achieving plant diversity. In order to provide maximum diversity at any point in time, it is desirable that most stages of the rotation be represented. Thus where a 20 yr fire rotation is practised (Bands 1977), the area should be subdivided into 20 compartments and one should be burnt each year.

Vegetation diversity also results from sharp topographic, soil and climatic variations, where a superimposed burning programme may further increase the diversity. For instance, parts of southern aspects, which favour forest development, could be protected from fire to allow forests to develop, while other portions of these slopes could be burnt occasionally to maintain a forest precursor stage. Vlei areas may be burnt in alternate halves to cater for birdlife, and similar considerations may be applied to the grasslands on the warmer northern aspect. These areas also provide a valuable pool of plant and animal genetic material.

In recreation areas burning in many seasons, even those considered undesirable in farming areas, might be the best means of achieving the desired diversity of vegetation. In previous chapters the effects of such fires on the vegetation and on soil and water loss have been discussed.

SYSTEMS FOR INCREASING WATER YIELD

Situations may exist in mountain catchments where the primary use of land is for water production. However, in the vast majority of instances water yield is but one factor in a multiple land-use system. In the Cape mountains water yield, conservation of resources, flower production and recreation are the main management objectives (Bands 1977). In other areas the water yield objective is combined with afforestation and certainly nearly all farmers require a sustained water yield from their properties.

Water for industry, urban use and farms is usually stored in dams or reservoirs. In South Africa, because of the seasonal nature of the rain which in the summer rainfall areas falls at high intensities over short periods, it is necessary to store water because stream flow is variable and normally inadequate. This applies particularly to the high rainfall eastern parts of the country with their steep topography. However, sustained water yield from catchments reduces the required storage capacity and cost, and so this should be encouraged. Here, burning practices for optimum quality and for sustained streamflow would be those which encourage a dense cover for the greatest part of the rain season (chapters 6, 14 and 15). Thus, management of the catchments must be aimed at obtaining a high infiltration and percolation rate as opposed to a rapid runoff rate in order to provide for sustained yield. Also, the effects of this management are not confined to the mountains but are also evident in the silt loads deposited in dams, estuaries and the sea.

Because burning affects the canopy and basal cover and species composition of vegetation it is a powerful tool in influencing the pattern of water release from a catchment. Even in the winter rainfall area, where the type of vegetation has little effect on infiltration because rainfall intensity is normally low and water percolates freely through the soil, the removal of vegetation by fire does, in the short term, increase streamflow because of reduced evapotranspiration (Bosch et al, this volume, chapter 15).

The frequency of burn required to achieve optimum patterns of water release from catchments and to meet other goals in multi-use systems may vary from annual burns in the Drakensberg (Edwards 1968) to burns once in 20 yr in arid parts of the western Cape (Bands 1977).

THE PROTECTION OF PROPERTY

Firebreaks are one of the most effective means of limiting the spread of fire in vegetation. A burnt area within a system also provides sanctuary for animals in time of fire. For firebreaks to be effective they must be burnt before the period of high fire hazard. Fire hazard rating systems, based on fuel loads, fuel moisture and climatic conditions, are employed in some areas as an aid in fire control (Bosch and Rogers 1980).

In summer rainfall areas firebreaks are usually burnt in early winter. In frost areas, burning before frosts makes it difficult to achieve a clean burn while burning after frosts requires considerable care. In order to simplify the procedure of burning firebreaks, several techniques have been developed. Trollope (1979) lists burnt, mown, cultivated and herbicide strips as aids to burning firebreaks. He also lists the advantages and disadvantages of each method and the procedures that should be followed. The continued application of firebreaks and strips to the same site year after year can lead to deterioration of the vegetation on these sites, particularly when they are open to grazing. To overcome this, firebreaks should be rested frequently and be protected from grazing.

Periodic controlled fires with the specific intention of reducing fuel load and consequently frequency and intensity of wildfires have a place in many systems where the herbage is not intensively used (Haigh 1977).

SYSTEMS IN WHICH PLANTS ARE HARVESTED FOR DIRECT SALE

Some veld flowers, particularly those in fynbos, are picked and sold commercially, and veld plants are used for medicines, herbal teas, perfumes, thatching and haymaking. The optimum fire management for each of these uses varies. Many of the spring geophytes will not flower on areas not burnt annually, while proteaceous communities require fire at less frequent intervals unless they are to be succeeded by taller communities (chapters 5 and 13). The reduced hay yields obtained from burnt as opposed to unburnt veld have been discussed in chapter 11. Similar reductions in yield have been recorded on planted pastures (Smit 1969).

AS AN AID TO THE INTRODUCTION OF EXOTICS

Although fire is often used to control undesirable invading species (chapters 5 to 8) it also aids in introducing improved exotics into the veld. Burning together with other manipulations of the cover and soil is used, for example, to aid in the establishment of overseeded pastures (Edwards 1978).

FIRE LEGISLATION

In view of the potential value of fire as a management tool over much of South Africa and the detrimental effects which often accompany its misuse, leglislative control has been introduced. Essentially, this control has been based on an acknowledgement of the role of fire in achieving only some of the objectives listed earlier in this chapter. For example, it is accepted as a means of removing surplus vegetative material, of reducing fuel load and so the intensity and frequency of accidental fires, for making firebreaks, to control changes in plant composition, both in the herbaceous layer and in the control of woody species, to facilitate the introduction of exotic plant species, to improve the acceptability and nutritional value of forage produced by certain communities, to control water production from catchments, to assist in the creation of specific habitats for different species of wildlife and to assist in inducing the movement of large game. Many of these objectives are interrelated and a number can often be achieved simultaneously within the same

burning programme. However, throughout, control is often needed
to ensure that fire is used wisely and hence the need for legis-
lative control.

Burning of vegetation over most of the Republic of South
Africa is governed by two acts of Parliament. These are "The
Forestry Act" (No 72 of 1968) and the "Soil Conservation Act" (No
76 of 1969). Further legislation pertaining to specific areas is
also contained in other acts such as the "National Parks Act" (No
57 of 1976), the "Mountain Catchment Areas Act" (No 13 of 1970)
and various other local ordinances.

THE FORESTRY ACT

The prevention of wild-fires and the restriction of damage
caused by them would appear to be the main objective of this
act. The act states that the Minister of Forestry may prohibit
open-air fires in specified areas by proclamation in the Government Gazette, and that the owner, occupier or person in charge of
any land is required to clear a fire-belt on the common boundary
with other properties but the Minister may prohibit the use of
fire for this purpose at certain times. In Natal, for example,
no burning of slash or boundary fire-belts is usually permitted
during the particularly dangerous period from 1 August to 31
October inclusive, nor are fires allowed (except in demarcated
areas) between 16h00 on Fridays and 06h00 on Mondays because of
the lack of sufficient supervision often associated with weekend
burning. Similar restrictions apply in the forest areas of the
eastern Transvaal. The act also defines the procedures for burning and penalties for transgression (Anon 1968) in an attempt to
reduce the frequencies of runaway fires.

THE SOIL CONSERVATION ACT

The object of this act is to regulate the burning of "grasslands" in order to obtain optimum use and to guard against burning practices which would lead to increased soil erosion. This
act makes provision for the declaration of fire protection areas,
schemes and committees.

The committee may propose to the Minister of Agriculture schemes
for:

(a) the regulation of prohibition of veld burning and (b) the
prevention, control and extinguishing of veld and forest fires,
provided that (c) no such proposals are in conflict with the
Forestry Act. (Several committees have been appointed in the
Cape Fynbos biome in order to monitor the administration of this
act) (Anon 1969).

General provisions in line with the objectives of the Soil
Conservation Act have been published under notice R495 of
26/3/1970. With regard to veld burning these are:-

"Subject to the provisions of the Forest Act, 1968 –

(1)   sweet grassveld may not be burnt except where this is necessary for the control of invader plants on veld sufficiently rested beforehand;

(2)   mixed and sour grassveld types may be burnt only if –

   (a)   rested for the full preceding growing season or if a considerable amount of plant material has accumulated, the moisture content of soil is sufficient to allow veld growth, and the veld already shows early signs of sprouting; or if
   (b)   burning is necessary for the control of invader plants on veld sufficiently rested beforehand;

(3)   veld in fire protection areas declared in terms of the Soil Conservation Act may be burnt only in accordance with the provisions of the fire protection scheme applicable to such areas; and

(4)   macchia (fynbosveld) outside fire protection areas may be burnt only in accordance with such directions as the Minister may from time to time declare applicable to such veld" (Anon 1970).

Various regions have published guidelines as aids in interpreting these provisions. For example, the latest from Natal (which are frequently amended as new research results become available) are summarized in Table 1 and are supplemented by a number of notes.

These are supplemented by further recommendations to the Soil Conservation Committee:-

1   That the last date for burning may be brought forward at least 15 days (ie in cold moist areas from 15th October to 30th September).

2   A dry burn during August be allowed in exceptional cases in the cool moist grassveld areas, but only on veld rested from January to the end of May. Such permission to be granted on written application only, and in areas where such requests are normally made, farmers should be informed of the conditions.

3   No more than a third of the veld on a farm should be burnt before 31st August in cold moist areas or 31st July in the warm moist areas, and no more than two thirds of the veld on a farm should be burnt in any one year.

Table 1   Summarized veld burning guidelines for Natal, 1979 (Anon 1979b).

| Area | Burning permitted | |
	After rain	Without rain
1. Warm, moist grassveld (>800 mm on sourveld and mixed veld)	1 July–15 Sept (>15 mm in 24 hr)[a]	1 Aug–15 Sept
2. Cool, moist grassveld (>800 mm on sourveld and mixed veld)	1 Aug –15 Oct (>15 mm in 24 hr)	1 Sept–15 Oct
3. Dry tall grassveld (<800 mm on mixed veld) upland	15 Aug – 31 Oct (>25 mm in 24 hr)	Nil
vleis	1 Aug –31 Oct	1 Aug–31 Oct
4. Dry thornveld (<800 mm on sweetveld)	Only with permission in exceptional circumstances	

[a]Burning permitted only after 15 mm of rain have fallen in a period of 24 hr.

Notes:

1   Grazing burnt veld too early can cause more damage than the burn itself. Therefore burnt sourveld or mixed veld may be grazed only after sufficient regrowth to permit normal rotational grazing practices (ie a minimum regrowth of 10 cm of most of the new leaves).

2   Sweetveld which is burnt shall not be grazed by primarily grass-eating domestic livestock before the majority of grasses are in the full flower stage and have attained a leaf height of 25 cm.

3   Veld may be burnt under exceptional circumstances and at other times than are specified for the areas mentioned above only after written application (stating the reasons for burning) has been made to and written permission has been obtained from the Department of Agriculture after consultation with the local Soil Conservation Committee.

4   It is noted that northern and western aspects are particularly vulnerable to mismanagement and should be considered carefully when granting exemptions, particularly when included in same camp as other aspects.

5   No general exemption to the burning regulations should be made without consultation with all other Chief Extension Officers". (Anon 1979b).

The Soil Conservation Act also makes provision for "directions" to be applied to land (usually that which has been misused) with regard to actions such as the time and frequency of burning.

In the Kruger National Park "according to the present policy almost 80% of the Park shall be burnt every three or four years, in rotation. These burns will be applied alternatively before rain in spring, after rain in the spring and in mid-summer. Each year, burnt blocks are scattered over the whole park. Certain areas are burnt annually or bienially in spring and autumn (mainly Pretoriuskop and Punda Maria areas) and riverbanks and other areas where the grass cover is sparse, will be burnt less frequently (from 4 to 8 yr). Areas set aside as 'Wilderness areas' will receive no fire treatment other than fire caused by lightning" (Gertenbach 1979).

The main objectives of these regulations are to supply short grazing for the declining black wildebeest *(Connochaetes gnou)* and Burchell's zebra *(Equus burchelli)* populations, facilitate burning management and minimize the detrimental effects of erratic spring rains on recently burnt veld (Gertenbach 1979).

In the mountain fynbos of the Cape, the Department of Forestry policy calls for prescribed burning in a rotation of about 12 yr. Burns are normally applied in late summer, although some flexibility in choice of rotation and season is permitted, particularly while large tracts of largely unused veld still exist. Certain types of ecosystems such as relict forests in kloofs, "the true sponges," and the higher peaks, often snow-covered in winter, are not to be burnt, nor are catchments in dry areas (Bands 1977).

These examples show how the appropriate fire legislation in three biomes (grassveld, savanna and fynbos) has been applied to suit the optimum land use for each site.

It is of interest to note that much of the legislation has been amended within the last 10 yr to cater for more recent research results and policies. Whereas fire was at one time almost totally prohibited (chapter 4), the value of controlled burning is now recognized (chapters 4 to 8). The regular amendment of veld burning guidelines in recent years indicates that both legislators and scientists accept that veld burning legislation must allow for the specific requirements of each site and each type of land use.

Concluding Remarks.
Fire Research – A Perspective for the Future

P. DE V. BOOYSEN

Whatever good may eventuate from the preparation and publication of this book, one important benefit will surely be the realization amongst ecologists that there is much still not known, and to be learnt, regarding the ecology of fire in the biomes of South Africa. Certainly, for some this realization will not be a new experience, either because of an earlier acknowledgement of ignorance or because of a state of penetrating insight and wisdom. However, equally certainly, there are many practising ecologists, probably mainly in the field of agriculture, forestry and conservation, who have been of the view that this management tool, fire, has been well researched and consequently is well understood. This belief probably emanates from the circumstances of fairly narrow management objectives and of familiarity with a specific ecological system. I believe the preceding chapters will have dispelled the notion that fire as an ecological factor is well understood. In certain circumstances, particularly certain management circumstances, fire as a tool may be fairly well researched and, as a consequence, present little difficulty in the successful management of the specific system, but the mechanisms of action of fire as a factor in the ecology of the varied and ever-changing biomes which constitute South Africa, are clearly very imperfectly understood. Indeed, not only in terms of mechanisms but also in terms of effects on the structural and functional dynamics of the ecosystem, is there still much to be learnt. Hopefully this book will stimulate further research in the quest for a more complete understanding of our biomes and the myriad ecosystems of which they are composed. Appropriately then, these remarks will focus on the gaps in our knowledge of fire ecology in an attempt to aid in the development of programmes seeking a better understanding of the ecological effects and mechanisms of fire.

It would be possible, at least theoretically, to construct from the contents of all the preceding chapters a list of influences and processes related to the occurrence of fire in our biomes and requiring elucidation in review of the various authors. Apart from being difficult, the compilation of such a list in any comprehensive or complete manner would be tedious and hardly helpful to prospective researchers. Instead, it is my intention to discuss fire in the perspective of the structural and functional elements of the ecosystem – no particular ecosystem. Such an approach will hopefully focus attention on the holistic nature of the ecosystem – a viewpoint essential to the understanding of these complex systems. While there is value in research programmes which study individual ecological factors in isolation from other variables, and assess the effects of these factors on specific components of the ecosystem in isolation of other components, such narrowly designed and executed programmes of research tend to overlook the interactive

nature of the multiple elements of the ecosystem. The wider
vision is essential to the better understanding of the ecosystem
itself and also the influence upon the system of the factors
which are part of the whole.

Before the influences of fire upon the stucture and function
of the ecosystem can be meaningfully studied it is necessary to
be able to describe fire itself in the full range of its forms -
and preferably quantitatively. And, in turn, this process of
description, if it is to be unambiguous, requires a clear and
precise terminology. If there is to be effective communication
amongst fire ecologists, if effects of particular fires are to be
meaningfully compared and if universal principles regarding the
effects of fire are to be developed, then both the fire and its
effects must be measured and reported in comparable terms. In
the literature terms such as fire regime, fire behaviour, fire
intensity, fire characteristics, and many others are variously
used, sometimes defined, and then not consistently. This is not
helpful to an understanding of fire and its ecological effects.
If terms such as characteristics and behaviour were used in the
general and colloquial sense then little harm would be done.
However, in an effort to become quantitative these terms have
become defined with respect to their components and in the
absence of consistency, confusion develops. Fire intensity, for
example, seems to me to be inappropriately defined as an element
of fire regime. Rate of spread of fire has been defined as a
component of both fire behaviour and fire characteristics - so,
too, fire intensity. Thus, this subject of fire terminology is
deserving of critical evaluation and standardization.

There can be no doubt that an adequate and preferably quantitative description of all fires in accordance with a standard
terminology, such as that suggested above, would assist materially in identifying its role in the ecosystem.

Perhaps it would be useful to define **Fire Regime** in terms of
the frequency, season and time of fires which are characteristic
of the area. **Fire Circumstances** relate to the environment within
which the fire occurs and could be described in terms of the fuel
properties of the vegetation, the weather conditions at the time
and the physiography of the site. **Fire Types** could be descript-
ively defined either according to vegetation or fuel type being
burnt (eg grass fire, bush fire), according to layer of fuel
being burnt (eg crown fire, surface fire) or according to the
direction of the fire in relation to the direction of the wind
(eg head fire, back fire). The term **Fire Characteristics** could
be used to describe the flame in the spatial sense - the major
variables being size (height, depth and length), shape (angle)
and pattern (the progressive change in size and shape over
time). On the other hand, **Fire Behaviour** could reasonably refer
to dynamic properties such as rate of spread, the energy profile
and the rate of energy release (intensity). Then, of course, the
Fire Effects would include all the consequences of the fire on
all components and functions of the ecosystem. These six phrases
seem to adequately cover the variables of fire which have relev-
ance to a study of its ecological role in ecosystems. A greater
consistency in the use of these terms, perhaps on the basis of
the above definitions, would facilitate communication and understanding in this field.

This kind of information is urgently needed in the South African situation. It would not be difficult for all fire researchers to agree on a Terminology, a quantitative formulation of each parameter and a field procedure for measurement of the elements contained in the formulation so that fires, wherever and whenever they occur, can be monitored. This will aid not only the documentation of the variability of fire but also in the interpretation and prediction of the effects of fires according to their properties.

The ecosystems in which fire occurs must, in the first instance, be seen as an integrated system of structural components and functional processes. The **structural** components of the ecosystem can be broadly classified as abiotic or biotic. The abiotic component is constituted of the physical environment comprising the soil and atmosphere (climate). Each of the soil and atmosphere, in turn, shows a precise and complex structure. The biotic component of the system is comprised of the living assemblage of biological organisms - plants, animals and micro-organisms. These, too, are structurally complex and can be variously classified. The ecologist often finds it useful to classify them in terms of producers, consumers and decomposers according to their fundamental function in the ecosystem. All these structural components of the system, abiotic and biotic, are both inter-dependent and interactive.

It is primarily in the **functions** within the ecosystem that the essential inter-dependence of the structural components, and thus the unity of the ecosystem, is revealed. Three primary functional threads link inextricably the components of a typical terrestrial ecosystem - the flow of energy through the components of the system, the flow of water through the system, and the flow of nutrients.

We tend to see man as outside of, and not an integral part of, the ecosystem. It is true that the ecosystems with which we deal today developed under conditions of little or no influence by pre-settlement man. But, wherever he occurred he formed part of the biotic structure of the ecosystem and influenced the intergrative functions of the ecosystem in no less significant a way than the other biotic components. Today the influence of man is far more drastic - some of his activities are more akin to perturbations than influences. But he is none the less an inherent part of the ecosystem and each of his actions must be seen in terms of its effects upon all structural and functional elements of the system. Seldom do any of his acts of ecosystem management cause less than a ripple through the cyclical functions of the system and consequent modifications of the structural components. More often his influences take the form of drastic perturbations in respect of one of the structural or functional elements of the system, producing a shudder through all the functions linking all the structures. His tools in these actions are varied, including the axe, the mower and fire. So in this sense fire is part of the arsenal of the biotic component of the ecosystem.

However, fire is not always to be seen as a tool of man. Fires are sometimes caused by lightning, and have been for as long as there has been lightning and inflammable vegetation. In this sense, then, fire must be seen as a climatic factor, like hail or snow, and not of biotic origin. Here too the effect of fire can be equally traumatic, irrespective of the energy source. But, despite this, fire still remains a factor inherent in the ecosystem and not external to it.

The purpose of this elaboration of the nature of the ecosystem and the plea for fire to be seen as part of the ecosystem, is to emphasize that any future research on the ecological effects of fire will be the less successful if it is designed and interpreted on the basis of a factor/product relationship without due regard to the complexities of the integrated multiple factor - multiple process system. The starting point in many future fire research programmes will continue to be direct and apparently simplistic - as in the factor/product relationship. Examples could well be an investigation into the effects of spring burning of various frequencies on the botanical composition of savanna communities or the influence of infrequent burning on biotic succession in the humid grasslands. The objectives of such research programmes may well be narrowly defined but the full value of such research will be achieved only if the nature of the fire is carefully and quantitatively described in terms of regime, circumstance, type, characteristics, behaviour and effect; and, further, if the effects are measured in terms not only of the immediate impact on the fauna and flora but in terms of the cyclical functions and interrelated structures which constitute the ecosystem.

Clearly then, the key to a better understanding of the effects of fire upon the ecosystem lies in the elucidation of the influences of fire upon the functional processes within the system. Very little research in the past has been directed toward these fundamental relationships - the influence of fire on the energy cycle in the ecosystem; its influence on the hydrological cycle in the ecosystem; and its influence on the bio-geochemical cycle in the ecosystem. Only when these relationships are better understood will we be getting close to the heart of the matter. However, even then the complete understanding will not be achieved. Only when the relationship of these intergrative cyclical functions to the structural dynamics of the system is understood will the ecosystem be sufficiently well understood to clarify the nature and mechanism of the influence of fire upon the system. All ecological research, however narrow and specific its immediate objectives, should be perceived in the perspective of these central functional threads of the ecosystem.

References

Acocks J P H   1975.   Veld types of South Africa.   Memoirs of the Botanical Survey of South Africa 40, 1-128.

Adamson R S   1935.   The plant communities of Table Mountain III.   A six years' study of regeneration after burning.   Journal of Ecology 23, 44-55.

Agricola   1947.   Geskiedenis van veldbrand in die Unie.   Landbouweekblad 31 Desember, 47.

Agricola   1948.   Uit die geskiedenis van die veldbrand verskil. Landbouweekblad 8 Desember, 64-65.

Ahlgren I F   1974.   The effect of fire on soil organisms.   In: Kozlowski T T and Ahlgren C E (eds)   Fire and ecosystems.   Academic Press, New York, pp 47-92.

Ahlgren I F and Ahlgren C E   1960.   Ecological effects of forest fires. Botanical Review 26, 483-533.

Ahlgren I F and Ahlgren C E   1965.   Effects of prescribed burning on soil microorganisms in a Minnesota jack pine forest. Ecology 46, 304-310.

Albini F A   1976.   Estimating wildfire behaviour and effects.   USDA Forest Service General Technical Report INT-30.

Alexander M   1961.   Introduction to soil microbiology.   Wiley, New York, 239 pp.

Anderson K L   1965.   Time of burning as it affects soil moisture in an ordinary upland bluestem prairie in the Flint Hills.   Journal of Range Management 18, 311-316.

Anderson R B   1965a.   Lightning research in the power electrical engineering field.   CSIR National Institute of Mathematical Science, Power Electrical Engineering Division Formal Colloquium series 1966, No. 6.

Anderson R B, van Niekerk H R, Meal D V and Smith M A   1978.   Tenth Progress Report on the development and testing of lightning flash counters in the Republic of South Africa during 1977/78.   CSIR Special Report ELEK 148 National Electrical Engineering Research Institute, CSIR, Pretoria 1978.

Andrag R H   1977.   Studies in die Sederberge oor (i) die status van die Clanwilliam Sedar *Widdringtonia cedarbergenis* Marsh (ii) buite-lugontspanning. MSc Thesis, University of Stellenbosch.

Anon   1934.   Journal of the Mountain Club of South Africa 37, 8.

Anon   1961.   Veld burning in the karoo mountains with special reference to sour grassveld areas.   Farming in South Africa 37(5), 36-37.

Anon   1968.   The Forest Act 72 of 1968. Government Printer, Pretoria.

Anon   1969.   Soil Conservation Act 76 of 1969.   Government Printer, Pretoria.

Anon   1970.   General provisions in pursuance of the objects of the Soil Conservation Act, 1959. No R495. Government Printer, Pretoria.

Anon 1974.   Annual report, N-U1 21.   Department of Pasture Science, University of Natal.

368

Anon 1977. Thunderstorms. Lightning - the second piece of a pattern. Scientiae 18(4), 12-25.

Anon 1979a. Cutting down the wood with the trees. New Scientist 81 (1143), 557.

Anon 1979b. New veld burning guidelines: Natal region: 1979. Department Agricultural Technical Services, Natal Region, Cedara.

Anon 1973/74. Progress report N-U1 21. Department of Pasture Science, University of Natal.

Arend J L 1941. Infiltration rates of forest soils in the Missouri Ozarks are affected by woods burning and litter removal. Journal of Forestry 39, 726-728.

Aucamp A J, Howe L G, Smith D W W Q and Mostert J M 1978. Die struik-weidingswaarde van die Oos-Kaap-valleibosveld. Proceedings of the Grassland Society of Southern Africa 13, 91-93.

Austen B 1971. The history of veld burning in the Wankie National Park, Rhodesia. Proceedings of the Tall Timbers Fire Ecology Conference 11, 277-296.

Austin R C and Baisinger D H 1955. Some effects of burning on forest soils of western Oregon and Washington. Journal of Forestry 53, 275-280.

Backhouse J 1844. A narrative of a visit to the Mauritius and South Africa. Hamilton, Adams and Co, London.

Bagshawe-Smith L 1937. Rhenoster bush in the district of Albany. South African Journal of Science 33, 355.

Bands D P 1977. Prescribed burning in Cape fynbos catchments. In: Mooney H A and Conrad C E (technical coordinators) Proceedings of the symposium on the environmental consequences of fire and fuel management in Mediterranean ecosystems (August 1-5, 1977, Palo Alto, California). USDA Forest Service General Technical Report WO-3, Washington D C, 245-256.

Bands D P 1980. Policy memorandum for the Cedarberg Mountain catchment area. Department of Water Affairs, Forestry and Environmental Conservation.

Banks C H 1961. The hydrological effects of riparian and adjoining vegetation. Forestry in South Africa 1, 31-45.

Banks C H 1962. Effects of phreatic vegetation on baseflow in selected Jonkershoek streams. MSc Thesis, University of Stellenbosch.

Banks C H 1964. Further notes on the effect of autumnal veld burning on stormflow in the Abdolskloof catchment, Jonkershoek. Forestry in South Africa 4, 79-84.

Bayer A W 1955. The ecology of grasslands. In: Meredith D (ed) The grasses and pastures of South Africa. Central News Agency, Union of South Africa, pp 539-550.

Beadle N C W 1940. Soil temperatures during forest fires and their affect on the survival of vegetation. Journal of Ecology 28, 180-192.

Bean P A 1962. An enquiry into the effects of veld fires on certain geophytes. MSc Thesis, University of Cape Town.

Beard J S 1961. Further evidence on burning versus non-burning in wattle silviculture. Journal of the South African Forestry Association 38, 7-10.

Beard J S and Darby G D 1951. An experiment on burning in wattle silviculture. Journal of the South African Forestry Association 20, 53-77.

Beaton J D 1959. The influence of burning on the soil in the timber range area of Lac Le Jeune, British Columbia. Canadian Journal of Soil Science 39, 1-11.

Beaufait W R 1965. Characteristics of backfires and headfires in a pine needle fuel bed. US Forest Service Research Note INT-30.

Beaumont P B 1978. Border cave. MA Thesis, University of Cape Town.

Bentley J R and Fenner R L 1958. Soil temperatures during burning related to postfire seedbeds on woodland range. Journal of Forestry 56, 737-740.

Berry A and Macdonald I A W 1979. Fire regime characteristics in the Hluhluwe-Corridor-Umfolozi Game Reserve Complex in Zululand I. Area description and an analysis of causal factors and seasonal incidence of fire in the central complex with particular reference to the period 1955 to 1978. Unpublished report.

Bews J W 1916. An account of the chief types of vegetation in South Africa, with notes on the plant succession. Journal of Ecology 4, 129-159.

Bews J W 1925. Plant forms and their evolution in South Africa. Longmans, London.

Bigalke R C 1978. Mammals. In: Werger M J A (ed) Biogeography and ecology of southern Africa. Junk, The Hague, pp 981-1048.

Bigalke R C 1979. Aspects of vertebrate life in fynbos, South Africa. In: Specht R L (ed) Ecosystems of the World, Vol 9A. Heathlands and related shrublands. Descriptive Studies. Elsevier, Amsterdam, pp 81-95.

Bigalke R C and Pepler D 1979. Unpublished records. Department of Nature Conservation, University of Stellenbosch.

Bishop E J B 1980. Unpublished data. Faculty of Agriculture, University of Fort Hare, Alice.

Biswell H H 1974. Effects of fire on chaparral. In: Kozlowski T T and Ahlgren C E (eds) Fire and ecosystems. Academic Press, New York, pp 321-364.

Blommaert K L J 1972. Buchu seed germination. Journal of South African Botany 38, 237-239.

Blommaert K L J and Bartel E 1976. Chemotaxonomic aspects of the buchu species *Agathosma betulina* Pillans and *A. crenulata* Pillans from local planting. Journal of South African Botany 42, 121-126.

Bond W J 1979. Unpublished research reports.

Bond W J 1980. Fire and senescent fynbos in the Swartberg, southern Cape. South African Forestry Journal 114, 68-71.

Bond W, Ferguson M and Forsyth G 1980. Small mammals and habitat structure along altitudinal gradients in the southern Cape mountains. South African Journal of Zoology 15, 34-43.

Booysen P de V, Tainton N M and Scott J D 1963. Shoot apex development in grasses and its importance in grassland management. Herbage Abstracts 33, 209-213.

Borman F H and Likens G E 1979. Pattern and process in a forested ecosystem. Springer-Verlag, 253 pp.

Bosch J M and Rogers F 1980. Fire hazard rating system for Natal. Mimeo.

Bosch J M 1979. Treatment effects on annual and dry period streamflow at Cathedral Peak. South African Forestry Journal 108, 29-38.

Bosch J M 1980. 'n Ontleding van die hidrologiese eksperimente in die Cathedral Peak opvanggebiede. MSc Thesis, University of Stellenbosch.

Bosch J M and Hewlett J D 1981. A review of catchment experiments to determine the effect of vegetation changes on water yield and evapotranspiration. Journal of Hydrology 55, 3-23.

Botha C G 1924. Note on early veld burning in the Cape Colony. South African Journal of Science 21, 351-352.

Botha J P 1938. The digestibility and nutritive value of Karoo pasture plants. Farming in South Africa February to November 1938.

Botha J P 1945. Veld management in the Eastern Transvaal. Farming in South Africa 20, 537-541.

Botha J P 1953. Veldbeheerstudies op die suurveld van Oos-Transvaal. DSc Thesis, University of Pretoria.

Boucher C and McCann G D 1975. The *Orothamnus* saga. Veld and Flora 61, 2-5.

Broadley D G 1966. The herpetology of south-east Africa. PhD Thesis, University of Natal.

Bronowski J 1973. The ascent of man. British Broadcasting Corporation, London.

Brooks H 1876. Natal; a history and description of the colony. Reeve and Co, London.

Brooks P M 1974. The ecology of the four-striped field mouse, *Rhabdomus pumilio* (Sparrman, 1784), with particular reference to a population on the van Riebeeck Nature Reserve, Pretoria. DSc Thesis, University of Pretoria.

Brooks P M and Berry A 1980. The responses of 18 ungulate species to fire in the central complex, Zululand, between October 1975 and September 1977. Unpublished report, CSIR.

Brown A A and Davis K P 1973. Forest fire: control and use. McGraw-Hill, New York.

Brown J C 1875. Hydrology of South Africa. Henry King and Co, London, 260 pp.

Brown J C 1877. Water supply of South Africa. Oliver & Boyd, Edinburgh.

Brown N A C and van Staden J 1971. Germination inhibitors in aqueous seed extracts of four South African Proteaceae. Journal of South African Botany 37, 305-315.

Brown N A C and van Staden J 1973. The effect of scarification, leaching, light, stratification, oxygen and applied hormones on germination of *Protea compacta* R. Br. and *Leucadendron daphnoides* Meisn. Journal of South African Botany 39, 185-195.

Bryant A T 1949. The Zulu people as they were before the white man came. Shuter and Shooter, Pietermaritzburg.

Brynard A M 1964. The influence of veld burning on the vegetation and game of the Kruger National Park. In: Davis D H S (ed) Ecological studies in southern Africa. Junk, The Hague, pp 371-393.

Brynard A M 1971. Controlled burning in the Kruger National Park - history and development of a veld burning policy. Proceedings of the Tall Timbers Fire Ecology Conference 11, 219-321.

Brynard A M and Pienaar U de V 1960. Annual Report of the biologist, Kruger National Park. Veld burning. Koedoe 3, 173-194.

Buckhouse J C and Gifford G F 1976. Sediment production and infiltration rates as affected by grazing and debris burning of chained and seeded pinyon-juniper. Journal of Range Management 29, 83-85.

Bunting C B and Wright H A 1974. Ignition capabilities of non-flaming firebrands. Journal of Forestry 72, 10.

Burchell W J 1822. Travels in the interior of southern Africa, vol 1. Longman, Hurst, Rees, Orme and Brown, London.

Burger A E, Siegfried W R and Frost P G H 1976. Nest-site selection in the Cape sugarbird. Zoologica Africana 11, 127-158.

Burtt E D 1951. The ability of adult grasshoppers to change colour on burnt ground. Proceedings of the Royal Entomological Society of London (A) 26, 45-48.

Burtt-Davy J 1922. The suffrutescent habit as an adaptation to environment. Journal of Ecology 10, 211-219.

Byram G M 1959. Combustion of forest fuels. In: Davis K P (ed) Forest fire control and use. McGraw-Hill, New York, pp 61-89.

Cable J H C, Scott K and Carter P L   1980.   Excavations at Good Hope Shelter, Underberg District, Natal.   Annals of the Natal Museum 24, 1-34.

Cameron M J   1980.   Fynbos islands in the Knysna forests.   South African Forestry Journal 112, 27-29.

Campbell B M and van der Meulen F   1980.   Patterns of plant species diversity in fynbos vegetation, South Africa.   Vegetatio 43, 43-47.

Carlquist S   1977.   A revision of Grubbiaceae.   Journal of South African Botany 43, 115-128.

Carpenter F L and Recher H F   1979.   Pollination, reproduction and fire.   American Naturalist 133, 871-879.

Carter P L   1970.   Late Stone Age exploitation patterns in southern Natal.   South African Archaeological Bulletin 25, 55-59.

Carter P L   1978.   The prehistory of eastern Lesotho.   PhD Thesis, Downing College, Cambridge University.

Cass A   1978.   Chemical characteristics of selected plots at the Ukulinga long-term burning trials.   Unpublished report, Department of Soil Science and Agrometeorology, University of Natal, 1-4.

Cass A and Collins M   1983.   Effect of burning and mowing on soil physical and chemical properties, paper in preparation.

Cesar J   1971.   Etude quantitatife de la strate herbac e de la savane de Lamto (moyenne Cote d'Ivoire).   Th se de Doctorat de 3e cycle, Paris, 125 pp.

Chapman J D and White F   1970.   The evergreen forests of Malawi.   Commonwealth Forestry Institute, Oxford University Press.

Cheney N P   1981.   Fire behaviour.   In: Gill A M, Groves R H, and Noble I R (eds)   Fire in the Australian biota.   Australian Academy of Science, Canberra, pp 151-175.

Cheney N P and Vines undated.   Recommended units for fire research.   CSIRO, Australia.

Christensen N L   1973.   Fire and the nitrogen cycle in California chaparral.   Science 181, 66-68.

Christensen N L and Muller C H   1975.   Effects of fire on factors controlling plant growth in Adenostoma chaparral.   Ecolological Monograph 45, 29-55.

Christian D P   1977a.   Effects of fire on small mammal populations in a desert grassland.   Journal of Mammalogy 58, 423-427.

Christian D P   1977b.   Diurnal activity of the four-striped mouse *Rhabdomys pumilio*.   Zoologica Africana 12, 238-239.

Christian D P   1979.   Comparative demography of three Namib desert rodents: responses to provision of supplementary water.   Journal of Mammalogy 60, 679-690.

Cilliers P J H   1972.   Population structure and social relationships in a confined population of multimammate mice, *Praomys (Mastomys) natalensis*.   MSc Thesis, University of Pretoria.

Clancey P A   1964.   The birds of Natal and Zululand.   Oliver and Boyd.

Clark F E and Paul E A   1970.   The microflora of grassland.   Advanced Agronomy 22, 375-435.

Clark G C and Dickson C G C   1971.   Life histories of the South African Lycaenid butterflies.   Purnell, Cape Town.   272 pp.

Clark J D   1959.   The prehistory of southern Africa.   Penguin Books, London.

Clark J D   1969.   Kalambo Falls prehistoric site, vol 1.   Cambridge University Press, Cambridge.

Clark O R   1940.   Interception of rainfall by prairie grasses, grasses, weeds and certain crop plants.   Ecolological Monographs 10, 243-277.

372

Clary W P, Malchus B B Jr, O'Connel P F, Johnson T N Jr, and Campbell R E
1974. Effects of pinyon-juniper removal on natural resource products
and uses in Arizona. USDA Forestry Service Research Paper, RM-128.
Rocky Mountain Forest and Range Experimental Station, Fort Collins,
Colorado, 1-28.

Clements F E 1916. Plant succession. Carnegie Institute, Washington,
Publication 242.

Clements F E 1936. Nature and structure of the climax. Journal of
Ecology 24, 552-584.

Cody M L 1975. Towards a theory of continental species diversities: bird
distribution over mediterranean habitat gradients. In: Cody M L and
Diamond J M (eds) Ecology and evolution of communities. Kelknap
Press, Harvard University, Cambridge, Massachusetts, pp 214-257.

Coetzee C G 1969. The distribution of mammals in the Namib desert and
adjoining inland escarpment. Science Papers Namib Desert Research
Station 40, 23-36.

Coetzee P J S 1942. Fire and veld management. Veld burning as an agent
in the "ngongoni" sourveld. Forestry of South Africa 17, 107-116.

Cohen C 1937. *Stoebe vulgaris*, Levyns. MSc Thesis, Witwatersrand
University.

Cohen C 1949. The occurrence of fungi in the soil after different
grazing and burning treatments of the veld. Part 1. South African
Journal of Science 46, 260-265.

Coles J M and Higgs E S 1969. The archaeology of early man. Faber and
Faber, London.

Colinvaux P A 1973. Introduction to ecology. Wiley, New York.

Commission of Enquiry into Water Matters, Republic of South Africa 1970.
Official report. Government Printer, Pretoria.

Conklin H C 1969. An ethnoecological approach to shifting agriculture.
In: Vayda A P (ed) Environment and cultural behaviour. The Natural
History Press, New York, pp 221-233.

Connell J H 1978. Diversity in tropical rain forests and coral reefs.
Science 199, 1302-1310.

Connell J H and Slatyer R O 1977. Mechanisms of succession in natural
communities and their role in community stability and organization.
The American Naturalist 111, 1119-1144.

Cook L 1938. Some experiments and observations on veld burning. BSc Hons
Thesis, Witwatersrand University.

Cook L 1939a. A contribution to our information on grass burning. MSc
Thesis, Witwatersrand University.

Cook L 1939b. A contribution to our information on grass burning. South
African Journal of Science 36, 270-282.

Cook R E 1979. Patterns of juvenile mortality and recruitment in
plants. In: Solbrig O T, Jain S, Johnson G B and Raven P H (eds) Topics
in plant population biology. Macmillan Press, London, pp 207-231.

Cook S F Jr 1959. The effects of fire on a population of small
rodents. Ecology 40, 102-108.

Cooke H B S 1964. The Pleistocene environment in southern Africa. In:
Davis D H S (ed) Ecological studies in southern Africa. Junk, The
Hague, pp 1-23.

Cooper J P 1970. Potential production and energy conversion in temperate
and tropical grasses. Herbage Abstracts 40, 1-15.

Corbet A S   1934.   Studies in tropical soil microbiology.   II.   The bacterial numbers in the soil of the Malay Peninsula.   Soil Science 38, 407-416.

Corbett E S   1968.   Rainfall interception by annual grass and chaparral. USDA Forestry Service Research Paper, PSW-48.   Pacific Southwest Forest and Range Experimental Station, Berkeley, California, 1-12.

Countryman C M and Philpot C W   1970.   Physical characteristics of chamise as a wildland fuel.   USDA Forest Service Research Paper PSW-66/1970, 1-16.

Coutts J R H   1945.   Effect of veld burning on the base exchange capacity of a soil.   South African Journal of Science 41, 218-224.

Cumberland K   1963.   Man's role in modifying island environments in the south-west Pacific.   In: Fosberg F R (ed)   Man's place in the island ecosystem.   Bishop Museum Press, Honolulu, pp 187-205.

Curtis B A and Perrin M R   1979.   Food preferences of the vlei rat *(Otomys irroratus)* and the four-striped mouse *(Rhabdomys pumilio)*. South African Journal of Zoology 14, 224-229.

Cushwa C I, Martin R E and Miller R L   1968.   The effects of fire on seed germination.   Journal of Range Management 21, 250-254.

Cutler M R   1979.   Fire management and land management.   Putting them into perspective.   Proceedings of the fire working group society, American foresters.   USDA Forest Service General Technical Report INT 49, 1-2.

Dahlgren R   1963.   Studies of *Aspalathus:* phytogeographical aspects. Botaniska Notiser 116, 431-472.

Daitz J   1953a.   Some measurements of the CO_2 produced by microorganisms in soil collected from a veld burning experiment.   BSc Hons Thesis, Witwatersrand University.

Daitz J   1953b.   A further report on the seasonal burn experiment at Bethal.   Annual Report for 1953 of the Frankenwald Field Research Station, Witwatersrand University, 33-34.

Daitz J   1954.   Available carbohydrate reserves in the roots of *Themeda triandra* from a seasonal burn experiment at Bethal.   Annual Report of the Frankenwald Field Research Station, Witwatersrand University, 27-29.

Danckwerts J E   1980.   Unpublished data.   Dohne Research Station, Sutterheim.

Daubenmire R   1968.   Ecology of fire in grasslands.   In: Cragg J B (ed) Advances in ecological research volume 5.   Academic Press, London, pp 209-266.

Davidson R L   1950.   Veld burning experiments at Bethal.   Annual Report of the Frankenwald Field Research Station, Witwatersrand University, 23-26.

Davidson R L   1951a.   Further analysis of a veld burning experiment at Bethal.   Annual Report of the Frankenwald Field Research Station, Witwatersrand University, 39-46.

Davidson R L   1951b.   A long term seasonal burn experiment near Standerton.   Annual Report of the Frankenwald Field Research Station, Witwatersrand University, 47-49.

Davidson R L   1952a.   Herbage yield from a seasonal burn experiment near Standerton.   Annual Report of the Frankenwald Field Research Station, Witwatersrand University, 30-31.

Davidson R L   1952b.   Herbage yields from a seasonal burn experiment at Bethal.   Annual Report of the Frankenwald Field Research Station, Witwatersrand University, 32-34.

Davidson R L 1953. A seasonal burn experiment in sour/mixed bushveld. Annual Report of the Frankenwald Field Research Station, Witwatersrand University, 29-32.

Davidson R L 1954. Further herbage yields from a seasonal burn experiment near Standerton. Annual Report of the Frankenwald Field Research Station, Witwatersrand University, 25-27.

Davis K P 1959. Forest fire: control and use. McGraw-Hill, New York.

Davis R M 1973. The ecology and life history of the vlei rat, *Otomys irroratus* (Brants, 1827), on the van Riebeeck Nature Reserve, Pretoria. DSc Thesis, University of Pretoria.

de Villiers G Du T 1975. Reenval onderskeppingsverliese in die Republiek van Suid-Afrika - 'n streekstudie. PhD Thesis, University of the Orange Free State.

de Wit C 1972. An ecological study of a small mammal community with emphasis on the status of *Praomys* (Mastomys) *natalensis*. MSc Thesis, University of Pretoria.

Deacon H J 1976. Where hunters gathered. South African Archaeological Society Monograph No 1, 1-232.

Deacon H J 1978. Palaeoecology of the fynbos biome. Mimeo, 1-11.

Deacon H J 1979. Excavations at Boomplaas Cave - a sequence through the Upper Pleistocene and Holocene in South Africa. World Archaeology 10 (3), 241-257.

Deacon H J, Brooker M and Wilson M L 1978. The evidence for herding at Boomplaas Cave in the southern Cape. South African Archaeological Bulletin 33, 39-65.

Deall G B and Brown N A C 1981. Seed germination in *Protea magnifica* Link. South African Journal of Science 77, 175-176.

Dean W R J 1974. Breeding and distributional notes on some Angolan birds. Durban Museum Novitates 10, 109-125.

DeBano L F 1966. Formation of non-wettable soils involves heat transfer mechanism. USDA Forest Service Research Note PSW-132. Pacific Southwest Forest and Range Experimental Station, Berkeley, California, 1-8.

DeBano L F 1981. Water repellent soils: a state-of-the-art review. USDA Forest Service General Technical Report PSW-46, 21 pp.

Delaney M J 1972. The ecology of small rodents in tropical Africa. Mammal Review 2, 1-42.

Dethier V G 1970. Chemical interactions between plants and insects. In: Sandheimer E and Simeone J B (eds) Chemical ecology. Academic Press, New York, pp 85-102.

Dillon R F 1979. Research reports of the Department of Pasture Science, University of Natal.

Donaldson C H 1966. Control of blackthorn in the Molopo area with special reference to fire. Proceedings of the Grassland Society of Southern Africa 1, 57-62.

Donaldson C H 1967. Further findings on the effects of fire on blackthorn. Proceedings of the Grassland Society of Southern Africa 2, 59-61.

Donaldson C H 1969. Bush encroachment with special reference to the blackthorn problem of the Molopo area. Government Printer, Pretoria.

Donaldson C H and Mostert J W C 1958. Alarming encroachment of bitterbos in the Orange Free State. Forestry in South Africa 34 (9), 53-55.

Donaldson C H, Kelk D M and West K N 1972. *Anthephora pubescens* Nees. Proceedings of the Grassland Society of Southern Africa 7, 112-116.

Downing B H 1966. The plant ecology of Tabamhlope vlei. MSc Thesis, University of Natal.

Downing B H 1972. A plant ecological survey of the Umfolozi Game Reserve, Zululand. PhD Thesis, University of Natal.

Downing B H 1974. Reactions of grass communities to grazing and fire in the sub-humid lowlands of Zululand. Proceedings of the Grassland Society of Southern Africa 9, 33-37.

Downing B H 1979. Grass protein content and soils as factors affecting area-selective grazing by wild herbivores in the Umfolozi Game Reserve, Zululand. Proceedings of the Grassland Society of Southern Africa 14, 85-88.

Downing B H 1980. Woody and grass community ratios in parts of Zululand subsequent to Henkel's research in 1936. Paper delivered at South African Association of Botany Conference, Pietermaritzburg.

Downing B H, Robinson E R, Trollope W S W and Morris J W 1978. The influence of macchia eradication techniques on botanical composition of grasses in the Dohne Sourveld of the Amatole Mountains. Proceedings of the Grassland Society of Southern Africa 13, 111-115.

Drewes R H 1979. The response of veld to different removal treatments. MSc Thesis, University of Natal.

Drury W H and Nisbet I C T 1973. Succession. Journal of the Arnold Arboretum 54, 331-368.

du Plessis M C F and Mostert J W C 1965. Afloop en grondverliese by die Landbounavorsingsinstituut, Glen. Suid Afrikaanse Tydskrif vir Landbouwetenskappe 8, 1051-1060.

du Plessis S S 1972. Ecology of blesbok with special reference to productivity. Wildlife Monographs 30, 1-70.

du Toit P F 1972a. *Acacia karroo* intrusion. The effect of burning and sparing. Proceedings of the Grassland Society of Southern Africa 7, 23-27.

du Toit P F 1972b. The goat in a bush-grass community. Proceedings of the Grassland Society of Southern Africa 7, 44-50.

du Toit P J, Louw J G and Malan A I 1940. A study of the mineral content and feeding value of natural pastures in the Union of South Africa (final report). Onderstepoort Journal of Veterinary Science and Animal Industry 14, 123-327.

Dunn P and DeBano L F 1977. Fire's effect on biological and chemical properties of chaparral soils. In: Mooney H A and Conrad C E (technical coordinators) Proceedings of the symposium on the environmental consequences of fire and fuel management in Mediterranean ecosystems (August 1-5, 1977, Palo Alto, California). USDA Forest Service General Technical Report WO-3, Washington D C, 75-84.

Dunn P H, DeBano L F and Eberlein G E 1979. Effects of burning on chaparral soils. II. Soil microbes and nitrogen mineralization. Soil Science Society of America Journal 43, 509-514.

Dyer R A 1932. Control of *Selago corymbosa*. Forestry in South Africa 6, 511-512.

Dyrness C T and Youngberg C T 1957. The effect of logging and slash-burning on soil structure. Soil Science Society of America Proceedings 21, 444-447.

Edwards D 1963. A plant ecological survey of the Tugela River Basin, Natal. PhD Thesis, University of Natal.

376

Edwards D 1967. A plant ecological survey of the Tugela River Basin. Memoirs of the Botanical Survey of South Africa 36, 1–285.

Edwards D 1977a. Biomes of South Africa. Unpublished manuscript submitted to the National Programme for Environmental Sciences, CSIR, Pretoria, 1–6 and map.

Edwards D 1977b. Monitoring the extent and occurrence of fire in the different veld types of South Africa with particular reference to its ecological role and role in veld management. Unpublished Final Report to NASA.

Edwards D, de Vos W H, Hartkopf D, Hattingh D J, Scheepers J J and Wilby A F 1983. Monitoring of veld burns using satellite imagery. Proceedings of the Grassland Society of Southern Africa 18, 131–134.

Edwards P J 1961. Studies in veld burning and mowing in the Tall Grassveld of Natal. MSc Thesis, University of Natal.

Edwards P J 1968. The long term effects of burning and mowing on the basal cover of two veld types in Natal. South African Journal of Agricultural Science 11, 131–140.

Edwards P J 1969. Veld burning in the Giant's Castle Game Reserve. Lammergeyer 10, 64–67.

Edwards P J 1978. Methods of veld re-enforcement their action and adaptability to various sites. Proceedings of the Grassland Society of Southern Africa 13, 71–74.

Edwards P J, Jones R I and Tainton N M 1979. *Aristida junciformis* Trin et Pupr: A weed of the veld. Weeds 3, 25–32.

Endrody Younga S 1978. Coleoptera. In: Werger M J A (ed) Biogeography and ecology of southern Africa. Junk, The Hague, pp 797–821.

Eriksson A J 1978. Lightning and tall structures. Transactions of South African Institute of Electrical Engineers, Research Paper No. 4.

Evans W G 1971. The attraction of insects to forest fires. Tall Timbers Conference on Ecological Animal Control by Habitat Management 3, 115–127.

Everson C S 1979. Autecological studies on *Philippia evansii* M E Br with particular reference to water relations. MSc Thesis, University of Natal.

Fantham H B 1924. Some protozoa found in certain South African soils. IV. South African Journal of Science 21, 445–479.

Fenn J A 1980. Control of hakea in the western Cape. In: Neser S and Cairns A L P (eds) Proceedings of the third national weeds conference of South Africa. Balkema, Cape Town, pp 167–173.

Fernow B E 1902. Forest influences. U S Forestry Service Bulletin No 7, Department of Agriculture, Washington D C, 1–197.

Field-Dodgson J 1976. A study of seed production in weeping lovegrass, *Eragrostis curvula* (Schrad.) Nees. Proceedings of the Grassland Society of Southern Africa 11, 109–114.

Fisher M J 1978. The recovery of leaf water potential following burning of two droughted tropical pasture species. Australian Journal of Experimental Agriculture and Animal Husbandry 18, 423–425.

Fitzpatrick R W 1980. Effect of forest and grass burning on mineralogical transformations in some soils of Natal. Report No 952/139/80. Soil and Irrigation Research Institute, Department of Agriculture and Fisheries, Pretoria.

Foran B D, Tainton N M and Booysen P de V 1978. The development of a method for assessing veld condition in three grassveld types in Natal. Proceedings of the Grassland Society of Southern Africa 13, 27–33.

Forestry Department 1959/60 to 1977/78. Annual reports.

Fourcade H G 1889. Report on the Natal forests. Pietermaritzburg, Government Printer. pp 197.

Freeze R A 1972. Role of subsurface flow in generating surface runoff, 1. Base flow contributions to channel flow. Water Resources Research 8, 809–823.

Frost P G H 1979. A review of the adaptive responses of organisms to fire regime in South Africa. Progress report. National Programme for Environmental Sciences, CSIR, Pretoria.

Fugler S R 1979. Some aspects of the autecology of three *Hakea* species in the Cape Province, South Africa. MSc Thesis, University of Cape Town.

Fulton R E and Carpenter F L 1979. Pollination, reproduction, and fire in California *Arctostaphylos*. Oecologia (Berlin) 38, 147–157.

Galpin E E 1926. Botanical survey of the Springbok Flats. Memoirs of the Botanical Survey of South Africa 12, 1–100.

Gandar M V 1982. Description of a fire and its effects in the Nylsvley Nature Reserve: a synthesis report. South African National Scientific Report Series 63, 1–39.

Garnett T F F 1973. The Department of Forestry and its functions. South African Department of Forestry Pamphlet 107, 1–38.

Gates D M and Papian L E 1971. Atlas of energy budgets of plant leaves. Academic Press, New York, 277 pp.

Geiger R 1957. The climate near the ground. Harvard University Press. Cambridge, Massachusetts, 494 pp.

Gertenbach W P D 1979. Veld burning in the Kruger National Park: history, development, research and present policy. Department Nature Conservation, Kruger National Park.

Gertenbach W P D and Potgieter A L F 1979. Veldbrandnavorsing in die struikmopanieveld van die Krugerwildtuin. Koedoe 22, 1–28.

Gill A M 1974. Fire and the Australian flora: a review. Australian Forestry 38, 4–25.

Gill A M 1977. Plant traits adaptive to fires in Mediterranean land ecosystems. USDA Forest Service General Technical Report WO-3, 17–26.

Gill A M 1981. Adaptive responses of Australian vascular plant species to fires. In: Gill A M, Groves R H and Noble I R (eds) Fire and the Australian biota. Australian Academy of Sciences, Canberra, pp 243–272.

Gill A M, Groves R H and Noble I R (eds) 1981. Fire in the Australian biota. Australian Academy of Science, Canberra.

Gill A M and Ingwerson F 1976. Growth of *Xanthorrhoea australis* R. Br. in relation to fire. Journal of Applied Ecology 13, 195–203.

Gill G A 1936. Veld burning experiments. Farming in South Africa 2, 134.

Gillon D 1971a. The effect of bush fire on the principal pentatomid bugs (Hemiptera) of an Ivory Coast savanna. Proceedings of the Tall Timbers Fire Ecology Conference 11, 377–417.

Gillon D and Pernes J 1968. Etude de l'effet du feu de brousse sur certains groups d'Arthropodes dans une savane guin enne. Annales de l'Universit d'Abidjan, serie E 1, 113–198.

Gillon Y 1971b. The effect of bush fire on the principal acridid species of an Ivory Coast savanna. Proceedings of the Tall Timbers Fire Ecology Conference 11, 419–471.

Gimingham C H 1972. Ecology of heathlands. Chapman and Hall, London, 266 pp.

Glover P E and van Rensburg H J 1938. A contribution to the ecology of the highveld grassland at Frankenwald in relation to burning and grazing. South African Journal of Science 35, 274-279.

Gordon-Gray K D and Wright F B 1969. *Cyrtanthus breviflorus* and *Cyrtanthus lutens* (Amaryllidceae). Observations with particular reference to Natal populations. Journal of South African Botany 35, 35-62.

Grace J 1977. Plant response to wind. Academic Press, London, 204 pp.

Granger J E 1976a. The vegetation changes, some related factors and changes in the water balance following 20 years of fire exclusion in Catchment IX, Cathedral Peak Forest Research Station. PhD Thesis, University of Natal.

Granger J E 1976b. A plant ecological survey of the Cathkin Key Area. Unpublished data.

Granger J E 1980. A pilot study to investigate the effects of burning in protea savanna. Internal Research Report of the Department of Forestry.

Greene S W 1935. Effect of annual grass fires on organic matter and other constituents of virgin longleaf pine soils. Journal of Agricultural Research 50, 809-822.

Greig J C and Burdett P D 1976. Patterns in the distribution of southern African terrestrial tortoises (Cryptodoera: Testudinidae). Zoologica Africana 11 (2), 249-273.

Grier C C 1975. Wildfire effects on nutrient distribution and leaching in a coniferous ecosystem. Canadian Journal of Forestry Research 5, 599-607.

Guilloteau J 1957. The problem of bush fire and burns in land development and soil conservation in Africa south of the Sahara. African Soils 4, 64-102.

Gulmon S L 1977. A comparative study of the grassland of California and Chile. Flora 166, 261-278.

Haigh H 1977. Burning branchwood under *Pinus patula*. South African Journal of Forestry 102, 91-92.

Hall A V 1959. Observations on the distribution and ecology of Orchidaceae in the Muizenberg Mountains, Cape Peninsula. Journal of South African Botany 25, 265-278.

Hall A V and Boucher C 1977. The threat posed by alien weeds to the Cape flora. In: Proceedings of the second national weeds conference of South Africa. Balkema, Cape Town, pp 35-45.

Hall M 1980. The ecology of the Iron Age in Zululand. PhD Thesis, University of Cambridge.

Hall M and Vogel J C 1980. Some recent radiocarbon dates from southern Africa. Journal of African History 21 (4), 43-455.

Hall T D 1934. South African pastures, retrospective and prospective. South African Journal of Science 31, 59-97.

Hall-Martin A J and Basson W D 1975. Seasonal chemical composition of the diet of Transvaal lowveld giraffe. Journal of the South African Wildlife Management Association 5, 19-21.

Halpin Z T and Sullivan T P 1978. Social interactions in island and mainland populations of the deer mouse *Peromyscus maniculatus*. Journal of Mammalogy 59, 359-401.

Hamilton E L and Rowe P B 1949. Rainfall interception by chaparral in California. US Forestry Service, Californian Forest and Range Experimental Station, 1-43.

Hamner D A 1978. Dickinson's Kestrels hawking birds at cane fires. Bokmakierie 30, 78.

Hanney P 1965. The Muridae of Malawi (Africa: Nyasaland). Journal of Zoology 146, 577–633.

Harr R D 1977. Water flux in soil and subsoil on a steep forested slope. Journal of Hydrology 33, 37–38.

Harrison T D 1978. Report on maximum temperature measurements during the Nylsvley veld fire of 5 September 1978 and on postfire micrometeorological measurements. Unpublished report to the National Programme for Environmental Sciences, CSIR, Pretoria, 19 pp.

Haylett D G 1960. Run–off and soil erosion studies at Pretoria. South African Journal of Agricultural Science 3, 379–394.

Haynes R A 1976. Aspects of the ecology and life–history of *Protea arborea* Houtt. Unpublished report, Department of Zoology, University of Rhodesia, 1–68.

Haynes R A and Kruger F J 1972. The effect of protection on basal cover in microphyllous scrub communities of the fynbos on Marloth Nature Reserve. Jonkershoek Forestry Research Station Report 72-01, 1–5.

Henkel J S 1912. The indigenous high forest situated in the Division of George, Knysna and Humansdorp, Cape Province. South African Journal of Science 9, 68–76.

Henrici M 1935. Fodder plants of the Broken Veld. Part I. Science Bulletin No 142, Department of Agricultural Technical Services, Pretoria.

Henrici M 1940. Fodder plants of the Broken Veld. Part II. Science Bulletin No 213. Department of Agricultural Technical Services, Pretoria.

Hervey D F 1949. Reaction of a California annual plant community to fire. Journal of Range Management 2, 116–121.

Hewlett J D 1961. Soil moisture as a source of base flow from steep mountain watersheds. USDA Forest Service Station Paper SE-132, 1–11.

Hewlett J D and Troendle C A 1975. Non-point and diffused water sources: A variable source area problem. In: Watershed Management Proceedings of Irrigation and Drainage Division Symposium. ASCE, Logan, Utah, 21–46.

Hewlett J D, Lull H W and Reinhart K C 1969. In defense of experimental watersheds. Water Resources Research 5, 306–316.

Heyward F D 1937. The effect of frequent fires on profile development of longleaf pine forest soils. Journal of Forestry 35, 23–27.

Heyward F D 1938. Soil temperatures during forest fires in the longleaf pine region. Journal of Forestry 36, 478–491.

Hibbert A R 1967. Forest treatment effects on water yield. In: Sopper W E and Lull H W (eds) International symposium for hydrology. Pergamon Press, Oxford, pp 527–543.

Hibbert A R 1971. Increases in streamflow after converting chaparral to grass. Water Resources Research 7, 71–80.

Hibbert A R 1979. Managing vegetation to increase flow in the Colorado River Basin. USDA Forestry Service General Technical Report RM-66, 1–27.

Hillel D 1971. Soil and water. Physical principles and processes. Academic Press, New York, 288 pp.

Hinnells J R and Sharpe E J (eds) 1972. Hinduism. Oriel Press, Newcastle.

Hobbs L D 1980. Warning to hydrologists re water resources: future supply will pose problems. South African Water Bulletin. September 1980, 1.

Hocking B 1964. Fire melanism in some African grasshoppers. Evolution 18, 332–335.

Holden W 1855. History of the colony of Natal. London.

Holling C S 1973. Resilience and stability of ecological systems. Annual Review of Ecology and Systematics 4, 1–23.

Holling C S 1974. Fail-safe or safe failure? Proceedings of the International Congress of Ecology 1, 121.

Horne I P 1981. The frequency of fires in the Groot Swartberg mountain catchment area, Cape Province. South African Forestry Journal 118, 56–60.

Horton R E 1945. Erosional development of streams and their drainage basins: hydrological approach to quantitative morphology. Bulletin of Geological Society of America 56, 275–370.

Howe G E 1976. The evolutionary role of wildfire in the Northern Rockies and implications for resource managers. Proceedings of the Tall Timbers Fire Ecology Conference 14, 257–265.

Huleatt-James N C 1979. A survey of the insect fauna of experimental grassland plots at Ukulinga research farm, Natal, South Africa. Unpublished report, University of Natal.

Humphreys F R and Craig F G 1981. Effects of fire on soil chemical, structural and hydrologicl properties. In: Gill A M, Groves R H and Noble I R (eds) Fire and the Australian Biota. Australian Academy of Science, Canberra, pp 177–200.

Hunter J S 1905. Studies in grasshopper control. Agricultural Experimental Station Bulletin, Berkeley, California 170, 8 pp.

Hursh C R 1944. Report of the subcommittee on subsurface flow. Appendix B. EOS Transactions of the American Geophysics Union 25, 743–746.

Huston M 1979. A general hypothesis of species diversity. American Naturalist 113, 81–101.

I'Ons J H 1960. Studies on veld burning. MSc Thesis, University of Natal.

Inskeep R R 1978. The peopling of southern Africa. David Philip, Cape Town.

Irvine L O F 1943. Bush encroachment in the northern Transvaal. Farming in South Africa 18, 725–729.

Isaac L A and Hopkins H G 1937. The forest soil of the Douglas-fir region and the changes wrought upon it by logging and slash burning. Ecology 18, 264–279.

Jackson G 1974. Cryptogeal germination and other seedling adaptions to the burning of vegetation in savanna regions: the origin of the pyrophytic habit. New Phylologist 73, 771–780.

Jackson I J 1975. Relationships between rainfall parameters and interception by tropical forest. Journal of Hydrology 24, 215–238.

Jackson W P U 1976. Fire and flora on Constantia ridge, Table Mountain. Veld and Flora 62, 24–27.

Jacobson J 1979. Recent developments in southern Asian prehistory and protohistory. Annual Review of Anthropology 8, 467–502.

Jansen P F 1959a. A study of *Margarodes* on grasses of the *Trachypogon/* other species veld. BSc Hons Thesis, Witwatersrand University.

Jansen P F 1959b. The influence of burning on grasses and soil structure of *Trachypogon/* other species veld. BSc Hons Thesis, Witwatersrand University.

Jarvis J U M   1979.   Zoogeography.   Fynbos ecology: a preliminary synthesis.   In: Day J, Siegfried W R, Louw G N and Jarman M L (eds) South African National Scientific Programmes Report 40, pp 82–87.

Jelinek A J   1977.   The Lower Palaeolothic: Current evidence and interpretations. Annual Review of Anthropology 6, 11–32.

Johnston R S, Tew R K and Doty R D   1969.   Soil moisture depletion and estimated evapotranspiration on Utah mountain watersheds.   USDA Forestry Service Research Paper INT-67, 1–13.

Jordaan P G   1949.   Aantekeninge oor die voorplanting en brandperiodes vir *Protea mellifera* Thunb. Journal of South African Botany 15, 121–125.

Jordaan P G   1965.   Die invloed van 'n winterbrand op die voortplanting van vier soorte van die Proteaceae.   Tydskrif vir Natuurwetenskappe 5, 27–31.

Jorgensen J R and Hodges C S   1970.   Microbial characteristics of a forest soil after twenty years of prescribed burning. Mycologia 62, 721–726.

Jorgensen J R and Wells C G   1971.   Apparent N fixation in soil influenced by prescribed burning.   Soil Science Society of America Proceedings 35, 806–810.

Jorgensen J R, Wells C G and Metz L J   1975.   The nutrient cycle: key to continuous forest production. Journal of Forestry 73, 400–403.

Joubert J G V, Stindt H W and Perold I S   1969.   The nutritive value of natural pastures in the districts of Calitzdorp, George, Knysna, Mossel Bay, Oudtshoorn and Uniondale in the winter rainfall area of the Republic.   Technical communication No 82, Department of Agricultural Technical Services, Pretoria.

Jungius H   1971.   The biology and behaviour of the reedbuck (*Redunca arundinum* Boddaert 1785) in the Kruger National Park. Parey, Hamburg.

Junod H A   1962.   The life of a South African tribe.   University Books, New York.

Kayall A J   1963.   A technique for studying the fire tolerance of living tree trunks.   Publication of the Department of Forestry, Canada 1012, 1–22.

Kayall A J   1974.   Use of fire in land management.   In: Kozlowski T T and Ahlgren C E (eds) Fire and ecosystems.   Academic Press, New York, pp 483–511.

Keay R W J   1959.   Vegetation map of Africa.   Oxford University Press, London.

Keeley J E and Zedler P H   1978.   Reproduction of chaparral shrubs after fire: a comparison of sprouting and seeding strategies.   American Midland Naturalist 99, 142–161.

Kennan T C D   1971.   The effects of fire on two vegetation types of Matopos.   Proceedings of the Tall Timbers Fire Ecology Conference 11, 53–98.

Kenworthy J B   1963.   Temperatures in heather burning. Nature 200, 12–26.

Kern N G   1978.   The influence of fire on populations of small mammals of the Kruger National Park. MSc Thesis, University of Pretoria.

Kidd M M   1973.   Wild flowers of the Cape Peninsula.   Oxford University Press, Cape Town, 100 pp.

Killick D J B   1963.   An account of the plant ecology of the Cathedral Peak area of the Natal Drakensberg.   Memoirs of the Botanical Survey of South Africa 34, 1–178.

King J A   1957.   Meteorological aspects of forest fire danger rating. Journal of South African Forestry Association 29, 31–38.

King N and Vines R 1969. Variation in the flammability of the leaves of some Australian forest species. Division of Applied Chemistry, CSIRO, Australia, 1-14.

Kingdon J 1974. East African mammals. Vol IIB (hares and rodents). Academic Press, London.

Klapwijk M 1974. A preliminary report on pottery from the N E Transvaal, South Africa. South African Archaeological Bulletin 29, 19-23.

Klein R G 1972a. Preliminary report on the July through September 1970 excavations at Nelson Bay Cave, Plettenberg Bay (Cape Province, South Africa). Palaeoecol Africa 6, 177-208.

Klein R G 1979a. Stone Age exploitation of animals in southern Africa. American Scientist (March-April), 151-160.

Klein R G 1979b. Environmental and ecological implications of large mammals from Upper Pleistocene and Holocene sites in southern Africa. Paper prepared for "Towards a better understanding of the upper Pleistocene in sub-Saharan Africa," South African Association of Archaeology, Workshop, Stellenbosch, 27-29 June, 1979, 1-61.

Komarek E V 1962a. The use of fire, an historical background. Proceedings of the Tall Timbers Fire Ecology Conference 1, 7-10.

Komarek E V 1962b. Fire ecology. Proceedings of the Tall Timbers Fire Ecology Conference 1, 95-108.

Komarek E V 1965. Fire ecology. Grasslands and man. Proceedings of the Tall Timbers Fire Ecology Conference 4, 169-220.

Komarek E V 1966. The meteorological basis for fire ecology. Proceedings of the Tall Timbers Fire Ecology Conference 5, 85-128.

Komarek E V 1967. Fire and the ecology of man. Proceedings Tall Timbers Fire Ecology Conference 6, 143-170.

Komarek E V 1969. Fire and animal behaviour. Proceedings of the Tall Timbers Fire Ecology Conference 9, 161-208.

Komarek E V 1971a. Lightning and fire ecology in Africa. Proceedings of the Tall Timbers Fire Ecology Conference 11, 473-511.

Komarek E V 1971b. Principles of fire ecology and fire management in relation to the Alaskan environment. Proceedings of the Symposium on Fire in the Northern Environment. USDA, Portland, Oregon.

Komarek E V 1976. Fire ecology review. Proceedings of the Tall Timbers Fire Ecology Conference 14, 201-216.

Kozlowski T T and Ahlgren C E (eds) 1974. Fire and ecosystems. Academic Press, New York, 542 pp.

Krige E J 1965. The social system of the Zulus. Shuter and Shooter, Pietermaritzburg.

Kroninger H 1978. Newsletter, National Lighting Recording Scheme, No. 2, November 1978. CSIR, Pretoria, National Electrical Engineering Research Institute, Special Report ELEK 161, 1-18.

Kruger F J 1972. Jakkalsrivier catchment experiment: investigation of the effects of spring and autumn burns on vegetation. Jonkershoek Forestry Research Station Progress Report.

Kruger F J 1974. The physiography and plant communities of Jakkalsriver catchment. MSc Thesis, University of Stellenbosch.

Kruger F J 1977a. A preliminary account of aerial plant biomass in fynbos communities of the mediterranean-type climate zone of the Cape Province. Bothalia 12, 301-307.

Kruger F J 1977b. Ecology of Cape fynbos in relation to fire. In: Mooney H A and Conrad C E (technical coordinators) Proceedings of the symposium on the environmental consequences of fire and fuel management in Mediterranean ecosystems (August 1-5, 1977, Palo Alto, California). USDA Forest Service General Technical Report WO-3, Washington D C, 75-84.

Kruger F J 1978. A description of the fynbos biome project. South African National Scientific Programmes Report 28, 1-25.

Kruger F J 1979a. Fire. In: Day J, Siegfried W R, Louw G N and Jarman M L (eds) Fynbos ecology: a preliminary synthesis. South African National Scientific Programmes Report No 40, pp 43-57.

Kruger F J 1979b. South African heathlands. In: Specht R L (ed) Ecosystems of the world, Volume 9A. Heathlands and related shrublands. Descriptive studies. Elsevier, Amsterdam, pp 19-80.

Kruger F J 1980. Research reports. Department of Forestry, Pretoria.

Kruger F J 1981. Seasonal growth and flowering rhythms: South African heathlands. In: Specht R L (ed) Ecosystems of the World, Vol 9B. Heathlands and related shrublands. Analytic studies. Elsevier, Amsterdam, pp 1-4.

Kruger F J 1982. Unpublished research reports. Department of Forestry, Pretoria.

Kruger F J and Haynes R A 1978. Preliminary results of studies on the demography of *Widdringtonia cedarbergensis* Marsh and its interaction with fire. Department of Environment Affairs. Jonkershoek Forestry Research Station Report 78-05, 1-16.

Kruger F J and Lamb A J 1978. Conservation of the Kogelberg State Forest. Preliminary assessment of the effects of management from 1967 to 1978. Department of Environment Affairs. Jonkershoek Forestry Research Station Report 79-02, 1-20 + appendices.

Krupko I 1961. An experimental study of *Stoebe vulgaris* in relation to grazing and burning. Empire Journal of Experimental Agriculture 29, 175-180.

Krupko I and Davidson R L 1954. *Stoebe vulgaris* control experiments. Annual Report for 1954, Frankenwald Field Research Station. Witwatersrand University, 29-33.

Lamont B L 1981. Strategies for maximizing nutrient uptake in mediterranean-type ecosystems. In: Kruger F J, Mitchell D T and Jarvis J U M (eds) Mediterranean-type ecosystems. The role of nutrients. Springer-Verlag, Heidelberg, 552 pp.

Lamotte M 1975. The structure and function of a tropical savanna ecosystem. In: Golley F B and Medino E (eds) Tropical ecological systems. Trends in terrestrial and aquatic research. Springer-Verlag, Berlin, pp 179-222.

Lawrence R F 1953. The biology of the cryptic fauna of forests. Balkema, Cape Town.

Lawson L W 1979. The effect of fire on Natal coast forest: The Umlalazi Monitoring project. Project 10. Relative abundance of birds, burned to unburned sections, Mtunzini-Umlalazi Nature Reserve. Unpublished interim report, Natal Parks Board, 1-2.

Lawton R M 1978. A study of the dynamic ecology of Zambian vegetation. Journal of Ecology 66, 175-198.

le Maitre D C 1980. Unpublished research reports. Jonkershoek Forestry Research Station.

le Maitre D C 1981. Kogelberg season of burn trial II. The experimental fires. Report 81-02. Directorate of Forestry and Environmental Conservation, Jonkershoek Forestry Research Station.

le Roux C J G 1968. Veldbrand en maai sonder beweiding in die langgrasveld van Natal. Final report. South African Department of Agricultural and Technical Services, Pretoria.

le Roux C J G 1979b. The grazing of the plains in the Etosha National Park. Proceedings of the Grassland Society of Southern Africa 14, 89-93.

le Roux P J 1969. Brandbestryding in Suid-Kaapland met spesiale verwysing na chemiese metodes van beheer. MSc Thesis, University of Stellenbosch.

le Roux P J 1979a. The occurrence of fires in the southern Cape fynbos. Paper presented at the conference on terrestrial ecology of the southern Cape, George, 1-13.

Lecatsas G 1962. The effect of mowing and burning on the vegetative growth of *Stoebe vulgaris*. South African Journal of Science 58, 301-304.

Lee R B 1968. What hunters do for a living or, how to make out on scarce resources. In: Lee R B and DeVore I (eds) Man the hunter. Aldine, Chicago, pp 30-48.

Lee R B and DeVore I (eds) 1968. Man the hunter. Aldine, Chicago.

Lem K H L 1930. Preliminary ecological notes on the Acridiidae of the Cape Peninsula. South African Journal of Science 27, 406-413.

Lemon P C 1967. Effects of fire on herbs of the southeastern United States and central Africa. Proceedings of the Tall Timbers Fire Ecology Conference 6, 113-127.

Lemon P C 1968. Fire and wildlife grazing on an African plateau. Proceedings of the Tall Timbers Fire Ecology Conference 8, 71-88.

Leuthold W 1977. African ungulates. A comparative review of their ethology and behavioural ecology. Springer-Verlag, Berlin.

Levyns M R 1929a. The problem of the rhenoster bush. South African Journal of Science 26, 166-169.

Levyns M R 1929b. Veld burning experiments at Ida's Valley, Stellenbosch. Transactions of the Royal Society of South Africa 17, 61-92.

Levyns M R 1935b. Germination in some South African seeds. Journal of South African Botany 1, 89-103.

Levyns M R 1956. Notes on the biology and distribution of the rhenosterbush. South African Journal of Science 52, 141-143.

Levyns M R 1966a. *Haemanthus canaliculatus*, a new fire-lily from the western Cape Province. Journal of South African Botany 32, 73-75.

Levyns M R 1966b. A guide to the flora of the Cape Peninsula. Juta, Cape Town, 310 pp.

Levyns S 1924. Some observations on the effects of bush fires on the vegetation of the Cape Peninsula. South African Journal of Science 21, 346.

Levyns S 1927. A preliminary note on the rhenoster bush *Elytropappus rhinocerotis* and the germination of its seed. Transactions of the Royal Society of South Africa 14, 383-388.

Levyns S 1935a. Veld burning experiments at Oakdale, Riversdale. Transactions of the Royal Society of South Africa 23, 231-244.

Lewis H T 1972. The role of fire in the domestication of plants and animals. Man (New Series) 7(2), 195-222.

Lewis S 1975. Unpublished records. Department of Nature Conservation. University of Stellenbosch.

Lewis S 1978. Unpublished records. Department of Nature Conservation, University of Stellenbosch.

Lewis W M   1974.   Effects of fire on nutrient movement in a South Carolina pine forest. Ecology 55, 1120–1127.

Leyton L, Reynolds E R C and Thompson F B   1967.   Rainfall interception in forest and moorland.   In: Sopper W E and Lull H W (eds) International symposium for hydrology. Pergamon Press, Oxford, pp 163–178.

Linnartz N E, Hse C, and Duvall V L   1966.   Grazing impairs physical properties of a forest soil in central Louisiana. Journal of Forestry 64, 239–243.

Little S   1974.   Effects of fire on temperate forests: north-eastern United States.   In: Kozlowski T T and Ahlgren C E (eds)   Fire and ecosystems. Academic Press, New York, pp 225–250.

Lombaard H B   1971.   'n Ekologiese studie van aspekte van die generatiewe voortplanting van *Protea mellifera* en *Protea pulchella*. MSc Thesis, University of Stellenbosch.

Louw G N   1969.   The nutritive value of natural grazings in South Africa. Proceedings of the Southern African Society for Animal Production, 57–61.

Louw G N, Steenkamp C W P and Steenkamp E L   1967.   Die verwantskap tussen die eterekstrakinhoud van karoobossies en hul smaaklikheid vir skape. Suid Afrikanse Tydskrif vir Landbouwetenskap 10, 867–873.

Louw G N, Steenkamp C W P and Steenkamp E L   1968a.   Chemiese samestelling van die vernaamste plantspesies in die Noorsveld. Tegniese Mededeling Nr. 77. Departement van Landboutegniese Dienste, Pretoria.

Louw G N, Steenkamp C W P and Steenkamp E L   1968b.   Chemiese samestelling van die vernaamste plantspesies in die Westelike Berg karoo in die distrik Fraserburg. Tegniese Mededeling Nr. 78.   Departement van Landboutegniese Dienste, Pretoria.

Louw G N, Steenkamp C W P and Steenkamp E L   1968c.   Chemiese samestelling van die vernaamste plantspesies in die Dorre, Skyn-dorre, Skyn-sukkulente en Sentrale Bo Karoo. Tegniese Mededeling Nr. 79. Departement van Landbou Tegniese Dienste, Pretoria.

Lowes J J   1963.   A preliminary investigation into the relative merits of pre-rain and post-rain burning in the sourveld in spring. MSc Thesis, Witwatersrand University.

Luckhoff H S   1971.   The Clanwilliam cedar *Widdringtonia cedarbergensis* Marsh: its past history and present status.   Journal of Botanical Society of South Africa 57, 17–23.

Luke R H and MacArthur A G   1978.   Bushfires in Australia.   Australian Government Publishing Service, Canberra, 1–359.

Lunt H A   1950.   Liming and twenty years of litter raking and burning under red and white pine. Soil Science Society of America Proceedings 15, 381–390.

Lyle A D and Brockett G M   1974.   Progress report.   Project N-Ko/5, Kokstad Research Station, Department of Agricultural Technical Services, Kokstad.

Macdonald I A W   1978a.   Report on the present condition of that portion of the dune forest in Umlalazi Nature Reserve accidentally burnt in August, 1975, with recommendations for the future monitoring and management of the area. Report dated 5 April 1978, Natal Parks Board, 1–13.

Macdonald I A W   1978b.   Proposed monitoring projects for the dune forest in Umlalazi Nature Reserve with particular reference to measuring the effects of the accidental forest fire. Mimeo report. Natal Parks Board, 1–22.

Macdonald I A W 1978c. Pattern and process in a semi-arid grassveld in Rhodesia. Proceedings of the Grassland Society of Southern Africa 13, 103–110.

Macdonald I A W 1980. The effects of single fires on three woody plant species in Hluhluwe Game Reserve. National Programme for Environmental Sciences Report. CSIR, Pretoria.

Macdonald I A W 1982. Unpublished research reports.

Macdonald I A W and Pammenter N W 1979. The regeneration of the tree and shrub components of a coastal dune forest following fire. Unpublished report to Natal Parks, Game and Fish Preservation Board, Pietermaritzburg, 15 pp.

Macdonald I A W, Furniss P R, Scholes R J and Berry A 1980. Fire regime characteristics in the Hluhluwe–Corridor–Umfolozi Game Reserve Complex in Zululand. 2. Analysis of the areas burned in the period 1955–1978. Mimeo report to National Programme for Environmental Sciences, CSIR, Pretoria, 1–6.

MacLean G L and Kemp A C 1973. Neonatal plumage patterns of Three-banded and Temminck's Coursers and their bearing on Courser genera. Ostrich 44, 80–81.

Maertens H 1964. Bible themes. Darton, Longman and Todd, London.

Maggs T 1976. Iron Age communities of the southern Highveld. Natal Museum, Pietermaritzburg.

Maggs T 1977. Some recent radiocarbon dates from eastern and southern Africa. Journal of African History 17(2), 161–191.

Maggs T 1980. The Iron Age sequence south of the Vaal and Pongola Rivers: some historical implications. Journal of African History 21(1), 1–15.

Maggs T and Ward V 1980. Driel Shelter: rescue at a late Stone Age site on the Tugela River. Annals of the Natal Museum 24, 35–70.

Malajczuk A and Lamont B 1981. Specialized roots of symbiotic origin in heathlands. In: Specht R L (ed) Ecosystems of the World, Vol 9B. Heathlands and related shrublands. Analytic studies. Elsevier, Amsterdam, pp 165–182.

Malajczuk N and Glenn A R 1981. *Phytophthora cinnamomi* – a threat to the heathlands. In: Specht R L (ed) Ecosystems of the World, Vol 9B. Heathlands and related shrublands. Analytic studies. Elsevier, Amsterdam, pp 241–247.

Malherbe H L et al 1968. Report of the Committee of Investigation into the afforestation and water supplies in South Africa. Mimeo report, 1–132.

Manry D E 1982. Habitat use by foraging bald ibises *Geronticus calvus* in western Natal. South African Journal of Wildlife Research 12, 85–93.

Manson J 1974. Aspekte van die biologie en gedrag van die Kaapse grysbok *Raphicerus melanotis* Thunb. MSc Thesis, University of Stellenbosch.

Marais F J 1974. The behaviour and population dynamics of a confined colony of striped mice (*Rhabdomys pumilio*). MSc Thesis, University of Pretoria.

Marloth R 1924. Notes on the question of veld burning. South African Journal of Science 21, 342–345.

Marshall L 1976. The !Kung of Nyae Nyae. Harvard University Press, Cambridge.

Martin A R H 1966. The plant ecology of the Grahamstown Nature Reserve: II. Some effects of burning. Journal of South African Botany 32, 1–39.

Marwick B A 1940. The Swazi. Cass, London.

Mason H 1972. Western Cape Sandveld flowers. Struik, Cape Town, 203 pp.

Mason R 1969. Prehistory of the Transvaal. Witwatersrand University Press, Johannesburg.

McArthur A G 1962. Control Burning in Eucalypt Forests. Forestry and Timber Bureau, Leaflet No. 100.

McArthur A G 1966. Weather and Grassland Fire Behaviour. Forestry and Timber Bureau, Leaflet No. 106.

McArthur A G 1967. Fire Behaviour in Eucalypt Forests. forestry and Timber Bureau, Leaflet No. 107.

McKenzie B 1978. A quantitative and qualitative study of the indigenous forests of the south-western Cape. MSc Thesis, University of Cape Town.

McKenzie B, Moll E J and Campbell B M 1977. A phytosociological study of Orange Kloof, Table Mountain, South Africa. Vegetatio 34, 41-53.

McLachlan C R and Liversidge R 1957. Roberts birds of South Africa. Trustees of the South African Bird Book Fund.

McMaster C 1976. *Protea simplex*, is it an endangered species? Veld and Flora 62, 21-22.

McMurphy W E and Anderson K L 1965. Burning Flint Hills range. Journal of Range Management 18, 265-269.

Meester J A J 1978. The effect of fire on Natal coast forest. The Umlalazi monitoring report. Project 8. A comparison of the small mammal populations of burnt and unburnt portions of the dune forest. First report, Natal Parks Board, 1-2.

Meester J A J, Lloyd C N V and Rowe-Rowe D T 1979. A note on the ecological role of *Praomys natalensis*. South African Journal of Science 75, 183-184.

Meiklejohn J 1955. The effect of brush burning on the microflora of a Kenya upland soil. Journal of Soil Science 6, 111-118.

Mendelsohn J M 1981. A study of the black shouldered Kite *Elanis caeruleus*. PhD Thesis, University of Natal.

Menhenett R and Wareing P F 1975. Possible involvement of growth substances in the response of tomato plants (*Lycopersicon esculentum* Mill.) to different soil temperatures. Journal of Horticultural Science 50, 381-397.

Mentis M T 1972a. Game on the farm. Part 8. Quail. The Farmers Weekly, 2 August 1972, 31.

Mentis M T 1972b. Game on the farm. Part 4. Cover for guinea-fowl. The Farmers Weekly 21 June 1972, 22.

Mentis M T 1972c. A review of some life history features of the large herbivores of Africa. Lammergeyer 16, 1-89.

Mentis M T 1973. A comparative ecological study of greywing and redwing francolins in the Natal Drakensberg. MSc Thesis, University of Stellenbosch.

Mentis M T 1977. Stocking rates and carrying capacities for ungulates on African rangelands. South African Journal of Wildlife Research 7, 89-98.

Mentis M T 1978. Population limitation in grey rhebuck and oribi in the Natal Drakensberg. Lammergeyer 26, 19-28.

Mentis M T 1979a. Veld condition and status of blesbok in the experimental paddocks of Coleford Nature Reserve. Report of the Natal Parks Board, Pietermaritzburg.

Mentis M T 1979b. The effects of anti-nagana game eradication on the veld of Umfolozi Game Reserve. Workshop on vegetation dynamics of the Hluhluwe-Umfolozi-Corridor Complex, Natal Parks Board.

Mentis M T 1980. The effect of animal size and adaptation on defoliation, selective defoliation, animal production and veld condition. Proceedings of the Grassland Society of Southern Africa 15, 147-151.

Mentis M T and Bigalke R C 1973. Management for greywing and redwing francolins in Natal. Journal of South African Wildlife Management Association 3, 41-47.

Mentis M T and Bigalke R C 1979. Some effects of fire on two grassland francolins in the Natal Drakensberg. South African Journal of Wildlife Research 9, 1-8.

Mentis M T and Bigalke R C 1980. Breeding, social behaviour and management of greywing and redwing francolins. South African Journal of Wildlife Research 10, 140-149.

Mentis M T and Bigalke R C 1981a. Ecological isolation in greywing and redwing francolins. Ostrich, 84-97.

Mentis M T and Bigalke R C 1981b. The effect of scale of burn on the densities of grassland francolins in the Natal Drakensberg. Biological Conservation 21, 247-261.

Mentis M T and Collinson R F H 1979. Management goals for wildlife reserves in grassveld and bushveld. Proceedings of the Grassland Society of Southern Africa 14, 71-74.

Mentis M T and Duke R R 1976. Carrying capacities of natural veld in Natal for large wild herbivores. South African Journal of Wildlife Research 6, 65-74.

Mentis M T and Rowe-Rowe D T 1979. Fire and faunal abundance and diversity in the Natal Drakensberg. Proceedings of the Grassland Society of Southern Africa 14, 75-77.

Mentis M T, Meiklejohn M J and Scotcher J S B 1974. Veld burning in Giant's Castle Game Reserve, Natal Drakensberg. Proceedings of the Grassland Society of Southern Africa 9, 26-31.

Mes M G 1958. The influence of veld burning or mowing on the water, nitrogen and ash content of grasses. South African Journal of Science 54, 83-86.

Midgley D C and Pitman W V 1969. Surface water resources of South Africa. University of the Witwatersrand, HRU 2/69.

Miles J 1979. Vegetation dynamics. Chapman and Hall, London, pp 80.

Miller R M 1979. The effect of fire on Natal coast forest. The Umlalazi Monitoring Project. Project 6. Comparison of the insect faunas of burnt and unburnt portions of the Umlalazi dune forest with special reference to selected taxonomic groups. Progress Report, May 1979. Natal Parks Board, 1-6.

Milton S J 1980. Australian acacias in the S W Cape: pre-adaptation, predation and success. In: Neser S and Cairns A L P (eds) Proceedings of the third national weeds conference of South Africa. Balkema, Cape Town, pp 69-78.

Mitchell M R 1922. Some observations on the effects of a bush fire on the vegetation of Signal Hill. Transactions of the Royal Society of South Africa 10, 213-232.

Moffett R O and Deacon G J 1977. The flora and vegetation in the surrounds of Boomplaas Cave, Congo Valley. South African Archaeological Bulletin 32, 127-145.

Mogg A O D 1918. Some preliminary observations on unseasonal veld burning and its possible relation to some stock diseases. South African Journal of Science 15, 653.

Moll E J 1967. Forest trees of Natal. Wildlife Protection and Conservation Society of South Africa, Pietermaritzburg.

Moll E J 1972. A preliminary account of the dune communities at Pennington Park, Mtunzini, Natal. Bothalia 10 (4), 615–626.

Moll E J 1976. The Three River Region – A vegetation study. Natal Town and Regional Planning Report No 33. Natal Town and Regional Planning Commission, Pietermaritzburg, 1–127.

Moll E J, McKenzie B and McLachlan D 1980. A possible explanation for the lack of trees in the fynbos, Cape Province, South Africa. Biological Conservation 17, 221–228.

Monnig H O 1967. The Pedi. Van Schaik, Pretoria.

Mooney H A and Conrad C E (eds) 1977. Symposium on the environmental consequences of fire and fuel management in mediterranean-climate ecosystems. USDA Forest Service General Technical Report WO-3.

Moore A W 1960. The influence of annual burning on a soil in the derived savanna zone of Nigeria. Transactions of the 7th International Congress on Soil Science, Madison, Wisconsin 4, 257–264.

Moreau R E 1952. Africa since the Mesozoic: with particular reference to certain biological problems. Proceedings of the Zoological Society of London 121, 869–913.

Moreau R E 1966. The bird faunas of Africa and its islands. Academic Press, London.

Mostert D P, Siegfried W R and Louw G N 1980. Protea nectar and satellite fauna in relation to the food requirements and pollinating role of the Cape Sugarbird. South African Journal of Science 76, 409–412.

Mostert J W C and Donaldson C H 1956. Veld burning: Observations in the central Orange Free State. Farming in South Africa 32 (6), 34–39.

Mostert J W C, Roberts B R, Heslinga C F and Coetzee P G F 1971. Veld bestuur in doe O V S Streek. Departement Landbou Tegniese Dienste, Pamphlet No 391.

Muller C J, Hanawazlt R B and McPherson J K 1968. Allelopathic control of herb growth in the fire cycle of California chaparral. Bulletin of the Torrey Botanical Club 95, 225–231.

Nanni U W 1956. Forest hydrological research at Cathedral Peak research station. Journal of South African Forestry Association 27, 2–35.

Nanni U W 1960. The immediate effects of veld-burning on streamflow in Cathedral Peak catchments. Journal of South African Forestry Association 34, 7–12.

Nanni U W 1969. Veld management in the Natal Drakensberg. Journal of South African Forestry Association 28, 5–15.

Nanni U W 1970. Trees, water and perspective. South African Forestry Journal 75, 9–17.

Nanni U W 1972. Water-use by riparian vegetation at Cathedral Peak. South African Forestry Journal 80, 1–10.

National Parks Board of Trustees 1967/68. Annual report.

Naveh Z 1974a. Effects of fire in the Mediterranean region. In: Kozlowski T T and Ahlgren C E (eds) Fire and Ecosystems. Academic Press, New York, pp 401–434.

Naveh Z 1974b. The ecology of fire in Israel. Proceedings of the Tall Timbers Fire Ecology Conference 13, 131–170.

Naveh Z 1975. The evolutionary significance of fire in the Mediterranean region. Vegetatio 29, 199–208.

Neal B R 1970. The habitat distribution and activity of a rodent population in western Uganda, with particular reference to the effect of burning. Revue de Zoologie et de Botanique Africanes 81, 29–50.

Noble I R and Slatyer R O 1977. Postfire succession of plants in Mediterranean ecosystems. In: Mooney H A and Conrad C E (eds) Proceedings of the Symposium on the Environmental Consequences of fire and fuel management in Mediterranean ecosystems. USDA Forest Service General Technical Report WO-3, pp 27-36.

Noble I R and Slatyer R O 1981. The use of vital attributes to predict successional changes in plant communities subject to recurrent disturbance. Vegetatio 43, 5-21.

Norton B E and McGarity J W 1965. The effect of burning of native pasture on soil temperature in northern New South Wales. Journal of the British Grassland Society 20, 101-105.

Novellie P A 1978. Comparison of the foraging strategies of blesbok and springbok on the Transvaal highveld. South African Journal of Wildlife Research 8, 137-144.

Nursey W R E and Kruger A H G 1973. The effect of spring mowing and burning on seed and dry matter production of *Anthephora pubescens* Nees. Proceedings of the Grassland Society of Southern Africa 8, 123-127.

Oates F 1889. Matabeleland and the Victoria Falls. Kegan Paul, Trench, London.

Odum E P 1971. Fundamentals of ecology, 3rd edn. W B Saunders, Philadelphia.

Old S M 1969. Microclimate, fire and plant production in an Illinois prairie. Ecological Monograph 39, 355-384.

Oliver M D N, Short N R M and Hanks J 1978. Population ecology of oribi, grey rhebuck and mountain reedbuck in Highmoor State Forest Land, Natal. South African Journal of Wildife Research 8, 95-105.

Orput P A and Curtis J T 1957. Soil microfungi in relation to the prairies continuum in Wisconsin. Ecology 38, 628.

Owensby E and Wyrill J B 1973. Effects of range burning on Kansas Flint Hills soils. Journal of Range Management 26, 185-188.

Packham D R 1969. Heat transfer above a small ground fire. Australian Forest Research 5, 19-24.

Pammenter N W 1979. Umlalazi monitoring project. Seed germination characteristics of some species common in the burnt area. Final report 1, Natal Parks Board.

Parkington J 1972. Seasonal mobility in the Late Stone Age. African Studies 31, 221-343.

Parkington J 1977. Soaqua: Hunter-fisher-gatherers of the Olifants River Valley, Western Cape. South African Archaeological Bulletin 32, 150-157.

Parmeter J R 1977. Effects of fire on pathogens. In: Mooney H A and Conrad C E (technical coordinators) Proceedings of the symposium on the environmental consequences of fire and fuel management in Mediterranean ecosystems (August 1-5, 1977, Palo Alto, California). USDA Forest Service General Technical Report WO-3, Washington D C, 58-64.

Pase P and Lindenmuth A W 1971. Effects of prescribed fire on vegetation and sediment in oak-mountain mahogany chaparral. Journal of Forestry 69, 800-805.

Passmore N I and Carruthers V C 1979. South African frogs. Witwatersrand University Press, Johannesburg.

Patric J H, Douglass and Hewlett J D 1965. Soil absorption by mountain and piedmont forests. Soil Science Society of America Proceedings 29, 303-308.

Perrin M R 1980. The feeding habits of two co-existing rodents, *Rhabdomys pumilio* (Sparrman, 1784) and *Otomys irroratus* Brants, 1827 in relation to rainfall and reproduction. Acta Ecologica 1, 71-89.

Perrin M R and Curtis B A 1980. Comparative morphology of the digestive system of 19 species of southern African myomorph rodents in relation to diet and evolution. South African Journal of Zoology 15, 22-33.

Pexton J 1979. Changes in small mammal populations in selected forest precursor communities in the Natal Drakensberg in response to burning. Mimeo report, Department of Forestry, Pietermaritzburg.

Phillips E P 1919. A preliminary report on the veld burning experiments at Groenkloof, Pretoria. South African Journal of Science 16, 286-299.

Phillips E P 1920. Veld burning experiments at Groenkloof. Second report. Science Bulletin 17: Department of Agriculture, Union of South Africa.

Phillips J F V 1930. Fire: its influence on biotic communities and physical factors in South and East Africa. South African Journal of Science 27, 352-367.

Phillips J F V 1931. Forest succession and ecology in the Knysna region. Memoirs of the Botanical Survey of South Africa 14, 1-327.

Phillips J F V 1963. The forests of George, Knysna and the Zitzikama. A brief history of their management, 1778-1939. Bulletin 40, Department of Forestry, Government Printer, Pretoria.

Phillips J F V 1965. Fire - as master and servant: its influence in the bioclimatic regions of trans-Saharan Africa. Proceedings of the Tall Timbers Fire Ecology Conference 4, 6-110.

Phillips J F V 1971. Fire in Africa: A brief re-survey. Proceedings of the Tall Timbers Fire Ecology Conference 11, 1-7.

Phillips J F V 1973. The agricultural and related development of the Tugela Basin and its influent surrounds. Natal and Regional Planning Commission, Pietermaritzburg, 1-299 and maps.

Phillips J F V 1974. Effects of fire in forest and savanna ecosystems of sub-Saharan Africa. In: Kozlowski T T and Ahlgren C E (eds) Fire and ecosystems. Academic Press, New York, pp 435-481.

Pienaar A J 1959. Bush encroachment not controlled by veld burning alone. Farming in South Africa 35 (9), 16-17.

Pienaar U de V 1968. The use of fire as a tool in wildlife management in the Kruger National Park. In: Golley F B and Buechner H K (eds) A practical guide to the study of the productivity of large herbivores. IBP Handbook No 7, Blackwell, Oxford, pp 274-280.

Pillans N S 1924. Destruction of indigenous vegetation by burning in the Cape Peninsula. South African Journal of Science 21, 348-350.

Pitman C R S 1932. Notes on the breeding habits and eggs of *Rhinoptilus chalcopterus*. The Oologists Record 12, 16-24.

Plathe D J R and van der Zel D W 1969. 'n Veldbrand experiment op meervoudige opvanggebiede in Jakkalsrivier, Lebanon. Forestry in South Africa 10, 63-71.

Plug I 1978. Die latere steentydperk van die Boesmansrotsskuiling in Oos-Transvaal. MA Thesis, University of Pretoria.

Porter R N 1975. The production utilization and effects of grazing on some of the pastures in the Umfolozi Game Reserve, Zululand. MSc Thesis, University of Witwatersrand.

Potgieter A 1974. Temperatures of veld fires in the Kruger National Park as influenced by burning frequency, season and weather conditions. Unpublished report. University of Zimbabwe, Salisbury.

Poynton J C 1964. The amphibia of southern Africa. Annals of the Natal Museum 17, 1-334.

Poynton J C and Broadley D G 1978. The herpeto fauna. In: Werger M J A (ed) Biogeography and ecology of southern Africa. Junk, The Hague, pp 925-948.

Poynton R J   1971.   Sylvicultural map of the Republic of South Africa. Government Printer, Pretoria.

Puzo B   1978.   Patterns of man-land relations. In: Werger M J A (ed) Biogeography and ecology of southern Africa. Junk, The Hague, pp 1049–1112.

Raison R J   1979.   Modification of the soil environment by vegetation fires, with particular reference to nitrogen transformations: a review. Plant and Soil 51, 73–108.

Renbuss M, Chilvers G A and Pryer L D   1973.   Microbiology of an ashbed. Proceedings of the Linnean Society of New South Wales 97, 302–310.

Reynolds G W   1974.   The aloes of South Africa. A A Balkema, Cape Town, 534 pp.

Reynolds H G and Bohning J W   1956.   Effects of burning of a desert grass-shrub range in southern Arizona. Ecology 37, 769–777.

Rice E L and Parenti R L   1978.   Causes of decreases in productivity in undisturbed tall grass prairie. American Journal of Botany 65, 1091–1097.

Richards A I   1939.   Land, labour and diet in Northern Rhodesia. Oxford University Press, London.

Roberts A   1951.   The mammals of South Africa. Trustees, "The mammals of South Africa" book fund, Johannesburg.

Roberts B R   1981.   Sweet and mixed grassveld. In: Tainton N M (ed) Veld and pasture management in South Africa. Shuter and Shooter in association with Natal University Press, Pietermaritzburg, pp 383–391.

Robinson E T, Gibbs-Russel G E, Trollope W S W and Downing B H   1979. Assessment of short-term burning treatments on the herb layer of False Thornveld of the eastern Cape. Proceedings of the Grassland Society of Southern Africa 14, 79–84.

Rodel M G   1950.   A preliminary report on the veld experiments at Ukulinga. Experiment PMSC 1. Natal Agricultural Research Institute. BSc Thesis, Natal University.

Roth H H and Osterberg R   1971.   Studies on the agricultural utilization of semi-domesticated eland (*Taurotragus oryx*) in Rhodesia. 4. Chemical composition of eland browse. Rhodesian Journal of Agricultural Research 9, 45–51.

Rothermel R C   1972.   A mathematical model for predicting fire spread in wildland fuels. USDA Forest Service Research Paper INT 115.

Rourke J P   1972.   Taxonomic studies on *Leucospermum* R. Br. Journal of South African Botany Supplementary Volume 8, 1–194.

Rourke J P   1976.   Beyond redemption: the story of *Mimetes stokoei*. Veld and Flora 62, 12–16.

Rourke J P   1980.   The proteas of southern Africa. Purnell, Cape Town, 236 pp.

Routledge D A   1951.   A second report on investigations into the effects of burning and mowing of veld. BSc Agriculture Thesis, University of Natal.

Roux E R   1969.   Grass, a story of Frankenwald. Oxford University Press, Cape Town.

Roux E R and Middlemiss E   1963.   The occurrence and distribution of *Acacia cyanophylla* and *Acacia cyclops* in the Cape Province. South African Journal of Science 59, 286–293.

Roux P W and Smart C W   1980.   Fire in the Karoo. Unpublished report to the Symposium on the ecological effects of fire in South Africa, CSIR, Pretoria.

Rowe P B and Reimann L F   1961.   Water use by brush, grass and grass forb vegetation compared. Journal of Forestry 59, 175–181.

Rowe-Rowe D T   1977.   Mammal survey of the Cathedral Peak area of the Natal Drakensberg. Unpublished report, Natal Parks Board, 1–13.

Rowe-Rowe D T   1980.   Mammal distribution and density in relation to fire.   Report of the Natal Parks Board, Pietermaritzburg.

Rutherford M C   1975.   Aspects of ecosystem function in a savanna woodland in South West Africa.   PhD Thesis, University of Stellenbosch.

Rutherford M C   1978.   Primary production ecology in southern Africa.   In: Werger M J A (ed)   Biogeography and ecology of southern Africa, Junk, The Hague, pp 621-659.

Rutherford M C   1979.   Aboveground biomass subdivisions in woody species of the Savanna Ecosystem Project study area, Nylsvley.   South African National Science Progress Report No. 36.   Pretoria, CSIR.

Rutherford M C   1980.   Annual plant production-precipitation relations in arid and semi-arid regions.   South African Journal of Science 76, 53-56.

Rutherford M C   1981.   Survival, regeneration and leaf biomass changes in woody plants following spring burns in *Burkea africana* - *Ochna pulchra* savanna.   Bothalia 13, 531-552.

Rycroft H B   1947.   A note on the immediate effects of veld burning on stormflow in a Jonkershoek stream catchment.   Journal of South African Forestry Association 15, 80-88.

Rycroft H B   1955.   The effects of riparian vegetation on water loss from an immigration furrow at Jonkershoek.   Journal of South African Forestry Association 26, 2-8.

Sampson A W   1944.   Effect of chaparral burning on soil erosion and soil moisture relations.   Ecology 25, 171-191.

Sampson C G   1974.   The Stone Age archaeology of southern Africa.   Academic Press, New York.

Sanson B   1974.   Traditional rulers and their realms.   In: Hammond-Tooke W D (ed)   The Bantu-speaking peoples of southern Africa.   Routledge and Kegan Paul, London, pp 246-283.

Savage M J   1979a.   Report on veld burning and its effect on the microclimate.   Unpublished report, Department of Soil Science and Agrometeorology, University of Natal, Pietermaritzburg, 1-29.

Savage M J   1979b.   Use of international system of units in the plant sciences.   Hort Science 14, 492-495.

Savage M J   1980.   The effect of fire on the grassland microclimate.   Herbage Abstracts 50, 589-603.

Savage M J and Vermeulen K   1983.   Microclimate modifications of tall moist grasslands of Natal by spring burning.   Journal of Range Management 36, 172-174.

Schapera I   1930.   The Khoisan peoples of southern Africa.   Routledge and Keagan Paul, London.

Schelpe E A   1976.   Veld burning and veld and flora conservation.   Veld and Flora 62, 24-25.

Schelpe E A C L E   1946.   The plant ecology of the Cathedral Peak Area.   M Sc Thesis, Natal University College, University of South Africa.

Schirge G U and Penderis A H   1978.   Fire in South African ecosystems: an annotated bibliography.   South African National Scientific Programmes Report 33.   CSIR, Pretoria.

Schonland S   1927.   On the reclamation of ruined pasturage on the Amatolas near Keiskamma Hoek.   Science Bulletin 55, Department of Agriculture, Union of South Africa.

Schulze B R 1965.   Climate of South Africa.   Part 8: General survey.   South African Weather Bureau WB 28.

Schulze R E 1975. Catchment evapotranspiration in the Natal Drakensberg. PhD Thesis, University of Natal.

Schulze R E 1980. The land use component in hydrological modelling: an evaluation. University of Natal, Department of Agricultural Engineering. ACRU Report 9, 1–38.

Schulze R E and McGee O S 1978. Climatic indices and classifications in relation to the biogeography of southern Africa. In: Werger M J A (ed) Biogeography and ecology of southern Africa. Junk, The Hague, pp 19–54.

Schulze R E, Scott-Shaw C R and Nanni U W 1978. Interception by *Pinus patula* in relation to rainfall parameters. Journal of Hydrology 36, 393–396.

Schutte K H 1960. Trace element deficiencies in Cape vegetation. Journal of South African Botany 26, 45–49.

Schweitzer F R and Scott K D 1973. Early occurrence of domestic sheep in sub-Saharan Africa. Nature 241, 547.

Schweitzer F R and Wilson M L 1978. A preliminary report on excavations at Byneskranskop, Bredasdorp District, Cape. South African Archaeological Bulletin 33, 134–140.

Scotcher J S B 1980. Fire ecology in the Natal Drakensberg game and nature reserves. Mimeo report to National Programme for Environmental Sciences, CSIR, Pretoria, 1–49.

Scotcher J S B and Clarke J C 1980. The effect of fire on grasslands in Giant's Castle Game Reserve. Unpublished report, Natal Parks Board.

Scotcher J S B and Clarke J C 1981. Effects of certain burning treatments on veld condition in Giant's Castle Game Reserve. Proceedings of the Grassland Society of Southern Africa 16, 121–127.

Scotcher J S B, Clarke J C and Lowry P B 1980b. The effect of fire on herbage production and quality in Giant's Castle Game Reserve. Unpublished report, Natal Parks Board.

Scotcher J S B, Rowe-Rowe D T and Clark J 1979. Fire ecology in the Natal Drakensberg. Report of the Natal Parks Board, Pietermaritzburg.

Scotcher J S B, Rowe-Rowe D T, Clarke J C and Lowry P B 1980a. Fire ecology in the Natal Drakensberg game and nature reserves. Unpublished report.

Scott J D 1938. Veld burning experiments at the Athole Research Station. Pasture Research in South Africa, Progress Report No 1. Department of Agriculture and Forestry, Union of South Africa, 48–52.

Scott J D 1940a. Veld burning experiments in the Highland Sourveld at the Tabamhlope Research Station. Pasture Research in South Africa, Progress Report No 1. Department of Agriculture and Forestry, Union of South Africa, 357–370.

Scott J D 1940b. Veld burning experiments in the Highland Sourveld at the Tabamhlope Research Station. Pasture Research in South Africa, Progress Report No 2. Department of Agriculture and Forestry, Union of South Africa, 365–366.

Scott J D 1947. Veld management in South Africa. Bulletin 278, Government Printer, Pretoria.

Scott J D 1952a. A contribution to the study of the problems of the Drakensberg Conservation Area. Science Bulletin No. 324. Department of Agriculture, Union of South Africa.

Scott J D 1952b. Management of range lands (veld) in Africa. Proceedings of the Sixth International Grassland Congress (1), 477–483.

Scott J D 1955. Principles of pasture management. In: Meredith D (ed) The grasses and pastures of South Africa. Central News Agency, Johannesburg, pp 601–623.

Scott J D   1956.   The study of the primordial buds and the reactions of
roots   to   defoliation   as   the   basis   of   grassland   management.
Proceedings of the Seventh International Grassland Congress, 479-487.

Scott J D   1970.   Pros and cons of eliminating veld burning.   Proceedings
of the Grassland Society of Southern Africa 5, 23-26.

Scott J D   1971.   Veld burning in Natal.   Proceedings of the Tall Timbers
Fire Ecology Conference 11, 33-51.

Scott J D and van Breda N G   1940.   Effects of burning on indigenous veld
shrub at the Worcester Veld Reserve.   Pastoral Research in South Africa
Progress Report No 2, Department of Agriculture and Forestry, Union of
South Africa, 373-374.

Scott-Shaw C R   1976.   Rainfall interception by *Pinus patula* Schlect. and
Cham. in the Natal Drakensberg.   Unpublished seminar, Department of
Geography, University of Natal.

Scotter D R   1970.   Soil temperatures under grass fires.   Australian Journal
of Soil Research 8, 273-279.

Scriba J H   1976.   The effects of fire on *Widdringtonia nodiflora* (L) Powrie
on Mariepskop.   South African Forestry Journal 97, 12-17.

Scudder T   1971.   Gathering among African woodland savannah cultivators.
Zambian Papers 5, 316-324.

Sharrow S H and Wright H A   1977.   Proper burning intervals for tobosa-grass
in West Texas based on nitrogen dynamics.   Journal of Range Management
30, 343-346.

Shortridge G C   1934.   The mammals of South West Africa.   Volume I.
Heinemann, London.

Siegfried W R   1980.   The incidence of fire at Etosha National Park,
1970-1979.   Unpublished report.

Sim T R   1907.   The forests and forest flora of the Colony of the Cape of
Good Hope.   Taylor and Henderson, Aberdeen.

Simmons I G   1969.   Evidence for vegetation changes associated with
Mesolithic man in Britain.   In: Ucko P J and Dimbleby G W (eds)   The
domestication and exploitation of plants and animals.   Duckworth,
London, pp 111-119.

Skaife S H   1953. African insect life.   Longmans, Green and Company.

Slingsby P and Bond W   1982.   Of ants and proteas.   African Wildlife 36,
104-107.

Smit I B J   1954.   Some notes on the effects of burning on two veld types
at Frankenwald.   Annual Report of the Frankenwald Field Research
Station, Witwatersrand University, 35-36.

Smit I B J   1969.   The *Eragrostis curvula* ley: effect of burning and mowing
on seasonal herbage yields.   Annual Report, Department Agricultural
Technical Services Project H-BL 56/6.

Smith F R   1978.   Determination of the effects of veld burning treatments
on the major plant communities of the Natal Drakensberg catchment:
responses of four shrubs to fire regime.   Department of Forestry, Natal,
conservation   research   subproject   1/3/06/04/01   unpublished   progress
reports Nos 1, 2 and 3.

Smith F R   1979.   Determination of the effects of veld burning treatments on
the major plant communities of the Natal Drakensberg catchment: responses
of   four   shrubs   to   fire   regime.   Department   of   Forestry,   Natal,
conservation   research   subproject   1/3/06/04/01   unpublished   progress
reports Nos 4 and 5.

Smith F R   1982.   Responses of four shrub species to timing and behaviour of
fire in the Natal Drakensberg.   MSc Thesis, University of Natal.

Smith F R, Everson T M and Everson C S 1983. The study of fire behaviour in grasslands and woody vegetation of the Natal Drakensberg. Poster session. Jonkershoek Forest Research Station, 18 March.

Sonntag E E 1960. The protection of veld and forest against fire. African Wildlife 14, 117–123.

Specht R L and Morgan D G 1981. The balance between the foliage projective covers of overstorey and understorey strata in Australian vegetation. Australian Journal of Ecology 6, 193–202.

Specht R L, Rayson P and Jackman M E 1958. Dark Island heath (Ninety-Mile Plain, South Australia). VI. Pyric succession: changes in composition, coverage, dry weight, and mineral nutrient status. Australian Journal of Botany 6, 59–88.

Spring P E, Brewer M L, Brown J R and Fanning M E 1974. Population ecology of loblolly pine *Pinus taeda* in an old field community. Oikos 25, 1–6.

Squires V R and Trollope W S W 1979. Allelopathy in the Karoo shrub *Chrysocoma tenuifolia*. South African Journal of Science 75, 88–89.

Staples R R 1926. Experiments in veld management. First report. Science Bulletin 49, Department of Agriculture, Union of South Africa.

Staples R R 1930. Studies in veld management. A second report on certain veld burning and grazing experiments. Science Bulletin 91, Department of Agriculture, Union of South Africa.

Start H M 1977. Fire and nutrient cycling in a Douglas-fir/larch forest. Ecology 58, 16–30.

Stayt H A 1931. The Bavenda. Cass, London.

Steward F R 1974. Fire spread through a fuel bed. Fire Service Centre, University of New Brunswick, Canada 22, pp 316–377.

Stewart C T 1972. A report on the progress of the rodent and insectivore survey of the Andries Venter Research Station, Jonkershoek Valley. Cape Town: Unpublisehd report Cape Provincial Administration Department of Nature and Environmental Conservation.

Stewart J B 1977. Evaporation from the wet canopy of a pine forest. Water Resources Research 13, 915–921.

Stewart O C 1956. Fire as the first great force employed by man. In: Thomas W L (ed) Man's role in changing the face of the earth. University of Chicago Press, Chicago, pp 115–133.

Stewart O C 1963. Barriers to understanding the influence of use of fire by aborigines on vegetation. Proceedings of the Tall Timbers Fire Ecology Conference 2, 117–126.

Stindt H W and Joubert J G V 1979. The nutritive value of natural pastures in the districts of Ladismith, Riversdale and Heidelberg in the winter rainfall area of the Republic of South Africa. Technical Communication No. 154. Department of Agricultural Technical Services, Pretoria.

Stinson K J and Wright H A 1969. Temperatures of head fires in the southern mixed prairie of Texas. Journal Range Management 22, 169–174.

Story R 1951. A botanical survey of the Keiskammahoek district. Memoirs of the Botanical Survey of South Africa 27, 1–184.

Swynnerton C F M 1920. An examination of the tsetse problem in north Mossurise, Portuguese East Africa. Bulletin of Entomological Research 11, 315–386.

Tainton N M 1963. Burning or mowing – which is more profitable. Farming in South Africa 39 (8), 24–25.

Tainton N M 1978. Fire in the management of humid grasslands in South Africa. Proceedings of the First International Rangeland Congress, Denver, Colorado, pp 684–686.

Tainton N M 1981a. The grass plant and its reaction to treatment. In:
  Tainton N M (ed) Veld and pasture management in South Africa. Natal
  University Press, and Shuter and Shooter, Pietermaritzburg, pp
  218-238.

Tainton N M 1981b. Introduction to the concepts of development, production
  and stability of plant communities. In: Tainton N M (ed) Veld and
  pasture management in South Africa. Shuter and Shooter in association
  with Natal University Press, Pietermaritzburg, pp 3-24.

Tainton N M 1982. Response of the humid sub-tropical grasslands of South
  Africa to defoliation. In: Huntley B J and Walker B H (eds) The
  ecology of tropical savannas. Springer-Verlag, Berlin, pp 405-414.

Tainton N M and Booysen P de V 1963. The effects of management on
  apical bud development and seeding in *Themeda triandra* and *Tristachya
  hispida*. South African Journal of Agricultural Science 6, 21-30.

Tainton N M and Booysen P de V 1965a. Growth and development in
  perennial veld grasses, I. *Themeda triandra* under various systems of
  defoliation. South African Journal of Agricultural Science 8, 93-110.

Tainton N M and Booysen P de V 1965b. Growth and development in perennial
  veld grasses, II. *Hyparrhenia hirta* tillers under various systems of
  defoliation. South Africa Ibid 8, 745-760.

Tainton N M, Booysen P de V, Bransby D I and Nash R C 1978. Long term
  effects of burning and mowing on tall grass veld in Natal: dry matter
  production. Proceedings of the Grassland Society of Southern Africa
  13, 41-44.

Tainton N M, Groves R H and Nash R C 1977. Time of mowing and burning
  veld: short term effects on production and tiller development.
  Proceedings of the Grassland Society of Southern Africa 12, 59-64.

Tarrant R F 1956. Effects of slash burning on some soils of the
  Douglas-fir region. Soil Science Society of America Proceedings 20,
  408-411.

Taylor H C 1961. Ecological account of remnant coastal forest near
  Stanford, Cape Province. Journal of South African Botany 27 (3),
  153-165.

Taylor H C 1969a. The vegetation of the Cape of Good Hope Nature
  Reserve. MSc Thesis, University of Cape Town.

Taylor H C 1969b. Pesplante en natuurbewaring. Forestry in South Africa
  10, 41-46.

Taylor H C 1972. Notes on the vegetation of the Cape Flats. Bothalia
  10, 637-646.

Taylor H C 1977. Aspects of the ecology of the Cape of Good Hope Nature
  Reserve in relation to fire and conservation. In: Mooney H A and
  Conrad C E (technical coordinators) Proceedings of the symposium on the
  environmental consequences of fire and fuel management in Mediterranean
  ecosystems (August 1-5, 1977, Palo Alto, California). USDA Forest
  Service General Technical Report WO-3, Washington D C, 483-487.

Taylor H C 1978. Capensis. In: Werger M J A (ed) The biogeography and
  ecology of southern Africa. Junk, The Hague, pp 171-229.

Taylor H C and Kruger F J 1978. A first attempt to measure temperature of
  fire in fynbos. Bothalia 12, 551-553.

Theron G C 1932. Veld burning in the western Transvaal. Farming in South
  Africa 7, 244-254.

Theron G C 1937. Veld management investigations at the School of Agriculture, Potchefstroom. Preliminary Report. Bulletin 166, Department of
  Agriculture, Union of South Africa, 1-23.

398

Theron G C 1946. Research in connection with veld control at the Potchefstroom College of Agriculture. Science Bulletin 266, Department of Agriculture, Union of South Africa.

Theron G K, Morris J W and van Rooyen N 1983. Ordination of the herbaceous stratum in savanna in the Nylsvley Nature Reserve, South Africa. Vegetatio 36, in press.

Theron J N 1974. The seismic history of the south-eastern Cape Province. In: van Wyk W L and Kent L E (eds) The earthquake of 29 September 1969 in the south-western Cape Province, South Africa. Geological Survey, Department of Mines, Pretoria. Seismologic Series 4, 12-18.

Thiollay J-M 1971. L'exploitation des feux de brousse par les oiseaux en Afrique Occidentale. Alauda 34, 54-72.

Thompson W R 1936. Veld burning: its history and importance in South Africa. Publications of the University of Pretoria, Series L: Agriculture No 31, 1-19.

Thorud D B 1967. The effect of applied interception on transpiration rates of potted Ponderosa Pine. Water Resources Research 3, 443-450.

Tinley K 1977. Framework of the Gorongosa ecosystem. DSc Thesis, University of Pretoria.

Tinley K L 1982. The influence of soil moisture balance on ecosystem patterns in southern Africa. In: Huntley B J and Walker B H (eds) Ecology of tropical savannas. Springer-Verlag New York, pp 175-192.

Tiwari V K and Rai B 1977. Effect of soil burning on microfungi. Plant and Soil 47, 693-697.

Toes E 1972. Tellingen van kleine zoogdieren en vogels in de Jonkershoek Vallei, Zuid-Afrika. Unpublished report, Landbouwhogeschool te Wageningen.

Tomlinson D N S 1980. Seasonal food selection by waterbuck *Kobus ellipsiprymnus* in a Rhodesian Game Park. South African Journal of Wildlife Research 10, 22-28.

Tothill J C 1960. Soil temperatures and seed burial in relation to the performance of *Heteropogon contortus* and *Themeda australis* in burnt pastures in eastern Queensland. Australian Journal of Botany 17, 269-275.

Trapnell C G 1959. Ecological results of woodland burning experiments in northern Rhodesia. Journal of Ecology 47 (1), 129-168.

Trimble G R and Tripp N R 1949. Some effects of fire and cutting on forest soils in the lodgepole pine forests of the northern Rocky Mountains. Journal of Forestry 47, 640-642.

Troendle C A 1979. A variable source area model for stormflow prediction on first order forested watersheds. PhD Thesis, University of Georgia.

Trollope W S W 1970. A consideration of macchia (fynbos) encroachment in South Africa and an investigation into methods of macchia eradication in the Amatola Mountains. MSc Thesis, University of Natal.

Trollope W S W 1971. Fire as a method of eradicating macchia vegetation in the Amatola Mountains of South Africa - experimental and field scale results. Proceedings of the Tall Timbers Fire Ecology Conference 11, 99-120.

Trollope W S W 1973. Fire as a method of controlling macchia (fynbos) vegetation on the Amatole Mountains of the eastern Cape. Proceedings of the Grassland Society of Southern Africa 8, 35-41.

Trollope W S W 1974. Role of fire in preventing bush encroachment in the eastern Cape. Proceedings of the Grassland Society of Southern Africa 9, 67-72.

Trollope W S W 1978a. Fire behaviour - a preliminary study. Proceedings of the Grassland Society of Southern Africa 13, 123-128.

Trollope W S W 1978b. Fire - a rangeland tool in southern Africa. Proceedings of the First International Rangeland Congress, 245-247.

Trollope W S W 1979. Veld burning as a veld management practice in livestock production. Unpublished report.

Trollope W S W 1980a. Unpublished data. Department of Agriculture, University of Fort Hare, Alice.

Trollope W S W 1980b. The ecological effects of fire in South African savannas. In: Huntley B J and Walker B H (eds) Ecology of tropical savannas. Springer-Verlag, New York, pp 292-306.

Trollope W S W 1980c. Controlling bush encroachment with fire in the savanna area of South Africa. Proceedings of the Grassland Society of Southern Africa 15, 173-177.

Trollope W S W and Booysen P de V 1971. The eradication of the macchia (fynbos) vegetation on the Amatole mountains of the eastern Cape. Proceedings of the Grassland Society of Southern Africa 6, 28-38.

Trollope W S W and Potgieter A l F 1983. Characteristics of fire behaviour in the Kruger National Park Research Report, University of Fort, Hare, Alice.

Tunstal B R, Walker J and Gill A M 1976. Temperate distribution around synthetic trees during grass fires. Forest Service Center, University of New Brunswick, Canada 22, 361-377.

Turcott G L 1976. Fire management - a vital factor in land-use planning. Symposium, Bureau of Land Management, Alaska State Office.

Tyson P D 1964. Berg winds of South Africa. Weather 19, 7-11.

Tyson P D 1978. Rainfall changes over South Africa during the period of meteorological record. In: Werger M J A (ed) Biogeography and ecology of southern Africa. Junk, The Hague, pp 55-70

Tyson P D and Dyer T C J 1975. Mean annual fluctuations of precipitation in the summer rainfall regions of South Africa. South African Geographic Journal 57, 2.

van Daalen J C 1981. The dynamics of the indigenous forest-fynbos ecotone in the southern Cape. South African Forestry Journal 119, 14-28.

van der Merwe N J and Killick D J 1979. Square: an iron smelting site near Phalaborwa. South African Archaeological Society Goodwin Series 3, 86-93.

van der Merwe P 1966a. Datering van veldbrande met behulp van *Protea mellifera* Thunb. Tydskrif vir Natuurwetenskappe 9, 251-254.

van der Merwe P 1966b. Die flora van Swartboschkloof, Stellenbosch en die herstel van die soorte na 'n brand. Annale Universiteit van Stellenbosch 41 Serie A(14), 691-736.

van der Merwe P and van der Merwe D 1968. Fire in the Swartboskloof Nature Reserve. African Wildlife 22, 147-157.

van der Schijff H P 1957. Bush encroachment in South Africa. In: Hand-book for farmers in South Africa, vol III. Government Printer, Pretoria, pp 732-741.

van der Schyff H P 1958. In leidende verslag oor veldbrandnavorsing in die Nasionale Krugerwildtuin. Koedoe 1, 60-93.

van der Schyff H P 1964. 'n Hervaluasie van die probleem van bosindringing in Suid Afrika. Tydskrif vir Natuurwetenskappe 4, 67-80.

van der Westhuizen F G J, van den Berg J A and Opperman D P J 1978. Die benutting van grasveld in die sentrale Oranje-Vrystaat met skape. Proceedings of the Grassland Society of Southern Africa 13, 83-89.

van der Zel D W 1974. Catchment research at Zachariashoek. Forestry in South Africa 15, 23–30.

van der Zel D W and Kruger F J 1975. Results of the multiple catchment experiments at the Jonkershoek Research Station, South Africa. II. Influence of protection of fynbos on stream discharge in Langrivier. Forestry of South Africa 16, 13–18.

van Lill W S, Kruger F J and van Wyk D B 1980. Preliminary report on the effect of afforestation with *Eucalyptus grandis* Hill ex Maiden and *Pinus patula* Schlecht. et Cham. on streamflow from experimental catchments at Mokobulaan, Transvaal. Journal of Hydrology 48, 107–118.

van Rensburg W L J 1962. Die aandeel van grasse in veldtipes rondom Stellenbosch. MSc Thesis, University of Stellenbosch.

van Staden J 1966. Studies on the germination of seed of Proteaceae. Journal of South African Botany 32, 291–298.

van Staden J and Brown N A C 1972. Characterization of germination inhibitors in seed extracts of four South African species of Proteaceae. Journal of South African Botany 38, 135–150.

van Staden J and Brown N A C 1973. The role of covering structures in the germination of seed of *Leucospermum cordifolium* (Proteaceae). Australian Journal of Botany 21, 189–192.

van Wilgen B W 1981a. An analysis of fires and associated weather factors in mountain fynbos areas of the southwestern Cape. South African Forestry Journal 119, 29–34.

van Wilgen B W 1981b. Some effects of fire frequency on fynbos plant community composition and structure at Jonkershoek, Stellenbosch. South African Forestry Journal 118, 42–55.

van Wilgen B W 1982. Some effects of post-fire age on the aerial plant biomass of fynbos (macchia) vegetation in South Africa. Journal of Ecology 70, 217–225.

van Wyk D B 1977. Die invloed van bebossing met *Pinus radiata* op die totale jaarlikse afvoer van die Jonkershoek strome. MSc Thesis, University of Stellenbosch.

van Wyk D B 1982. Influence of prescribed burning on nutrient budgets of mountain fynbos catchments in the S W Cape, Republic of South Africa. In: Conrad C E and Oechel W C (technical coordinators). Proceedings of the Symposium on Dynamics and Management of mediterranean-type Ecosystems. USDA Forest Service General Technical Report PSW-58, Berkeley, California, pp 390–396.

van Wyk P 1971. Veld burning in the Kruger National Park, an interim report of some aspects of research. Proceedings of the Tall Timbers Fire Ecology Conference 11, 9–31.

van Wyk W L and Kent L E 1974. The earthquake of 29 September 1969 in the south-western Cape Province, South Africa. Geological Survey, Department of Mines, Pretoria. Seismologic Series 4.

van Zinderen Bakker E M 1978. Quaternary vegetation changes in southern Africa. In: Werger M J A (ed) Biogeography and ecology of southern Africa. Junk, The Hague, pp 131–143.

Veihmeyer F J and Johnson C N 1944. Soil moisture records from burned and unburned plots in certain grazing areas in California. Transactions of the American Geophysics Union 1, 72–88.

Versfeld D B 1978. Rainfall interception in stands of *Pinus radiata* D Don. Unpublished report, Jonkershoek Forestry Research Station, 1–15.

Versfeld D B 1981. Overland flow on small plots at the Jonkershoek Forestry Research Station. South African Forestry Journal 119, 35–40.

Vesey-Fitzgerald D F 1966. The habits and habitats of small rodents in the Congo river catchment region of Zambia and Tanzania. Zoologia Africana 2, 111-122.

Vesey-Fitzgerald D F 1971. Fire and animal impact on vegetation in Tanzania National Parks. Proceedings of the Tall Timbers Fire Ecology Conference 11, 297-317.

Viro P J 1974. Effects of forest fire on soil. In: Kozlowski T T and Ahlgren C E (eds) Fire and ecosystems. Academic Press, New York, pp 7-45

Vogl R J 1974. Effects of fire on grasslands. In: Kozlowski T T and Ahlgren C E (eds) Fire and ecosystems. Academic Press, New York, pp 139-182

Vowinckel E 1958. Fire danger rating. Journal of South African Forestry Association 31, 58-73.

Walker B H 1974. Ecological considerations in the management of semi-arid ecosystems in south-central Africa. Proceedings of the International Congress of Ecology 1, 124-129.

Walker B H 1980. Stable production versus resilience : a grazing management conflict? Proceedings of the Grassland Society of Southern Africa 15, 79-83.

Walker B H 1982. Is succession a viable concept in African Savanna ecosystems? In: Proceedings of the workshop on forest succession, 8-14 June 1980, Mountain Lake, Virginia, USA.

Walker B H and Noy-Meir I 1982. Aspects of the stability and resilience of savanna ecosystems. In: Huntley B J and Walker B H (eds) Ecology of tropical savannas. Springer-Verlag, New York, pp 556-590.

Wallis F M and Price W J 1979. Fire ecology microbial responses. Unpublished report, Department of Plant Pathology and Microbiology, University of Natal, Pietermaritzburg.

Walsh B N 1968. Some notes on the incidence and control of driftsands along the Caledon, Bredasdorp, and Riversdale coastline of South Africa. Department of Forestry Bulletin 44, 1-79.

Walter H 1971. Ecology of tropical and subtropical vegetation. Oliver and Bond, Edinburgh.

Ward C J 1962. Report on scrub control in the Hluhluwe Game Reserve. Lammergeyer 2 (1), 57-62.

Weather Bureau, Department of Transport 1957. Climate of South Africa. Part 4. Rainfall maps. WB 22. Pretoria, Government Printer.

Webber C N 1979. The effects of fire on soil plant ecological relation-ships in the southern part of the Kruger National Park: a study in soil geography. MSc Thesis, University of Pretoria.

Weinmann H H 1955. The chemistry and physiology of grasses. In: Meredith D (ed) The grasses and pastures of South Africa. Central News Agency, Johannesburg, pp 571-600.

Wells C G 1971. Effects of prescribed burning on soil chemical properties and nutrient availability. In: Prescribed Burning Symposium Proceedings. USDA Forestry Service Southeast Forestry Experimental Station, Asheville, North Carolina, 86-99.

Wells C G et al 1979. Effects of fire on soil. General Technical Report WO-7. Forest Services, U S Department of Agriculture, Washington D C, 1-35.

Werger M J A (ed) 1978. Biogeography and ecology of Southern Africa. Junk, The Hague.

West O 1943. The vegetation of Weenen County - an ecological account of the vegetation of the Estcourt and Weenen districts. DSc Thesis, Witwatersrand University.

West O 1951. The vegetation of Weenen County, Natal. Memoirs of the Botanical Survey of South Africa 23, 1-160.

West O 1952. Plant succession and veld burning considered particularly in relation to the management of bushveld grazing. In: Veld gold. National Veld Trust, Johannesburg, pp 65-80.

West O 1955. Veld management in the dry, summer-rainfall bush. In: Meredith D (ed) The grasses and pastures of South Africa. Central News Agency, Johannesburg, pp 624-636.

West O 1965. Fire in vegetation and its use in pasture management with special reference to tropical and subtropical Africa. Mimeographed Publication No 1. Commonwealth Bureau of Pastures and Field Crops, Hurley, Berkshire, 1-53.

West O 1969. Fire: its effect on the ecology of vegetation in Rhodesia, and its application in grazing management. Proceedings of the Veld Management Conference Bulawayo, Rhodesia. Government Printer, Salisbury.

West O 1971. Fire, man and wildlife as interacting factors limiting the development of climax vegetation in Rhodesia. Proceedings of the Tall Timbers Fire Ecology Conference 11, 121-145.

Wharton C H 1966. Man, fire and wild cattle in North Cambodia. Proceedings of the Tall Timbers Fire Ecology Conference 5, 23-65.

Whateley A and Porter R N 1979. The woody plant communities of the Hluhluwe-Corridor-Umfolozi Game Reserve Complex. Unpublished paper, Natal Parks Board, Pietermaritzburg.

White F 1976. The underground forests of Africa: a preliminary review. Gardens' Bulletin 39, 57-71.

White R E and Grossman D 1972. The effect of prolonged seasonal burning on soil fertility under *Trachypogon-* other species grassland at Frankenwald. South African Journal of Science 68, 234-239.

Wicht C L 1943. The variability of Jonkershoek streams. Journal of South African Forestry Association 10, 13-22.

Wicht C L 1945. Report of the committee on the preservation of the vegetation of the south-western Cape. Special publication of the Royal Society of South Africa, Cape Town, 1-56.

Wicht C L 1948a. Hydrological research in South African forestry. Journal of South African Forestry Association 16, 4-22.

Wicht C L 1948b. A statistically designed experiment to test the effects of burning on a sclerophyll scrub community. I. Preliminary account. Transactions of the Royal Society of South Africa 31, 479-501.

Wicht C L 1949. Forestry and water supplies in South Africa. Department of Forestry Bulletin 33, Pretoria.

Wicht C L 1971. The influence of vegetation in South African mountain catchments on water supplies. South African Journal of Science 67, 201-209.

Wicht C L and de Villiers Y R 1963. Weerstoestande en brandgevaar by Hermanus. Journal of Geography 2, 25-36.

Wicht C L and Kruger F J 1973. Die ontwikkeling van bergveldbestuur in Suid Afrika. South African Forestry Journal 86, 1-17.

Wicht C L, Meyburgh J C and Boustead P G 1969. Rainfall at the Jonkershoek Forest Hydrological Research Station. Annale Universiteit Stellenbosch 44, Serie A(1), 1-66.

Wicklow P T 1973. Microfungal populations in surface soils of manipulated prairie stands. Ecology 54, 1302.

Willan K 1982. Social ecology of *Otomys irroratus, Rhabdomys pumilio* and *Praomys natalensis*. PhD Thesis, University of Natal.

Willan K and Bigalke R C 1982. The effects of fire regime on small mammals in S W Cape montane fynbos (Cape macchia). In: Conrad C E and Oechel W C (technical coordinators). Dynamics and management of mediterranean-type ecosystems. USDA Forest Service General Technical Report PSW-58, pp 207-212.

Willan K and Meester J 1978. Breeding biology and postnatal development of the African dwarf mouse. Acta Theriological 23, 55-73.

Williams G C 1966. Adaptation and natural selection. Princeton University Press, Princeton N.J.

Williams I J M 1972. A revision of the genus *Leucadendron* (Proteaceae). Contributions of the Bolus Herbarium 3, 1-425.

Winterbottom J M 1963. Avian breeding seasons in Southern Africa. Proceedings of the Thirteenth International Ornithological Congress, 640-648.

Winterbottom J M 1972. The ecological distribution of birds in southern Africa. Monographs of the Percy FitzPatrick Institute for African Ornithology 1, 1-81.

Woodruff J F and Hewlett J D 1970. Predicting and mapping the average hydrologic response for the eastern United States. Water Resources Research 6, 1312-1326.

Wright H A 1978. Use of fire to manage grasslands of the Great Plains: Central and Southern Great Plains. Proceedings of the International Rangeland Congress 1, 694-696.

Zinke P J 1967. Forest interception studies in the United States. In: Sopper W E and Lull H W (eds) International symposium for hydrology. Pergamon Press, Oxford, pp 131-161.

Zon R 1927. Forests and water in the light of scientific investigation. U S Forestry Service Bulletin, Government Printing Office, Washington D C, 1-106.

Index of Plants and Animals (Scientific)

Index of Plants and Animals (Common)

Subject Index

Ecological Studies
Analysis and Synthesis

Editors: **W.D.Billings, F.Golley, O.L.Lange, J.S.Olson, H.Remmert**

Springer-Verlag
Berlin
Heidelberg
New York
Tokyo

Ecological Studies

Analysis and Synthesis

Editors: W.D.Billings, F.Golley, O.L.Lange, J.S.Olson, H.Remmert

Springer-Verlag Berlin Heidelberg New York Tokyo